Laws, men and machines

Laws, men and machines
Modern American government and the appeal of Newtonian mechanics

Michael Foley

London and New York

First published 1990
by Routledge
11 New Fetter Lane, London EC4P 4EE

Simultaneously published in the USA and Canada
by Routledge
a division of Routledge, Chapman and Hall, Inc.
29 West 35th Street, New York, NY 10001

© 1990 Michael Foley

Typeset by NWL Editorial Services, Langport, Somerset

Printed and bound in Great Britain by
Billings & Sons Limited, Worcester

All rights reserved. No part of this book may be reprinted or
reproduced or utilized in any form or by any electronic, mechanical, or
other means, now known or hereafter invented, including photocopying
and recording, or in any information storage or retrieval system,
without permission in writing from the publishers.

British Library Cataloguing in Publication Data
Laws, men and machines : Modern American government and the
appeal of Newtonian mechanics.
1. United States. Politics. Influence of science, history
I. Title
320.973

ISBN 0-415-04273-9

Library of Congress Cataloging in Publication Data
Applied for

To my mother

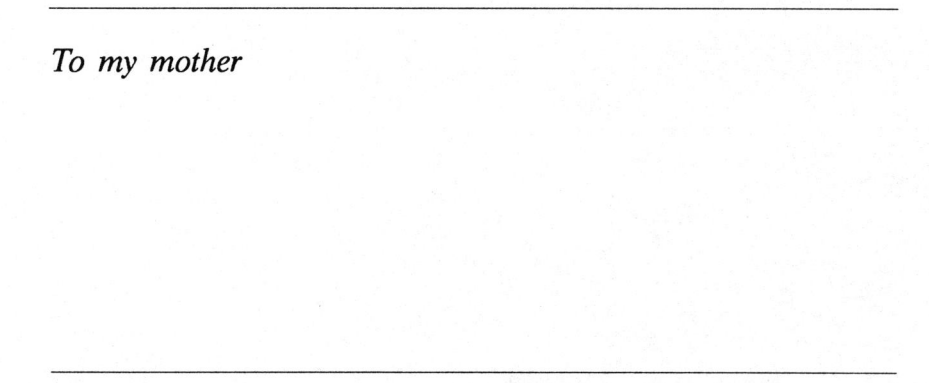

Contents

	Acknowledgements	ix
1	Newtonian mechanics and American constitutionalism	1
2	The death of constitutional Newtonianism?	21
3	The perpetuation of constitutional mechanics	45
4	The Presidency, the Congress and the separation of paradigms	80
5	A government of laws, men and machines	186
	Epilogue	232
	Notes	238
	Index	281

Acknowledgements

This work had a long period of gestation during which I was repeatedly led to ruminate upon the extraordinary wealth of mechanical references in American politics. I must, therefore, thank all those who were patient enough to listen to my speculations and to allow me to formulate thoughts on the wing. I am especially indebted to my past and present students, who could always be relied upon to make the sort of innocent, but penetrating, remarks that would topple towers of previously impregnable argument.

I must also pay tribute to those who provided me with more structured appraisals and with the benefit of their opinions and advice. In addition to one anonymous referee, who helped me to tighten the analysis, I am especially indebted to Professor Aaron Wildavsky of the University of California, Berkeley and to Dr John Zvesper of the University of East Anglia. My gratitude also goes to Professor Anthony King of th University of Essex, who provided encouragement and practical help at a strategic point in the work's passage into print.

It is one thing to produce a work that is publishable; it is quite another to make it into a published work. For that I have to thank Ray Offord and Robert Tarling, but most of all my thanks go to Routledge's social science editor, Alan Jarvis. Without his efforts, I can honestly say that this book would not have been brought into existence. Technical support came in the form of Susan Blair who typed the footnotes, Doreen Hamer who typed innumerable letters, and my wife, Frances, who produced the index. Personal support and encouragement was, of course, provided by my family who ensured that Newtonian mechanics did not turn me into an automaton!

MF
University of Wales, Aberystwyth

Chapter one

Newtonian mechanics and American constitutionalism

One of the most enduring, yet least well understood, characterizations of American society is that it is mechanistic in nature. This reputation is not derived simply from the fact that so many of America's great bequests to the world have been new mechanical devices (e.g. telephone, computer) or new production techniques (e.g. assembly line, automation, mechanized agricultural production). It is rather that America is believed to have been so affected by the forms and purposes of mechanical processes that they have come to represent the principal features of American life. As a result, the United States is conventionally described as being the 'culture of machine living'.[1] Mechanical metaphors (e.g. machine politics), mechanical concepts (e.g. countervailing force, domino theory), mechanical symbols (e.g. dynamo, railroad), and mechanical cults (e.g. automobiles, firearms, spacecraft) are conspicuously prominent in American life. American history has been described as not only a process by which 'a rustic and in large part wild landscape was transformed into the site of the world's most productive industrial machine',[2] but a process which in itself was prompted and directed by technological change – 'technological determinism, as an inescapable aspect of the modern American way, has been an implicit American assumption'.[3] Accordingly, American society has often been either applauded or decried on the basis of whether the observer either condones a mechanized society as being dynamic, progressive, and emancipated or deplores it as being rootless, aimless, divisive, and spiritually arid. In both respects, the actual existence of a highly mechanistic society is assumed as a fact of American life.

The United States is probably not dissimilar to any of the other Western industrial states in this respect. The sheer scale of its technological capacity gives it a prominence within the community of advanced industrialized societies, but it can be argued that this particular distinction is one of degree and not of kind. What does differentiate the United States substantively from comparable societies, however, is the extent to which mechanistic concepts and values are believed to have penetrated society and to have become established as traditional criteria of perception and normative assessment. This peculiarly American trait, which was no mere adjunct to the industrial revolution but which preceded the process of industrialization, is probably given its most emphatic expression in the way that Americans tend to associate the principles of mechanical energy with the design and workings of their political system. Mechanical terms of reference are commonly employed to define the framework and to characterize the operation of the governmental system of institutions and powers. For example, the institutions are commonly seen as constituent units that move in relation to one another in accordance with a stated order of mechanical sequence; they are assumed to check and to balance each other as they proceed in motion; and they are portrayed as accommodating stress through such mathematically precise formulae as a two-thirds majority for a veto override in Congress and a three-quarters majority of states for a constitutional amendment. The analogy to a machine is further strengthened by the many references that are made concerning the purpose underlying the constitution's design. It is a widely acknowledged assertion that the Founding Fathers' objective was geared towards producing a multiplicity of parts operating with and against one another at different levels and at different times deliberately, in order to generate a framework of continuous material interaction. The purpose of the constitution, therefore, was not merely physically dependent upon institutional dynamics, but was in essence defined by them as well. While the institutions exist to perform certain specific functions, their collective role is commonly concluded to be the provision of a system of indigenous forces that serve to regulate the constituent structures and, thereby, to produce an autonomous form of control for the system as a whole.

This conception of government represents an integral part of what can be termed a mechanistic tradition in American politics. Like all traditions, it is characterized by an intuitive allegiance to a set of long-standing principles. In this case, the principles in question are mechanical in nature and purpose. They constitute a conspicuous American propensity to employ mechanically based precepts and premises as working assumptions about politics and government. Of course, it is impossible to say exactly how individuals come to have certain conceptions regarding politics. Nevertheless, it is possible to observe the manifestations of these conceptions of political evaluation and analysis. It is possible to detect the way in which, for example, a constitutional issue is comprehended, and the conceptual and ethical grounds on which it is examined and discussed. Through observations of this type, one can trace certain regularities in the way individuals view and discuss political events and certain patterns in the way they construct and present their opinions and arguments. This does not mean that one can ever draw definite conclusions as to *why* they think about politics in the way they appear to. But it does mean that one can discern the steps revealed by individuals in the course of arriving at conclusions on political matters. In other words, while it is impossible to know the mysteries of the mental processes providing views, opinions, conceptions, etc., it is at least possible to observe what these processes produce and to examine the premises and perceptions to which such products are clearly related.

In this case, it is clear that one of the chief characteristics that distinguish the American approach to comprehending political and constitutional developments is a dependence upon modes of thought that are remarkable for their attachment to closed and repetitious systems of physical cause and effect. This mechanical tradition is so deeply embedded in the processes of American political discourse that it is instinctively employed as a method of political conceptualization, as a scheme of political analysis, as a device for resolving political problems, and even as a means of political evaluation.

The content and ramifications of this tradition will be examined more closely at a later point. What is important to note at this stage is the way in which these various allegiances to mechanical principles have led to a blurring of the distinction between the belief in a constitutional framework resembling a machine and the belief in a constitution that possesses real mechanical properties. In the United States this distinction is not one that arouses much in the way of explicit recognition. On the contrary, it requires a considerable effort to resist what has become an accustomed disposition to construe the operation of American constitutional processes as a self-evidently mechanical exercise.

Nothing exemplifies this mechanical tradition more, or provides it with fuller expression, than the common American practice of attaching Newtonian terms of reference to the political system. The summoning up of the name of Isaac Newton and his scheme of classical mechanics as a vehicle of political description and definition is a peculiarly idiosyncratic feature of American life. The practice obviously lends itself to the mechanistic tradition, but less obviously it helps to sustain, and even to cultivate, that tradition by reinforcing its principles with the timeless fixity of Newton's clockwork world. The source of the special relationship between Newtonianism and American politics is normally identified as the cultural and intellectual context of the eighteenth century from which the American constitution was drawn. In particular, the constitution's reputation for possessing mechanical properties is derived from the widespread belief that the Founding Fathers were men of the Enlightenment, who could not fail to have been inspired by the contemporary cult in natural science and, in particular, by the pervasive salience of Newtonian mechanics at the time. The very centrality of Newton and of classical mechanics to the Enlightenment has been taken as offering conclusive evidence that the Founders were motivated in their endeavours by a desire to incorporate the principles of mechanics into their scheme of government. By the same token, the nature of what the Founding Fathers bequeathed to the United States has been used to corroborate an exact matching of Newtonian results with Newtonian intentions and techniques.

As a result of these general associations, it is not uncommon to find in the literature on American politics the most explicit affirmations of a direct causal relationship between Newtonian physics, the Founding Fathers, and the composition of the constitution. For example:

> The Constitution was fabricated by men who believed that the laws of Newtonian physics could be applied to the construction of a government. They accepted as a first principle, the law of gravitation in politics – the inexorable gravitation of power from small centers of authority by the attraction of larger ones. So they designed a government as though it were a ship for use in rough waters.[4]

> As the principle of self-regulation was embodied in nature by the science of Newton, the principle of self-government was now to be embodied in society by the science of politics.... The machinery of government was thereby forced to repeat itself ... grinding out results as the mechanism of the heavens endlessly repeats its nocturnal orbits. But it was not itself a mechanism for change, for it presupposed a repetitious cycle of nature with no real change.... In its structure, therefore, the republic was a mechanism; not simply an instrument of government, but a political machine, the structure of which was determined by the universal reign of law, and regulated by a cosmic constitution.[5]

> The constitution-makers, it appears, were eminently 'rational'. They chose wisely and they did so under hazardous conditions. They knew that they were 'organizing' a system in the face of great uncertainty.... In fabricating the constitution, the architects were ever mindful of the grave possibility of failure and sought a system which could perform in the face of error – which could manage to provide a stable set of decision rules for an exceedingly unstable circumstance. And they found their answer in Newton's Third Law.[6]

> The Founders were elitists, and realists about human nature.... Their task was to make passion subject to reason. If men could be expected to be selfish, or worse, then said James Madison 'ambition must be made to counteract ambition'. The Newtonian principles of action and reaction were applied to politics.[7]

> The political theory to which the Fathers had subscribed ... was Newtonian.... The ideal toward which all rational lawmakers aspired was a government which should reduce the merely human factor to a minimum.... Government which was bound by natural law could no more transgress that law than the tides could reverse themselves or the stars depart from their fixed courses.[8]

These passages reflect a popular belief in the Founding Fathers' allegiance to the Enlightenment tenet of the existence of a natural order of universal cause and effect which was intellectually accessible to man and also directly applicable to him in a practical sense. According to Enlightenment principles, if the world could be conceived in Newtonian terms as a clockwork mechanism, then there was every justification for believing that human society might be made to conform to its own discoverable laws of dynamics. In this respect, governments could be constructed on mechanical foundations and, thereby, become an integral part of the self-sustaining and self-regulating universe. They could literally become governments of law and not of men, for they would be incorporated into the fixity and harmony of predetermined natural processes.

That the Founding Fathers consciously subscribed to such a conception of the world, and proceeded upon such a basis in the formulation of their governmental system, has become one of the traditional interpretations of the roots of American constitutionalism. What should not be overlooked, however, is that this interpretation is a quite exceptional one. It has led to Isaac Newton and to the ethos of classical mechanics being given an extraordinary prominence in an area of social life which has ostensibly no very obvious relationship to physics or to mechanical principles at all. Whether the allusions are direct or indirect, explicit or implicit, they constitute a distinguishing characteristic of the subject of American government, but one that is very rarely examined in any depth or even acknowledged with anything like the degree of self-consciousness that such a characterization warrants. It is noticeable, for example, that the figure of Newton and the principles of Newtonianism barely arise in British political history. Even though Newton was a Member of Parliament, a social contemporary of John Locke, a discoverer of the centrality of balanced forces in nature at a time when the British constitution was increasingly being interpreted as an ancient equilibrium of powers, and a progenitor of the 'Age of Reason' with all its attendant political ramifications, the imprint of Newton or Newtonianism on the British political tradition has never been claimed to be anything other than minimal. As for Newton's significance to modern British politics, again it is not so much dismissed as never even raised as a serious topic of discussion. Among his own countrymen, Newton's long-term political significance seems as little regarded as his career in Parliament, where he was reputed to have spoken only once and that being a request to have the windows of the chamber closed.[9] In Britain, Newton's status is exclusively that of a great natural scientist. His name, and the concepts and principles associated with it, are not drawn upon to support propositions on the nature of political activity and thought. Newtonianism in this environment has had no history of affording characterizations of constitutional dynamics or institutional relationships. To suggest otherwise would seem to British observers so misplaced as to be almost aberrational.

This is not the case in the United States. Far from being aware of any anomaly involved in such a linkage, Americans have actively sought to integrate

Newton and Newtonianism into their conception of government. There is a seminal and heroic quality to Newton in the American context. It is felt that Newtonian principles lie near the root of American politics, in the generative sense of having shaped the design of the constitution and, thereby, the subsequent operation of America's political processes. Accordingly, the Enlightenment figure of Newton is afforded an elevated status in the pantheon of American heroes. In many respects, he is regarded as being as much of an honorary Founding Father as John Locke.

Isaac Newton and Newtonian mechanics

Isaac Newton (1642–1727) was a seventeenth-century figure whose celebrated work *Philosophia Naturalis Principia Mathematica (Mathematical Principles of Natural Philosophy)* was published in 1687.[10] In it he sought to answer the key intellectual issue that had preoccupied Europe's burgeoning scientific community. The riddle that needed to be resolved was what kept the planets in motion round their orbital paths, given that the Aristotelian device of concentric crystalline spheres had become implausible. The astronomy of Nicholas Copernicus (1473–1543), Johannes Kepler (1571–1630), and Galileo Galilei (1564–1642), combined with the seventeenth century's intensive experimentation on the nature of terrestrial motion, had totally undermined the old Aristotelian orthodoxy, but had not replaced it with a comparable system of explanation.[11] Terrestrial physics had now to be accommodated to the phenomenon of a mobile earth, at the same time that celestial dynamics had to be accommodated to a sky apparently devoid of any vehicular structure by which the planets could remain in motion within their peculiarly elliptical orbits. Partial theories and disconnected ideas abounded as to the material or metaphysical nature of motion. Until Newton's *Principia*, they remained mostly pockets of unco-ordinated experimental data or unverified rationalist speculations. It was Newton who, in a combination of empirical observation and theoretical insight, synthesized the diverse strands together and established a coherent science of motion which embraced both terrestrial and celestial movement within the same framework of physical laws. Furthermore, by providing mathematical verification of his system of motion, Newton made it all the more compulsive as a conceptual focus to the notion of a pervading physical unity of the universe.

Newton based his achievement upon three laws of motion[12] that at the outset established the study of motion on an idealized level of abstraction. At its heart was the principle of inertia by which any moving body would continue in a straight line unless it was compelled to change by forces acting upon it. Motion, therefore, was a fixed state as much as rest, and one that required no force and no explanation. The only phenomenon that needed to be taken into account was a change in motion, or a change from rest to motion. The fact that no such perfect and uninterrupted motion of a weightless object moving freely and uniformly in a straight line through space had ever been observed on earth was irrelevant to Newton. He wanted to use the conception of inertia as an idealized basis from which to identify and measure those forces that necessarily had to exist – even unobservable forces at a distance – in order to account for *changes* in motion.[13] Newton's definitive law of inertia represented 'the repudiation of a belief which had blocked the progress of physics for two thousand years'.[14] It cleared away all the medieval and Aristotelian clutter of objects possessing natural forces and purposes of their own; of motion requiring force; and of circular movement representing the self-explanatory norm of celestial perfection.[15] What now remained were the geometrical properties of motion, either in a fixed state, or else in the departure from such a condition through the application of force. Force was definable and measurable only in terms of the degree of change wrought in the motion of an object to which force had been applied. Specifically, force was directly proportional to the mass and to the acceleration of the body concerned. This stark correlation underlined the direct linkage between what Newton regarded as being significant (1) in the behaviour of a body – acceleration; (2) in its physical property – mass; and (3) in its relationship between itself and other bodies – force.

Newton's three laws of motion created a framework of interrelated concepts that were dependent upon each other in terms of both physical phenomena and terminological definition. They stipulated a set of relationships between such notions as inertia, changes in motion, force, mass, action, and reaction – and in so doing they collectively determined not only what physical phenomena could be explained in the light of the three laws, but what physical phenomena required explanation through the identification of a cause. The three laws of motion were a testament to Newton's own belief that the purpose of science was to account for those physical changes that were attributable to a physical agency with a separate physical identity. According to Newton, those changes in the material world that required a causal explanation (i.e. acceleration/deceleration) could only be understood and accounted for by the behaviour of another entity that 'must lie "outside of", or be "external to" or "independent of" the change (changing event, changing entity) itself'.[16] Thus, whenever a change of motion was observed, then, in accordance with Newton's laws of motion, the change had to be attributable to a force which necessarily had an independent physical existence, not just in its effect, but in its being an actual derivative of another physical entity – whether the latter's posited effect was directly and visibly discerned or not.

Newton took these three laws and applied them to the problem of what prevented the planets from drifting 'at the mercy of chance in the ocean of boundless space'.[17] Many allusions to the existence of a central force emanating from the sun and pushing the planets around their orbits had been made by such natural philosophers as William Gilbert (1540–1603), Gilles Roberval (1602–75), Giovanni Borelli (1608–79), and Kepler.[18] But all these assertions suffered from a lack of material and mathematical corroboration. Theories concerning central, continuous, and unseen forces also suffered from being regarded as retrograde steps towards a dependence upon magical properties. René Descartes (1596–1650) sought to overcome that difficulty by claiming that space was really densely packed with material and that planetary motion could be explained by a series of giant whirlpools of matter supporting planets in their journeys around the sun, which lay at the centre of the vortices.[19] Newton poured scorn upon such a notion and mathematically demolished the Cartesians' materialist construction of the universe.

In its place, Newton relied purely upon the measurement of planetary movements and the posited existence of forces to account for them. Newton believed that the planets' retention of their orbits had to be due to a sustained balance between the sun's gravitational force drawing the planets' masses inwards to the greater mass of the sun, and the centrifugal force of the planets' own orbital motion. Without the sun, the planets would immediately relinquish their orbital paths for rectilinear flight into empty space. Without their centrifugal force, on the other hand, they would collapse into the sun. Centrifugal forces could be readily envisaged and, with the assistance of the mathematical advances made by Christian Huygens (1629–95), precisely measured as well. The other half of the equation, however, could not be grasped with the same assurance. And yet, according to Newton, a central unseen force had to exist as a causal agent exerting a corrective pull on the planets. Newton deduced that this motive force exerted upon the planets was gravity – the selfsame force that kept the moon in its orbit around the earth and the apples falling from his trees at Woolsthorpe Manor. This was not gravity as the Cartesians understood it, whereby a body was pulled to the centre of a rotating form of liquid matter as a result of its circular motion. Newton was suggesting something much more abstract and integral to the nature of matter – namely that a body would fall to earth as a result of the mutual attraction of their masses in proximity to one another.

In contrast to nearly all his predecessors, Newton felt no need to devise a mechanism by which the planets could be driven around the sun mechanically. Newton's inertial physics persuaded him that nothing pushed the planets around their orbits. On the contrary, he believed that, after being given an initial transverse velocity, planetary motion could be explained by this linear inertia in combination with the mutual gravitation of each individual planet and the sun. As the sun's gravitational pull could not be regarded as magically self-correcting to account for the orbit of every planet irrespective of its positional and constituent properties, Newton concluded that each planet had to have a speed, a mass, and a distance from the sun that was in some way proportional to the attraction of the sun, since those factors were providing the critical counterweight to it. In this way, Newton's concepts of planetary motion and of gravity became dependent upon one another. Just as the idea of mutual attraction seemed to explain the motion of the planets, so the latter had the capacity to serve as the dynamic and visual means by which the actual force of gravity might be not only established but precisely calculated.[20]

After twenty years overcoming the prodigious technical and mathematical problems involved in such an exercise, Newton presented his celebrated law of mutual gravitation. The law stated that two bodies would attract one another with a force proportional to the product of the two masses and inversely proportional to the square of the distance between them. Newton was able to prove his law by showing that the centrifugal force necessary to keep the moon in orbit was equal in proportion to the gravitational force exerted on an object near the earth, i.e. within the realm of direct and calculable observation. Newton was convinced that his law of mutual gravitation was an integral and immutable feature of the property of matter anywhere and at any time. This belief was vindicated, as far as contemporary knowledge of the solar system was concerned, by the astronomical observations recorded over the preceding two hundred years. Newton and his elegant formula had not only solved the puzzle of planetary motion, but he had proved he had done so with such a level of precision that in the process he demonstrated that nature possessed inherent properties which could be mathematically unlocked, and which were constant across time and as true for the University of Cambridge as they were for worlds unseen and unknown across the magnitude of space.

At first, Newton's mathematical triumph did not receive general acclaim. This was partly because of its technical complexity but, more significantly, because of Newton's refusal to explain the physical means by which gravity acted as a force. Newton replied that the 'main business of natural philosophy was to argue from phenomena without feigning hypotheses, and to deduce causes from effects'.[21] The thrust of contemporary physics, particularly among the influential Cartesian centres of Europe, had been based upon a progressive mechanization of the universe by way of material cause and effect. Newton's unexplained propositions of inertial motion through a void and of action at a distance between two masses in empty space were unacceptable, since they were in effect unintelligible. Newton might have shown how the planets conformed to a fixed pattern of motion in relation to their respective masses and distances from the sun. But, because he omitted to venture reasons why they adhered to such a pattern in the absence of any material medium, his law was regarded for some time in Europe as a misplaced return to pure mysticism.

Newton consistently attempted to emphasize the fine distinction between 'mathematical forces' that provided an abstract description of gravity in terms of a force mathematically related to two masses, and 'physical forces' that not only accounted for phenomena but were directly and materially connected to them in a tangibly causal manner. Newton wanted to explain gravitational action *as if* there was an attraction between the two masses as a result of their masses. He did not want to endow matter with the physical yet incomprehensible and unproved power of actual physical attraction. This inhibition was a reflection of Newton's overall objective: to discern the mathematical properties of nature, and from those properties – and within the limits of those properties – to account for the physical features of the universe as a whole. In Newton's own words, 'to us it is enough that gravity really does exist, and acts according to the laws which we have explained, and abundantly serves to account for all the motions of the celestial bodies'.[22] It was not his purpose to advance the physical causes of these motions. He openly acknowledged that they were unknown.

In spite of Newton's elaborate distinctions and his mathematically circumscribed form of explanation, his work was none the less popularly accepted as proof of the physical existence of a force attributable to the physical properties of matter. The concept of a mathematical force was simply too nebulous in meaning to allow it to become readily distinguishable from the world of real physical forces and, as a result, they became not merely analogous to each other but conceptually interchangeable. This may have clarified the edifice of Newtonian science, but it also invested it with a mysterious foundation – the unexplained mechanics of instantaneous action at a distance. And yet, despite the riddle of a physical force without a physical form, Newtonian mechanics quickly acquired the status of being a fundamental key to God's universe. The sheer elegance, scale, and accuracy of Newton's inverse square law succeeded in diverting attention away from its deficiency in explaining the causes of the universe's central dynamics. Its appeal lay in its dramatic revelation of a factual relationship at the heart of nature – a relationship which came to be regarded as being no less factual or valid because of its inexplicability. Eventually, with the popularization of Newton's work in summarized versions, the meaning of universal gravitation lost its mystery by a process of familiarization. 'Once used to it, people – with very few exceptions – did not speculate about it any more.... Eighteenth century thought became reconciled to the ununderstandable.'[23]

While it is true that gravitation represented an affront to the seventeenth-century structure of matter, motion, and impact by which all natural phenomena could be exclusively accounted for in terms of material cause and effect, Newton's laws more than made up for their mechanical deficiencies by the sheer scale of their explanation, precision, and applicability. Newton himself regarded the forces between particles of matter 'not as a denial of the mechanical philosophy, but as a conception to perfect it'.[24] While the conception of 'action at a distance' had at one time 'been rejected by the greatest physicists as essentially unmechanistic',[25] Newton's success in setting such a force within an explicitly mechanistic context of precisely determinable changes in motion allowed it to acquire a physical and universal reality that was not merely consistent with mechanical philosophy but, ultimately, amounted to that philosophy's fullest expression and most productive achievement.

The Newtonian tide swept into the eighteenth century and over the old cosmos with its hierarchical states of being, its qualitative material differentiation, and its distinctive physical laws for different areas and different things. Through the 'simplest possible law'[26] and the 'only one that could be uniformly and universally applied to large and small bodies, to apples and to the moon',[27] Newton had shown that the physical universe not only had an order, it had a rational order. As a result, the diverse and precise aspects of nature's interior structure were now believed to be discoverable by man, attentively examining nature's uniformly basic physical characteristics. Although Newton himself had always objected to the atheistic potential of a self-motivating and self-regulating mechanistic universe, he could not prevent his works and laws from being used to develop just such a world picture in the eighteenth century. As Newton's 'mechanical laws' became increasingly extended, and absorbed ever greater numbers of phenomena within their rubric, the conception of the universe began to be dominated by a configuration of matter and motion conforming to set laws of dynamics. 'Newtonianism' came to represent the culmination of a process which converted physics into a comprehensive framework of classical mechanics. According to E. J. Dijksterhuis, 'the mechanisation of the world picture had in principle been accomplished; natural scientists had been furnished with an aim which they were to pursue for two centuries as the only conceivable one'.[28] In other words, contrary to Newton's own scientific methodology, Newtonianism in the eighteenth century became a compulsive *a priori* scheme to which empirical evidence was fitted, in order to corroborate still further the validity of the scheme. In the view of Jacob Bronowski, Isaac Newton

> had produced a single system ... ordered it seemed, by a single divine edict, the law of inverse squares.... From this moment it was felt that here plainly was the order of God. And plainly therefore the mathematical method was the method of nature, a model for all scientific orders.... To eighteenth century thinkers, at least in England, the universe was settled once and for all.[29]

Irrespective of Newton's own personal doubts, the effect of his revelation of the mathematical logic and geometrical precision inherent in the motion of material objects was to make him a central figure of inspiration in the drive to reduce nature to nothing other than an aggregate of its mechanical and geometrical characteristics. The stimulus received from Newton's synthesis of physical dynamics and his disclosure of an intelligible system of planetary motion analogous to the regularity of clockwork proved to be decisive. It became the foundation of the eighteenth century's preoccupation with conceiving the world as a clockwork mechanism, whose structure and processes could be understood only through Newton's own mechanistic principles.

Newtonianism, the Enlightenment, and the American republic

According to Isaiah Berlin, the influence of Newton was the 'strongest single factor'[30] in the eighteenth century's predominant disposition towards the use of nature's observed and calculable properties not merely in providing knowledge of the world, but in elevating that knowledge to the position of the only true knowledge available to man. The simplicity and range of Newton's laws revealed nature to be so harmonious and rational that it could now legitimately be regarded as a single entity. Nature became recognized as a coherent system. Jean Lerond d'Alembert (1717–83) called it 'the system of the world and the collection of all created things'.[31] The form and operation of this natural order were deemed discoverable precisely because of this belief that nature entailed permanent and objective principles. Furthermore, it was a system that embraced all finite reality. This rendered all phenomena potentially reducible to an analytical unity and it made an overall science of nature a plausible undertaking. It was assumed that the physical world could be broken down into its ultimate constituent nature of uniform units for the purpose of examination. In like manner, what could be explained in terms of those units and the causal relationships between them constituted, by definition, the nature of the world. Just as the world could be made explicable in terms of mechanics, so whatever could be treated mechanistically in the world could be said to constitute its real nature. Newton's demystification of nature and his revelation that the keys to nature's previously secret harmonies were available stood as a permanent inspiration to the furious inquisitiveness of the eighteenth-century Enlightenment. There was an almost obsessive impulse to vindicate Newton, not merely in his own field, but in a wide range of systematic studies into subjects that Newton would not have imagined to be related in any way to natural science. He may have been only indirectly responsible for the proliferation of such widely ranging enquiries, but he was, nevertheless, a major motive force behind the Enlightenment's broad assault upon established thought and expression. Newton became the symbol of the Enlightenment's strident faith in scientific revelation that would not only assure human progress, but determine its very course.

The Newtonian gospel was received and applied in a profusion of different ways. Sometimes as an inspirational force in guiding and encouraging the emancipatory crusade of reason against the constricted orthodoxies of the past. At other times, as a direct model and methodology to be imitated and applied with mechanical precision to any subject of enquiry. On occasions the Newtonian spirit might even be used as a critical instrument of insight into the processes of empirical reasoning itself. David Hume (1711–76), for example, was noted for his efforts to be recognized as the 'Newton of the moral sciences'. Contrary to those zealous Newtonians who endorsed Alexander Pope's dictum that after Newton 'all was light',[32] Hume neither agreed that nature had been revealed *in toto* by Newton, nor believed that nature ever could be completely explained. Hume even denied the verifiability of cause-and-effect relationships. Nevertheless, he did support the Newtonian method of observation and induction from experience, in order to discover the regularities in men's passions, ethics, and politics. To Hume, the study of history, for example, was undertaken not for its own sake but to extract from the accumulation of human experience the regular springs of men's actions and behaviour. Hume stated his premise in the following way. 'Mankind are so much the same, in all times and places, that history informs us of nothing new or strange in this particular. Its chief use is to discover the constant and universal principles of human nature.'[33] Hume attempted to be far more rigorous than even Newton in his drive to be liberated from feigning hypotheses and from fabricating a false world of laws and morals derived from 'nature'. Hume's transformation of ideas and values into a more basic and accessible currency of experience laid the way open for a science of man and society founded upon a very strict empiricism, in which the basic assumption was that man could be systematically studied as a product of common experiences derived from common needs and conditions.[34] While Hume was under no illusions as to the comparability of the natural and the moral sciences in respect to the level and precision of understanding, he was nevertheless in the vanguard of the era's intellectual commitment to a reliable science of man, and the subsequent rise of this science *for* man in the functional sense.

Given that the eighteenth century was marked by 'an effervescence and a diffusion of ideas so remarkable in its nature, so far-reaching in its extent as to be without parallel in history';[35] given that many of these ideas bore the hallmarks of Newtonian natural philosophy; and given that the gestation period of the American republic occurred within such a context – then the conclusion is often drawn that the American constitution represented a culmination of Enlightenment thought and practice. Far from the Enlightenment being an intrinsically European phenomenon, it is widely claimed that the malleable conditions of the New World in the eighteenth century made Americans highly susceptible to the sculpture of progressive ideas. Put simply, it is that the foundation and subsequent development of the American colonies can, and have been, interpreted as not merely providing an additional non-European dimension to the Enlightenment, but in many respects as the social and political fruition of the Enlightenment's fundamental precepts. Theoretical experimentation and intellectual hope in Europe became practical experimentation and hope fulfilled in the distinctive conditions of the New World. According to this view, American society in the eighteenth century achieved, through the force of conscious and self-willed reason, such an advanced level of civilized tolerance, material prosperity, and political freedom that it was the New World rather than the Old World which truly embodied both the spirit and the objective of the Enlightenment.

This belief has remained deeply embedded in American society and it continues to represent a fundamental element in America's historical consciousness. The primacy of reason as an explanation of American development and of America's exceptional condition is given just as much emphasis today as it was in the era of the Founding Fathers. In America, enlightened reason has become an intellectual tradition central to America's historical understanding of the formative period of its society. According to Bernard Bailyn:

> The political and social ideas of the European enlightenment have had a peculiar importance in American history. More universally accepted in eighteenth century America than in Europe, they were more completely and more permanently embodied in the formal arrangements of state and society; and less controverted, less subject to criticism and dispute, they have lived on more vigorously into later periods, more continuous and intact.[36]

Peter Gay reiterates the same theme when he remarks that the Founding Fathers and their contemporaries experienced a 'deep-seated and widespread need to see the newly independent colonies as agents for the fulfillment of the reasonable and human program of the enlightenment applied'.[37] It is Henry Steele Commager, however, who provides the quintessential statement of this declared relationship between the Enlightenment in Europe and the Enlightenment in America. He states unequivocally that:

> the Old World imagined, invented and formulated the enlightenment, the New World – certainly the Anglo-American part of it – realized and fulfilled it.... It was the Americans who not only embraced the body of enlightenment principles, but wrote them into law, crystallized them into institutions and put them to work.[38]

To those seeking reasons why American politics is so impregnated with references to mechanics, therefore, the Enlightenment period of American history affords one compulsively simple and persuasive answer – namely, that Newtonianism is established in the ancestry of the American republic and, in particular, in the design of the federal constitution's structures and operational processes. This traditional interpretation of the constitution's dynamics and of its elevation of balanced government as an objective to be mechanically acquired and sustained through separated powers, and institutional checks and balances, is habitually juxtaposed with modern accounts of the American political system. The net effect of such an association has been to infer that the use of Newtonian terms of reference is wholly authentic in that they correctly allude to a mechanistic continuity in government stretching back to its inception in 1787, when Newtonian concepts and devices were implanted into the American constitution.

Evidence of just such an eighteenth-century accommodation of politics to mechanics is profuse and wide-ranging. The conditions to such a construction being placed upon the origins and design of the constitution can be found. Included in these would be the following:

1 An active interest in, and appreciation of, science within American society at the time.
2 A contemporary fascination with Newton's schema of the world as a model of the interplay of physical forces and also an aesthetic symbol of

the inner harmonies of nature.
3 The high status of science in American culture both as a vanguard and as a symbol of a generalized dependence upon reason that had fostered the political radicalism and social emancipation of the American revolution.
4 A concern for the practical application of scientific knowledge in the furtherance of human progress and in the cause of socially beneficial objectives.
5 The prevailing appeal of rational enquiry and empirical philosophy, which could provide alternative sources of knowledge through the Newtonian method of reasoned observation.
6 The existence of a compulsive Newtonian faith in an indigenous and universal order to nature whose regularities and general laws are ultimately accessible to the human intellect.
7 Signs of the immediacy of science to politics as witnessed by many of the Founding Fathers, who were not only philosopher statesmen but also amateur scientists and students of natural philosophy.
8 The contemporary belief in the accessibility of a 'political science' concerning the nature of government and the ways in which political arrangements might be consciously created to accommodate the effects of human motivations and behaviour.
9 The Founding Fathers as a representative selection of that educated leadership sector of American society most steeped in the Enlightenment passion for free enquiry, scientific discovery, and utilitarian knowledge; and most immersed in the contemporary obsession with the vocabulary and value of balance in eighteenth-century thought.[39]

Taking this background into account, and bearing in mind that the Founding Fathers were engaged in the task of deliberately devising a system of government, then it might be thought of as inconceivable that they were not strongly influenced by Newtonianism and that they did not draw upon the familiar principles of Newtonian mechanics in the structural arrangements which they concluded. On the contrary, the system of separated and balanced powers might justifiably be construed as an authentic extrapolation of Newtonian technique and substance into the sphere of institutional dynamics. According to many commentators the constitution does stand as a monument to the pervasive suggestiveness of Newtonian mechanics experienced in the epoch that gave rise to the document. This position is presented with differing degrees of force and argued to different levels of conclusiveness, but, as the following examples will show, the overall direction of the analysis is quite clear.

To I. Bernard Cohen, the distinguished historian of science, 'the Founding Fathers could not help but be imbued with Newtonian science'.[40] 'The debates on the constitution,' Cohen notes, 'were held up by questions on the meaning and possible applications of Newtonian physical properties.'[41] In the following extract Cohen uses the example of John Adams, who confessed himself to be 'in the habit of balancing everything':[42]

> In his defense of the American constitutions, Adams cited Isaac Newton as an authority when discussing the best form of constitutional government. Arguing against Franklin's desire for a unicameral or single-assembly system .... Adams remarked: 'The president of Pennsylvania might, upon such an occasion, have recollected one of Sir Isaac Newton's laws of motion, namely, – that reaction must always be equal and contrary, or there can never be any rest.'[43]

Richard Hofstadter draws attention to Newtonian science as a contemporary source of mechanical analogies to the Founding Fathers:

> The eighteenth century ... was dominated intellectually by the scientific work of Newton, and ... mechanical metaphors sprang ... naturally to men's minds.... Men had found a rational order in the universe and they hoped that it could be transferred to politics.... Madison spoke in the most precise Newtonian language when he said that such a 'natural' government must be so constructed 'that its several constituent parts may, by their mutual relations, be the means of keeping each other in their proper places'.[44]

Clinton Rossiter is also sharply aware of Newton's potent influence in shaping the Founding Fathers' general mental outlook and in inducing within them a receptivity to certain constitutional ideas:

> It is going a bit too far to look upon the American Constitution as a monument to Sir Isaac Newton, but certainly the widespread acceptance of his theory of a harmonious universe helped create an intellectual atmosphere in which a system of checks and balances would have special appeal to constitution-makers.[45]

Felix Gilbert, referring to late eighteenth-century America in more general terms, asserts the existence of an implicit link between the Newtonian ethos and contemporary constitutional ideas:

> The eighteenth century conceived life in terms of an artificial mechanism, thus the more complicated machine appeared as the more perfect one. Consequently involved mechanical concepts such as 'balance of power' and 'mixed government' were favorite principles of political thought.[46]

Martin Landau's interest in political metaphors and paradigms leads him to underline the inspirational significance of the eighteenth century's cult of balance to the formulation of the American constitution:

> One central unifying image seems to distinguish the way men think. In the eighteenth century it was the machine that provided this image, and it was

the Newtonian system that was taken as the model on which all rational inquiry was to be based. So strong were these influences that numerous scholars of the Enlightenment have regarded the form of the American constitutionalism as a direct product of mechanism.... What is to the point is the sense of certainty that was attached to the concept of balance, and the fact that this assurance reflected the triumph of mechanism. With but few exceptions the constitution-makers thought that the government they were constructing was in accord with nature's design: in establishing the separation and balancing of power they were following nature's way.[47]

Richard Mosier likewise draws attention to the constitutional repercussions of 'an age which indulged in Newtonian science and conceived the science of mechanics to be the foundation of the science of politics':[48]

> This approach to the science of politics clearly reveals the influence of the science of mechanics; for the principle of balance of power, of harmonization of sovereignties, is a reflection of the well-known principle of mechanics that action and reaction are equal.... A republican government, in brief, was like the world of Newton, a huge machine in perfect equilibrium, endlessly repeating, but never violating, a few stable and harmonious laws. It was no wonder that the young republicans insisted so universally on the principles of mechanism, or that they clung so tenaciously to the picture of the world which the science of mechanics had bequeathed to them; for they were building a government according to those principles which science had discovered to lie at the heart of reality.[49]

Stanley Pargellis is also very mindful of the implicit Newtonian orthodoxy that lay at the back of the Founding Fathers' perspective of the challenge that confronted them. They were immersed in the history and traditions of mixed government, the terms of which were in the eighteenth century 'taken from the realm of mathematics and physics':[50]

> However hardheaded they were in seeking the national and individual security they knew the country needed, however practical in adapting colonial and state constitutional experience, they still bathed willy-nilly in the stream of eighteenth century thought. Arguments for balance were all about them, in pamphlet and treatise, in legal commentary, in reports of parliamentary debates, in encyclopaedias, in classical works, in books on education, on morality, on philosophy, as well as in John Adams's book – the whole of it a learned defense of balance – which they were all reading in the spring of 1787, and in Madison's doctrinaire pronouncements on the convention floor.[51]

This influence of Newtonianism is enough for Winton Solberg to state categorically that 'the notion of government as a mechanical equipoise of powers which grew out of Newtonian thought captivated the delegates'.[52]

To Woodrow Wilson this notion of government did more than just grow out of Newtonian thought. It was explicitly 'conceived in the Newtonian spirit and upon the Newtonian principle'.[53] So much so, in fact, that the constitution of the United States might be said to have 'been made under the dominion of the Newtonian theory':[54]

> The government of the United States was constructed upon the Whig theory of political dynamics, which was a sort of unconscious copy of the Newtonian theory of the universe.... As Montesquieu pointed out to them in his lucid way, [the Whigs] had sought to balance executive, legislature, and judiciary off against one another by a series of checks and counterpoises, which Newton might readily have recognised as suggestive of the mechanism of the heavens. The makers of our federal constitution followed the scheme as they found it expounded in Montesquieu, followed it with genuine scientific enthusiasm.... Politics is turned into mechanics under his touch. The theory of gravitation is supreme.[55]

Laurence Tribe makes use of the eighteenth century's fascination with the clockwork mechanism of a Newtonian universe to make his point:

> The Madisonian clockwork would enable the forces and counterforces of government to mesh ... and to check one another as needed to shield the individual and community from governmental oppression and discrimination. The concerns that inspired the system's design were human; the design itself, mechanical.[56]

Although J. R. Pole discerns a definite historical affinity between the American constitution and Newtonian mechanics, he is inclined to attribute the constitution's Newtonian credentials to its form rather than to the manner of its inception:

> After the creation of the American constitution it became something of a commonplace to compare the system to the Newtonian cosmic order. The elements, each of which was impelled by a natural propensity to go in its own direction, were kept in place by the countervailing force of the others; in the federal system correct proportions were maintained by a similar balance, while the gravitational power of the federal government held the states in their orbits.[57]

Walter Lippmann, on the other hand, not only acknowledges the influence of Newtonianism upon both the origins of the constitution and upon the intention of the framers, but also draws attention to the way in which the constitution's mechanistic principles have induced in the popular mind the belief in the actual presence of a mechanical basis to the structure and operation of American government:

> They [i.e. Founding Fathers] worked with the philosophy of their age.

> Living in the eighteenth century, they thought in the images of Newton and Montesquieu.... Our own federal constitution is a striking example of [the] machine conception of government. It is probably the most important instance we have of the deliberate application of a mechanical philosophy to human ... affairs.... Is there in all the world a more plain-spoken attempt to contrive an automatic governor – a machine which would preserve its balance without the need of taking human nature into account.... Our theories assume, and our language is fitted to thinking of government as a frame.... We picture political institutions as mechanically constructed contrivances within which the nation's life is contained and compelled to approximate some abstract idea of justice or liberty.[58]

In his study of the constitution, suggestively entitled *A Machine that would go of Itself*, Michael Kammen also acknowledges the way in which the document became increasingly conceived as a Newtonian construct:

> The notion of a constitution as some sort of machine or engine had its origins in Newtonian science. Enlightened philosophers, such as David Hume, liked to contemplate the world with all of its components as a great machine.... Analogies between the U.S. constitution and a piece of machinery had appeared ever since 1787, but became more common after the middle of the nineteenth century, perhaps because technology began to pervade the public consciousness.[59]

This Newtonian tradition within the constitution is taken as read by Arthur Schlesinger, who, as a result, believes that the American system of government is sufficiently comparable to a machine to prompt concern as to how it could be made less like a machine:

> The Founding Fathers were good Newtonians, and their system of checks and balances, conceived almost as a mechanism, contained an inherent tendency toward inertia.... The question has always remained – and has provided a central theme of American political history – how a government based on the separation of powers could be made to work.[60]

From these observations it is evident that a distinctive element of American commentary upon the past adheres to the belief that Newton's influence was so pervasive at the time as to extend to the point of inspiring the Founding Fathers in the detailed formulation of their constitution. 'Historians of the enlightenment have quite properly recognised the importance of Newton as a symbol' of natural philosophy and as a 'rallying cry for radical politics and social reform'.[61] In America 'science became the lodestar for those who thought they were at the dawn of a new age; modern scientists, not ancient philosophers, guided them into the future'.[62] Significantly, many of the foremost scientific figures in the latter half of the eighteenth century were political activists in their own right. Likewise, many of that society's political leaders had scientific training and scientific interests. It was this fusion of science and politics which is thought to have received its ultimate expression in the constitution. It is claimed that, at a time when the 'dominant metaphors of the age constantly invoked the ideal of balance',[63] the Founding Fathers, as philosopher statesmen, drew their inspiration from Newton. They did so not merely in respect to the declared rationalism of their exercise in governmental design, nor simply in connection with the general undertone of mechanical analogies and similes in their several analyses, but in their implicit acknowledgement of Newtonianism as a model of political imitation in direct mechanistic terms. According to this view, it was a measure of the age that the Founding Fathers submitted to this compulsive idea that the constitution could, and should, emulate the properties of Newtonian natural law, which were seen as being so endlessly applicable in the universe. It was also a measure of the age that the Framers believed that they were changing the art of government into a science by the transmutation of the classical-corporatist conception of a constitution into a contrived autonomous mechanism of discrete yet interdependent parts held in a self-adjusting equilibrium.

The constitution, therefore, can be seen as representing one of the most significant and far-reaching developments of Newtonian mechanics and one of the most outstanding professions of faith in the force of reason to have emanated from the Enlightenment. If Newton and Newtonianism in its various guises served to embody much of the Enlightenment's meaning, then it would appear in this context that the United States' Enlightenment credentials were quite exceptional. The new republic acquired the reputation of having constructed its very constitution upon Newtonian principles in the most direct sense. From that point, a conspicuous Newtonian tradition is reputed to have been formally introduced into the American organization of political authority and, thereupon, allowed to ramify throughout American political history to the present day.

Chapter two

The death of constitutional Newtonianism?

There is an obvious appeal to the traditional Enlightenment solution to the puzzle of American constitutionalism's liaison with Newtonian mechanics. Such an interpretation is clear and clean. From this viewpoint, the formulation of the constitution can be made to appear as an exercise in reasoned enquiry and as a practical example of the utility of marshalled experience in arriving at the structural requirements necessary for an effective constitution. The Founding Fathers' claim to rationality was supported by the assumption that they intuitively reflected their era's adherence to Newtonian philosophy and, consequently, infused the constitution with mechanical principles of which the most important was that of balance. The concept of balance in the constitution, therefore, became attributed either directly or indirectly to the compulsive attraction of Newton's perspective of nature as an intrinsic harmony of maintained balances. Constitutional balance became not only a symbol but a physical manifestation of nature. Nevertheless, the main problem concerning such an interpretation is that it has been denounced in many quarters as wholly inaccurate and fundamentally untrue. The challenge comes from four main sources. Three of these are objections based upon historical grounds. The fourth is an empirical challenge to the existence of the constitution's mechanistic properties.

America's own experience

First, it is claimed that America was formed not through the medium of Enlightenment ideas but through an indigenous process that was facilitated by the imperative of America's own unique conditions. In this guise, America was a product not of the mind but of experience – ideas being subsequent to, and not prior to, circumstances. This objection to the notion of the Enlightenment in America is founded upon the belief that the conditions of the New World were so exceptional that they nurtured a society, naturally endowed with many of the arrangements and values to which the European Enlightenment could only aspire. While European *philosophes* might struggle against the forces of the *ancien régime* in their crusade to translate their intellectual prescriptions into reality, America proffered itself as an instinctive model of the *philosophes'* objectives. In other words, the American Enlightenment was not only a misnomer but a tautology, for America was instinctively enlightened.

The New World had achieved this distinction without recourse to the European Enlightenment and without recourse to any self-conscious assimilation of modernistic ideas. According to this view, American freedom 'was a matter of birthright and not of conquest'.[1] Americans had been 'born equal, instead of becoming so'.[2] Society was a collective idiosyncracy derived from America's unique geo-political position, its abundance of land and resources, its status as a sanctuary for so many nonconformists, its general lack of a traditional order of class deference, and its multi-faceted orientation to an ethos of the new – all of which rendered America a land apart and a people divorced from the categories of Europe. Through a purely spontaneous and indigenous process, Americans evolved towards a state which could be characterized as enlightened in European terms, but whose enlightened condition could not in any way be regarded as a related product of the European Enlightenment. It was in effect an enlightenment related to circumstances and to native instinct.

This view of American history is given a most resolute form by Louis Hartz in *The Liberal Tradition in America*.[3] In this influential work, Hartz asserts that the constitutions of the New World led to a natural commitment among Americans to those liberal virtues associated in the Old World with John Locke, but which in the New World appeared to be nothing other than the outgrowth of social experience – a mostly unconscious and unexpressed consensus of values. Without the distraction of either a revolutionary tradition or a reactionary tradition, Americans were permitted to proceed intuitively towards a self-enclosing circle of values and perceptions lying within the only available dimension of bourgeois liberalism. According to Hartz, the middle class was so ubiquitous and its dogma of possessive individualism so pervasive that American society quickly developed a 'submerged and absolute liberal faith'[4] in norms which were manifestly self-evident and which, therefore, required no intellectual rationalization of their effect or of their worth. The 'absolute and irrational attachment'[5] for Locke, born out of the ' "free air" of American life',[6] not only eliminated the stimulus to concerted social and political thought, but atrophied the very capacity of Americans for any serious philosophical speculation. This impulsive and emotional traditionalism rendered Americans free and enlightened irrespective of the Enlightenment itself.

An even more potent objection to the American Enlightenment notion is provided by Daniel Boorstin. He explicitly condemns the very idea that the American revolution or the American constitution can in any way be characterized as part of the undifferentiated international movement known as the Enlightenment. Like Hartz, he claims that America is an exceptional society which should not be categorized with European cultures and countries. Unlike Hartz, however, Boorstin is not prepared to entrust the anti-Enlightenment argument to purely geo-political or socio-economic factors. Boorstin claims unequivocally that America is special because it is divinely ordained – 'God himself drew the plans of our career and marked its outlines in our history.'[7] The result of this mystical exceptionalism (what Boorstin calls 'giveness') is that American history, to Boorstin, can be understood only in terms of working itself out from an original seed which had already determined all subsequent developments in a predefined manner – 'giveness is the belief that values in America are in some way or another automatically defined: given by certain facts of geography or history peculiar to us'.[8] Instead of the European Enlightenment providing the crucial injection of ideas into eighteenth-century America, therefore, the ideas themselves were already inherent in the New World and intrinsic to the autonomy of its historic processes:

> Our theory of society is conceived as a kind of exoskeleton, like the shell of the lobster. We think of ourselves as growing *into* our skeleton, filling it out with the experience and resources of recent ages. But we always suppose that the outlines were rigidly drawn in the beginning. Our mission, then, is simply to demonstrate the truth – or rather the workability – of the original theory.[9]

To Boorstin, neither the American revolution nor the American constitution were occasions for observing the susceptibility of America to absorbing European intellectual principles and translating them from the abstract into reality. They were rather more examples of a professed emancipation from European philosophy through the ineluctable passage of history designed to demonstrate not just the superfluity but the incongruity of externally conceived ideas within the context of an intellectually autonomous New World.

Such strident declarations of independence on the part of experience made Hartz and Boorstin exemplify a common theme in American history. The theme is variously presented, but its major characteristic has been to reduce the general significance attached to reason and abstraction, and to emphasize the role of history, tradition, indigenous circumstances, and even religious sentiment[10] in the evolution of late eighteenth-century American society. In contrast to those who envisage the Founding Fathers as a group of cerebral scholars steeped in the most recent advances in social analysis and 'political science', there are just as many historians who, for example, base the Founders' reputation firmly upon their practical open-minded commitment to achieving workable solutions to stated problems – even at the expense of accepting compromises and half measures in the cause of managing conflict.[11] John P. Roche, to quote one case in point, rejects the assertion that the Framers divided their time between philosophical discussions on government and reading classics in political theory. On the contrary, 'their concerns were highly practical'[12] and 'they spent little time canvassing abstractions':[13]

The constitution, then, was not an apotheosis of 'constitutionalism', a triumph of architectonic genius; it was a patchwork sewn together under the pressure of both time and events.... The careful observer of the day-to-day work of the convention finds no overarching principles.[14]

These sentiments are reiterated with differing emphases in a variety of contexts in much of the historical literature on the period. The point usually made is that the significance of rationally derived social and political principles in the emergence of America as an independent entity was due either to the way they justified already existing conditions, or to the fact that they were formulated by Americans on the basis of their own experience and in line with their personal motivations, aspirations, and interests.[15] Cecilia Kenyon, for example, states that in the 1780s Americans were drawn to Charles-Louis de Secondat Montesquieu's (1689–1755) espousal of the principle of the separation of powers because it 'reflected their own experience and inclinations'.[16] In like manner, James Conniff asserts that James Madison's sociological analysis and theories of politics were sufficiently home-grown to be understood in terms of a synthesis of ideas prompted and shaped by 'the lessons he drew from his extensive practical experience in American politics'.[17] These interpretations, and the many others like them, reflect a widespread movement on the part of many Americans to retrieve the integrity of their history from the compromising embrace of the European Enlightenment.

America's British experience

The second objection to the elevation of Enlightenment reason and of the Enlightenment's archangel, Isaac Newton, to the position of determinants of the American constitution comes from those who wish to emphasize the cultural continuity between the British and American political arrangements in the eighteenth century. By the second half of the century, when American interest in the British system was at its height, the imperial constitution had been processed into an object of virtue and stability primarily on account of its structural properties, which were persistently reduced to a construction of balance. And yet, if Britain's curious pastiche of institutions, powers, branches, social estates, and varying principles of governmental organization could be manageably reduced to the central objective of balanced government, then that balance was a very nebulous one. It represented only the merest outline of a framework and only the vaguest notion as to its actual operation. It was at best a belief in the *prima facie* existence of a balance within British government, but a balance with an imprecise nature and one, therefore, with enormous potential for varying interpretations.

In contrast to the customary picture of the eighteenth century as a tranquil era in which Britain enjoyed the benefits of settled government bequeathed by the Glorious Revolution, the century was characterized by a continual debate over just this issue of balanced government. Not only did the principle lend itself to heated constitutional argument, but political disputes were invariably translated into efforts to legitimize one interpretation rather than another concerning the real nature of the balance in the British constitution.[18] Appropriately, it was also a period when the constitution was subjected to intense scrutiny by commentators and observers each seeking to explain its mysteries and to account for the relationship of its constituent parts to one another. Montesquieu,[19] William Blackstone,[20] William Paley,[21] Jean de Lolme,[22] and Henry St John Bolingbroke[23] all produced popular theories about the manner in which three social orders, three political institutions, and three governmental functions were combined in one way or another to produce a framework of reciprocal restraint. It is true that 'if the theory was evident and unanimously agreed upon, the mechanics of the operation were not'.[24] Consequently, the theme of balance was subjected to varying interpretations, which were by no means devoid of political motivation, nor always sensitive to the distinction between description and prescription.

The different permutations of balance between and among a variety of components available in the British system became so central to the constitution's meaning that the principle of equilibrium ultimately provided the only common frame of reference for both traditionalists and radicals alike. How best to maintain an ancient equilibrium, or to restore the constitution's lost heritage of balance, exercised the most gifted political and legal minds of the day, as each sought to acquire legitimacy for its position by what had become the constitution's primary prescriptive feature. Balance permeated the political vocabulary of eighteenth-century Britain. It dominated the rules of engagement between political adversaries to such an extent that a structure of balanced powers and mutual control came to be recognized as the indispensable guarantor of Englishmen's rights and liberties.

This British theme of balanced government had a direct historical relevance to the colonists in North America. This was partly because, as British subjects, they were enamoured of a constitution which bestowed its blessings upon them in the New World. That this was so cannot be doubted. When John Adams referred to the British constitution as 'the most perfect combination of human powers in society which finite wisdom has yet contrived and reduced to practice for the preservation of liberty',[25] it was nothing more than a conventional eulogy for the time. The colonists customarily lent their voice to the praise heaped upon the constitution of the mother country during this period, and regarded themselves and their liberties as the living embodiment of the British system's capacity for balance and stability. Although there was, according to Bernard Bailyn,[26] no real understanding as to how the balanced government of the British constitution operated across the empire or within individual colonial societies, there was little doubt among the colonists that the principle of balance existed in British government and that it was this principle which was primarily responsible for the maintenance of their liberties.

It was against this landscape and in accordance with its main precepts that the American colonists challenged the British government on its own constitutional terms and justified the subsequent confrontation as an attempt to restore a stability that had been lost through an imbalance of its constituent forces – an imbalance which was debilitating the British constitution and endangering traditional liberties both at home and abroad in the imperial possessions. So immersed were they in the precedent and protocol of the British constitution, so entrenched in the established technique of dissent used by radicals on both sides of the Atlantic, and so conditioned into the infrastructure of British forms and conditions that the colonists can be seen as being unable, either emotionally or intellectually, to extricate themselves from the British influence even after they had secured independence. This view is often supported by the constitutional structures of the new states, most of which revealed an anxiety over unbalanced government by the provision of upper chambers with a membership drawn from the propertied sector of society. Some states allayed fears over the lost executive element of monarchy by the establishment of strong governors with varying levels of independence from, and with veto powers over, their respective legislatures. While these arrangements could not be said to have been motivated purely by a desire to reintroduce uncorrupted versions of the British constitution, they were, nevertheless, strongly reminiscent of the British model and were, at least partly, prompted by the genuine concern felt at the time over the lack of a monarchical and aristocratic element to serve as counterweights to the mass.[27]

The claim that American republicanism had been unable to disengage itself from the influence of British political culture, however, is given its strongest endorsement by the federal constitution of 1787. Far from being the product of unencumbered and autonomous reason, the constitution can appear as the fullest expression of American conditioning to past practices and old habits. It can be seen as a device by which the United States could regress to a central form of government after the revolutionary epoch when decentralization and dispersal of authority had become the touchstone of anti-imperial republicanism. The constitution was condemned by its critics at the time on precisely these grounds.[28] They detected a return to the internal forms and processes of the British constitution. Like the state governments', the rationale of the federal government's institutional structure was a separation of powers. This in itself represented a potentially radical and strenuously republican principle of government, which afforded supremacy to the law-making institution and which possessed little or no inherent capacity to generate checks and balances. In America's republican experience, however, the system of separated powers had become implicated with the self-regulatory objectives of mixed government. Although the country had no formal means of social differentiation to service a class-oriented system of checks and balances, America's indigenous political institutions provided the raw materials for a state of equilibrium, by which the popular assembly would be prevented from falling prey to its own impulsive excesses. In these most critical of exercises in governmental design, it was to be expected that basic American dispositions towards political authority would be revealed. On this basis, the claim is made that the federal convention betrayed a continued dependence by Americans upon the British constitution as a venerated and inspirational norm to which the Framers had been ineluctably drawn. Nowhere is the suspicion of cultural conditioning and political continuity greater than in the federal constitution, which gave sanction to a profusion of checks and balances in that most central and significant part of American government. Instead of reason and modernity, therefore, the constitution can be read as blind instinct and anachronism. The Founding Fathers can appear as radical antiquarians but antiquarian nevertheless who, while formally embracing popular sovereignty, sought to attach it to the traditional British accoutrements of balanced government.

The ancestry of balanced government

The third means by which the Enlightenment's infusion of Newtonian mechanics into the American constitution has been summarily ejected is through recourse to the history of balanced government as an idea. In essence, the argument here is that, even allowing for the Founding Fathers being motivated by a conscious intention to translate the idea of balanced government into the reality of government machinery, the idea itself can be shown to antedate the Newtonian cult by centuries. It should be stated at the outset that the idea of balance between differentiated constituent parts of a government, and between the differentiated principles embodied within a government, has had a wide currency in the literature of political thought. The idea can be traced back even as far as Plato (428–348 BC)[29] and Aristotle (384–322 BC),[30] who both lent their names to the principle of a mixed state within which the strengths and values of different classes could be fused together to maximum effect.[31] The theory of mixed government, however, only reached its mature and popularly identifiable form with Polybius (c. 201–118 BC).[32] Up to then, a mixture at the institutional level was seen as a consequence of the mixture of classes in society and, in particular, as an embodiment of the stabilizing force of a society's middle class. It was Polybius's study of the Roman republic that pushed mixed government to the point where it became a deliberate institutional device for achieving a mutual balance between all three social classes. The balance was to be secured by organizing the constituent units of government in such a way that they individually embodied the distinctive interests and passions of each class. These interests and passions would then be effectively offset against one another in the inevitable intermingling of powers and responsibilities on the part of these class-based units during the course of the normal functioning of government. In effect the three divisions of society were to be directly translated into government through separate class-based institutions, which would share in the process of government.

In contrast to Plato and Aristotle, Polybius placed a distinct emphasis upon the dynamic nature of the balance acquired by mixed government. The accent was not upon fusion, blending, or aggregation, but upon political competitiveness, reciprocal checks, and the interaction of institutional forces.[33] The purpose of Polybius's mixed government was also much more aligned to the problem of controlling and delimiting the power of the state than either Plato's or Aristotle's form of mixed government. With the assistance of Cicero (106–43 BC), who later endorsed it, and of Tacitus (AD 55–120), who subsequently celebrated it as a principle of government – albeit a largely unrealizable one – Polybius's instinctive exposition of mixed government became established as one of those fixtures of received classical wisdom in political science which was later to be rediscovered and adopted in social situations far removed from the ancient world.[34]

The individual to whom the modern resurrection of the mixed government principle is normally attributed is Niccolo Machiavelli (1469–1527). He led the Renaissance reinstatement of this classical doctrine through his comparative and historical assessment of past states, from which he concluded that the ideal form of government was constituted on the basis of a balance between classes and, to a lesser and more ambiguous extent, a balance between the functions of government. Machiavelli applauded the balance between the patricians and the plebeians as the key to the success of Rome.[35] He wished to capture the same inner social vigour through a socio-political balance, whereby the main groupings of society would achieve an equilibrium, either of their own accord under the aegis of a sovereign authority, or through the direct intervention of such an authority. This sort of shared responsibility, evocative of Polybius, would lead to stability and moderation. It was a very tenuous and a basically implausible synthesis of democracy and monarchy, yet it became an integral part of Machiavelli's 'classical bequest' to the political thought of the seventeenth and eighteenth centuries.

According to Kurt von Fritz, the author of the standard work on Polybius, 'no part of ancient political theory has had greater influence on political theory and practice in modern times than the theory of the mixed constitution'.[36] While this is a contestable claim, what cannot be doubted is the way the whole concept of mixed and balanced government became a focus of political argument during the seventeenth and eighteenth centuries. The term suffered or benefited, as the case may be, from being susceptible to a host of different interpretations, supporting a variety of positions and lending legitimacy to diverse social and political developments. In England, in particular, the term 'mixed government' floated through the turbulent waters of seventeenth-century political history like a half-submerged treasure from antiquity – clearly a very valuable classical artefact and one with the property of being endlessly manipulable in meaning. The term was already an obscure one, but in the seventeenth century it was complicated even further by the emergence of a separate constitutional doctrine, which was raised alongside the mixed state as a principle of government. This was the doctrine of the separation of powers, which sought to delimit the powers of each institution to the individual functions that needed to be performed in government.[37] The emphasis in the separation of powers doctrine was on matching functions explicitly to institutions and of matching institutions explicitly to functions. Thus, according to this scheme, monarchy would be stripped of its class connotations, its general authority, and its political power in other branches of government and be confined to the role of an executive office. This doctrine was amply suited to the Parliamentarians in their fight to reduce the power of the monarchy. It provided a rationale of government which replaced class privilege, and the need for mixture, with abstract functional requirements and the objective of co-ordinated yet separate specialist agencies of government. Instead of openly invoking a class attack upon the king, therefore, the separation of powers concept allowed a balance to be argued in the more abstract and less provocative language of functional analysis – even if the stimulus of the argument remained as class-oriented as it had been before.

Both these schemes of government, mixed government and the separation of powers, were geared towards the same basic principle of a system of checks upon the arbitrary exercise of governmental power. While mixed government was primarily associated with existing interfunctional agencies representative of different social sectors, the separation of powers format was associated with a division of specifically functional units devoid of particular social linkages. A key feature of the great disputes in seventeenth-century English history was precisely the attempt to work into the constitution either the precepts of mixed government, which would rationalize the status of monarchy, or the more radical separation of powers doctrine, which would tend to render the units and rationale of mixed government irrelevant.[38] In the cause of one sort of balance or another the century witnessed a crisis of political authority and constitutional legitimacy during which a profusion of arguments were presented that sought not only to define the elements of mixed government and the units of separated powers within the English constitution, but to establish the ways in which the relationship between the elements or the units could be represented as a balance.

In the confused aftermath of both the Puritan revolution and the Glorious Revolution, the principle of balance began to be developed within the disciplined categories of the separated powers doctrine, with the object of qualifying the newly concentrated power of Parliament, while at the same time preventing any recurrence of Stuart absolutism. It was left to the eighteenth century, however, to witness the full ramifications of the confluence of these two constitutional hybrids. One significant effect of the British constitution's transmutation into balanced government was the rise of the 'Commonwealthman tradition'. The term 'Commonwealthman' refers to those dissenters and radicals like John Trenchard, Thomas Gordon, Robert Molesworth, and Thomas Hollis who sought to redeem the historical perspective of the British constitution from what they took to be the enforced myopia and dangerous complacency of the Glorious Revolution's 'new beginning'.[39] They did this by reviving the spirit of ancient English liberty which had been so emotively and effectively exploited by the Commonwealth and republican apologists in the seventeenth century (e.g. James Harrington, Andrew Marvel, Algernon Sidney, John Milton, and Henry Neville). These writers had attempted to establish the concept of English liberty on a time scale stretching back to the Saxon period, which supposedly featured a system of freehold tenure, a free parliament, and a militia force. In this context, the Norman conquest was characterized as a form of tyranny which had shattered the idyll of Saxon gothic liberty under the 'yoke' of feudal tenure, canon law, and baronial power.[40] Gradually the original state of this indigenous freedom had been clawed back by centuries of struggle which had culminated in the deposition of the Stuarts. The 'Commonwealthmen' of the late seventeenth and eighteenth centuries extended this process of the progressive reinstatement of Saxon liberty by accepting the Glorious Revolution of 1688 as merely a constituent part of a continuing historical struggle. In contrast to many of their contemporaries, the 'Commonwealthmen' did not regard the Glorious Revolution as a climactic triumph of English liberty, which had raised the country to a permanent plateau of serene stability. On the contrary, their extended perspective of English history led them to conclude that the precious quality of freedom remained an extremely tenuous one, which was in constant danger of being eroded through lack of vigilance. In the apparent tranquillity of the Hanoverian monarchy, therefore, the 'Commonwealthmen' believed that the battle for liberty was still in progress and would continue to be so as long as men appreciated the value of liberty and understood the fragility of its nature.

The significance of the 'Commonwealthman' tradition to the study of the American colonists' disposition towards balanced government is twofold. First, the tradition might almost be said to reflect the prevailing view amongst Americans of themselves. Many colonists identified strongly with the idea of ancient Saxon liberty and with their own status as nonconformists who had fled tyranny, in order to establish a system of English liberty, public virtue, and Saxon simplicity in the New World. Americans were highly responsive to this theme of an ancient constitution, and highly sensitive towards any explicit or implicit assault upon the bequest of such a constitution. This being so, they developed a close affinity with just those dissidents, radicals, and independents in eighteenth-century England who were maintaining and developing an emphatically historical perspective of the British constitution, in order to use it as a cultural norm by which to evaluate and criticize contemporary conditions.[41]

The second way in which the 'Commonwealthman' tradition was significant to the subsequent history of American constitutional thought lay in the importance attached to balanced government in that tradition. These disciples of Whig continuity were acutely aware that the trend in all stable governments was that of degeneration into one of the three corrupt forms described by Aristotle. Like their more mainstream and establishment contemporaries, they shared a common desire that government should remain balanced. But this was not the balance that was safely assumed to exist by virtue of the revolutionary settlement of 1688. The concept of balanced government in the 'Commonwealthman' tradition was an integral part of the ancient constitution itself. As a result, the whole principle of balanced government became a historical standard against which the presumed mechanics of the officially and recently inaugurated balance could be assessed. According to J. G. A. Pocock, it was the 'classicising influence of Harringtonian ideas upon English thought'[42] which provided the link between Polybius on the one hand and Gordon and Trenchard on the other. Harrington came to be in this position not merely by recognizing the need for a form of mixed government in his *Oceana*, but by advocating a balanced commonwealth through a wide distribution of landed property. Since property to Harrington was synonymous with power and independence, a balanced distribution of property would secure the republic's political stability. In the hands of what Pocock terms the eighteenth-century 'Neo-Harringtonians' these ideas were converted from prescription into established historical fact and, subsequently, worked into the ancient constitution of Saxon freeholders:

> The essence of neo-Harringtonianism lay in its reconciliation of Harrington's vision of a balanced commonwealth of proprietors with the older English vision of the ancient constitution, and one result of this somewhat uneasy marriage was the importance of Polybian and Machiavellian ideas into the way in which Englishmen thought about their constitution. The seventeenth century saw the constitution as ancient; the eighteenth, as ancient and balanced.[43]

Through *Cato's Letters*, written by Gordon and Trenchard, 'the ideas of this school were passed to the American colonies',[44] where they permeated the conceptual landscape of the American revolutionaries. In this way it could be said that the American concern for balanced government was ultimately rooted in the classical past. The tradition of mixed government had successfully been transmitted from Greek and Italian Renaissance theorists into the British tradition by way of Milton, Harrington, and others during the Commonwealth period in the seventeenth century. Thereupon the tradition was conveyed through the radical-traditionalism and ancient libertarianism of the 'Commonwealthmen' and the 'Neo-Harringtonians' of the eighteenth century, who confronted the threat of courtly and ministerial executive power by recourse both to the principle of balanced government and to its assumed actuality in English history. From this foundation, the classical conception of balanced government crossed the Atlantic as part and parcel of the republican radicalism of the Walpole era.

Placed in this light, the position and role of balanced government in American constitutionalism become a product at least as much of ancient prescription and cultural custom as of empirical analysis and applied mechanics. The concept of balanced government emerges as an established principle of constitutional virtue which, through history, had generated such an infrastructure of accepted analysis and instinctive terminology that it came to constitute a paradigm of good government. Americans were no less susceptible to it than any one else, and it is in this context that the American system of differentiated and competing governmental powers can be seen as representative of an intuitive adherence to past experience and orthodox solutions. This is what Hannah Arendt was referring to when she reminded her readers that the balance of power in the American constitution was not an Enlightenment invention inspired by Newtonian mechanics, but the corroboration of something very much older:

> The idea [of the balance of powers] – far from being the outgrowth of a mechanical, Newtonian world view, as has recently been suggested – is very old; it occurs, at least implicitly, in the traditional discussion of mixed forms of government and thus can be traced back to Aristotle, or at least to Polybius.[45]

The same point is echoed by Norman C. Thomas in response to Harvey Wheeler's provocative essay on constitutionalism,[46] in which Wheeler lays particular emphasis upon the American constitution's Newtonian character. Thomas draws attention to the danger of obscuring the richness of the constitution's manifold sources by shrouding it with a purely mechanical rationale. In conclusion, he provides the archetypal dismissal of those who would foist Newtonian mechanics upon the constitution's ancestry – namely, that 'the concept of the balanced constitution has been a persistent and recurring theme in American constitutional politics and is more than mere political Newtonianism'.[47]

The modern dissipation of balanced government

The main assaults on the Newtonian construction of the American constitution have up to this point been challenges made on the basis of historical research into the period prior to, and before, the year 1787. The final blow to strike at the Enlightenment vision of a continuity of self-perpetuating constitutional dynamics comes in the form of changes in American society which are claimed to have rendered the Newtonianism in the constitution altogether less convincing as an explanatory cause and less relevant as a binding condition of government. In short, the manner in which American society and government have evolved during the twentieth century, in particular, has allowed for a different way of looking at both the present and the past.

The effects of economic, social, and political developments in the United States can be construed as being directly contrary to the ethos and operation of balanced government. The progressive centralization of resources, ownership, and direction in the economy have led to an ever tighter concentration of industrial integration and financial control. The unceasing tide of corporate mergers has turned America not only into a society of wage and salary earners living and working in urban conditions, but also into a land of closed frontiers, mass markets, integrated communications networks, standardized products, cultural commonality, and a genuinely national economy.[48] A concomitant development has been a decline in the traditional diversity of American life-styles and attitudes. The onset of greater social integration has witnessed a consequent weakening of some of those barriers which have historically divided the American population into different sectors. And one of the chief results of this reductionism in experience and behaviour produced by the conditions of a mass society has been the stimulus it has provided to a growing national consciousness.

In the specific field of political organization and behaviour, the increasing nationalization of American culture has brought with it an increased nationalization of politics.[49] The old blocs of regional and social power that used to be largely insulated from shifting political loyalties elsewhere have fragmented in the face of changing social and economic conditions. The south, for example, still remains the most distinctive region in the country, yet it is no longer the political bloc apart from the rest of America that it once was – 'the fall of the white supremacists means that poor farmers in southern Appalachia are more like poor farmers elsewhere; big farmers like big farmers elsewhere; and urban workers like urban workers elsewhere'.[50] It would seem that even the south, the old citadel of conspicuous exceptionalism that used to be notorious for immunizing itself against the practices and attitudes of surrounding regions, has had to succumb to the new forces of commonality and uniformity.[51]

The increasing homogenization of conditions has led not just to the steady erosion of often anomalous regional loyalties to one party or another. It has also led to the dissipation of popular attachment to the two national political parties *per se*. Herein lies an apparent paradox – namely, a process of nationalization in the culture coinciding with a weakening of just those very popular organizations that one would have expected to reflect the national shift in political conditions most of all. The key to much of this paradox is provided in the following passage from Frank Sorauf's book *Political Parties in the American System*:

> Increasingly it is difficult to isolate and quarantine a local party system from the influences of national politics.... Radio, television, the magazines, and newspaper chains and syndicates bring the same political figures, debates, and opinions to all parts of the country.... In the nationalisation of American culture local ways of life, local identification and pride, even local folkways, yield their place. Increasingly, the same political symbols,

the same political issues and appeals, the same political personages dominate American politics.[52]

It is noticeable that Sorauf lays stress upon national symbols, national issues, and national candidates, but not upon national parties. In one sense, the breakdown of old and often anachronistic geo-political barriers has made the parties more coherent as national organizations. But, in another sense, it has revealed them to be more the products of change than the active agents of change. They have not only done very little to precipitate such a nationalization in the pattern of voter support and opposition, they have been merely incidental to its development.

What had been a discernible change in the 1960s had become an evident transformation by the end of the 1970s. Far from being the primary means by which a new nationalistic orientation in political attitudes manifested itself, the national party system followed in its wake and, in the process, lost much of its continuity, its identity, and its stability. This was because the motivating forces and organizational facilities that lay behind voter choices and electoral campaigns were, during the 1970s and 1980s, being determined less and less by party loyalty and collective party effort, and more and more by the common appeal of issues, movements, and candidates. This may have led to a 'nationalization of electoral coalitions'.[53] But it has also led to reduced rates of party identification, a greater volatility in voter support for parties, an increase in the incidence of split-ticket voting, larger swings between the parties in national elections, a decline in the scale and effectiveness of the party organizations, and to numerous analyses of electoral behaviour suggesting that the electorate was 'dealigning' itself to the parties and that the parties themselves were in a process of 'decomposition'.[54] The nationalization of American politics, therefore, is reflected, rather than contradicted, by the condition of the two national parties. What has become 'nationalized' has been the nature of the surges to one candidate instead of another, or to one set of policy positions in contrast to another. The result is 'a mobilized population – active and involved – but a populace with weaker institutional ties ... where neither demographic characteristics nor partisan ties guide the vote'.[55] Under these conditions, one of the classical functions ascribed to parties has been reversed. The national parties no longer formulate policies and recruit leaders. Leaders with policies recruit parties. The parties are then aligned to take advantage of those swings in candidate and issue interest that currently exist in the country. The subsequent victory or defeat may be ascribed to the party, but it is a performance of party in name only.

The configuration of the government would seem to have responded in like fashion to the changing nature of American society and its economy. Whether the stimulus prompting this change in government is seen as coming from the enlarged scale of established areas of central concern, or from new – or newly recognized – problems requiring a central and co-ordinated response, the result has been once again a developing concentration of activity and responsibility. The federal government has grown in actual and relative terms. Its budget in 1932, for example, was a mere $4.3 billion, whereas in 1986 it had grown to more than $979 billion. The number of people directly employed by the federal government grew in the same period from 601,000 to a combined civilian and military total of 5,039,000. But it is in relation to the state and local levels of government that these other increases in the scale of the federal government can best be assessed. In the period from 1932 to 1983, for example, the federal government's share of public expenditure grew from 34.3 per cent to 58.2 per cent.

At the beginning of the century Washington had been responsible for only 27.2 per cent of domestic expenditures, but fifty years later it was accounting for as much as half these expenditures. In 1984 its share stood at 58.1 per cent. In many respects, the federal government had grown into a *de facto* central government, issuing funds, recommendations, regulations, incentives, and reforms not just to states but also direct to local governments. The old formalistic structures of 'dual federalism' – by which the federal relationship was conceived as two mutually exclusive spheres of authority reserved to the federal and to the state governments irrespective of the financial capacity, administrative competence, and political will of the respective governments to fill their allotted fields – has withered away under the pressure of both the economic need and the social desire for expanded federal intervention. In 1932, for example, grants-in-aid to state and local governments amounted to $32 million and accounted for 2.9 per cent of their revenue, but by 1980 the grants had increased to $88,000 million, which represented 21.7 per cent of their income. By this time, a fifth of the federal budget was being channelled into the states, and with it a vast profusion of centrally imposed conditions, standardized rules, and common procedures.[56]

As a result of these developments, federalism is no longer perceived as a static legal concept, but as a highly fluid set of relationships which accommodates constant social and economic change, and which acknowledges the *de facto* interdependence between the federal and state levels of government.[57] But for all the emphasis upon reciprocal obligation and mutual leverage within the federal system, the fact cannot be disguised that the relationship between the states and the central government has changed to a point where they can no longer be regarded as equal partners. The underlying force that has characterized the development of the federal system over the past fifty years has been that towards the centre. Reflecting 'the whole secular drift towards the concentration of power'[58] in this century, the pattern of this federal–state interdependence has become one that seems irrevocably oriented to the federal sector at the expense of the state governments. According to M. J. C. Vile, the government in Washington had become by the end of the 1960s the pre-eminent partner in the federal relationship. Within all major fields of government responsibility:

the Federal Government laid down policies, sometimes in considerable detail, and the States and localities were required to implement them, usually under close Federal supervision. During this period the constitutional issue seems to have been settled in favour of the exercise of national power ... ; the administrative and financial power of the Federal Government is potentially overwhelming.[59]

Whether it has been the emergence of new national problems; or the increased urgency accorded to established fields of federal concern; or the transference of old localized problems; or the elevation of certain issues like inflation, defence, and energy into a position of paramount significance, it has been the federal government to which crises and demands have tended to gravitate. It is this level of government which has increasingly been recognized as the only organization capable of providing the type of response warranted by the magnitude of the problems. The simple imperative of popularly perceived or officially declared necessity, along with the size and resources of the federal government, its accumulation of precedents and statutory powers, and its enlarged capacity for centralized management and leadership through an institutionalized Presidential apparatus, have together fostered the impression that the shape of American government has come to correspond to the contemporary patterns of centrism and concentration experienced in the economy and in American society at large.

These centripetal developments have been further reinforced by the emergence of a fervent American nationalism characterized by an inner conviction of mission, destiny, and social exceptionalism.[60] Nationalistic awareness on this scale acquired dramatic fulfilment with the United States' emergence first as an international power at the beginning of the century and, subsequently, as a global superpower after World War II.[61] The tangible vindication of its belief in its own republican virtue and strength has acted as a powerful binding agent upon the indigenous population. The inspiration of American mission, combined with the constant spectre of a hostile, dangerous, and critical world has remained a powerful factor in the sustained vigour of national purpose present in America and in that society's ready capacity for uninhibited patriotism. Whether or not American national identity is seen as being derived primarily from Americans' belief in their own social distinctiveness, or from the solidarity induced by the United States' world responsibilities, or by the dangers perceived in the international environment, the end result remains the same – namely, a very high degree of popular attachment to, and identification with, the nation as an embodiment of shared values, beliefs, experiences, and goals. Indeed, apart from some occasional lapses, the United States has become renowned for a social solidarity moulded around a formidable set of national themes and symbols – a feature of American life confirmed by cross-national opinion surveys, which, according to one such study, revealed that the United States not only 'has a highly supported sense of national identity ... [but is]

ranked first among the countries studied'.[62]

Finally, the increase in economic, social, political, and national centralization has been thought to have nourished a greater social cohesion and sense of conscious community and reciprocal obligation among Americans. Instead of the anarchically competitive individualism of the nineteenth century, in which society was conceived as an agglomeration of ruthlessly acquisitive agents of property, the twentieth century has witnessed a movement away from the licentiousness of *laissez-faire* and towards the obligations of the organic and positive state.[63] Under pressure from social unrest and political instability, the philosophical assumptions underlying the principles of *laissez-faire* economic freedom were finally permitted to be publicly and effectively confronted during the New Deal by those critical ideas and alternative perspectives that had been prompted by America's accelerated industrialization. The net result and subsequent bequest to the future was a redefinition of liberty away from its purely negativist and individualist connotations to an ethos oriented more towards the several interests of the community. Such a construction of liberty allowed for the community actively to intervene in individuals' lives for the purpose of ensuring the minimum practical means by which each citizen could effectively exercise his liberty in real, rather than in purely notional, terms.[64] As a result of this transmutation of liberty from an incidental attribute of a declared law of social dynamics into more of a socially assured substantive right, the New Deal is claimed to have rediscovered, or to have recreated, the sense of social harmony and community consciousness which has reputedly been institutionalized into America since the Roosevelt era.

The principle established by the New Deal, that the 'liberty safeguarded ... is liberty in a social organization',[65] was extended and enlarged in succeeding years to produce modern America's vast infrastructure of welfare programmes and regulatory devices. Although this edifice is far from being a coherent and co-ordinated structure of social provision and planning, it has shown the communal virtue of collective endeavour in the cause of improved general welfare and greater fairness in the allotment of opportunities to individuals. It could be claimed that the increase in the American welfare state reflects the United States' emerging social consciousness. If that is true, then it is significant that the greatest increases in federal government over the last twenty years have been in precisely that sector most concerned with the provision of social benefits and entitlements. While the growth in the 'welfare' area aroused the greatest controversy – not least because 'welfare' is that sector of governmental activity furthest removed from the traditional Lockian ethos of individual sufficiency and property rights – public opinion polls have, nevertheless, revealed a solid level of support for the main elements of public care. Notwithstanding the conservative invective of the late 1970s and 1980s, polls show that over 80 per cent of Americans approved of food stamps and health care for the poor and aid to impoverished families with dependent children. In 1982, 59 per cent thought that the government should do more for the poor.[66]

The support given to such federal programmes lends credence to the notion that the factors of social concentration, national solidarity, political centralization, and community consciousness are in reality not merely interlinked, but interdependent upon one another. According to Samuel Beer, the New Deal acted as a nationalizing force in the United States, for it not only centralized governmental power in order to solve problems more general than individual states could contain, it also integrated the national community around the entity of the federal government. The American people became more of a political community and, as such, the federal government was closer to it than those local and state governments whose contact with the nation was only partial. In Beer's view, the liberalism of the New Deal 'consisted of a combination of the national idea and the democratic idea which was unique in our history'.[67] It has been continued and developed in the succeeding period as a result of those conditions and relationships both embodied and promoted by the federal government.

> National government and national community, like the processes of unification and integration from which they emerge, are interdependent.... It is legitimate and logical that as the process of integration of the national community goes forward, the content of the common good with whose promotion the central government is charged should likewise develop.[68]

Despite differences of opinion concerning the exact nature of the relationship between the social, economic, and political factors referred to above, there does seem to be real substance to the widespread impression that the United States is no longer the hostage to unbridled individualism and uninhibited group antipathies it once was. At the very least, it does appear that the coexistence of these centralist conditions has fused Americans together into a greater spirit and system of co-operative interdependency than ever before, and in a way which suggests that the aggregative process will continue into the future – whether by conscious choice or through the inertial force of established practices.

If what has been described above is generally accurate and the United States has been undergoing a substantial metamorphosis in respect to its economic structures and social values, then nothing seems to exemplify this passage into modernity more conclusively than the commonly declared dissipation of the separation of powers, both as a scheme of government organization and as a principle of constitutional benevolence. For most of the latter half of the nineteenth century the constitution was received as a repository of fixed principles and self-regulating mechanics. Contemporary social relationships and arrangements were seen as analogous to the constitution's closed world of action and reaction between atomized bodies. For most of the twentieth century, however, the constitution has been seen in an ever more organic light of interdependence, adaptation, and faded distinctions. Given that the separation of powers format has always been the most conspicuously mechanistic aspect of the constitution, then the erosion of that format has understandably been regarded as a measure of the extent to which the document's avowed mechanical character has weakened in the face of a changed public consciousness concerning the constitution and its institutional arrangements.

The principle of the separation of powers has been eroded by two main agents. The first has been a renewed analytical and logical assault upon the doctrine's premises and conclusions. It should be pointed out that the separation of powers has always been susceptible to tautology and circular argument. For example, in the history of the doctrine, it has often been difficult to determine (1) whether institutions have been defined in terms of perceived governmental functions, (2) whether governmental functions have been identified in reference to the physical presence of institutions, or (3) whether it has been a joint process through which both the structures and the functions progress to a fused identity by a form of conceptual and empirical osmosis. Moreover, it has always been something of a conundrum as to whether the three distilled abstract functions of government are in fact completely discrete phenomena. Assuming that they are, then the question is still raised as to the source of their identity. Their distinctiveness may well be based upon the existence of three empirically discernible, and/or logically demonstrable, functions that are intrinsically exclusive to one another. On the other hand, the identity of the three functions may be attributable more to their direct association with the presence of three coexisting institutions which appear to be distinct and separate from one another. The difficulty of definitions and descriptions has never been far away from the separated powers doctrine. And it is this problem which has always made the doctrine susceptible to the threat of a logical nonsense. For example, it is one of the most commonly asserted corollaries of a separation of powers scheme that each functional branch requires the possession of certain checks on the remaining two branches, in order to ensure the maintenance of a balance assuring the independence of each branch. And yet this requirement can be seen as not only contradictory, as it undermines the original principle of separated powers, but superfluous, as it seeks to prevent something (i.e. the functional independence of one branch being compromised by another branch) from occurring, which, according to the assumptions of the doctrine, is implausible. Since the separation of powers takes it as read that specialist institutions and specialist functions go hand in hand with one another, then legislatures in actuality cannot be executives, in the same way that executives cannot literally embody judiciaries, or assume the idiosyncratic function of legislatures. As a result, there is no need for checks, for no branch can perform the function of another without compromising itself and undermining its own functional identity.

In addition to these traditional flaws which have always made the principle of separated powers susceptible to logical dispute, the principle has suffered during recent years from more advanced forms of critical analysis which owe much of their force to the conceptual rigour of modern political science. For example, it has become readily apparent that Montesquieu's three celebrated functions are not performed exclusively by those government agencies with which they are nominally related. In effect, this is saying that, irrespective of theories to the contrary, each government function does not, and cannot be, monopolized by any single institution. Institutions, therefore, are multi-functional. A further conceptual assault on the separation of powers has come with the realization that the functions themselves are no longer distinguishable from one another even in the abstract. A taxation officer, for instance, may be an executive but the decisions he makes and the way that he makes them could well be seen as constituting a collective form of behaviour which at one and the same time embraces the adjudication of existing rules, the formulation of new rules, and the implementation of those rules. Thus Montesquieu's classification of functions is held up to severe attack on the grounds that not only are institutions indistinguishable on the basis of functions, but that the functions are themselves conceptually indistinguishable from one another.

This great artefact of eighteenth-century political science has had to suffer several further indignities in the sceptical atmosphere of twentieth-century political analysis.[69] Among these assaults has been the indictment that much of modern government concerns policy discretion and delegated authority, which places it outside the procedural and sequential ambit of formal law-making, law application, and law adjudication. Second, is the suggestion that there may well have evolved new modern functions (e.g. administration, communication) or new institutions (e.g. bureaucracy, press, military) whose significance warrants them being qualitatively differentiated from the old categories of government. Last, the doctrine has had to undergo a rigorous critique of its declared utility in preventing centralized tyrannical rule. According to the theory, because 'the accumulation of all powers in the same hands would lead to severe deprivations of natural rights and hence to tyranny',[70] it is necessary to avoid such an accumulation by the establishment of reciprocal checks between the branches. Nevertheless, this basic assumption stands as an assertion and not a fact. The Founding Fathers never proved that the accumulation of the three powers in the same hands would inevitably produce tyranny. They also failed to realize that the division of governmental power into separated functional entities does not prevent the capture of the three branches by one faction or another of the populace. It may be made more difficult, but it does not make it a physical impossibility, as is implied in the theory. The causes of tyranny and the substance of tyranny are more complex and involve factors not within the immediate sphere of the separation of powers paradigm. According to Robert Dahl, the Madisonian rationale for a separation of powers scheme is faulty, for the presence or absence of tyranny is nowhere proved to be dependent upon the presence or absence of a constitutional separation of powers:

> The Madisonian argument exaggerates the importance, in preventing tyranny, of specified checks to governmental officials ... ; it underestimates the importance of the inherent social checks and balances.... Without these social checks and balances, it is doubtful that the intergovernmental checks on officials would in fact operate to prevent tyranny.[71]

The conceptual clarity and logical force of the doctrine have clearly suffered from the attention given to it in recent analysis. Nevertheless, the real damage wrought in the modern epoch has come less from conceptual criticism and more from the observational evidence of its apparent demise. It is this weakening of its official position in the formal framework of institutional arrangements and processes which constitutes the second main agent in the erosion of the separation of powers principle in American government.

The proposition that the history of the modern Presidency is the story of its aggrandisement[72] has become an almost truistic piece of conventional political wisdom. Whether the origins of this expansion of Presidential power are seen principally in terms of the pressure of individual events, or the changes in socio-economic conditions, or the force of historical precedent, or the granting of entrusted statutory responsibilities, or the inspiration of executive leadership, the fact remains that there has occurred an almost universally acknowledged shift in the distribution of actual powers behind the formal allocation of authority in the constitution. It would appear from recent history that the dynamism of modern Presidential leadership has redeemed the excessively mechanistic format of constitutional organization by demonstrating the system's potential capacity for co-operation and productive interaction. According to Woodrow Wilson, the fragmentation, divisiveness, and irresponsibility induced by the separation of powers rendered the President 'at liberty both in law and conscience to be as big a man as he could',[73] in order to provide a much needed element of central co-ordination, enlightened leadership, and recognizable accountability within American government. The development of the modern Presidency has for the most part been characterized by precisely this Wilsonian spirit of working within and amongst multiple restraints to establish an authority made necessary by the very profusion of those restraints. Accordingly, the essential condition of the modern Presidency has come to be that of heroic self-assertion in circumstances of political adversity and constitutional imposition.

The success that the modern Presidency has achieved in accumulating authority has been reflected in a corresponding decline in the power and prerogatives of the other two branches. After the constitutional imbroglio of the New Deal, it can be claimed, for example, that the Supreme Court has been more than sympathetic to the Presidency in respect to the amount of executive discretion it has been prepared to approve. This discretion has been derived mainly from the delegation of legislative powers by the Congress and from the Court's acknowledgement of the 'delicate, plenary and exclusive power of the Presidency as the sole organ of the federal government in the field of international relations' – allowing for a 'freedom from statutory restriction which would not be admissible were domestic affairs alone involved'.[74] As for the Congress, it is reputed to have had neither the will nor the capacity to maintain its co-equal position in relation to the Presidency. Instead, its unremitting parochialism, its decentralization of internal power, its ambiguous party system, and its ineffectual leadership have by most accounts made it incapable of drawing its own disaggregated parts into a coherent, responsible, and consistent agency of government. The modern Congress has become noted more for its unpredictable lurches into transient political fashion, its apparently arbitrary obstructiveness, and its timorous inhibition over sensitive policy matters. Bearing in mind Congress's dispersed structure, its penchant for specialization, and its labyrinthine procedures, it is understandable that it has a reputation for depending upon the Presidency for legislative proposals which the formal legislature will then react to and evaluate accordingly in a stimulus–response fashion. The Congress has come to rely upon the Presidency for a programme of policies, in order to provide the legislature with both the provocation and the substance by which it will be prompted into performing its primary legislative function of making laws. Whether this shift in legislative initiative has been due more to an increasingly assertive and informative executive branch, or to sheer Congressional default in the face of the complexity of modern legislation and the executive's superior resources to cope with detailed laws, the end result has been a Congress whose modern role in policy-making has been markedly reduced. It is often seen as either a critical and obstructionist reviewer of executive proposals, or an overly passive and submissive recipient of the bureaucracy's suggestions. Samuel Huntington underlines this aspect of Congress's modern condition in the following well-known dictum. 'If Congress legislates, it subordinates itself to the President; if it refuses to legislate, it alienates itself from public opinion.'[75] It is this condition which is seen as the clearest representation of the way modern political developments can diverge from formal constitutional norms. Just as common opinion suggests that the executive has assumed the initiative in legislation, so the Congress is seen as having been derogated to the subordinate position of a general consultant, or, at the most, just a partner in law-making. Either way, it adds up to 'the breakdown of the principle of the separation of powers as defining the relationship of President and Congress in lawmaking'.[76]

Although the assumption of law-making powers by the executive branch represents the most obvious example of the modern fluidity that belies the professed fixity of constitutional premises and arrangements, it by no means exhausts the number of features which cast doubt upon the modern relevance of the separated powers doctrine. Other examples include the officially sanctioned mixture of law-making, law enactment, and law adjudication within the commission structure of economic and social regulation; the vastly expanded scope of discretionary authority ceded by the legislature to the executive branch that permits bureau officials to make laws and issue regulations; the so-called 'iron triangles' of interaction and co-operation between individual interest groups, executive agencies, and Congressional committees that collectively constitute a set of 'permanent sub-governments' in the American system; the emergence of Congressional committees that conduct themselves in the manner of judicial tribunals, complete with presented evidence, subpoenaed witnesses, legal counsel, cross-examinations, and penalties for contempt; the periods of exaggerated Presidential success in securing legislative proposals from a compliant Congress through the use of legislative liaison techniques which, according to one highly successful President, made him 'a hyphen which joined, a buckle which fastened the legislative part of the state to the executive part';[77] the sharp increase in the use of the legislative veto which has 'blurred ... the theoretically crisp lines of authority'[78] by allowing Congress not just to invalidate specific instances of executive discretion, but also to make its objections binding by suspending the President's constitutional prerogative of veto over Congressional actions; the Supreme Court's appearance in the forefront of public policy-making, which during the Warren era enabled the Court to redeem the inadequacies and failures of other institutions by assuming responsibility for the protection of several basic civil rights and liberties; and, finally, the elevation of the administrative bureaucracy to a position described by its apologists as a bulwark of constitutional democracy – more representative, more responsive to public demands, more sensitive to individual liberties, and more attuned to the national interest than the Congress and, as such, representing in effect a 'great fourth branch of government ... [which] in a real and important sense ... provides a constitutional check on both the legislature and executive'.[79] The accumulation of examples like these seem to bear testament to the apparent demise of the separation of powers in the modern context. The decline in the doctrine has occurred in terms of both its conceptual symmetry and its actual operation. It would seem that, whereas the intellectual challenge posed by the doctrine used to be one of showing how the different powers might act together, the challenge has now changed to one of examining whether it is possible to differentiate and separate out the original powers. According to Mr Justice Holmes, in *Springer v. Government of the Philippine Islands* (1928), such a possibility does not exist and, moreover, never has existed:

> The great ordinances of the Constitution do not establish and divide fields of black and white. Even the more specific of them are found to terminate in a penumbra shading gradually from one extreme to the other.... It does not seem to need argument to show that however we may disguise it by veiling words we do not and cannot carry out the distinction between legislative and executive action with mathematical precision and divide the

branches into watertight compartments, were it ever so desirable to do so, which I am far from believing that it is, or that the Constitution requires.[80]

This being so, the modern centralizing tendencies of society and government have served to highlight the anomalies already implicit in the doctrine rather than to generate qualitatively distinct and innovatory challenges. In the face of modern conditions, the separation of powers principle appears in most respects to stand revealed as a scheme offering few real barriers to any concerted social demand for sustained governmental activism requiring collaboration between the branches.

Two principal conclusions can be drawn from what has been presented above. First, that the assertion of a direct Newtonian influence upon the design of the American constitution is an impression conspicuously out of proportion with the historical evidence supporting it. The conscious infusion of Newtonian principles into the United States' constitutional processes not only remains unproved but, in many quarters, is flatly dismissed as a figment of later imaginations – particularly those of the nineteenth century, which wished to develop the constitution into a cult of fixed mechanical perfection. The first conclusion centres upon the dismissal of an outmoded historiography to the effect that Newtonianism had never been a significant part of the history of balanced government as an idea, or as a practical model of government in eighteenth-century America. The second conclusion suspends judgement as to whether Newtonian mechanics were or were not in the minds and work of the Founding Fathers. Even if they had been an integral part of the Framers' intellectual repertoire, by whatever means and with whatever results, the noteworthy point here is that the purportedly mechanical properties of America's scheme of balanced government stand revealed either as being mechanically unsound and conceptually insupportable, or else as a set of mechanical relationships which have simply faded away with time.

Chapter three

The perpetuation of constitutional mechanics

The difficulty with abandoning the historical dimension of Newtonianism's reported contribution to the American constitution by rejecting one set of influences in favour of another is that the same problem of establishing causality and verification is merely being repeated rather than being resolved. It would appear that the folly lies in assigning responsibility for the adoption of balanced government to any one set of circumstances, or to any one era, or to any single reason whatsoever. To adopt such a unidimensional interpretation is tantamount to assuming that it is possible, among other things (1) to unravel the complexities of historical cause and effect; (2) to differentiate active forces from incidental developments, from unrelated yet parallel phenomena, and from diffuse and ambiguous associations; (3) to separate description from prescription; (4) to distinguish clear and positive causative factors from the symmetry of *ex post facto* rationalizations; (5) to determine the real significance both of explicit and declared values and beliefs, and of implicit and assumed values and beliefs; (6) to discern the point at which prior ideas and preceding experience can be differentiated from active ideas and immediate experience; and (7) to know the precise relationship between ideas and experience, i.e. to be able to answer 'the great basic question of all philosophy ... that concerning the relationship of thinking and being'.[1]

It is possible, for example, to attribute the principle of balanced government in the American system to the constitution's 'classical ancestry'. Contemporary references to Cicero, Tacitus, and Polybius can lend weight to the argument that classical ideas on political stability and governmental organization were so ingrained in the colonists' ideology of dissent against Britain that later they became the authoritative source of balanced government within their own constitutional arrangements.[2] The lineage of an idea, however, does not account for its use, or its salience, or the conditions of its adoption as an active political principle. The question that still requires an answer in these circumstances is what led such an ancient device of government to be incorporated into the constitution. Put this way, it is quite plausible that Newtonian mechanics may well have had a role to play in the reconstitution of balanced government into a more thoroughgoing system of dynamics, and also in the reanimation of interest and belief in balanced government because of its mechanical connotations in an era noted for its propensity to a mechanistic universe. It would not be unreasonable to suppose that the centrality of Newton's cosmology in the conditioning processes of the eighteenth-century mind contributed towards the Founding Fathers' susceptibility to an appreciation of those very lessons from antiquity which preached the virtues of equilibrium and stability, to a revival of interest in the dynamic properties of the British constitution, and to a renewal of confidence in America's own evolved practices in balanced government. In this light, the influence of Newtonian mechanics on the structure and processes of the American constitution should perhaps be seen more as a sort of cultural inspiration regenerating interest in allied ideas from both the past and the present; as a key metaphor of nature and, thereby, of government and society, which lent renewed authority and vigour to differently, and more ambiguously rooted, concepts of balance; as an imprimatur of rationalism lending cosmological sanction to established practice and previous experience; and as a conceptual lightning rod, drawing varied principles and ideas together into a common frame of interrelated relevance marked by a heightened awareness of balance as a central property of nature. At the very least, it might be said that the eighteenth century's near obsession with balance was unlikely to be entirely dissociated from the evocative splendour of Newton's triumphant exposition of nature's physical constitution.

Whether the counter-arguments are based upon classical roots, cultural traditionalism, negotiated compromise, chance circumstances, institutional socialization, or on economic determinism, the problems behind claiming any one of these factors as the exclusive source of American balanced government are the same. In undermining the Enlightenment vision of the American constitution, the several lines of attack also succeed in devaluing one another in a profusion of partial causes and disputed effects. This being so, there must remain some room at least for the Newtonian theme to be acknowledged in such a highly problematic issue, to which there is no assurance of ever acquiring conclusive answers. It may well be that the link between Newtonian mechanics and the constitution does exist, but that it is obscured by the way the evidence is construed, or by the ambiguity attached to what can be classified as evidence, or to the many ways that evidence can fall victim to the entanglements of conflicting methodologies and disputed analytical priorities.

An illustrative example of the complexities generated by the variety of criteria affording explanation is provided by a dispute between James A. Robinson[3] and Martin Landau[4] on this very issue of Newton's purported influence upon the constitution. Robinson objects not only to the 'impressive list of writers on American political ideas' who see 'a relationship between the philosophy of the Founding Fathers and Newtonianism',[5] but also to the 'generations of scholars [who have] read Newtonianism into the constitution'.

He bases his objection initially on the acknowledged fact that the doctrine of balanced government preceded Newton, thereby affording the Founding Fathers the opportunity to have derived their concepts and working assumptions of balanced power from sources other than Newton. Robinson then goes on to make his substantive objection. From a survey of the Framers' political writings, little is revealed of 'acknowledgements of intellectual debts to Newton or to a stream of thought which may be regarded as Newtonian'.[6] The few direct references to Newton or to mechanics are dismissed by Robinson as 'probably mere window-dressing',[7] or as 'little more than literary flourishes'.[8] According to this interpretation, those writers who had been 'attributing Newtonianism to the Founding Fathers' possessed 'precious little evidence to support their claims' and that, consequently, 'the influence of Newtonianism had been exaggerated'.[9]

And yet, with a different perspective, it is precisely what Robinson classifies as the absence of evidence affirming the Newtonian influence upon the constitution that can be construed as consistent with the nature of evidence substantiating the presence of just such an influence. By confining Newtonianism's effect purely to cited and explicit acknowledgements, Robinson's analysis precludes the possibility of the Newtonian influence being discerned by any means other than through the conscious and articulate expression of such an influence on the part of the Founders. It is this dependence upon such a unidimensional form of evidence which Landau takes issue with. He does not believe that the nature of influence can be measured in such an insensitive manner. He criticizes Robinson for transforming the 'problem from that of the influence of mechanics on the Founders to whether or not they "acknowledge" Newton'.[10] Landau makes a case for seeing Newtonianism as a 'central unifying image'[11] of the way men thought in the eighteenth century. The sheer success of the Newtonian model in science prompted its unconscious transference into a dominant metaphor of social enquiry and prescriptive thought. It is in the nature of such an orthodoxy that men remain unaware that their thoughts and observations are 'shaped and directed by a particular image'.[12] That image in the eighteenth century was Newtonianism and, therefore, Landau concludes, the absence of the sort of explicit references to Newtonianism which Robinson demands as proof of its influence misunderstands 'the nature of a dominant metaphor'.[13] This is because 'metaphors may be so implicit that a lack of acknowledgement means only a lack of awareness that a transfer is in process'.[14]

A dispute like this reflects many of the deeply problematical and, arguably, insoluble issues that characterize the history of ideas. At this level of enquiry the possibilities of explanation are legion – as varying and occasionally contradictory constructions can be placed upon the same evidence, and as different forms of evidence become available to satisfy the criteria of particular methodologies. For example, where the level of conscious dependence upon Newtonianism may be found wanting, the deficiency can be made up with references to an unconscious and intuitive attachment to its principles. If economic incentive and motivation threaten to derogate reason to a mere adjunct of material forces, then an alternative interpretation can cast the Founding Fathers as men of ideas who not only argued out and thought through their differences, but who employed techniques of political analysis and governmental construction drawn from history and experience, and sanctioned by allusions to natural science. By relying more on the factor of language and upon linguistic analysis, it is possible to interpret the written or spoken words of the Founding Fathers in terms not merely of what was expressed, but of the meaning being conveyed in accordance with the current paradigm of language in use. The notion of an organized political language in society opens up the content of the recorded word to an examination of its usage at the time, which may or may not correspond to the meanings and significance attached to the same words and phrases in the present day. If it is true that the same society can have varying linguistic conventions of political discussions and changing codes of language for political persuasion and analysis, then this in itself generates a profusion of interpretative possibilities where a theme like that of Newtonian influence on the constitution is concerned. For example, just as the absence of explicit references to Newtonianism may mean that Newton's influence was being expressed by other means and through other linguistic conventions, so the presence of allusions to Newtonian principles of mechanics may be coded references to something other than purely Newtonian or mechanical categories; they may be nothing other than empty digressions punctuating the elements of real meaning being transmitted by a passage of contemporary argument.[15]

A final twist is provided by the last example of how a theme like political Newtonianism can become irretrievably complex and, thereby, subject to a diversity of meanings and causal permutations. This refers to the commonly accepted premise that a Newtonian end presupposes a Newtonian cause and that, consequently, a Newtonian construction of the constitution's checks and balances requires, as a precondition, a reasoned and Newtonian-inspired exercise in institutional engineering on the part of the Founders. But the framework of government designed as Newtonian may not be necessarily and exclusively dependent upon an intellectual and rational base. Moreover, its sources may well be quite irrelevant to the finished product, which may legitimately be Newtonian in character, but which may have been prompted by all manner of motives, or precipitated by compromise and happenstance. In other words, the Founders may well have created a Newtonian constitution in spite of themselves and in spite of their intentions. Likewise, evidence of motivations to devise a constitution in the Newtonian spirit of reason and intellect can by no means be interpreted as ensuring that the final design faithfully reflected the driving spirit of the exercise.

Amidst this bewildering array of arguments, theories, claims, and provisos, only one aspect of this issue seems to have remained untouched – namely, that the reputed association between Newtonianism and American constitutionalism through the medium of the Founding Fathers is a position for which conclusive evidence – either for or against – is notoriously difficult to establish. On the one hand, given that Newtonianism represented an explanatory system of such compulsive authority during the eighteenth century, it would be difficult to discount it completely as an influence on the ideas and working assumptions of the Framers. On the other hand, it may be technically possible to account for both the idea of balanced government and its introduction into American government in terms that have no apparent relationship with, or approximation to, Newtonianism in any form whatsoever. Nevertheless, such accounts as these run the risk of securing clarity at the expense of veracity. As a matter of course, they overlook the less explicit meanings that can be attached to Newtonianism, and they fail to recognize the potential for ascribing influences to categories derived from, or allied to, Newtonianism.

The real significance of this issue lies in its very existence as a controversy. What is important, in the end, is not the relative merits or demerits of the arguments presented for and against. It is in the way that the controversy itself throws the widespread *belief* in the Newtonian character of the constitution into sharp relief. It is this belief – supported as it is by a sort of literate and articulate folklore sustaining the idea of a Newtonian legacy bequeathed by the Founding Fathers – that has provoked demands for evidence capable of substantiating the contention. As this study has shown, such evidence as is available can only be of a provisional nature and quite inadequate to support a conclusive affirmation of Newton's direct effect on the organization of American government. What makes this inconclusiveness remarkable is that it has no effect whatsoever on the belief in the Newtonian dimension which originally provoked the search for proof. Even in the face of a formidable array of historical, methodological, conceptual, and analytical objections, the Newtonian connection has remained intact. Through this intellectual adversity, the connection's cultural and affective durability has been revealed to its full extent. Despite the far from convincing evidence in its favour, the status of Newton in the field of American constitutionalism shows no signs of being diminished. The initiative in the controversy still lies with tradition in that the onus of proof is upon those who wish to refute the allegations of a Newtonian connection. It is this assumption of validity even in the absence of explicit proof which has offended the analytical sensibilities of individuals like James Robinson. It prompted him to undertake a highly critical appraisal of what he regarded as Newton's quite bogus reputation in this field. The ultimate significance of just such a concerted attack is not only that Robinson felt compelled to make such an assault by the conspicuous presence of Newton in the literature on the constitution, but that even after having subjected the Newtonian case to the most damning criticism and having apparently buried the issue for good, the references to Newton and to the influence of Newtonian mechanics in American politics show no signs of having declined in number or conviction.

Even if one were to cast aside the influence of Newtonian mechanics upon the design and construction of the American constitution, the key issue would still remain unresolved – i.e. the reason for the very question of Newtonianism's influence to continue being raised at all, and for the answer to continue to be regarded as a matter of significance to the present-day realities of American politics. What is it about the nature of American political perceptions and understandings that makes Newtonian dynamics seem so especially apposite as a term of operational description and as a generative source of American constitutionalism? Both the constitution's origins, and its modern form and function, can now be persuasively accounted for by factors which have no connection whatever with Newtonian mechanics. Furthermore, since the eighteenth century a profusion of cultural and intellectual developments have served in numerous respects to reduce the salience and authoritative force of the once ubiquitous world view of Newtonian physics. Nevertheless, in spite of all these developments that have ostensibly rendered Newtonianism an outmoded model of the universe and an eclipsed progenitor of the American constitution, there remains something about the nature of the American political process and about the composition of American political perspectives that makes them both susceptible to the invocation of the name of Newton.

It is clear that the historical arguments and counter-arguments concerning the Newtonian nature of the constitution's design and consequent function are not only inconclusive but largely unproductive. The belief in the constitution's mechanical nature is what counts as being truly significant. This may ultimately be rooted in the past, or it may not. It cannot be proved or disproved either way. What requires elucidation is not the roots of the issue, but what continues to arouse such an interest in the roots; what sustains and cultivates the mechanistic perspective of American government. The mechanical inflection to American constitutionalism is not a dead issue, but one that is continually raised and debated in the United States. It appears evident that the key to this propensity to visualize mechanical forms and purposes in government and to see the hand of Newton in the institutional relationships contained within the constitution lies far more in the present than in the past. It is the contention of this study that the generative source of the mechanistic conception of American government that fuses the past and present so firmly together lies in the most obvious and most overlooked part of the American political system; that part which 'generations of schoolchildren have been taught'[16] and which 'every schoolchild in America learns'[17] as a matter of course – namely, the separation of powers.

In spite of all the revisions to, and reassessments of, the separation of powers as a working principle of government, its imagery has nevertheless remained largely unblemished and its salience as a norm of institutional organization has continued undiminished. The schema of separated powers still provides the most readily distinguishable and the most characteristic feature of the national government. Furthermore, the separation of powers continues to be recognized and even celebrated as an integral condition of American democracy. In effect it can be said that, in the light of the myriad challenges to it, the separation of powers principle continues to command an extraordinary level of prominence in the political culture of the United States. Indeed, so tenacious has its hold been upon the political consciousness of the United States in terms of its status as a generally accepted factual truth and as a normative principle that the separation of powers framework has come to embody a constitutional paradigm which is intuitively adhered to as a readily accessible conceptualization of both the nature and the purpose of American political institutions.

It is precisely this conventional perception of organizational reality and constitutional virtue which has acted as the stimulus to many of the analyses that have sought to present a much more fluid, adaptive, and dynamic portrayal of the Founding Fathers' triumvirate of powers. The underlying appeal of constitutional orthodoxy has been so pervasive, however, that the descriptions of recent developments away from the norm of separated powers seem very often to be as much a vindication of the eighteenth-century format as a denial of it. Departures from the separation of powers tend not to be acknowledged as representing a refutation or a disavowal of the principle, so much as recognized either as aberrant deviations from a discernible, legitimate, and still viable base; or else as evolved forms of the original idea and, thereby, compatible with the Founders' strictures and purposes. Whichever way, the separation of powers survives as an established premise of institutional reality and value. The sheer familiarity and authority of the separation of powers is such that it makes almost any rigorous statement concerning the logic of divided powers sound much more significant and profound than it actually is. In his book on Presidential power, for example, one can almost feel Richard Neustadt trying to wrest his readers free from their customary thought patterns on the subject of the government's structure: 'The constitutional convention of 1787 is supposed to have created a government of "separated powers." It did nothing of the sort. Rather it created a government of separated institutions *sharing* powers.'[18] The declaratory tone and explicit assertiveness of the statement not only convey the point, but reflect the depth of public attachment to the conventional picture of separated powers – which in itself makes such a basic observation worthy of such emphasis. When it comes to the political critiques of the separation of powers and to calls for reform, then, as we shall see later on in this study, such exercises can often remain heavily influenced by the premises inherent in the principle of divided powers. In various ways, and under various guises, many reformers have unwittingly returned to the items and conditions associated with precisely that principle of governmental organization which they had sought to repudiate. It would appear that even those most critically disposed towards the principle have not always been able to divorce themselves from its influence as much as they would have liked, or as much as they may have supposed. Along with much, if not most, of the American public, reformers have tended to share an affinity with a principle which, despite being constantly surrounded by a heavy groundswell of analytical dispute and political controversy, continues nevertheless to generate a very strong instinctive, affective, and intellectual appeal in American political life.

Many reasons can be and have been advanced to account for the continued salience of the separation of powers and its attendant checks and balances in American politics. For example, institutional rivalries, separated constituencies, differences in tenure, pluralistic power centres, and even plain constitutional traditionalism have all been persuasively presented as explanations for the principle's perpetuation as a popular conception of American government. While it is true that these sorts of factors, which are often very loosely referred to as Newtonian influences, may well go some way towards explaining the principle's longevity, they not only fail to provide the full answer but largely misrepresent the one influence that can legitimately be ascribed to Newtonian mechanics. What is being contended here is that there exists a vitally important, yet largely overlooked, ingredient to the salience of the separation of powers in American political culture. It is an ingredient which, it will be argued, represents a virtually unacknowledged dimension to the separation of powers scheme, but a dimension which is critically important in comprehending the scheme's hold on political thinking in the United States. This dimension is clearly related to, and is a major contributory factor in, the widespread view of the separation of powers as both a portrayal of institutional dynamics and a statement of normative principle. In addition, it will be claimed that this dimension transcends empirical proof and value judgements concerning the separation of powers in contemporary American politics in such a way as to produce a perception of divided and interacting powers – almost irrespective of direct evidence to the contrary, and in the face of challenges to its value as a principle of modern government. The contention is that this extra dimension will not only throw light upon the real substance and manifold nature of the influence exerted by the separation of powers principle, but also provide a greatly improved context within which the much vaunted but little understood role of Newtonian mechanics in American politics can best be placed.

The particular perspective that is being referred to is both simple and complex. It is simple from the point of view of being probably the most obvious feature of the separation of powers format. But it also remains relatively complicated, first because of the ambiguity involved in defining its constituent parts, second because of the confused nature of the relationships between these parts, and last because of the profusion of ramifications which flow from it. This universally acknowledged yet almost invariably overlooked feature is the assertion that the power of the federal government is separated into a structure of three juxtaposed and interacting parts. That characteristic description of institutional organization sounds almost too banal and mundane to be anything but a prelude to something else – a preamble, perhaps, to some more detailed examination of the system's consequences and repercussions. And yet that basic assertion of divided powers represents a conceptual profundity which belies the innocent simplicity and axiomatic explicitness with which the separation of powers is normally associated. What will be contended in this section is that the very notion of separate and balancing powers represents a fundamental imagery of political relationships which acts upon the mind in a stimulus–response fashion so as to generate a chain reaction of related perceptions, ideas, judgements, and conclusions. Not the least of these reactions is the self-affirmation of the notion of separated powers in precisely those terms in which it was initially received. The net result, therefore, is a circular and self-perpetuating process in which the separation of powers remains intact as a perceptual reference point and an explanatory device.

Perhaps the best way of illustrating the extraordinary potential of the separated powers scheme for generating conceptual associations and for facilitating quickly drawn conclusions on political relationships is to examine the way that most of us were first informed about the separation of powers in American government. By studying the textbook accounts of the formal design of the national government, it is possible to experience the form in which the notion of separated and balanced powers is customarily absorbed and assimilated as one of the most basic building blocks of political knowledge – so basic a block that it is normally consigned to the back of an individual's mind until such time as he is prompted into contemplating its existence. Even then, it can be supposed that he will experience great difficulty in extricating himself from the well worn perceptions of the separation of powers' familiar and comfortable symmetry.

No doubt many readers at this point will be saying quizzically to themselves that there simply cannot be anything very significant to be revealed about so obvious a piece of mental furniture as the separation of powers. After all, just as it appears to make manifest sense of the way the federal government works, so the operation of the political system in Washington seems to amount to a generally sound working illustration of the separation of governmental powers. Yet this response is in itself an indication of the depth to which the separation of powers framework has become entrenched as a first principle of political observation. It is this aura of compulsive authenticity that makes the significance of the separation of powers so notoriously difficult to reassess, particularly from the elementary perspective advocated here. But in order to demonstrate its remarkably evocative and suggestive nature as a concept, it is important to adopt precisely this approach. It is necessary to look carefully at the textbook descriptions of the separation of powers, and to observe the ways in which the seeds of such a deceptively innocuous notion have been sown in the political consciousness of almost all Americans.

From an examination of a random selection of popular and widely used textbooks on American government published over a thirty-year period (1957–87),[19] it is possible to discern a number of common features concerning not merely what is conveyed in respect to the separation of powers, but, just as important, how it is conveyed to the reader. The first point that is clearly noticeable from these publications is the extraordinarily small amount of *space* given over to what they universally acknowledge to be a fundamental aspect of American government. Some books reserve several pages to the subject, but most often the theory of the separation of powers together with its particular application in the American context is usually given nothing but a cursory acknowledgement alongside a very brief description of the basic format. More often than not, these acknowledgements run to no more than a single page or an extended paragraph. And this is true even for very lengthy works of over 300 pages.[20] The general impression left by these brief descriptions is of an obvious reality which can be safely and adequately accounted for in very few words. One is encouraged to regard the principle of separated powers as so self-evident and so obvious that mention of it hardly needs to be made. The separation of powers emerges from these texts as an elementary formality of political knowledge which warrants as much space being given to it as any of those other features of life whose sheer familiarity makes descriptions seem necessarily prosaic and superfluous. For most textbook writers it would seem as if the existence of a system of separated powers is so orthodox an opinion and such an incontrovertible observation that the principle can be safely dismissed in a short allusion to its glaring presence.

While the first discernible feature of the textbook versions of the separation of powers is that of length, the remaining features concern content and style. These features are clearly related to the first one dealing with space in that what is conveyed concerning the separation of powers system and how it is conveyed are both a reflection of that system's susceptibility to descriptive brevity. The content and general tenor of the textbook portrayals serve in turn to reinforce the initial impression of the separation of powers as something axiomatic, elementary, and self-evident. It is not just how much is said, therefore, but also what is said and the way it is stated that allow the system of separated powers in American government to be thought of as something clear and simple – clearly in existence and simple in nature.

One of the most conspicuous features of the manner in which textbook writers present their message on the separation of powers is their tendency towards *historical oversimplification* in terms of both its origins as a political principle, and the circumstances surrounding its adoption by the Founding Fathers. The textbooks convey a sense of timelessness by their general style of portraying the constitution retrospectively as a historical *fait accompli*, as a finished product of reasoned enquiry, and as a vehicle of undisputed fact. Normally there is very little discussion of the manifold and complex historical roots to the whole theme of separated powers. Apart from certain passing references to Locke and Montesquieu, the texts in the main reveal a remarkable lack of historical perspective. Certainly, they contain nothing resembling the development of the idea of separated powers and its significance both in colonial politics and in the political thought of post-revolutionary America which have been plotted so attentively by such writers as Bernard Bailyn,[21] W. B. Gwyn,[22] Gordon Wood,[23] and M. J. C. Vile.[24] Likewise, the Founding Fathers tend to lose their individual identities and their differences of opinion concerning the appropriate form and role of separated powers. With the treatment they are afforded in most textbooks, they become a homogenized collectivity whose unanimity is fashioned by taking the constitution as a given singular entity and by extrapolating from this attribute the conclusion that the constitution was derived from a similarly singular source. Both these descriptive mannerisms – i.e. (1) the general dismissal of the separation of powers' historical context as a political idea, and (2) the reduction of the Framers to an almost uniform fountainhead of constitutional design – have the effect of lending great weight to the impression that the separation of powers scheme in American government is derived directly from an incontrovertible principle unambiguously employed by the Framers to produce an explicit and predictable effect.

The textbooks do very little to dissuade the reader from believing that the separation of powers format in the organization of American government is not the result of a highly analytical and abstract exercise in constitutional formulation inspired by the eighteenth-century belief in a science of empirical political knowledge. On the contrary, the style of textbook writing serves to intensify, and even to dramatize, the imagery of the Founding Fathers self-consciously and assiduously complying with what is made retrospectively to appear as the only rational option for a design in government. It is possible to contend that this imagery is as much if not more a product of the easily perceived and readily comprehended symmetry of the separation of powers scheme itself – rather than from any overall summation of the Framers' actual conduct. It would appear in this respect that the cart often tends to pull the horse, and does so in such a way that the horse comes to assume much of the character of the cart. In other words, the apparent simplicity and rationality of the separation of powers scheme seems to lead to a redefinition of its sources in terms of its own beguiling qualities, with the result that the Founders come to be portrayed as mere vehicles of the idea. Just as the idea itself tends to prompt unqualified declarations of certainty, so its formal adoption in 1787 is normally described in similarly terse and unambiguous terms. For example:

> The writers of the Constitution ... divided powers across three different branches of government, giving different powers and resources to the legislative, executive, and judicial branches.[25]

The Founding Fathers discerned three principal powers: legislative, executive, and judicial. To implement these powers they established three branches of government.[26]

Constitutional powers were divided by the framers among three branches – legislative, executive, and judicial – to prevent the accumulation of all powers in one hand.[27]

The framers hoped that two different but related arrangements – separation of powers and checks and balances – would achieve their supreme goal of preventing public officials from abusing their power and preventing any one group of people ... from capturing control of the government.... The first step was the separation of powers – that is, dividing power among the three branches of the national government.[28]

The delegates to the Constitutional Convention of 1787 had to decide what fundamental powers the government would need to govern the people, and how these powers would be divided among the branches of government. The Framers developed the practical arrangement of the separation of powers.[29]

The Constitution divided the national government into three branches, legislative, executive, and judicial. It created a government, therefore, based on the principle of separation of powers and checks and balances.[30]

Conspicuous by their general absence in these types of passage are the doubts, uncertainties, technical disputes, mixed intentions, philosophical arguments, conflicting predictions, and all the other complexities that characterized the real process of the separation of powers' actual adoption. Instead, the impression one is left with is of an almost unilinear and predetermined development towards separated powers. This impression not only tends to remake the Founding Fathers in the image of the separation of powers, but, in addition, simultaneously reinforces the clarity of that image by appearing to be the direct product of enlightened, dispassionate, and harmonious reason. Just as the Framers become submerged into the disembodied functionaries of a rationally designed governmental system, so the principle of the separation of powers is made to seem more historically rootless and, thereby, more of a unified and timeless abstraction of American government.

The third point that can be made in reference to the textbooks' treatment of the separated powers principle is their tendency towards the *conceptual oversimplification* of the three powers involved in the scheme. As some of the above quotations will already have revealed, there is a clear inference in the textbook descriptions of the separation of powers that each branch initially draws its identity and its role from the preconceived idea that there exists three distinct and discrete functions in the conduct of government. Building upon this commonly accepted eighteenth-century assumption that the power of government could be broken into three, and only three, abstract functions, the conventionally accepted achievement of the Founding Fathers is that they matched the three functions of government on a one-to-one basis to three new institutions specifically created to embody each of the discrete elements of government. This assumption of the constitution as a piece of abstract design made to come to life by the provision of actual units of government is clearly perceptible in the manner in which the doctrine of separated powers is presented in the constitution itself. The constitution establishes the separation of powers in terms of structures created. By doing so, it gives a convincing impression of transforming avowed theoretical distinctions into something physically real. It is doubly explicit, doubly dogmatic. The language of the first three articles makes this quite clear:

> All legislative powers herein granted shall be vested in a Congress of the United States.
>
> The executive power shall be vested in a President of the United States.
>
> The judicial power of the United States shall be vested in one Supreme Court.

It is noteworthy that the constitution does not state that the legislative power shall be generally associated with Congress or that the Presidency is to be mainly concerned with executive duties. Quite the contrary. The initial declaration and the central point of all subsequent departures is one of an emphatic differentiation of branches of government in terms of exclusive functions. This was not a case of muted shades or of ambiguous dividing lines. This was not a matter of incorporating something approximating to a separated powers scheme into an established system, nor was it an attempt to characterize an established system in terms of separated powers. The impression given in the constitution, and the one assiduously conveyed by the textbooks, is that of explicit conceptual differences converted into reality through institutions custom-built to facilitate the conversion. The institutions seem almost to be constructed around the concepts of legislative, executive, and judicial power and, as a result, amount to a reification of the idea of distinguishable and distinct functions of government. The initial product of this picture, therefore, is one of primary colours, certain boundaries, clear differentiation, and hard-and-fast identities – all based on the professed coincidence between separate institutions and separate functions with each affording the other corroborative evidence of its identity and each helping to validate the others' authenticity.

The separation of powers probably ranks as the most unequivocal statement of conscious creation in the constitution and, as it stands in stark legal definition, it provides very little scope for scepticism or for interpretation. In effect, it stands as the constitution's three commandments on the framework of the government. And in a nation much given to constitutional veneration the separation of powers possesses that quality of certitude which encourages a particularly fundamentalist attachment to its provisions. The die is effectively cast with the constitution's deceptively clear yet highly attractive construct of separated powers. It amounts to a direct and immediate invitation to the imagination to see the shape of the national level of government in terms of a most aesthetically appealing and intellectually gratifying simplicity. Namely, the idea of a government with three clearly perceived parts – a trinity substantiated not only by the provision of three differing institutions, but also by the provisions of a persuasively presented criterion of differentiation, which succeeds in giving those institutions every appearance of being three definite and separate entities divided in a comprehensible and purposeful manner. This idea must represent the most readily grasped and most easily understood feature of American government. Once assimilated, it is not easily dislodged. On the contrary, it can be claimed that it more normally amounts to a standing first principle of government organization, to a starting point of political analysis, and to a fixed and fundamental element in the general perception of American politics.

The fourth major point that can be drawn from the way the theme of divided powers is handled by the textbooks concerns their *general ambivalence towards the relationship between the principle of separated powers and the principle of checks and balances*. The treatment afforded to this subject by most of the textbooks surveyed is distinguished by the remarkable degree of inattention given to the relative meaning and comparative significance of the two principles. These varying forms of oversight are important because they reveal the extent to which the two principles have become so tightly combined in the American constitutional tradition that they are customarily acknowledged as being one and the same thing. Just as neither principle appears plausible without the other, so each seems to assume the other's existence. It is not simply that the separation of powers and the scheme of checks and balances are claimed to be mutually inclusive, but that they are perceived and portrayed as being mutually dependent upon one another.

These abbreviated textbook versions of the relationship are significant because they serve to perpetuate the formal constitutional logic of the governmental structure as enunciated by its founders and subsequent apologists. But the textbooks' coverage of the subject is also important in another and far more crucial respect. Their accounts reveal the extraordinary conceptual and logical effects that are produced by the incorporation of a device like checks and balances into a framework of government based upon the separation of powers. It is hoped to show that these effects encourage the individual to see institutions and institutional relationships in a particular way – independent of time and irrespective of formal prescriptions, or traditional perspectives, or academic instructions, or constitutional intentions. The contention will be that the principle of balanced government disposes the perception of both the nature and the purpose of the governing institutions in such a way as to make them appear far more simplified, stylized, and self-evident than they actually are, or ever could be. So potent and so persistent is this perspective that it can be claimed to be the key factor behind all the other distinctive features presented in this survey of how the separation of powers is customarily envisioned both by those who seek to teach and, thereupon, by those who wish to learn.

One of the chief effects of this perspective of separated and balanced institutions is the tendency for it to bury its own history. It should be recalled, at this point, that the principle of separated powers and the principle of checks and balances originally represented two quite distinct and different notions of government. At the time of its adoption by the Founding Fathers, the separation of powers had acquired a reputation for being a radical and democratic doctrine which reduced government to three separate departments directly dependent upon and accountable to the people. The notion of checks and balances, on the other hand, was closely associated with the old classical concept of mixed government in which different classes in society shared in the processes of government. This ensured a measure of self-protection for each class through the inevitable friction that would ensue from such joint participation. The distinguishing principle of mixed government was that of balance, which would be derived from all the devices for mutual restraint and reciprocal control built in to the relationships between the constituent parts of the system. The watchword of separated powers, however, was not balance so much as limitation. It was not balance because the idea of separated powers had evolved largely in response to, and as a device against, arbitrary monarchical powers – albeit powers often exercised in the name of 'balanced government'. The separation of powers became a major instrument in the drive to reduce such powers by confining the monarchy and those offices derived from it (e.g. colonial governors) to something which could be defined and, thereby, circumscribed in terms of an executive function. The doctrine of separated powers in America subsequently developed into a scheme of government which succeeded in reducing the traditional source of arbitrary and unaccountable power (i.e. the executive) to such an extent that it threatened to produce a quite different source of excessive and unchecked power – namely the legislature. Although the pure doctrine of separated powers assumes that some reciprocal control would be forthcoming from the mere existence of three separated branches of government, it did not and could not assume anything approximating to a balance. On the one hand, it was difficult to conceive of how distinct departments and rigidly differentiated branches could check one another without compromising their exclusive identities. On the other hand, it was apparent that the logic of a full separation of powers system did not in any way assure the existence of three branches of comparable power and authority. On the contrary, it was reasonable to conclude that the legislature, as the law-making body in a republic, would always rank as the senior, and even predominant, department.

It was these problems endemic in America's radical post-colonial separation of powers schemes that the Founding Fathers addressed themselves to in Philadelphia. To their satisfaction, the constitution succeeded not only in rectifying the organizational defects of a pure separation of powers, but also in resolving many of the conceptual problems associated with the principle. According to M. J. C. Vile, the Framers had achieved their objective of an effective but limited and responsible government by conjoining the ostensibly contradictory principles of separated powers, and checks and balances 'in a new, and uniquely American, combination'.[31] Vile continues:

> The ideas and vocabulary that had formally been applied to monarchy, aristocracy and democracy were firmly transferred to the legislative, executive and judicial branches of government.... In America the checks and balances became a necessary, but subordinate, element of a system in which functionally divided branches of government could maintain their mutual independence.... The checks and balances were not in conflict with, but necessary to, the effective maintenance of a separation of the powers of government.[32]

This complex combination amounted to a qualified separation of powers, to an acknowledged minimal sharing of functions by different branches, and to an array of internal checks between and amongst the three departments. Paradoxically, these features collectively represented a means of preserving the independence and power of precisely those original branches of government whose separate identities had appeared initially to be so threatened by the inclusion of balance as an objective of the system.

This 'new, and uniquely American, combination' appeared to square the circle. Its appeal lay in its portrayal of a successful reconciliation between balanced government and the separation of powers. So effective has the constitution been in presenting these two elements of government as a united front that it is common practice for their historical distinctions to be dismissed as irrelevant. The textbooks reflect this general lack of interest in distinguishing the separate meanings and differing roots of the two principles. Their descriptions of the framework of government mirror the orthodox constitutional position of an inherent and indisputable union between divided powers and checks and balances in which each party is given every appearance of being the logical condition of the other. The sheer success of the constitution's vision has meant that these two elements are now normally seen as being indivisible. To discriminate between them is consequently made to seem spurious and superfluous – at worst contrived attempts to create false dichotomies and at best digressions for interest's sake into constitutional prehistory. For the most part, the textbooks effortlessly avoid both pitfalls. They remain well immersed in the conventional viewpoint. Furthermore, by either refusing to unravel the separation of powers from the doctrine of checks and balances, or failing to acknowledge that there is anything to disentangle, the textbooks successfully perpetuate convention.

Many reasons might be advanced which could account for the successful union between separated powers and balanced government in the American constitution. For example, the compatibility of the doctrines may well have been suggested to the Framers and to their contemporaries by the coexistence of the two principles in the political thought and practice of the time. This is reflected in the difficulty of ascertaining which principle was regarded as being prior to and superior to the other in the minds of those instrumental in formulating and defending the constitution. It can be argued that the separation of powers was the controlling principle and that checks and balances followed on in a manner consistent with the original format. On the other hand, it is also possible to regard the more historically well rooted principle of balanced government as responsible for securing the final provision of different branches of government, in order to provide an acceptable raw material for a new American form of governmental balance.

Another source of the union's success may have been simply the difficulties involved in delineating the units of government required in a separation of powers scheme. The provision of checks and balances, in this context, may be seen as less of a deliberate compromise of the separation of powers principle and more a product of the impossibility of rigorously differentiating the three branches from each other. Madison was well aware of this difficulty and confided to Jefferson that the boundaries between the executive, legislative, and judicial powers 'though in general so strongly marked in themselves, consist in many instances of mere shades of difference'.[33] His doubts were made more explicit in *Federalist Paper 37*:

> Experience has instructed us that no skill in the science of government has yet been able to discriminate and define with sufficient certainty, its three great provinces – the legislative, executive, and judiciary;.... Questions daily occur in the course of practice which prove the obscurity which reigns in these subjects, and which puzzle the greatest adepts in political science.[34]

A not unreasonable conclusion to such uncertainty might be that Madison's defence of departments possessing 'partial agency'[35] in one another and of their being 'blended'[36] was tantamount to a disbelief in the attainability of complete separation. His subsequent justification of the constitution's arrangements for the three constituent institutions, therefore, may have been influenced as much by a recognition of their essential inseparability as by the need to rationalize the inclusion of reciprocal checks between institutions.

The content and style of the textbooks, however, reveal a simpler yet more profound explanation for the successful partnership between separated powers and balanced government. This may not have been, and most probably was not, the chief reason for the original amalgamation, but, with time, it has become arguably the most compelling cause of the two principles continually appearing as one. The factor in question is the basic conceptual appeal of two elements of government which, when placed in conjunction with one another, seem so logically integrated that they appear to be a mutually dependent duality. Each one seems simultaneously to be both a condition and a corollary of the other. As such, they appear to require each other as a matter of course. They seem to strengthen one another's weaknesses and to fill in each other's gaps. Indeed, so successful are they in complementing one another that they are readily perceptible as a thoroughly unified package of concepts, structures, and relationships. One can go further and claim that these two elements of government have become so closely allied to one another, in terms of reciprocal and logical requirements, that they are in the main *only* perceptible in the guise of a single entity.

The strength of this partnership in the American context is such that each party seems not only incomplete without the other, but practically inconceivable in isolation. Without the added ingredient of checks and balances, the separation of powers on its own would amount to three abstractly defined 'powers' existing *in vacuo* and relying wholly upon the three matching institutions for an impression of material substance. Within this scheme, there would be no assumption of any dynamic interaction between the powers or the institutions said to embody those powers; there would be no assurance of co-equality between the powers and between the institutions and no reason to regard co-equality as being in any way significant as a condition of the arrangement; and, lastly, there would be no real sense of an underlying regulatory purpose to the scheme and no implicit expectation that reciprocal forces would even disturb the movements of independent and freely floating departmental powers. The scheme might be envisioned as in Figure 1.

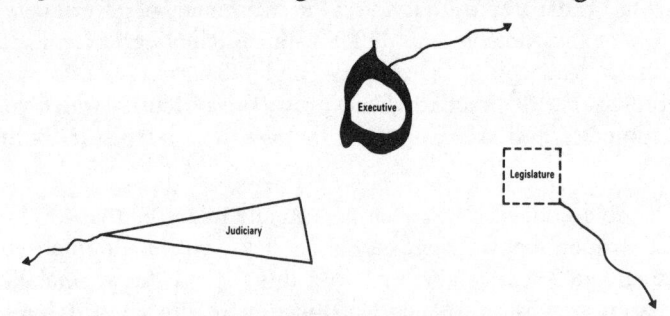

Some checks may occur, but in no predictably ordered, patterned, or purposeful manner. And, if checks do occur, they will be the result of fortuitous and arbitrary circumstances, for the system would in no way be motivated by the need to generate and to register exchanges of force. On the contrary, the rationale of the arrangement would be satisfied merely by the provision of three perceptibly distinct, unrelated, and unattached entities.

Checks and balances on their own would, of course, be unimaginable without the physical presence of a set of distinguishable parts interacting with one another. The necessary precondition of checks and balances is the provision of separately existing entities through which force can be transmitted and received. The separation of powers provides the checks and balances framework with that initial understanding of three differentiated elements being present in government – three constituents with sufficiently exclusive identities to possess the potential for being transformed into a full physico-kinetic framework of interacting parts.

The result of combining the principle of separated powers with the principle of political checks is to secure to each that aspect of itself which is implied, but whose actual existence is not assured. Both principles are compromised but strengthened at the same time by the fusion of both into one composite framework. For the checks and balances partner, the marriage provides the crucial prerequisite of three differentiated forms which can be projected into a dynamic relationship. For the separation of powers partner, the union provides the constituent parts with a greatly increased physical identity, a set of linkages between one another, an assumption of co-equal departments of government to produce a balance, and a newly acquired sense of purpose. Both partners have had to make sacrifices for the marriage. The separation of powers loses for good the pure and compartmentalized independence of its parts, while the checks and balances gain three related units whose very linkages threaten to undermine the basis of differentiation on which the checks depend. These compromises, however, are more than compensated for by the clarity and vigour afforded to both principles by their fusion.

The two principles, indeed, have become so bound up with one another in the American experience that they can seem quite indistinguishable. It takes a concerted effort not only to recall that they used to be seen as conflicting themes of governmental organization, but even to think coherently of one without the other. It has all the appearances of being a genuine symbiosis. It is not simply a case of independent *or* interdependent powers. The American system assimilates both simultaneously. The powers are different, but they are also the same. The powers are qualitatively distinguishable by function, but they are also quantitatively related in the physical dimension provided by the checks and balances theme. This can be demonstrated in the way shown in Figure 2.

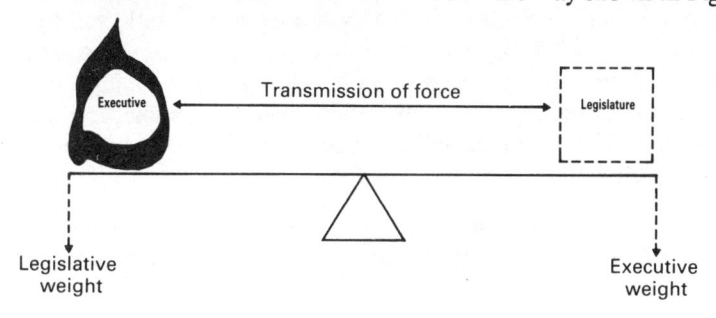

Using the executive and legislative powers as examples, it is possible from this illustration to see what effect the checks and balances concept has upon the concept of two different and separate abstract entities. At one and the same time, the executive and legislature are qualitatively separable but also linked by the common physical property of weight – an attribute imputed by the very idea of checks and balances. Just as checks and balances require objects, so the introduction of a concept of checks and balances not only presupposes but predetermines the existence of available objects. The two separate powers, therefore, become interrelated and interdependent by virtue of the common denominator of their imputed physical characteristics.

It was observed above that, without checks and balances, the separation of powers might be envisaged as in Figure 1. With the insertion of checks and balances, together with all its premises, the separation of powers scheme is more likely to be seen in the form shown in Figure 3.

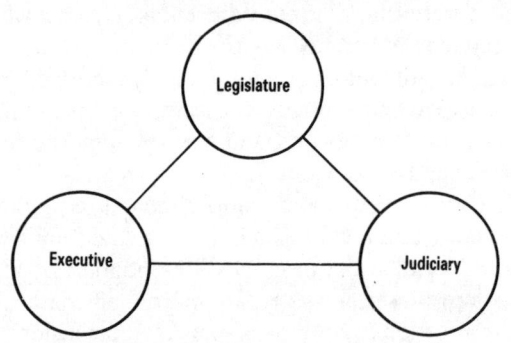

These entities are different and yet they are also the same: different from the point of view of functions; the same from the point of view of being material and co-equal constituents of a system designed and perceived with the virtue of balance in mind. What the powers might be said to lose in identity from having to share functions seems more than recouped from the powers becoming sufficiently concrete and hard-edged to play their role in the manifestly physical environment of checks and balances.

The net effect of this union of separated powers and checks and balances is to render them both a working premise of the other to the extent of becoming logically indivisible. Each appears to be the logical imperative of the other. This complex and compulsive interdependence is well reflected in the textbooks' accounts of the theme of separated powers in the American system. The various forms of expression employed to convey the nature of the relationship between separated powers and the principle of checks and balances illustrate the difficulty of explaining a duality which to all intents and purposes seems so much a unity:

> The principle of separation of powers is offset by the principle of checks and balances.... The principle of checks and balances ... actually enables one

branch to participate directly in the process that is supposedly the exclusive concern of one of the other two.[37]

Each branch checks and balances the others because each shares the lawmaking, administrative, and judicial powers with the other two.[38]

Even with separation of powers, the framers were still concerned that one element might dominate, so they provided each branch with the means to check the powers of the others.[39]

The separation of powers is spanned by the checks and balances which each branch of the government offers the other two.[40]

The key to the constitutional system is not the principle of separation of powers but the principle of checks and balances. The principle of checks and balances implies an intermixture of powers that will permit the several branches to check one another.[41]

... The third element – the principle of checks and balances – in the principle of separation of powers is what Madison ... called 'partial agency', which gives each branch enough power over the others to be able to check them.... This is the principle of checks and balances, designed to enable the three branches to protect themselves from each other's encroachments.[42]

The central government was divided among the executive, legislative, and judicial branches.... In addition to this separation of powers, the decision-making process was fragmented by a delicate system of checks and balances.[43]

Making laws, executing them, and judging are intertwined activities of government. As a result, the constitutional principle of separation of powers, along with checks and balances, really means sharing of powers.[44]

The government ... was one of balances and checks. Different branches of government were given different powers. But each branch was also given authority to involve itself in what were the primary responsibilities of the other branches.[45]

Separation of powers is reinforced by checks and balances.... The fact is that separation is intended to produce tension and friction between the branches.[46]

Checks and balances and separation of powers are distinct principles, but both are needed to ensure that one branch will not dominate the government. Separation of powers divides government responsibilities among the three branches; checks and balances prevent the exclusive exercise of those powers by any one branch.[47]

A checks and balances system permits each branch of government to intrude into the activities of the other branches.[48]

The [separation of powers] doctrine ... does not call for a total separation of powers. Although each of the three branches has the major responsibility for one of these processes ... each participates to some degree in the principal activities of the others.... By participating in one another's processes, the three branches are in a position to check and balance one another's influence and political power.[49]

The first step was the separation of powers.... But dividing up power in itself was not enough.... How could the framers use the separation of powers principle to prevent the governmental branches and officials from acting together in a tyrannical way? Their answer was to make these officials responsive to different pressures. This is the system of checks and balances.... Governmental power cannot be divided neatly into three separate categories, nor can the three departments be kept separate and distinct. That is not the intent of the maxim of separation of powers. What is required is a blending and mingling of powers.[50]

The three branches are independent of one another, but are at the same time interdependent.... The interdependence of the three branches is secured by what is the obverse of the separation of powers, namely the checks-and-balances system.[51]

The separation could not be complete, of course. Each branch would participate in the functions of the other, thus assuming communication among them and providing checks and balances.[52]

As a corollary and necessary consequence of this separation of powers, the three branches of government are designed to check and balance one another.[53]

The concomitant of the separation of powers is the system of checks and balances.... To assist in preserving ... distinction the branches are counterpoised against one another.... The separation of powers was designed to prevent a consolidation of political power; it was thought to be a mechanical arrangement for maintaining responsibility.[54]

Collectively these extracts display a remarkable degree of ambiguity and, at times, genuine confusion. Almost each one chooses to approach the relationship in a different way, with the result that there is an enormous variation in the descriptions and suppositions concerning the nature, origin, purpose, and consequences of the mixture of these two elements of governmental organization in the American constitution. Different verbs are used to describe the effects of one on the other. Different emphases are given to different aspects of the relationship. Different parts are implied as being superior or logically prior to others. And different degrees of consistency and inclusiveness are ascribed to the two principles. Despite the obscurity surrounding these diverse, and at times cryptic, allusions to the two principles, one thing remains constant, and that is their association with each other. Indeed, the confusion surrounding the relationship is itself a reflection of the proximity of the two principles to one another, which is so close that it is virtually impossible to extricate one from the other in any clear and coherent manner.

From these examples, it is evident that while the contents may be unpacked in many different ways, the end result is the same – namely, a synthesis between the separated powers and balanced government, which makes each one unimaginable and implausible without the other. This is, of course, another way of saying that explanations of this synthesis almost invariably slip into either starting where they intend to finish, or finishing at the point from which they departed. Thus the existence of separated powers tends to be seen as a result of checks and balances which in turn seem plausible only on the basis of a separation of powers. Likewise, checks and balances seem to be corroborated by a separation of powers which can be understood for no other reason than as a vehicle for checks and balances. Just as premises become entangled in conclusions, so proofs and assumptions become interchangeable. The result may be circular, but it is massively effective in building up a self-reinforcing and almost irresistible perception of separated powers operating literally in a physical environment. Without checks and balances, the three institutions of the Presidency, the Congress, and the Supreme Court help to lend weight and to provide an identity to the abstractly defined 'powers'. When the principle of checks and balances is combined with that of separated powers, however, the effect is reversed and the three institutions draw an identity and a purpose from becoming more the representational edifice of an underlying material framework of discrete units and physical contact.

The fifth point represents the final turn of the conceptual screw. Namely, the habit the textbooks have of *portraying America's scheme of national government in simple diagrammatic forms.* It may be true that the constitution's acceptance of three powers and its establishment of three departments invite pictorial representations of the government's structure for the sake of clarity. But it is also true that, by resorting to such graphic displays, the textbooks inevitably predispose the substance of their message to something which is compatible with being conveyed adequately in diagrammatic form. The effect of the partnership between separated powers and balanced powers is most

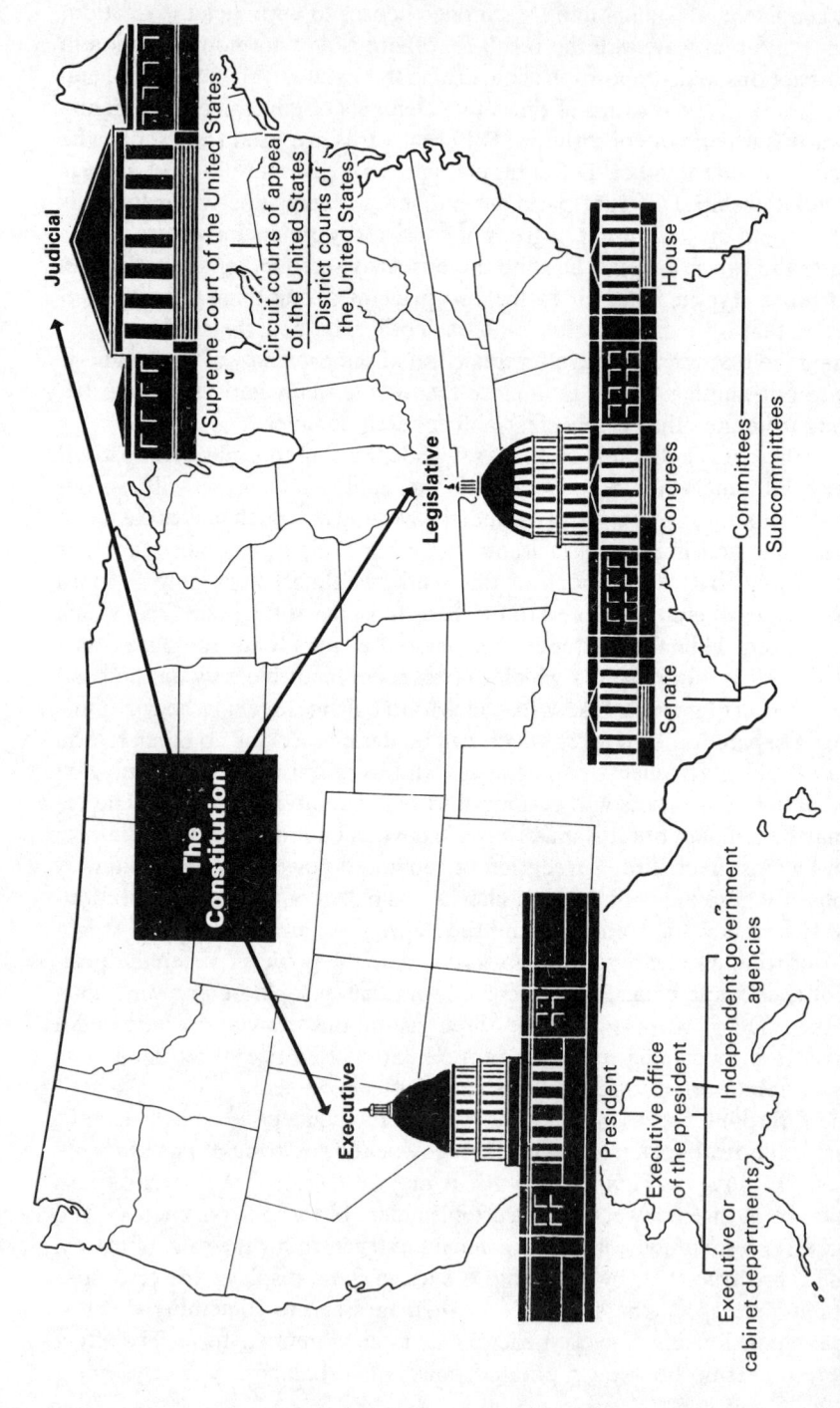

Figure 4 'The structure of the US government', from the end papers of K. Prewitt and S. Verba, *An Introduction to American Government*, 3rd edn (New York, Harper & Row, 1979); by courtesy of Harper & Row Inc.

clearly seen both in the textbooks' ready use of pictorial representation and in their customary depiction of the governmental structure. In these circumstances, all the complexities endemic to the separation of powers melt away before one's eyes. The separation of powers stands revealed as a structure reducible to a simple diagrammatic representation of three separate yet interconnected units. Furthermore, these units are equally sized, evenly weighted, and gracefully proportioned. The emphasis in such diagrams is on the comparability and even uniformity of the separate components. It is in the nature of diagrams to reduce characteristics and relationships to abstract and stylized forms. There is no exception to this general rule where the separation of powers is concerned.

Normally the separate powers are depicted as squares or boxes, or alternatively as circles or spheres. They are invariably portrayed as being equally sized entities. In reality, they are not. If one were to take architectural scale as the criterion, then the Congress would dwarf the Presidency and the Supreme Court. If one were to select another quantifiable criterion, that of annual costs and expenditures, then the executive branch would be a gargantuan size over 400 times as big as the Congress and over 1,000 times as big as the judiciary. Diagrams drawn according to these specifications, however, would destroy the symmetry and, thereby, the rationale for using diagrams in the first place. The pictorial representations are there to indicate not just separability but comparability – even if this impulse can lead to the architecture being strained to produce the required effect (Figure 4).

It is the physical solidity and dynamic equilibrium evoked by the checks and balances element in the partnership which induce the presentation of the entire separation of powers system in this highly stylized form. As a result, the separation of powers framework is made to seem not only more amenable to being depicted in this manner than it actually is, but also more subservient to its checks and balances partner than would otherwise be the case. The inclusion of checks and balances in the separation of powers scheme may make the framework of government appear reducible to an abstract form, but it does so in terms which very much favour the physical-mechanical mould of checks and balances. This is true partly because of what is depicted, and partly because diagrams are by their very nature a medium of exact amounts, precise movements, and measurable relationships. It is not simply that the pictures portray simplicity, it is that the very use of pictures betrays a belief in the simplicity of the message. Since diagrams are used as abbreviations and summations, the implication is always present that the essence of the subject is something that can be adequately reduced to pictorial form. Significance is attributed, therefore, not just to the diagrams themselves, but also to the decision to resort to pictures in the first place. Taken together, the effect is one of simple pictures speaking louder than wordy complexities – of uniform dynamics overriding qualitative distinctions. It is these compulsively simple portrayals that tend to fix the imagination, trap the mind, and finally close the conceptual circle

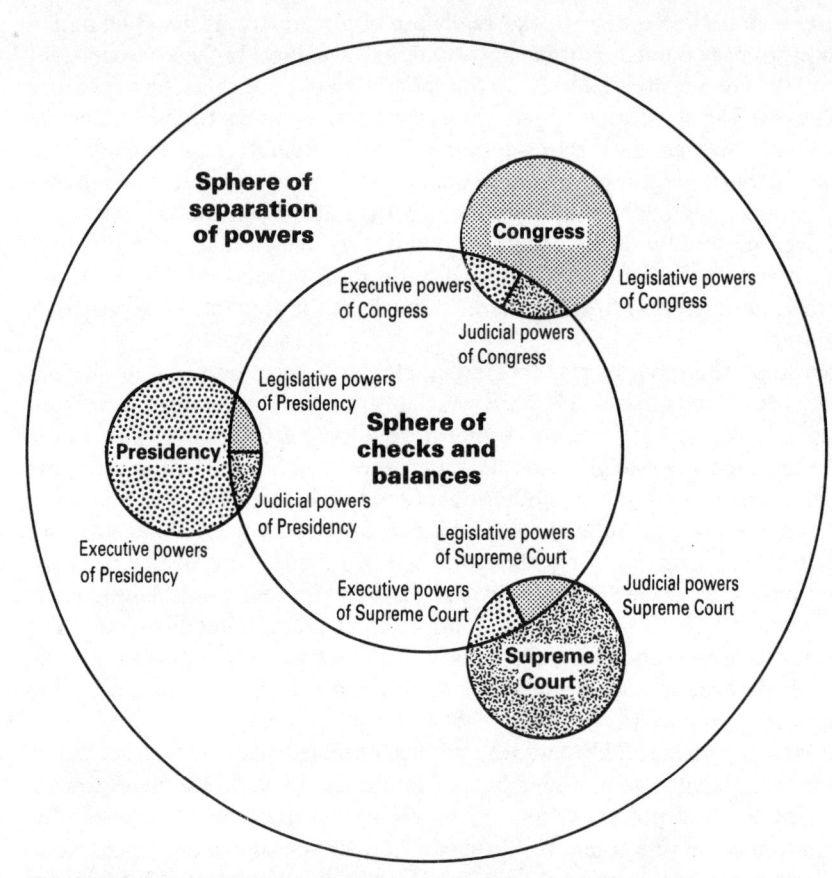

Figure 5 'The separation of powers and checks and balances', from A. de Grazia, *The American Way of Government* (Wiley, New York, 1957), p. 91; by courtesy of John Wiley & Sons Inc.

around the notion of a tightly closed system of self-balancing parts.

Even when efforts are made to portray the two dimensions of the separation of powers/checks and balances structure in equal measures, the results can often seem doomed to failure. In Figure 5, for example, Alfred de Grazia attempts to show the mixed nature of the system through the use of different shadings to depict a zone of shared functions between the three powers. This may seem a more subtle and penetrating portrayal of the relationship but it still fails to resolve many of the old issues and complexities which have always afflicted the separation of powers. Looking at this diagram, it is difficult to determine whether the sharing of functions is attributable to their inherent inseparability, or to their inherent comparability. In one way, the sectors of other functions depicted in each of the executive, legislative, and judicial powers can be seen as a means of satisfying the logic of the separation of powers by suggesting that the only linkage possible in such a system is one derived from the source of the original differentiation – namely, functional distinction. In this way, the President's executive veto, for example, is seen as part of the legislative process and, as such, qualitatively part of another branch of government. It is their functional attributes which bring the Presidency and the Congress into this relationship of different yet shared powers. Such a view is reminiscent of Aristotelian physics, as it supposes that for the Congress and the President to interact in any way it is necessary for Congress to be seen as having parts of an executive essence within it, just as it requires the Presidency to be shown possessing something of the legislative essence.

In another and quite different way, such a diagram can be seen primarily as a means of depicting the system of checks and balances. According to this perspective, the conditions of mutual control and reciprocal restraint between the three governmental powers require them to be portrayed as separate yet connected units. In this light, the shared sectors of powers represent not so much an intermixture of functions as a portrayal of points of contact. And the circular boundary intersecting the units represents not so much a sharing of functions as a sphere of influence in which force is received and transmitted.

Despite the genuine attempt to depict a synthesis between separated powers and checks and balances, such a diagram fails to reduce the confusion generated by the coexistence of two contrasting perspectives of the same subject suggested by each of the two principles incorporated in the scheme. A diagram like this may serve to illustrate many of the problems endemic to the subject, but it does not resolve them. The old problems and points at issue still persist. Problems as old as James Madison, who, as 'father of the constitution', not only questioned the plausibility of completely separating the three powers from each other, but equated functional intermixture ('partial agency') with checks and balances ('control').[55] In the end, even ambitious diagrams like de Grazia's reconcile qualitative distinction with physical uniformity and, as a result, fall prey to the same solution as other pictorial representations of the separation of powers. The issues are resolved only in those terms in which the structure can be depicted in diagrammatic form. As is the case with all such diagrams, the result is strongly suggestive of a closed, mechanistic system of physical cause and effect. In spite of the subtleties in presenting the sharing of functions, the physico-kinetic connections are so strong that the fundamental nature of the system is reduced to only one dimension – the dimension most susceptible to being portrayed through diagrams. The impression, even with de Grazia's diagram, is of a solid material structure with definite and ascertainable geometric properties. The three exactly equal spheres are juxtaposed in such a way as to represent either a three-way balance, or else a planetary system depending implicitly upon the balance of forces. As a consequence, the portrayal of both the nature and purpose of the structure is once again reduced to those physical-mechanical properties which not only encourage the use of such diagrams, but also determine their form.

The significance of such diagrams and of the textbooks' use of them lies in the meanings they convey and in the perceptions they stimulate. At one and the same time, they can be seen as (1) the quintessential distillation of a complex historical and conceptual phenomenon; and (2) an elementary assumption about American politics which pre-sets perspective into order and clarity, and despatches historical and conceptual problems into obscurity and irrelevance. Either way, the diagrams serve to emphasize how readily the organization and operation of the federal government can be, and habitually are, reduced into schemes of such geometrically definite form and proportion. Such visual encapsulations might be said to be the product of analytical certainty and exactitude, but it is perhaps more reasonable to surmise that they are the spontaneous and subconscious outcome of how the separation of powers system is both intuitively imagined and socially accepted. Whatever the reason for their use and form, the end result of such diagrams is normally the same – a highly abstract and mechanistic portrayal of the separate powers, which are presented, either implicitly or explicitly, as an expression of institutional reality rather than as an ideal model to which actual organizational entities and political relationships may approximate in varying degrees.

From this brief survey of the ways in which textbook writers tend to convey what the separation of powers is and how it works, it is clear that they conform to a general pattern of description and evaluation. This is not to say that the textbooks amount to a conspiracy which intentionally imparts a single and deceptive impression to the public. Quite the reverse. The value of the textbooks' coverage of the separated powers theme lies in the way they reveal not just the cultural acceptance of the scheme, but also the compulsively logical nature of its form and operation. Both the writers and their accounts are themselves a reflection of the way the separation of powers is traditionally perceived and understood in American politics. What they portray is further corroborated and reinforced by the suggestively mechanical format of the system. The internal logic of a separation of powers system incorporating a full complement of checks and balances leads almost invariably to certain set images, unavoidable corollaries, and irresistible conclusions. The textbooks contain little to challenge either cultural precepts or popular logic. On the contrary, they tend to reiterate and to confirm the products of both. It is for precisely this reason that such works are so useful. They reveal the way in which the great mass of the American citizenry – from those with the most meagre aptitude for political understanding to those with a lifetime's experience in political observation – have been encouraged by general contemporary sentiment and by force of reason to see government as not merely comparable to a machine but as a structure with real mechanical properties.

The accumulation of accustomed thought and traditional interpretation has given the separation of powers every appearance of being a real physical system composed of discrete units interconnected with one another to produce an enclosed pattern of direct physical contact, in which the positions of the constituent parts change in response to the forces exerted upon them by the others. Descriptions of the separate powers and reports of the institutions' relationships with one another generally serve to strengthen still further the whole concept of a system designed to generate and to sustain occurrences of physical cause and effect. The terms used and the vocabulary employed are normally redolent with mechanistic references. Whether it is 'the machinery of the national government',[56] or 'the engine of government',[57] or 'the mechanical arrangements for government',[58] or 'the machinery of constitutional limitation',[59] or 'the machinery of the system',[60] they, along with countless others like them, serve to maintain the imagery of moving shapes, political dynamics, and kinetic energy which pervades the general perspective of institutional relationships in American government. But such descriptions and references do more than this. Their allusions to physical interrelationships and to mechanics do not normally appear to be cases of poetic licence or examples of metaphor. Whether the mechanistic references are made consciously or unconsciously, the impression left is that of a widespread belief in the mechanical reality of the separation of powers. In short, the reason why the machine is called upon to supply so much descriptive material for the separation of powers is precisely because the latter is seen to be so much like a machine. There would appear to be enough in the American experience of the separation of powers, therefore, not merely to make a case for Newton's influence in the matter of the doctrine's constitutional origins, but also to substantiate the significance of Newtonian mechanics as an aid in perceiving and understanding how the arrangement works in actual day-to-day operation.

This perception of a mechanically arranged government is nowhere more revealingly displayed than in the way that the separation of powers is vigorously condemned for frustrating political developments in the face of a widespread desire for their establishment. The sentiment conveyed in most of these complaints is consistent with the idea of mechanical government – namely that, irrespective of popular will or social developments, the governmental framework has, through its own processes and in its own right, prevented the passage of strongly supported policies and inhibited the evolution of governmental structures and political organizations more congruent with a rapidly changing social order. The criticism is not just one of complaint over the nature and direction of changes in the government's institutional framework, nor is it one derived simply and directly from political bias over the system's policy output. An additional and powerfully intrusive dimension is provided by the idea that the government's scheme of checks and balances amounts to an autonomous mechanism which imposes an immutable form of structural self-limitation upon government, irrespective of the will of its members and regardless of society's needs. This idea of government inextricably imprisoned in the remorseless fixity of its own mechanical dynamics is clearly discernible in the following selection of complaints:

The fact is, from the 1950s on, American government has suffered from crippled leadership, from a slowdown of decision making, an impairment of its vital processes. The result has been an accumulation of unresolved problems and a buildup of public frustration so great that our quintessential American characteristics – our optimism and self-confidence – have now been shaken. Millions of Americans now feel that they have lost control of the government and that government has lost its capacity to act, to respond, to move on the challenges that confront our nation. In an era of rapid and accelerating scientific, technological, social, and cultural change, our governmental and political system has been operating in super-slow motion. Time has not stood still, but the processes of politics have.[61]

The United States is unique among the world's democracies in the extent to which the institutional system is weighted on the side of restraint regardless of the mandate of the people.... The total effect can be not just to delay action ..., but to forbid action. To the extent that the American institutional system cannot respond to a popular mandate for a change in the general course and direction of the government ..., it must be judged defective.[62]

This model was the product of the gifted men who gathered in Philadelphia over 175 years ago, and it deserves much of the admiration and veneration we have accorded it. But this is also the system of checks and balances and interlocked gears of government that requires the consensus of many groups and leaders before the nation can act; and it is the system that exacts the heavy price of delay and devitalisation.... We have underestimated the powerful balances and safeguards that are built into a system of majority rule and responsible parties.... We still underestimate the extent to which our system was designed for deadlock and inaction.... The Constitution has embodied the Madisonian model in giving the checks and balances a formidable grip on government.... The price of this radical version of checks and balances has enfeebled policy.... Hence we have lost control of our politics.... We lack popular control of the policy-making process.... Our government lacks unity and teamwork or, when it does exist, it is often the integration of drift.[63]

A particular shortcoming in need of a remedy is the structural inability of our government to propose, legislate and administer a balanced program for governing. In parliamentary terms, one might say that under the U.S. Constitution it is not now feasible to 'form a government'. The separation of powers between the legislative and executive branches, whatever its merits in 1793, has become a structure that almost guarantees stalemate today.... We cannot fairly hold the President accountable for the success or failure of his overall program, because he lacks the constitutional power to put the program into effect.... In each Administration, it becomes progressively more difficult to make the present system work effectively on the range of issues, both domestic and foreign, that the United States must now manage.... The most one can hope for is a set of modest changes that would make our structure work somewhat more in the manner of a parliamentary system, with somewhat less separation between the executive and legislature than now exists.... We need to do better than we have in 'forming a government' for this country, and this need is becoming more acute. The structure of our Constitution prevents us from doing significantly better.[64]

With our rigid government we have reached a point of public helplessness that is demeaning to a great nation. It is not merely demeaning but dangerous.... We face extraordinary shocks on the economic front and the President evidently does not know what to do, nor is there any quick way of replacing him.... No, we are helpless.... We need a more flexible system.[65]

Surely the concept of separated governmental powers has not fulfilled in any reasonably adequate manner either the preservation of liberty or the promotion of democracy. There is little liberty and little efficiency. Furthermore, if powers were in fact separated into three co-equal branches of government, the ineluctable consequence would be the crystallization of the *status quo* favoring those who wished to keep the existing political and economic orders unchanged – or changed as little as possible. Separation of powers is a profoundly conservative device to block innovations.[66]

If we are ever to regain the command of our situation, we must look first at our political and governmental institutions.... The sad truth is that today our political and governmental apparatus is rickety and inadequate. Even those Americans who are most interested in politics and government have tended to accept the limitations of the system as it now exists.... Under present conditions, our political and governmental machinery cannot serve anybody.... Even gifted leaders can't make the machinery work.... Problems are made harder to solve – or rendered wholly unsolvable – by breakdowns in the structure and process of government.[67]

Complaints about the U.S. system of government are a familiar litany from foreigners unaccustomed to the idea of checks and balances. Separation of powers ... is unique to the United States. Outsiders tend to believe either that it is not real or that it cannot work. For the first time in many years, however, some of the most thoughtful and experienced Americans in public life are coming to say that it doesn't work.... Government is bigger than ever and more muscle-bound. But the Constitution never did provide the lubrication to make its gears mesh. It is essentially a document setting limits to power and its concentration.... The loss of effective power [is] widely bemoaned in Washington at a time when Americans are demanding many more services of government.[68]

The crisis of 1973 had been foreshadowed. Presidential abuse of power, though seriously worsened, had been visible for decades; the inadequacy of Congress to provide an alternative to Presidential government had been shown from the close of the Civil War to the end of the nineteenth century and fitfully demonstrated again thereafter; and the malaise of public opinion had appeared in the late 1960s. In other words, the problems were long-standing and were rooted in structural faults.... Second, there was – there is – a way out, painful, difficult and dangerous as it may be. It will require constitutional surgery at least as severe as that of 1787.[69]

In the United States we find an almost total paralysis of political decision-making in connection with the life-and-death questions facing society.... Fully six years after the OPEC embargo ..., the U.S. political machinery still spins helplessly on its axis, unable to produce anything remotely resembling a coherent energy policy. This policy vacuum is not unique. The United States also has no comprehensive (or comprehensible) urban policy, environmental policy, family policy, technology policy. It does not even have – if we listen to critics abroad – a discernible foreign policy. Nor would the American political system have the capacity to integrate and give priority to such policies even if they did exist. This collapse of decision-making is, however, not the monopoly of one party or one President. It has been deepening since the early 1960s, and reflects underlying structural problems that no President ... can overcome within the framework of the present system.... The truly astonishing fact today is that our government continues to function at all. No corporation president would try to run a large company with a table of organisation sketched by the quill pen of some eighteenth-century ancestor.... Yet this is approximately what we are trying to do politically.[70]

Perhaps we shall be forced to conclude that the built-in tensions between Congress and the President make it impossible for us to act with the depth and dispatch that the urgencies of our problems require. Perhaps we shall eventually be compelled to turn to a parliamentary system.... My point is that we are in urgent need of effective, innovative government action to save ourselves and, within our capabilities, to help others. Fundamental to this is the strengthening of our governmental machinery.[71]

The 'separation of powers' concept ... may in fact be obsolete: an eighteenth-century theory turned late twentieth-century malfunction that is beginning to cause dangerous trouble.... In sum, we may have reached a point where separation of powers is doing more harm than good by distorting the logical evolution of technology-era government.[72]

It is apparent that the mechanistic framework in which these principles [i.e. separated powers] were conceived by the men of the eighteenth century is painfully inadequate for the more complexly intertwined constitutional and political problems arising in our time. In short, the adequacy of the American Constitution must be challenged.... Its tripartite provision for governmental powers is woefully inadequate and its mechanistic paradigm has become self-contradictory.... Government is now being charged with responsibility for the complete inventory of man's social problems rather than merely a few rudimentary functions of the negative state. This requires a constitution with a much fuller complement of functions than the eighteenth century allowed. But more important, it requires the application of a systemic approach to the political order.... This is not only because we must now deal with a fuller range of political problems than ever before but also because we must address ourselves to the qualitative element in politics rather than relying on unseen-hand types of constitutional mechanics.[73]

Our people are losing ... faith, not only in government itself, but in the ability as citizens to serve as the ultimate rulers and shapers of our democracy.... What you see too often in Washington and elsewhere around the country is a system of government that seems incapable of action.[74]

Thoughtful observers of our politics grow uneasy over the chronic inability of the United States to develop stable, coherent policies to deal with domestic problems and global dangers. Chaotic swings in the political fortunes of one President after another raise serious questions as to whether *anyone* can manage the U.S. store.... To expect the system to function otherwise is to ask for the impossible, for the founders intended Congress and the Presidency to be independent of each other.... The cost of separation, however, has grown proportionately with the cost to the nation in political drift, and in the government's inability to respond to seemingly intractable social, economic, and political problems.[75]

Separation of powers among the executive, legislative, and judicial branches seems to be one of the more settled questions in American politics.... But when the question of governability comes up, separation of powers often takes the brunt of the criticism.[76]

The idea of government irredeemably divided against itself, through the checks and balances integrated within it, is often so sharp a vision that it leads to serious doubt as to whether the government is in danger of failing to perform even the most rudimentary of its functions. To many, this is not simply a problem, but a deep, disquieting, and even threatening crisis. In the 1970s the question was 'Would the fragmented mechanism of government remain adequate for the needs of highly technological, complex and interdependent society?'[77] Could America 'run a Leviathan state with an eighteenth-century constitution?'[78] It is a testament to the continuity of the system that precisely the same anxieties were evident in the 1980s. 'Let us face reality. The framers have simply ... outwitted us. They designed separated institutions that cannot be unified by mechanical linkages.'[79] The questions were also the same. 'Can our 200-year-old constitutional blueprint meet policy demands and popular expectations that the constitutional framers could not possibly have envisioned?'[80] Whether or not the forceful complaints and the searching questions are prompted by a spirit of doom-laden fatalism or of outraged anguish, they are both founded upon the same central premise of a government having remained fixed in the eighteenth century's age of classical mechanics.

The partnership of separated powers and of checks and balances, therefore, still appears to be alive and well. In many respects, it seems more salient and controversial than ever. It could be said to be flourishing much more than conditions might ordinarily lead one to expect, especially when the many social and economic changes mentioned in the first section are taken into account. Under normal circumstances, these new conditions might have been sufficient to reduce the relevance and significance of the separation of powers in contemporary American politics. The attacks made by such Progressive critics as J. Allen Smith, Charles Beard, Vernon Parrington, and Herbert Croly upon the constitution's checks and balances as devices designed to debilitate popular government and to inhibit the use of government for collective social purposes were understandable and justifiable charges in the political context of the early twentieth century.[81] But with the arrival of large-scale bureaucracy, executive hegemony, managerial centralism, Cold War discipline, social integration, financial concentration, and national consciousness – together with the onset of demands for social policies, public services, and economic regulation – conditions appeared, at least, to be unconducive to the survival of divided and balanced powers. These expectations have not, however, been fulfilled. The idea of a political system operating in accordance with the principle of dynamic self-regulation continues to be a commonly acknowledged frame of reference. Mechanistic constitutionalism has remained in effect a central political perception sustained by a cultural consensus on its existence and by the mental trap of its self-contained and self-fulfilling logic. It may be arguable whether the Founding Fathers believed that the three powers were literally physical entities which 'if any one of them sought to get out of line ... would bump up against another element of public authority'.[82] What seems much less open to question is the subsequent acceptance of this mechanistic imagery in describing the behaviour and purpose of the three powers. The Founding Fathers may or may not have been Newtonian in the sense of allowing mechanics to inspire the design of their constitution. But what appears to be more certain is the extent to which the modern perception of the federal government is strongly influenced by the supposition that its working processes are mechanical in both form and substance.

Chapter four

The Presidency, the Congress and the separation of paradigms

The Presidency as a life science

It is evident from the previous chapter that there exists a dichotomy in the perceptions and conceptualizations of American government. On the one hand, it is asserted that the American system of government is a living entity responding to changing conditions in accordance with the imperative of necessity. On the other hand, American government can appear to be just as susceptible to a mechanistic frame of reference, in which remorselessly fixed patterns of exact interactions between mutually external units provide the main source of explanation. It was this dichotomy which Woodrow Wilson sought to eliminate in the celebrated appeal to his fellow Americans to reject the blind immutability of their formal conception of government and to accept its reality as a necessarily unified, purposeful, and constantly evolving organism:

> The Constitution was founded on the law of gravitation. The government was to exist and move by virtue of the efficacy of 'checks and balances'. The trouble with the theory is that government is not a machine, but a living thing. It falls, not under the theory of the universe, but under the theory of organic life.... It is modified by its environment, necessitated by its tasks, shaped to its functions by the sheer pressure of life.... Living political constitutions must be Darwinian in structure and in practice. Society is a living organism and must obey the laws of life, not of mechanics; it must develop.[1]

This was no mere prescription. Wilson exhorted his countrymen to acknowledge the actuality of government as an organism 'accountable to Darwin, not to Newton'.[2] Bearing in mind the conflicting perspectives of the nature of American government presented in the previous chapter, Wilson's famous assertion continues to be a highly debatable one. It is the terms of his declaration, however, that are of particular value, for they highlight the role of biology and physics in defining the duality of perceptions concerning American government. This is not to say that the contrasting impressions of the development of government in the United States can be literally reduced to the subject areas and working methods of these two sciences. What can be said is that Wilson's declaration gives stark emphasis to the contrast between the different cultural influences of Darwin and Newton as metaphors of description, as instruments of conception, and as representations of reality – influences which were clearly manifest to Woodrow Wilson and which are still just as salient to observers of American politics today.

The purpose of this chapter is not to resolve the dichotomy between Darwinism and Newtonianism as it relates to the structure and operation of American government. Its aim is to examine the nature of this duality and to explore some of its more important ramifications. In doing so, it will hopefully provide a major contribution to the overall objective of an improved understanding of the true role of Newtonian mechanics in the American system. With this ulterior motive very much in mind, the focus of this chapter will be centred upon the two institutions which together make up what is by reputation the most prominent example and the most characteristic feature of the American checks and balances system – namely the Presidency and Congress. What makes this example so very appropriate, however, is not simply its traditional association with mechanics, but also its recently developed parallels with the terms and concepts of biology. Indeed, as far as one of the institutions (the Presidency) is concerned, it may be said to have come to epitomize the most significant departure in American politics from the mechanistic format of known quantities and fixed relationships. Consequently, in studying the Presidency and Congress, one is in effect examining not just the professed showpiece of constitutional mechanics but, at the very same time, its reputed antithesis in the shape of the Presidency – the chief agent for and the chief embodiment of the idea of government evolving away from the steady-state dynamics of formal constitutionalism. The case of the Presidency and Congress, therefore, would appear to offer the prospect of a most fruitful insight into the dichotomy between what might be termed the Darwinian and the Newtonian elements of America's institutional framework.

To anyone who is conversant with the general style and descriptive techniques of studies of the United States' Presidency, it would not seem an undue exaggeration to say that they disclose a marked disposition towards biological terms of reference. Whether it is a case of biology being particularly apposite in studying the Presidency, or whether it is that the institution lends itself to biological forms of description, it remains a readily discernible fact that whenever the Presidency is being referred to it is not long before its position and role in government are defined in explicitly biological terms. The nature and significance of this association of the Presidency with biology will be examined in due course. But before such an examination can take place, it would be appropriate first to describe briefly the distinctive features of biology as a science.

Biology is the study of the structure and function of life forms. Living things have conventionally been identified by the following physiological characteristics.[3] First, the ability to extract from the environment the materials necessary for continued life (i.e. nutrition); second, the ability to absorb oxygen from the atmosphere to produce energy (i.e. respiration); third, the ability to change in substance and behaviour (growth); fourth, the ability to dispose of waste products and thereby complete an open system (excretion); fifth, the ability to create new generations (reproduction); and, last, the ability to respond to external stimuli (irritability). Collectively these attributes have served to characterize the phenomenon of life. They are portrayed as the distinguishing features of the massive profusion of diverse life forms in existence on earth – from the basic unit of the single cell to the prodigious complexity of the more advanced organisms. It is the processes and behaviour patterns of these many different vehicles of life which biologists attempt to examine and to explain.

It is claimed that biology is a qualitatively different science from physics because, while the latter is concerned with the ultimate reduction of all things to their irreducible material parts and to the purely physical relationships between them based on matter and energy, the former is more concerned with comprehending life as it stands – i.e. as a uniquely advanced and impregnably integrated order of composition and organization. It has to be acknowledged that there are many biologists, and even more physicists and chemists, who claim that biology is only a provisionally distinct science in so far as its subject matter is ultimately reducible to physico-chemical terms – i.e. that the diversity of life forms, together with all the apparent spontaneity and inner drives of their behaviour, can, in principle, be explained by the physico-chemical properties of the constituent materials of the cells in question.[4] The position of biology as an autonomous science concerned with the distinctive property of life has been, and continues to be, challenged by the spectre of Descartes's mechanistic world picture.[5] This perspective of the organism as a machine has led to a Cartesian biology which objectifies living things so that they become the passive registers of internal forces (genes) and external forces (environment). And yet, in spite of the pressures generated by those with materialist aspirations for explaining life, biology has revealed living matter to be extraordinarily resistant to such reductionism. Life has preserved much of its mystery. It continues to confound those who seek to reconstitute it into purely physico-chemical properties. As a result, it has succeeded – so far, at least – in retaining its identity as a qualitatively distinct element of nature.

Both the integrity of living matter as a distinguishable form of existence and meaning, and the integrity of biology as a science requiring distinctive approaches and strategies of enquiry, have been preserved from the materialist embrace of Descartes's modern disciples by three main lines of defence. First, is the sheer 'complexity and consequent uniqueness of biological systems'.[6] The complexity of living matter reaches such levels that it defies not only explanation, but also the imagination. Julian Huxley, for example, asserts that 'biology is much more complex than mechanics or physics'.[7] Some of his reasons for reaching this conclusion are as follows:

> Each single tiny cell has a highly complex organisation of its own, with a nucleus, chromosomes, and genes, and other cell organs.... But that is only the beginning, for larger higher mammals such as men and whales may have in their bodies over a hundred million million or even over a thousand million million cells of many different types, and organised in the most elaborate patterns.... The number of cells in our 'thinking parts' alone – the cerebral cortex of our brain – is about seven times the total human population of the world, and their organisation is of a scarcely conceivable complexity.[8]

It is true that recent advances in molecular biology have disclosed the existence of a fundamental structure to each cell, which determines both its nature and its function. This structure is the double helix chain of DNA (deoxyribonucleic acid), which stores and distributes genetic information in precisely coded combinations of linkages between the two strands of molecules that make up each unit of DNA. These linear sequences of links pass on the genetic instructions to each new cell by a process of self-replication.[9] The potential for a simple structural basis to living matter is further enhanced by the fact that each one of DNA's two molecular chains possesses only four types of available link. Such an apparently accessible simplicity, however, remains in reality an elusive and highly inaccessible complexity. This is because the four links constituting the inherited and the inheritable material of each cell can be placed in an almost infinite number of differing permutations. The net result is that while DNA's basic structure may be comprehensible, the prodigious scale and intricacy of the information contained within it is not. It continues to defy analysis. It has been estimated, for example, that if it were possible to transfer to a computer all the information stored in DNA which is required to make a human being, it would take 10,000 miles of paper to convey that information on to a computer print-out.[10] Clearly, then, it would appear that if biology might conceivably be reducible to physics and chemistry, the sheer magnitude of the subject matter would seem to ensure that such a technical possibility will continue to pale into unfulfilled potential.

The second line of defence for the idiosyncrasy of life can be referred to loosely as philosophical objections to the proposition that life can be accounted for in material and mechanistic terms. These objections are variously expressed and motivated by a variety of beliefs. For our purposes, it will be useful to refer to two of these objections. The first of these is the refusal to accept organisms as composite bodies formed from an aggregate of discrete parts existing simply in close proximity to one another. Organisms are claimed to be 'wholes' and, furthermore, idiosyncratic wholes with idiosyncratic histories. It is alleged that an organism is in essence a unity unto itself – a fundamental entity that gives life meaning by embodying a true system of internal and indivisible interdependence. The organism, therefore, amounts to that creative individuality, that persistent unified behaviour, and that singular agent of responsiveness to experience which serve to demarcate the reality of life and, therefore, to identify the genuine subject matter of the life sciences. In other words, an organism can be understood and explained only as an organism and not as a collection of sub-units. This idea of the cell or organism being an integrated unit of existence and meaning has had wide repercussions in philosophy. Perhaps one of the most noteworthy of these effects came with Alfred North Whitehead's insistence that the character of an organism ought not be confined to the non-material level, but should be permitted to define and to describe the nature of all material existence within an organism.[11] Instead of allowing mechanics to characterize the whole of inanimate nature and most of animate nature, Whitehead regarded the demarcation of life as so fundamental that it distinguished even the basic materials of the physical world between those lying within living bodies and those existing outside of them.

> An electron within a living body is different from an electron outside it, by reason of the plan of the body. The electron runs blindly either within or without the body; but it runs within the body in accordance with its character within the body; that is to say in accordance with the general plan of the body.[12]

Whitehead's 'theory of organic mechanism' leads to the second selected source of philosophical objection to the reduction of biology to physics. It was largely as a reaction to this doctrine that Whitehead devised his combination of organicism and materialism. The doctrine is that of vitalism. Although vitalism is not widely subscribed to by modern biologists, it does remain an important philosophical principle in the study of the meaning of life. The doctrine asserts that the form and behaviour of living things cannot be, and never can be, explained in purely materialist terms – not because of the complexity of the subject or because of the innate unity of the cell, but because life possesses a metaphysical dimension which has to be taken into account in any final analysis of a living body. Vitalists resist on principle the pretensions of those scientists who foresee the ultimate prospect of a capacity to break down the boundary between organic and inorganic matter, and who disregard the plausibility of supra-material factors in the existence of life. As a result, concepts like 'life force' or 'immanent energy' are presented by vitalists not only to fill in the areas of mystery left by the incomplete advances of biology, but also to explain why biology's advances will always remain incomplete.[13]

It would be inaccurate to say that biologists actively and enthusiastically embraced vitalism as a principle of explanation. On the contrary, 'one of the most pervasive of the presuppositions of biological research has been that organisms are to be regarded as physical mechanisms'.[14] Nevertheless, it is fair to say that many have felt resigned to abandon purely materialist categories and have, if somewhat reluctantly, resorted to some form of vitalism in order to account for the unfathomable nature of the phenomena under observation. This has been particularly true of those biologists researching in such fields as the central nervous system, embryonic development, and the biological chemistry of inheritance. It is in these advanced areas of research on the frontiers of life itself that the customary physico-chemical format of explanation has revealed its greatest deficiencies. The brain, for example, has been shown to possess an unpredictable and inexplicable capacity spontaneously to reassign responsibility for the control of a part of the nervous system from one area, which may have been damaged, diseased, or removed, to another having no previous association with that specialized function. Another example is provided by the 'central dogma' of molecular biology, which states that the information upon which the chemistry of life depends is provided by the genetic material DNA. But the refusal of biologists to regress further than this point and to confront the question as to where the information contained in DNA came from in the first place has, according to Stephen Black, reintroduced a quasi-vitalism into biology:

> Although Darwin's evolution by natural selection appeared to challenge the prevailing 19th century concept of a Divine Creation, the discovery of the structure of DNA and its role in the replication of genetic information has largely reinstated the Almighty as the Great Computer Programmer of the biosphere – and it is now a matter of 'In the beginning God created DNA'.[15]

Perhaps the field which has generated more doubts than any other over mechanistic reductionism in the life sciences has been embryology. 'Over and over again the great embryologists of the last century have begun as mechanists and have ended searching for the immortal hand that framed the symmetries they studied.'[16] The results of numerous experiments into the development of embryos have shown an unimagined capacity for living matter to grow according to a pre-set plan which remains intact in spite of efforts to intrude, to disrupt, or even to destroy the information network contained in the embryo. This exceptional ability of an organism to defy all mechanical precepts by reconstituting itself into its normal state of existence and by resuming its normal development as if by a conscious act of organizational purpose has led 'many biologists to believe in some mysterious force or inner will contained in living stuff'.[17]

The third, and probably the most important, line of resistance against the incursion of mechanics into biology lies with the Darwinian theory of evolution. It is difficult to overestimate the significance of Darwin to the development of biology as a science, for he not only showed how it was possible to synthesize a vast amount of separate and apparently disconnected observations on natural history into an interrelated whole, but provided biology with the prospect of a unifying theory which was applicable to all living things. Darwin's achievement was essentially one of offering a universal explanation of the causes of nature's evident profusion of diverse creatures – creatures which possessed an astonishing and inexplicable variety even between individuals within the same species. His suspicion was that there were simply too many variants and too much arbitrariness in nature to be comprehensible in terms of a divine plan. To Darwin, species did not seem to be the fixed categories which biblical orthodoxy insisted upon. Darwin looked at nature and saw change and mutability at a deeper level than anyone had done before. His theory was inspired by this sense of an undercurrent of change within nature and attributable to nature.[18]

Using an array of evidence based upon a relatively small number of selected examples, Darwin suggested that within the population of a given species there would always be a large measure of variation between individuals. This variation would be derived from genetic mutation. The variability would not be significant but for two facts. First, mutational differences would often either improve or reduce an individual's capacity to survive in its environment. Second, because nature always produced more individuals than the food supply could support, it meant that population pressure could be added to environmental constraints. This led to a selective process in which those variants whose differences gave them a higher chance of survival than other variants, would produce greater numbers of survivable offspring than the less well adapted individuals in the species. According to Darwin, these differentials in survival and reproduction could lead to a substantial change in the genetic composition of a species' population. Eventually, the changes might be sufficient to lead to the emergence of a new species out of the genetic material of an established species. In this way, what had originally occurred as spontaneous variations would become, with the process of natural selection, more permanent hereditary endowments to succeeding generations.[19] Nature, in this respect, could be seen as an active agent in its own mutability, for through genetic and environmental changes it continually produced changes in the living things that inhabit a continually changing world. These living forms represented both the inheritance of a lost past and the bequest to an unknown future.

Darwin's theory of natural selection could be, and subsequently was, extrapolated to account for the origin of all organisms and all species. While Darwinian theory has become a fundamental principle of biological science – a science with a dearth of theories, compared to physics – it has not yielded exact laws or mathematical rules about how species evolve. The theory has a built-in problem, for while it asserts the existence of certain processes (genetic mutation, differential survival, varied fertility), these processes are not amenable to direct and precise measurement. Thus the theory of evolution persuasively presents causes and effects, but just as the effects cannot be directly assessed in terms of their causes, so the causes cannot be precisely related to their effects. If Darwin succeeded in rationalizing the processes of organic development and in providing biology with a genuine universal principle, he also demonstrated that arbitrary randomness, blind chance, qualitative change, and unforeseen innovation were all integral to the subject matter of biology. In this respect, it would appear that the science of life, owing to the very nature of life itself, still eludes the rigour, constancy, and predictability which characterize the physical sciences. This continued distinction between the organic and the inorganic in nature is forcibly expressed by Jacob Bronowski:

> The living world is different because it is seen to be a world in movement. The creation is not static but changes in time in a way that physical processes do not. The physical world ten million years ago was the same as it is today, and its laws were the same. But the living world is not the same.... Unlike physics, every generalisation about biology is a slice of time; and it is evolution which is the real creator of originality and novelty in the universe.[20]

It can be said of Darwin that, in seeking to explain differences in nature, he converted it into a vast empire of flux whose only semblance of apparent order and purpose was provided by the theory of evolution. In the attempt to rationalize nature's multiplicity of individual mutations and the variability in its species, Darwin's theory became dependent upon the very disorder it was designed to clarify. Without it, the theory would become untenable and largely redundant. To the extent that Darwin's evolutionary theory represents the vanguard of biological enquiry, therefore, the nature of life with which biology concerns itself must of necessity be one premised upon incessant and ubiquitous change.

The significance of Darwin is not, of course, confined to biology. His success in providing biology with a scientific coherence led not only to the elevation of biology as a valued repository of general concepts and definitions available for the understanding of man and society, but also to the attempted application of the actual Darwinian theory of life to conceptions of society and social development.[21] It was a mixed tribute to Darwin, for while Darwinism undeniably became a major influence in sociology, economics, politics, and social philosophy, the coherence of his theory in biology could not be duplicated in its many extrapolations to other areas. It was not that his concepts or his terms lacked clarity or meaning. It was rather the difficulty of relating them to a social setting. It was difficult to know whether it was possible to identify precisely what features of society corresponded to which components of the evolutionary theory. For example, the distinction between an organism and its environment *seems* quite clear in the abstract, but in the case of man and society so much depends upon where the line is drawn. If the individual is classified as the base unit, then other individuals become part of the environment and, as a result, ruthlessly competitive individualism and self serving anti-social behaviour can be validated as biologically natural and systemically beneficial. But just as an individual cell may become part of the interdependent and co-operative structure of a multicellular organism, so the base unit of human society can likewise be taken at a more collective level – the family, the community, or the nation. If this is so, then the term Social Darwinism can take on a very different meaning from that with which it is normally associated. From this flexibility of interpretation, it can be seen why Darwin's theory has had a utility for socialists and anti-collectivists, and for Burkean conservatives and *laissez-faire* liberals alike.

Because of the sheer force of Darwin's concepts (e.g. spontaneous variation, adaptive improvement, natural selection, struggle for existence, survival value, inheritable advantages) and because of the promise, implicit within them, of a capacity to reduce the world to their terms, Darwinism has been accommodated, courted, and adopted by a host of differing interests and parties – each one seeking to invoke the authority of Darwin's natural selection in support of its basic social or political disposition. Darwinism offers analogies, metaphors, and accounts of reality to substantiate a vast range of political views and interpretations of society. This is not the place to examine the many ramifications of Darwinism. It is appropriate for the purposes of this study merely to record that Darwinism has developed into a genuinely universal conception of nature and, as a result, has acquired the trappings of a total philosophical system in which biology is presented as offering a different kind of explanatory reductionism from that offered by another *Weltanschauung* – namely, Newtonian mechanics.

From this brief survey of the terms and concepts of biology, and of Darwin's influence in bringing these terms and concepts to the forefront of social analysis and cultural awareness, it is possible to see that, while mechanics and biology are by no means mutually exclusive, they are not, however, the same as one another. The substance of their basic premises is different. The science of mechanics is founded upon the the blind purposelessness, yet determinable constancy, of objects interacting with one another in a closed system of purely material cause and effect. The working assumptions of biology, on the other hand, are those of a world of organic co-operation, growth processes, reactive structures, adaptive divergence, purposeful interdependence, and irreversible progression in an environment where changelessness is an implausible proposition. These concepts may not be totally exclusive to biology, but they are those with which biology is most strongly associated and which serve to give the science much of its identity. What is significant is that they are also the concepts which provide so much of the descriptive and analytical resources for studies of the United States Presidency.

There is no more appropriate way to begin a discussion of this theme of the connection between the Presidency and biology than by returning to Woodrow Wilson and his celebrated essay on the chief executive in American government. Through this essay, Wilson has become a de Tocqueville-like figure to the study of the Presidency not only because of the many Wilsonian aphorisms and dicta which are habitually employed by writers on the subject, but because Wilson succeeded in establishing a particular convention in the approach to analysing the office. According to Wilson, governments are living things ('political constitutions must be Darwinian in structure and practice'[22]). As a living thing, a governing structure possesses many specialized parts performing specialized functions in the service of the whole. The whole is given meaning only through the co-ordination of its parts by an active and purposive force of unifying control and central leadership. Wilson believed that in the American system this force could only ever be provided by the Presidency. This is because it is the only agency in the government which has the property of unity and centrality, and the only agency with the functional capacity to convert appearance into reality and, thereby, confer upon the system the characteristics of a real organism. In Wilson's view, the evolution of the Presidency 'from generation to generation ... as the unifying force in our complex system'[23] is both a cause and an effect of the government's existence as a living entity and not as a piece of machinery ('The influence of the President ... springs out of the very nature of government itself. It is merely the proof that our government is a living, organic thing, and must ... work out the close synthesis of active parts'.[24]).

The Presidency is not confined to being merely a force. Wilson views the office as the living embodiment of the entire community. Once again, it is a case of the Presidency being the only vehicle to register that collective consciousness and spirit which confirm the existence of a natural community. To the extent that the Presidency succeeds in this role, then the nation can be said to exist:

> The nation as a whole has chosen him, and is conscious that it has no other political spokesman. His is the only national voice in affairs.... He is the representative of no constituency, but of the whole people.... [The country's] instinct is for unified action, and it craves a single leader.[25]

Since the Presidency's relationship with the nation is alleged by Wilson to be organic in nature, the office is not merely the passive receptacle or symbol of nationhood, but an active force for its further integration into a corporate identity:

> He is not so much part of its organization as its vital link of connection with the thinking nation.... Let him once win ... the confidence of the country, and no other single force can withstand him.... A President whom it trusts can not only lead it, but form it to his own views.[26]

The Presidency, therefore, is not merely another unit in a government disaggregated into units. To Wilson, it is the central unit which by virtue of its position not only changes its significance within the system, but transforms both the nature of government itself and the conception of the society which is served by that government.

Another of Wilson's allusions to biology comes with his observation that it is easier to study Presidents than the Presidency. This is because the

Presidency has shown itself to have been a highly malleable office. It has varied with individual Presidents and with the conditions confronting them. Wilson makes it quite clear that, while the Presidency is not exactly a *tabula rasa*, it is sufficiently protean to allow individual incumbents to impress themselves upon the office. In doing so, they give the office an identity based upon the variability of individual Presidents. 'His office is anything he has the sagacity and force to make it. That is the reason why it has been one thing at one time, and another at another.'[27] The office in effect reveals the varied attributes of individual Presidents and, in so doing, is effectively characterized by the changes in the personal composition of the incumbents.

Finally, Wilson employs the biological notion of adaptation in response to environmental pressure to account for the necessary expansion of Presidential influence. Wilson sees it as a natural and inevitable development that Presidents have assumed increased powers, for it is only this office which has the potential capacity to make the required response to conditions on behalf of the American nation and people. ('His is the vital place of action in the system'.[28]) Because Wilson believed the constitution to be a living thing, he regarded a President's endeavours to fulfil the potential of the office to be within the spirit of the constitution. The Presidency would in essence be the proof of life and the touchstone of a living constitution – 'The President is at liberty, both in law and conscience, to be as big a man as he can.'[29] A President's impulse to exert himself to the maximum, therefore, would – in the best Darwinian tradition – facilitate the adaptation of the system to contemporary conditions.

Wilson's conversion of the study of the Presidency into one of the life sciences has reverberated through the literature on the office ever since. It is not the aim of this study to add to the stock of these biological references – although the temptation to discuss, for example, the system of Presidential primary elections as a process for producing the survival of the fittest is an enticing one.[30] Neither is the objective to pass judgement on the accuracy or validity of these allusions to the living world. The object of this section is simply to draw attention to the use of certain biological terms and concepts in the study of the Presidency, and to discuss their significance in what could be termed the conventional perspective of the Presidency. With this in mind, the proposal is to acknowledge the role of four themes which have been prevalent in Presidential analysis and which have their roots either specifically in biological science, or else in issues raised by biology. These themes largely represent the bequest of Woodrow Wilson to Presidential analysis in so far as at least three of them were first popularized by him in his essay on the office. The four themes are (1) organicism, (2) individual variability, (3) vitalism, and (4) evolution and adaptation.

The first theme is the commonly asserted notion that the Presidency is the embodiment of some form of *organic unity*. His specific functions, for example, of being chief of state, chief executive, commander-in-chief, chief diplomat, chief legislator, party leader, and economic manager have definite connotations of leadership and integration. They reflect what Alexander Hamilton argued to be the primary requisite of an executive – namely, the quality of unity. This was the reason why Hamilton pressed for the executive office to be conferred upon a single individual, rather than on a council of state or some other form of collective Presidency. He argued that a multiple executive would be detrimental to the system's capacity first to respond to the public, and second to provide clearly accountable government. According to Hamilton, unity was conducive to energy and efficiency – 'decision, activity, secrecy and despatch will generally characterise the proceedings of one man in a much more eminent degree than the proceedings of any greater number'.[31] It was Hamilton's view which prevailed at the convention, and it has been Hamilton's conception of executive government which has characterized the development of the office.[32] The single executive has certainly appeared to foster the creation of a centrality of purpose and direction in government which has permitted Presidents to perform their allotted functions, as well as enabling the system as a whole to benefit from the contribution of an adequate executive office.

The significance of the executive's singularity and individuality is not confined solely to the requirements of fulfilling the various executive functions and of integrating the executive branch of government. The President is not merely an executive officer but also the head of state, and as such his inherent unity as an individual has concentrated the symbolism of both the state and the nation around his central figure. The 'uniquely concentrated symbolic office'[33] of the Presidency, therefore, can be said not only to represent the degree of integration present in the executive branch and in the federal government, but also the level of integration achieved in the nation as a whole. Whether the process is interpreted as primarily one of the Presidency being simply the most appropriate and the most available agency in the system to symbolize patriotism and national aspiration, or of an office receiving its rightful prominence on the basis of its active association with the development of a national government and a national identity, the fact remains that the Presidency has a very close relationship with the rise of America as a national community. For example, American history is broken up into units corresponding to Presidential administrations. Surges of national spirit are associated with surges of support for the Presidency and with a general willingness to interpret Presidential strength as an unmitigated virtue. Likewise, the high points of the Presidency tend to be associated with national drama, epic developments, and increased national fervour. Taken together, the impression received is one of joint development and mutual identity.

The 'unifying quality of the Presidency'[34] in respect to the nation is a particularly strong theme in studies of the office. The theme is variously expressed and examined in differing ways. For example, the relationship can be seen as simply one of mutual advantage and reciprocal support in so far as what is beneficial to one is generally seen as being beneficial to the other. This view is presented to its best effect by Richard Neustadt's succinct conclusion that 'what is good for the country is good for the President, and *vice versa*'.[35] A different form of interpretation of the relationship has tended to lay stress upon the President's status as the nation's most prominent symbol. According to Clinton Rossiter, the Presidency is 'a priceless symbol of our continuity and destiny as a people. Few nations have solved so simply and yet grandly the problem of finding and maintaining an office of state that embodies their majesty and reflects their character.'[36] A closer linkage between the office and the country can be made by emphasizing the Presidency's role of genuinely representing the nation rather than merely symbolizing it. An example of this more substantive connection is provided by James MacGregor Burns, who asserts that:

> as the modern Presidency has become increasingly the expression of a consensus over political goals ... the holder of the office has come increasingly to represent the same kind of national unity and harmony in his political role as in his symbolic and ceremonial.[37]

A further strengthening of the linkage comes with those interpretations which assert that, in being 'the major innovative force within government',[38] the Presidency becomes in effect the active 'force that shapes the national mood and direction'.[39] Robert Hirschfield, for example, sees the Presidency as possessing an explicit mandate to act on behalf of the nation:

> The modern President can draw upon extraordinary power because he is the democratic symbol of national unity and the necessary instrument of national action.... As a result, ... democracy and necessity allow the President to transcend the limitational principle and to assert his full authority as trustee of the nation's destiny.[40]

Another variation, and perhaps the ultimate one, is the attempt to simplify the whole relationship by resorting to absolute terms and proclaiming the Presidency the actual embodiment of the nation. Joseph Califano believes that because 'the central executive today touches every American every day of his life'[41] the United States is undergoing a process of transformation into 'a Presidential nation'.[42] George Reedy agrees, and believes that the modern President cannot escape the process of becoming the 'personification of the people'.[43] According to Reedy, the Presidency and the nation are already so closely connected to one another in the American mind that the 'President becomes the nation'.[44]

> Often the terms 'nation' and 'president' are used interchangeably without any awareness of the fact. When we say that 'the nation' is doing something we usually mean that it is acting in accord with presidential directives.... When we speak of a 'buoyant, confident' nation, our mental image is

usually that of a buoyant, confident president. Conversely, when we speak of a 'strong' president, we mean one who has mobilized the nation in his behalf.... The state of the presidency can be regarded as the state of the nation.... We are committed to the presidential concept in a manner which leaves us virtually incapable of thinking of the United States in other terms.[45]

Clearly, there are many different ways in which the theme of the Presidency and the nation can be seen. In the literature, the relationship is variously described, given varied gradations of emphasis, and is evaluated in varying terms. The fusion of identities may be a cause for celebration, contentment, and satisfaction, or it may lead to criticism and anxiety. What cannot be denied is the existence of the association. Despite the diverse ways in which it is referred to, the matter of its underlying presence seems quite settled and has become one of the chief descriptive conventions in accounts of the Presidency.

A number of factors may be said to have contributed to the emergence of this organic quality in the Presidency, but three in particular stand out in the literature as being significant. They are the most commonly referred to elements in the Presidency's development as the nation's chief agent for unity. The first element concerns the nature and format of the President's election. With the 'nationalization of electoral coalitions',[46] Presidential elections have become more genuinely national elections – with nationally recognized candidates, nationally debated issues, and an electorate which, while still formally divided up into states, has become increasingly national in the manner of its choice. A Presidential election has come to assume more the character of a direct act of national decision. As a result, a President can draw upon an authority derived from his position as being not merely a nationally elected individual, but the *only* nationally elected office holder in the system. Louis Heren explains the significance of this distinction in the following terms:

> The Presidency has a mystique for Americans which Charles I would have recognised. All power flows from the people, but the President is the only national representative. National life begins anew when a new President is inaugurated. To that extent, the election is a rebirth.[47]

It is upon this distinction that Presidents have based their assertion of being the 'people's choice', the 'tribune of the people', the 'personification of the people', the 'people's representative', etc. It is on the basis of the nature of their election that Presidents have sought to identify themselves with the welfare of the American people and with the destiny of the nation. The techniques and circumstances of this process of identification are many and varied. They include the studied invocation of national themes and ideals in their public addresses and speeches; the development of the pomp and majesty of the office (e.g. the Presidential seal of office, the Presidential anthem, Air Force I); the drawing of constant historical parallels between Presidential responsibility and national crises, and between Presidential leadership and new departures in the pattern of national life; and the continual presentation of the President's persona through the national and international media. These practices have resulted in a modern Presidential cult, by which incumbents have sought to extract the fullest possible meaning from the manner of their election.

It is primarily through the election that Presidents have tried to substantiate their claim of being the choice of the people and to secure the maximum stature and leverage from that position. This strategy has been so successful, it has led Theodore Lowi to assert that the Presidency's 'power is great precisely because it is truly the people's power'.[48] While Presidential declarations of power on behalf of the people, in their interests, and with their consent may be contested, what does seem quite definite is the indispensability of public support to a President's power. According to Elmer Cornwell, popular support for the chief executive represents the 'very essence of the power to influence the process of governance'.[49] Presidents have used the initial momentum of their election victory to attempt to sustain their direct linkage with the public and, thereby, to build an enduring empathy between themselves and the concept of the American people. Presidents do this in the full knowledge that just as Presidential power is dependent largely upon integrating government and society around the office, so the loss of power is not only registered by, but precipitated by, a loss of support from the people at large ('the judgements of all historians of the Presidency concur that the loss of the people's trust is the one mortal disaster from which there can be no real recovery'[50]).

The second significant factor in the composition of the President's organic quality has been his strong association with the modern practice of employing the state to ensure certain minimum standards of welfare and opportunity to the individual. The objective of such actions has been to intervene on behalf of those individuals whose condition cannot be thought of as free, in order to raise them to an economic level at which liberty is transformed from an abstract principle to a real opportunity for personal action, individual fulfilment, and moral self-development. This form of state intervention in support of certain marginal groups, and the subsequent provision of welfare services as a social right, represented a radical departure from the accepted American orthodoxy of much of the nineteenth century. At the very least, it amounted to a principled qualification to the dogmatic individualism of *laissez-faire* liberalism, for by their very nature positive liberty and the positive state are premised upon the existence of a corporate dimension to society. In this light, society is seen much more as a collective entity of organic interdependence, mutual identity, and common traditions. As a result, the sovereignty of the individual becomes no longer unequivocal but contingent upon the legitimate requirements of agreed social need.

The idea that a community existed, that government gave expression to such a community, and that government could genuinely act in the interests of the community, all tended to converge upon the office of the Presidency.[51] This was, first, because the transformation in American attitudes to the state had been actively inspired by several prominent Presidents. Second, the responsibility for the maintenance and development of the framework of regulation and welfare tended to fall upon the Presidency for reasons of precedent and political leadership. And, third, much of the identity, continuity, and purpose of the modern Presidential office has been provided by the existence of the positive state and by its connotations of community, welfare, and social integration. The association is described by one observer in the following manner:

> Government ... by its own actions could enormously expand equality of opportunity and hence collective freedom by egalitarian policies.... And this is precisely what American government – and especially the American President – has been doing in the years since World War II.... Part of the nation's consensus over freedom and equality is a common commitment to federal action against depression and poverty. And because that commitment first and foremost binds the President ... it is part of the edifice of Presidential government.[52]

Since its original inception the positive state has expanded enormously and has come to encompass a vast array of services and agencies to cater for the ever increasing demands for protection, regulation, security, and supervision in a modern industrial economy. The net effect of this elaboration has been the creation of a large bureaucracy which has in itself become a persistent and central issue in American politics. The concept of the people *as* the state is regularly confronted by the concept of the people *against* the state. Presidents have been equally adept at associating themselves with both positions. But, either way, Presidents cannot escape the positive state, and by virtue of that fact alone they cannot avoid the traditions, responsibilities, and expectations of such an accumulated social inheritance. The positive state remains the patrimony of modern Presidents – and a very valuable patrimony, for it represents the conjunction of civil society and the government under the aegis of the Presidential office.

The third theme in the modern Presidency which is generally referred to in such a way as to leave a strong impression of the office's organic nature is the increased importance of foreign affairs and national security in modern American society. There has always been a strong association between the Presidency and the welfare of the nation in respect to the outside world. This association has largely been derived from the belief that defence and foreign affairs are executive by nature, and that much of the executive's inherent function is based upon the need to resort to some unified locus of decision and direction wherever and whenever the nation's basic interests are at stake. It has even been claimed to be an 'axiom of political science that the more deeply a nation becomes involved in the affairs of other nations, the more powerful becomes the executive branch'.[53] The perception of the necessary relationship between the executive role and the area of foreign relations had been recognized as self-evident and inevitable as early as the seventeenth century, when John Locke acknowledged the existence of the executive's 'federative power'. This term referred to the executive's inherent responsibility for supervising society's security and managing its interests overseas – a power 'less capable to be directed by antecedent, standing [and] positive law ... ; and so must necessarily be left to the prudence and wisdom of those whose hands it is in'.[54] Many of the United States' early leaders, including both Thomas Jefferson and Alexander Hamilton, also recognized that a nation's affairs with other countries was executive in nature. With the onset of total war and the elimination of America's geographical security, however, the twentieth century has witnessed a rapid extension of the Presidential responsibilities as the 'sole organ of the federal government in the field of international relations'.[55] As the world has impinged more and more on the affairs of the United States, so the Presidency has been elevated to an increasingly higher vantage point of perspective, from where the chief executive is expected to respond to the imperatives of security, to the priorities of the nation, and to the protection of the West in general.

Since World War II the continuing international tension of superpower rivalry, combined with the anxiety generated by the potential for apparently inconsequential events to escalate into global nuclear destruction, have together made the Presidency into an office of central significance for the very survival of American society. This has concentrated the minds of Presidents, but it has also concentrated the spirit of basic community within the nation – surrounded as it is by a much more complex and dangerous world. It is this context of instability and high stakes that has, in Aaron Wildavsky's view, made executive vigilance and response so important:

> We are interested in what happens everywhere because we see these events as connected with larger interests involving, at the worst, the possibility of ultimate destruction.... Since small causes are perceived to have potentially great effects in an unstable world, ... Presidents must be interested in relatively 'small' matters.[56]

Given the potential precariousness of the international system, as well as continuing strides made in the accuracy, speed, and destructive force of ever more advanced weapon systems, it has now become a recognized imperative that America should have the most sensitive, informed, and effective decision-making apparatus that its political system is capable of providing. It is a reflection of the trust placed in the functional reliability of American governmental organization that such an apparatus is assumed to be provided and operated by the Presidency. In what has become largely a profession of faith in the American system of government, the public has accepted the need for the President to possess the ultimate responsibility for the nation's vital interests, and has condoned the existence of a large Presidential organization and of an extensive degree of Presidential discretion to attend to those interests.[57] As for Presidents themselves, they have benefited in stature from the consensus that foreign policy and national security has normally evoked from the public. Much of the power of the modern Presidency has been derived from the imprint of this consensus upon the office.

The office, however, has not just been the passive mouth of a foreign-policy consensus. The Presidency in the past and the modern Presidency today has been renowned for infusing the people with national spirit; for reminding them of their providential position in the family of nations; for inspiring them with the themes of manifest destiny and global mission; for invigorating their ideological resolve and national self-esteem; and for mobilizing them into positive action on behalf of the nation and its beliefs.[58] National spirit and public demand may well be channelled into the Presidency, but it is also true that Presidents have skilfully tapped the element of cultural unity which maintains an underlying presence in this field of policy. Presidential success in eliciting a consensus around their foreign policies, and thereby around themselves, was particularly evident during the Cold War. It was in this period that much of the American people's *raison d'être* and its collective interest lay in what seemed an irrefutable necessity to confront every manifestation of communism in the world.[59] Since that time the orthodoxy and discipline generated by the Cold War's vigilant strictures have declined. The precarious uncertainty of the superpowers' rivalry has likewise subsided. Nevertheless, acute international tension has continued and has become compounded by the sheer growth in the complexity and interdependence of the world and by the subsequent decrease in American economic autonomy and military superiority. It seems likely that Presidents in the future, just as much as Presidents in the past, will seek to generate that heightened public regard for nationhood and for community purpose in a way that is not only consistent with the Presidency's symbolic presence as the representative of the nation, but sufficient to substantiate the widespread impression that Presidential action in this field is taken on behalf of the people and in recognition of its unitary essence.

Taken together, these three factors of the Presidential election process, the Presidency's association with the positive state, and the Presidency's responsibility for national security, make for an executive office with an immediate national and political identity to the broad mass of the American public. The Presidency has become so central to the political life of the nation that the office has been widely acknowledged to be an essential component of the political socialization process.[60] According to David Easton and Jack Dennis, it is probable that 'the first recognisable shadow that flickers across the wall of the cave of the child's unformed political mind is that of the President'.[61] From that first 'initial visible object of the political world',[62] the child goes on to construct a more comprehensive and complex view of politics around that central core. From an early age American children are encouraged to view both the occupant and the role of the Presidency in a highly idealized manner (e.g. omniscience, infallibility, diligence, omnipotence, protectiveness) and while these images tend to fade and judgements become less categorical and more qualified, it is argued that the early emotional appeal of the Presidency is crucial in the development of the individual's subsequent acceptance of the legitimacy of the political system as a whole. Furthermore, it is claimed that although the adult may become a lot more equivocal in his appreciation of the Presidency compared to his childhood view, Americans discard the 'adult overlays of skepticism to return to childhood images in times of national emergency'.[63] During such times, the President can normally draw upon a great stock of public support, a public expectation of leadership and direction, and a rise in national spirit which almost invariably finds its outlet in the Presidential office – irrespective of whether the incumbent is deemed responsible or not for the crisis.[64] This intuitive linkage between the public and the Presidency is also strongly in evidence when the office itself experiences some form of crisis. So much so, in fact, that whenever the President has been placed in jeopardy the occasion has constituted a national crisis in its own right. The assassination of President Kennedy, for example, brought about a vast outpouring of genuine public emotion and national anxiety which at once drew the country together around the Presidential office both in commemoration of a lost President and in a spirit of rededication to the principles of American government and the values of American society. The positive response of the public to the President during times of crisis does lend support to the convention of historians and commentators in relating the Presidency directly with the existence of a larger entity encompassing the American people, and its culture, society, and nationhood.

The second theme in Presidential observation and analysis which has close links with biology is that of *individual variation*. Woodrow Wilson observed that the nature and meaning of the Presidential office would change in relation to the individual incumbents. It is an observation which has consistently been made ever since. With the vast increase in the extent to which the office has been personalized in the modern era, the impression of individuality and of its significance in defining the office has grown accordingly. To the extent that the Presidency has been moved to the centre stage of political attention, the President himself has been cast as a singular force of uniqueness which forms an individual imprint upon both the office and the government. The government becomes *his* administration, and *his* policies become the administration's programme. The President's personal resources of leadership skills and persuasive subtlety are believed largely to determine that element of activism or energy in government upon which will hang the fate of so many policies. In matters involving national security, the relationship between the President as an individual and the policy-making process becomes even more marked. The well documented case of the Cuban missile crisis of 1962, for example, has become a classic piece of Presidential analysis in which President Kennedy's individual qualities are seen as being crucial to the outcome of the crisis.[65] But the Cuban crisis is by no means unique. The history of the modern Presidency is littered with momentous decisions revolving around the judgement of a single person at the centre of a vortex of conflicting advice and information. Whether it is President Johnson personally agonizing over the North Vietnam bombing halt in October 1968,[66] or President Nixon deciding in the autumn of 1972 to engage in a massive aerial offensive against North Vietnamese cities and ports in the face of considerable pressure from the Pentagon and from his staff against such a campaign,[67] or indeed President Truman's almost private decision to order the use of atomic weapons over Hiroshima and Nagasaki in 1945,[68] the impression left is one that strengthens the assumption underlying the basic notion of Presidential decision-making: namely, that critical choices in government are not just made in the name of the President, but are determined by him to the extent of being personal decisions. It is this assumption which is central to the common practice of measuring the success or failure of an administration in terms of the individual President acting as an individual: a practice which sustains the popular view of the office as one which responds to the variation in individual incumbents to the maximum extent possible within the constraints of institutional continuity. Others would go even further and claim, like Erwin Hargrove, that 'the Presidential office is shapeless and [that] each President fills it out to suit himself'.[69]

It would seem, therefore, that the President in many respects not only sets the style of Washington and the direction of the government, but also sets the terms in which the office is generally observed and understood. There can be fewer more emphatic endorsements of such an impression than the modern vogue for examining the Presidency from the point of view of the underlying personalities of the individual incumbents. Such studies proceed on the premise that if the nature of the Presidency is one of personal power, then the office can best be explained by studying not merely the individual President but what lies beneath the person and determines his character, his behaviour, and, ultimately, his decisions. This form of study attempts to go one step further than conventional biography by seeking to explain the developmental process in character formation and then to examine the ways in which character or personality determine a President's actions in office.[70] According to James Barber, who must be regarded as representing the vanguard of this form of study, a President's character is crucial to the understanding of the office – 'the connection between his character and his Presidential actions emerges as paramount'.[71] The basic objective of this type of analysis is to trace a line of causation from childhood to adulthood, from personality to action, and from the subconscious to political decision. It has been claimed that such analysis can even provide a predictive capacity and that this could be, and moreover should be, used to assess the suitability of prospective Presidential candidates.

The claims of personality theorists and character analysts like Barber have aroused a great debate over the reliability of their premises and methods, and over the validity of their conclusions and explanations.[72] Whether this type of analysis is or is not as fruitful as its defenders assert, it is a reflection in its own right of the abiding interest in Presidents not merely as individuals, and not even as different individuals, but as significantly different individuals. Herein lies the irony in this new vogue in psycho-biography and character categorization, for just as these forms of study attempt to advance Presidential analysis towards new standards of scientific rigour and systemization, so their results reinforce the traditional view of the Presidency as the embodiment of the incumbent's individuality. In other words, such analysis leads right back to the cultural fascination and public preoccupation with Presidents as discrete entities.

Many reasons have been advanced to account for the extensive public attention given to Presidents and for the entire cult of the modern Presidency. For example, it is possible to speculate that the American public has been conditioned into an active interest in individual Presidents by the massive media coverage given over to them, and by the tendency of American historians to stress the role of heroic leadership and the salience of great men in American history and society. It has also been claimed that, given America's democratic and individualist culture, there exists a need among the public to believe in the individuality of the office for the purposes of (1) simplifying the complexity of government; (2) providing the citizen with a form of surrogate participation; (3) giving him an identifiable element of responsiveness and accountability in government; (4) affording an accessible object of emotional and affective attachment to the political system as a whole; and (5) generally satisfying the American ideal of the individual forcing changes upon what would otherwise remain an unyielding landscape of immovable structures and intractable problems. Whatever the reason, it is clear that a modern Presidential cult exists within American society and that it is reflected in the ways in which the office is observed and analysed by commentators and political scientists.

The third theme which is detectable in contemporary Presidential analysis, and which can be included in Woodrow Wilson's tradition of organic constitutionalism, is that of *vitalism*. It is true that Wilson never alluded to such a concept or discussed the Presidency explicitly in terms of it. To that extent, this theme cannot be regarded as specifically Wilsonian in origin. Nevertheless, the concept of vitalism is difficult to dismiss if one accepts, like Wilson, the idea that government is a living being. It may be true that Wilson implicitly recognized the difficulties of explaining the Presidential office as a living thing. What is beyond doubt is that these difficulties have been openly recognized by many of those who seek to account for the modern Presidency.

It will be recalled that vitalism refers to the belief that living things cannot be adequately explained without recourse to some force or spirit which complements the purely material and behavioural aspects of life's existence. In other words, vitalism amounts to a recognition that living things are, in essence, ultimately inexplicable in the normal empirical terms which are customarily employed in analysis. Personality theory and character studies might be said to represent a form of vitalism in Presidential analysis in so far as, while they seek to convert the Presidency into a science, they do so by reducing it to that level which poses the gravest problems in respect to explanation. Individual variability may well represent the final essence of the office, but whether that essence can be successfully defined and accounted for may well depend in the long run upon whether psychology can ever completely break down the old Cartesian duality of mind and matter.

The psycho-biographers and personality typologists do at least hold out the prospect of answers, even if they have not yet secured them. Many of their colleagues in Presidential scholarship, however, tend to proceed upon the assumption that the Presidency is something which will never be really knowable. At its minimum, this attitude is normally represented by statements like Richard Pious's assertion that 'the only certain forecast about the Presidency is that no forecast is certain'.[73] But there are others who leave the distinct impression that the Presidency has a mystique all its own which is by no means confined to the dimension of behavioural predictability. Grant McConnell and John E. Hughes are two who make their position on the incomprehensibility of the Presidency quite explicit:

> The office is not a given quantity and never a known factor in any political equation.... The Presidency is ultimately elusive and almost insubstantial.... The office remains almost impossible to define in any but the most superficial terms. Its powers can never be stated with certainty and precision.... The nation ... is always something of an abstraction, a diverse inchoate multitude of men spread across a vast expanse of land. To mobilize these men is to give shape, to organize, to create and recreate the nation. This process is inevitably touched with mystery. Yet here is the essential dimension of the Presidency.[74]

> Perhaps all the sweep of Presidential leadership becomes more visible and sensible when looked upon as a political mystery rather than a political institution. And all the trial of the Presidency may come to be seen less as a naked play of powers than an obscure play of paradoxes.... To speak of the office as a *mystery*, moreover, ... is only to observe a political fact.... [The Presidency] warns watchers of the White House against all sweeping propositions and summary definitions which, by facile analogy or theory, would take the office out of its ever-changing context, and its ever-elusive place, in the Republic's history. There may be, I suspect, but one immutable fact of Presidential life: there are no immutable patterns to describe it, no invincible strategies to govern it.[75]

A number of writers on the Presidency have reacted against such declarations of mysticism and analytical defeatism, and have attempted to place the study of the institution upon a more empirically sound basis.[76] Despite the profusion of problems over methodologies and information availability, certain limited advances have been made. However, these are conspicuous by their meagre presence in the literature and by their failure to make any real inroads into the general style of Presidential analysis, which continues to depend upon the premise that the office is 'a seamless unity ... a whole greater than and different from the sum of its parts'.[77]

While vitalism or a form of vitalism may well lie in the background of most social and political analysis, in the case of the Presidency it can be said to lie in the foreground almost as warning to those whose zealous reliance upon empiricism threatens to overcome the prudent caution required in this particular field. Just as the complex subject matter of biology 'cries out for a special kind of explanation',[78] so the nature of the Presidency also seems to demand some element of uncertainty and unpredictability to be integrated into any explanation of the office. This feature of Presidential study may be derived from a genuine belief in the inscrutability and mystery of history and politics. On the other hand, it may be born out of a sophisticated analytical sensitivity to the problems involved, and a reluctant admission of the final elusiveness of the Presidency's true nature. Either way, from the point of view of *not* offering the prospect of explicability, the literature for the most part tends to support the Wilsonian view of the office as a living thing. In doing so, it satisfies the prevailing cultural preoccupation with seeing the office as alive – as vital as the incumbent and, as such, 'the vital center'[79] of government.

The fourth and final biological theme associated with the Presidency is perhaps the most significant one. It certainly pervades the literature on the Presidency and is widely recognized as a crucial feature in the nature of the office. The theme in question is that of the Presidency as an *adaptive and evolving institution*. There are essentially two dimensions to this theme. The first pertains to the Presidency itself as a living, sentient, conscious, and purposive body which changes in response to conditions and adapts itself to changing circumstances. The second dimension pertains to the Presidency's role as the chief agent of adaptation for the political system as a whole. In this guise, the office becomes the register of social and economic change and the active force in moulding the government's response to such change and, consequently, in adapting government to the needs of its environment.

The operative concept in Darwinism is necessity. Evolution occurs in response to the inner need to survive and the imposed need to adapt to the environment. The Presidency has successfully managed to assume for itself the mantle of representing, in visible and personal terms, the social will to survive and to adapt in order to do so. The office has also acquired the modern responsibility for generating responses to new conditions and for contriving changes in the light of shifting constraints. In adapting his Presidency to conditions, the individual President is seen as accommodating government to social and economic change within the United States, and secondly accommodating American government and society to the wider environment and greater flux lying outside America's borders. The more urgent and manifest the requirement for response, the more likely it is that the requirement will be focused upon the President – irrespective of constitutional prescription and institutional protocol. This is often couched in terms of a necessity finding its own outlet. A crisis generates an imperative which can be acted upon only in the terms in which it presents itself and by a body with a capacity to react in accordance with those terms. The development of the modern President's role is very much regarded in this light and is widely seen as the necessary means of reacting to a recognized and declared necessity.

Oliver Cromwell was well known for asserting that 'necessity knoweth no law'. This dictum has proved to be particularly salient in the search for an understanding of the Presidency. This is because one of the chief characteristics that the office has become noted for is its sanctioned licence to act on its own initiative when needs must. It can be argued that, by their very nature, the function of the executive and the concept of constitutionalism are as distinct as oil and water. Implicit in the constitution is the principle of defined and, therefore, demarcated and limited government. As such, the role and purpose of the executive office have traditionally been the subject of great dispute concerning its proper position in a constitutional framework. The landmarks in what is commonly described as the evolution of the modern Presidency have been those occasions when the essentially active capacity of the executive has been deployed to meet the categorical requirements of a demonstrable necessity – i.e. on those occasions when the political system had to respond to the 'real world' on its own terms by allowing the nature of a crisis to determine the means of the response. The forcible intrusion of the 'real world' with its own schedules and cycles into the settled formalism and tranquil legalism of a constitutional system has provided the stimulus for an almost continual re-examination of the relationship between the Presidency's actual powers and its formal responsibilities.

As a result of these enquiries and investigations, it has become an established tradition to view the executive as possessing an indigenous source of power and an authority peculiar to the institution. This concept of a constitutional Presidency with the capacity to generate power from within itself, rather than simply relying upon what could be explicitly derived from the constitution, tends to be based upon two constitutional foundations. The first is the assertion that there has existed all along a hidden reserve of Presidential powers which becomes apparent only as and when circumstances and their concomitant pressures warrant. This foundation is based essentially upon the lack of specific constraints in the constitution. Theodore Roosevelt's celebrated theory of the Presidency's stewardship role was very much embedded in this notion of an absent negative. Roosevelt rebutted the idea that, if some course of action was necessary for the country, it could not be taken by the President unless 'he could find some specific authorization'.[80] He went on to declare that:

> it was not only his right but his duty to do anything that the needs of the Nation demanded unless such action was forbidden by the Constitution or by the laws.... I acted for the common well-being of all our people, whenever and in whatever manner was necessary, unless prevented by direct constitutional or legal prohibition.[81]

The other foundation to the expansion, or alternatively the revelation, of Presidential power has been the doctrine that the existence of the executive office necessarily infers a substantial power from the very nature of the office itself. This argument springs from the notion that the utility of a modern executive is primarily that of immediacy, responsiveness, and action in the public interest. Accordingly, it is assumed that a chief executive worthy of the name cannot adequately respond to the unexpected and the unpredictable if the office is restricted to tightly defined standards of conduct and to previously drawn areas of activity. The general statement in Article II conferring executive power on the President, therefore, has become a cornerstone of the office. It has been regarded as being no mere nominal introduction to the article, but an acknowledgement of the substantive power and authority inherent in the function of the office. This intrinsically extra-constitutional attribute of the Presidency has even been recognized by the Supreme Court in a number of crucial judgements. Of these, the *In re Neagle* (1890) case is arguably one of the most significant. This is because in his judgement Justice Miller declared that the President's basic constitutional duty of 'faithfully executing the laws' was not limited to Acts of Congress or to United States treaties according to their express terms, but included 'the rights, duties and obligations growing out of the Constitution itself, our international relations, and all the protection implied by the nature of the government under the Constitution'.[82]

Given that this potentiality for expansion exists within the office, most modern Presidents have been unable to resist the temptation of exploring the possibilities of power further than their respective predecessors. The development of the modern Presidency has been generated by the active cultivation of the inherent reserves of power by Presidents in response to national problems and social needs. The office's capacity for changing its shape and altering its function has been nowhere more evident than in that field which has always been closely associated with the role of a chief executive and which can be said to be the very *raison d'être* of the executive office – namely the field of foreign relations and national security. The Presidency's development in this area has been well documented and requires no additional reappraisal here, except to say that, whether it is Lincoln's virtual suspension of the constitution in order to save the union, or the extraordinary powers over the economy granted to Woodrow Wilson by Congress in World War I, or F.D.R.'s destroyer deal with the British government in 1940, individual Presidents have built up a vast array of precedents which in a cumulative manner have changed the nature of the office. It is Presidents who have enriched the meaning of Article II, who have established powers for their successors, and who have ramified their responsibilities to match the ramifications of foreign policy and national security matters within American society at large.[83]

While it is true that the 'nature of foreign policy' requires 'a minimal kind of continuity and coordination in both policy formation and execution ... that Executives and not legislatures can provide', it is also true that the Presidency's discretion and prerogative in this field where 'the nation must speak with only one voice'[84] is not significantly out of character with the office's general properties of action and adaptability. Foreign-policy responsibilities and competence, therefore, tend to be not so much an exception to the Presidency's nature, but rather its exemplification. The office has become the object of a public expectation of development in the cause of emancipating the rest of the political system from the constraints that often threaten to engulf it in the name of constitutional propriety. Under the auspices of Presidential guidance, the requirements of domestic policy have become recognized as being just as urgent and just as much in need of direct government attention as disruptions to the international balance of power. Crises at home are not seen as any the less critical than crises abroad simply because they are domestically motivated. The public interest becomes conjoined to the national interest. In this way, Presidents have secured or assumed authority to address themselves to various domestic issues by treating them as critical either in the sense of their possessing a national security dimension, or in the sense of their being comparable in magnitude and seriousness to an external threat to the United States. On these grounds, Presidents have taken foreign policy-style initiatives in domestic affairs by treating them as emergency survival-threatening problems requiring effective attention from that element of government most able to adapt both itself and the government to the needs of the situation.

As a consequence of these strategies, the office is not only recognized as being mercurial in nature, but celebrated as such. This is because it is this quality which provides the office with the potential for adaptive innovation and for providing the necessary direction to shape the country to new conditions. The New Deal and its subsequent development of the whole infrastructure of the positive state, for example, have been interpreted as a Presidentially orchestrated response to need and as representing as imperative a reaction to conditions as any foreign-policy emergency. Likewise, the emergence of such extra-constitutional roles as guardian of the American economy, chief formulator and patron of policy, public opinion mobilizer, and leader of the Western world have come to represent a similar process of the Presidency changing by assimilating change and, by doing so, embodying the substance of what is seen as a systemic response to contemporary circumstances. In these respects, it is not difficult to understand why great Presidents have customarily been distinguished by such criteria as 'their mastery of events, their influence on history, their shaping of their country's destiny ... [and] their ability to magnify their own department, and their own powers'.[85] The 'great' Presidents are feted as such because through their achievements they have given dramatic and substantive weight to the idea of government as a living and responsive being. They have proceeded upon and acted out this idea through their inner capacity to emit change and, by doing so, to give the system that spark of adaptive vitality which, without active Presidents, might well have been absent to a dangerous degree.[86]

The final expression of the vital and adaptive nature of the Presidency comes with the belief that, notwithstanding apprehension or criticism, the office has been one of growth and will ineluctably continue to be so. Owing to the sheer weight of historical precedent and to the growing burdens placed upon government by an increasingly advanced industrial society, it has become a common assumption of American government in the modern era that the Presidency is inextricably set in an upward direction of power and responsibility. According to one noted commentator, 'the enlarged role of the President is the product for the most part of conditions which appear likely to continue operative for an indefinite future'.[87] It may be the cause of approval or disapproval, but there seem to be few exceptions to the general pattern of Presidential 'aggrandisement'[88] in one form or another. The office is seen quite simply as the only one capable of following the dynamics of social advance and of responding in such a way as to become part of that progression of constant and irrepressible change in American society. The Presidency is in essence seen as evolving through necessity into a necessarily improved form, better able both to perform its functions and to allow the system at large to undergo similar processes of extensive and long-running adaptation.

While it is difficult to assess whether the 'imperial Presidency' episode represents a significant departure from the trend of executive centrism, or merely a temporary decline in the pace of its development, it is clear that prior to this period of ambiguity the modern Presidency had for over a generation been recognized as an office with an underlying continuity of development. Clinton Rossiter provides perhaps one of the best examples of this form of resignation to the steady evolution of the Presidency. Rossiter maintained a conservative distrust of an office with such a manifest capacity for disturbing the fabric of the constitution. He wrote in his book *Conservatism in America* that:

> The American conservative remains fundamentally anti-statist in mood and philosophy.... He remains a cultist, a strict-constructionist, and an exponent of divided and balanced government.... As to the Presidency, even the sight of one of his own kind in this highest office [i.e. Eisenhower] for eight years has not allayed his suspicions of executive power. The yearning for Coolidge cannot be suppressed.[89]

Despite his conservative suspicions, however, even Rossiter ultimately felt the need to defer to the weight of historical progress and to the direction of evolution. Rossiter, who may well have yearned for Coolidge, felt obliged in *The American Presidency* to recognize and to accept the burgeoning power of the modern Presidency as a fact of life. In his well known and influential study of the office, Rossiter concluded that:

> All this evidence leads me to suggest that the outstanding feature of American constitutional development has been the growth of the power and the prestige of the Presidency.... In the face of history, it seems hard to deny the inevitability of the upward course of the Presidency – discontinuous, to be sure, but also irreversible.... All the great political and social forces that brought the Presidency to its present state of power and glory will continue to work in the future.[90]

Rossiter, along with very many of his fellow observers, conceded that the Presidency, like any other living thing, could proceed in no way other than forwards. There could be no going back to Coolidge. There could be no settled and static existence in the present. The Presidency produced the very plausible impression that its manifold changes were nothing less than a process of evolution which in turn provided additional corroboration to the proposition that the Presidency amounted to a form of life and that the best way to understand the office was to employ the same biological approach which Wilson had suggested at the beginning of the century.

Congress and the spectre of mechanics

The preceding review of Presidential analysis has been conspicuous by its almost total preoccupation with the office in isolation. A whole aspect of the Presidency has been missing. It is a crucial dimension, for without it the significance of the modern emphasis upon the institution as 'the vital place of action' might well be lost. It can be argued that the Presidency possesses several intrinsic qualities which make it particularly amenable to biological terms and concepts. This may indeed be so, but it is the effect of the institution's permanent partnership with an ostensibly comparable and co-equal institution which makes the terms and concepts of the life sciences seem so conclusively appropriate to the Presidency. Indeed, it might be said that, in many respects, the main stimulus to perceiving the Presidency in active, dynamic, and biological terms is provided by this institution, which the constitution has positioned adjacent to the Presidency as the executive's chief political co-participant in the framework of the national government. The institution in question is, of course, the United States Congress, which together with the Presidency accounts for the 'most striking example of the separation of powers afforded by the American Constitution'.[91]

It is precisely because these two institutions are structured into proximity to one another in the separation of powers framework that they generate comparisons. Owing to the institutional arrangements of the constitution, the Presidency and Congress are habitually viewed as two almost mutually inclusive bodies. Constitutionally, the two institutions are commonly regarded as the primary unit of reciprocal control and shared authority in a system dedicated to the principle of structural self-limitation. Culturally, the Presidency and Congress are instinctively referred to together as a composite entity – almost as a binary unit by which one would be incomplete without the other, and an understanding of one would not be possible without recourse to its partner. It was noted in the previous chapter that the American amalgamation of the separation of powers principle with the checks and balances principle served both to differentiate the Presidency and Congress into two institutions, and also to draw them together and reduce them to the same plane on which they could interact with one another. It was the checks and balances requirement, therefore, which introduced the notion of co-equality between the two branches. As a result, the separation of powers framework has fostered a presumption of a certain basic similarity in the nature of the two bodies. Although the Presidency and Congress are distinct in one respect, the rationale of the scheme is based upon the assumption that they are also the same. It is this feature of the separation of powers structure which infuses its observers with what could be called a heightened expectation of comparability. Given this implicit assumption, together with the way that the institutions are normally portrayed as two adjacent blocs of the same abstract form, then any differences between the two tend to be given a clarity and a significance that might otherwise have been obscure. In this way, the relationship provides a service of mutual definition for the two institutions in so far as their respective natures seem to be disclosed by the contrast of one institution with the other against a background of assumed similarity. In other words, by pulling the two 'separate' and 'separated' bodies together into an uncomfortable duality, the checks and balances principle makes their differences all the more vivid and throws the contrast in their respective natures into high relief. What makes for a calculable convergence, therefore, also makes for a qualitative divergence.

This process of mutual definition has been particularly salient to analysts and observers of the Presidency. In seeking to comprehend the nature of the office, to rationalize its role in contemporary society, and to confirm its overall vitality, these President watchers have been indebted to the Congress for being, in their eyes at least, everything that the Presidency is not and, in the process, for being the natural point of contrast and comparison. The substance underlying this view is that the previously stated attributes associated with the Presidency (e.g. action, unity, coherence, responsiveness, speed, leadership, decisiveness) owe much of their salience and credence to the fact that they do not appear to be so applicable to the Congress. The Presidency has taken on both the impression and the substance of being lifelike because of Congress's tendency of appearing to be a basically moribund institution. The more Congress has slipped into this reputation for lifelessness, so the Presidency has seemed more vital in comparison. And because of Congress's apparent dereliction of the massive responsibilities of the modern state, so Presidents have increasingly had to act out the office's reputation for innovation and adaptiveness – thereby making Congress even paler by comparison. It has become one of the most established pieces of conventional wisdom on the current state of the separation of powers that the modern Presidency has both the functional capacity and the will to compensate for the declining competence and motivation of Congress, even to the extent of absorbing much of Congress's own major role and traditional *raison d'être* in government (i.e. law-making). It has been contended that the Presidency now provides the legislature with a direction and leadership that would otherwise be absent. According to Robert Hirschfield, for example, 'executive leadership of the legislature has become an established feature of our system, though the effect of Congress's reliance on Presidential initiative and of its delegations of authority to the executive is to enhance his domination over the legislative process'.[92] Hirschfield, along with many of the chief executive's other observers and defenders, see the nature of the Presidency and the nature of the Congress as being sufficiently different to have led to Congress's law-making facility being largely co-opted by the Presidency as part of the grand integrative process of executive centralism that has characterized the development of twentieth-century government in general.

The divergent natures of the Presidency and Congress may well have led to the latter's subordination as a constitutional partner, but what remain to be ascertained are the views as to what these differences in their respective natures might be. The nature of the Presidency has already been examined in some depth. The nature of Congress is reputed to be different. The Presidency has developed a reputation for vitality, innovation, and organic awareness – a reputation which becomes so much more explicit in direct comparison with Congress. This leads to the question as to what it is about Congress that makes it appear so lifeless as an institution and which, thereby, makes the comparison with the Presidency so unflattering a contrast. Although it is true that some of Congress's reputation is derived simply from not being able to compete with the dynamic imagery of the Presidency, it is not altogether a matter of negative identity. In the same way that there is a conventional view of the modern Presidency, so there is also a similarly conventional view of the Congress in the modern era. This view revolves around a number of set themes and has been subscribed to by a wide variety of both observers and active participants in the political process. It would be useful as well as enlightening to dismantle this reputation and to enquire into precisely what there is about it and its component parts which renders Congress so dissimilar from the Presidency in nature. In order to discern the relative difference between the institutions and to understand why such an apparent contrast should exist, it is proposed to examine the Congress from the perspective of the same categories which were used in the examination of the Presidency (i.e. organicism, individual variation, vitalism, and evolution).

Organicism

While the Presidency may be perceived as an organism, Congress generally is not. On the contrary, Congress is more often noted for its particulate nature than for its coherence as a unified whole. The explicitly pluralist dimension of Congress is derived from several sources. For example, the Congress is often compared unfavourably to the Presidency because, while the latter is thought to embody the nation, the former is seen as the expression of all the diverse sections, regions, group loyalties, sovereignties, and sub-cultures which represent not so much the constituent elements of the nation as the countervailing forces to nationality. It is 'the idea that the people are *represented* in the Legislature *versus* the idea that they are *embodied* in the Executive'.[93] While the two institutions may both be popularly elected, 'as the elected choice of the whole people, the President, in Rousseau's language, represents the general will as against the mere aggregate of particular wills represented in Congress'.[94] This mere aggregate is not thought of as in any way amounting to a corporate identity because – owing to the decentralized structures of the parties, the localistic orientation of elections, and the general cultural adherence to the principle of popular sovereignty which reduces representatives to formal agents of their constituencies – the individual components of Congress are seen as necessarily discrete entities reflecting the separate interests and loyalties of their individual political bases. As a result, the popular reputation of the Congressman is that of a figure who 'is supposed to represent his constituents, not the nation at large' and who 'over the long run ... must behave like a toy wound up by his constituents to go their pointed way'.[95] It is this reputation which lies at the heart of Congress's folklore that representatives 'vote their districts first'. It is also a reputation which, in David Mayhew's judgement, is largely deserved, for, in their enthusiasm to impress their constituents and to secure re-election, members engage in the universal practice of associating themselves with particularized governmental benefits in such a way that a single Congressman can be 'recognised as the claimant for the benefit' and as having had 'a hand in the allocation of the benefit'.[96] This notion of Congressmen as merely ciphers acting on behalf of their constituents and in pursuit of their constituencies' interests has been a central assumption underlying many of the accounts and theories of Congressional behaviour in general and of legislative–executive relations in particular. The influence that sectional interests and localistic concerns are reputed to have in Congress, for example, has in many instances acted as a rationale and motivation for Presidential assertion on behalf of the nation. The Congress is often seen as embodying the centrifugal forces and the fissiparous tendencies of

American politics in general and, thereby, providing every justification for the Presidency to emerge as a self-styled redemptive force, independent of such dissident chauvinism and capable of providing a necessary balance in favour of national direction and central policy. 'The function of the President in our system,' writes Wilfred Binkley, 'is to discover and somehow or other to promote the public welfare amid the mosaic of conflicting interests represented in Congress.'[97]

The decentralization of Congress, however, is not limited to its multiple base or to its representational ethos. Its fragmentary nature is further compounded by the committee system. It is no exaggeration to say that Congress is synonymous with committees. The committee system is the Congress's major distinguishing characteristic. The committees are not only the chief means by which Congress performs its functions, but to a large extent the committees determine what functions Congress is capable of performing and, consequently, what kind of legislature it is. The committee system is so central to Congress that Clem Miller described the institution as 'a collection of committees that come together in a chamber periodically to approve of one another's actions'.[98] While these committees may well be defended as centres of legislative expertise for policy-making competence, or as specialist units for the effective supervision of the executive branch, the fact remains that the committees compartmentalize the structure and authority of Congress into quasi-autonomous fortresses from which members defend their privileges and their power. This 'device of disintegration',[99] as Woodrow Wilson termed it, breaks up the *esprit de corps* of new members, deters the formation of effective trans-committee groupings, and dissipates the institution's potential for collective action.

The committees seem to instil into the Congress a natural predisposition towards decentralization, for, while they provide the organizational structure of the institution, they do little to retard the indiscipline and political licence of individual members. They might even be said to facilitate the release of these discordant energies. It is that 'they excel at pulling things apart, not putting them together'.[100] Certainly, the Congress, in contrast to the British Parliament, with its emphasis on party loyalty, party voting, and party authority, is characterized by its centrifugal forces of committee careerism, policy specialization, entrepreneurial individualism, and proliferating enclaves of insulated hierarchies. Samuel Huntington complains that Congress:

> has failed to combine increasing specialization of function with increasing centralization of authority.... As a result, Congress lacks the central authority to integrate its specialized bodies. In a 'rational' bureaucracy authority varies inversely with specialization. Within Congress authority varies directly with specialization.... Reciprocity among specialists replaces co-ordination by generalists.[101]

What is more, the selfsame forces of decentralization which used to give such power to the committee chairmen instead of the party leaders have worked to undermine the position of even the chairmen as committees have become more democratic, more open, and more fragmented into sub-committees with substantial independence from the parent committees. Consequently, 'the specialization of function and dispersion of power, which once worked to the benefit of the committee chairmen, now work against them'.[102] It is true that the parties in Congress cannot be lightly dismissed, especially as they represent the best predictive guide to voting behaviour within the institution and, moreover, are said to mitigate 'the fractionalizing effects of persistent policy cleavages among members'.[103] Nevertheless, the structural landscape of the committee system, together with its associated ethos of amplified disaggregation, tends to reduce party leaders to being not 'program salesmen or vote mobilizers, but ... brokers, favor-doers, agenda setters and protectors of established institutional routines'.[104] It is on only very rare and short-lived occasions that party organizations or individual party leaders have been able to generate sufficient group empathy and collective coherence to retard the development of committee decentralization. It is more normally the case that the parties in Congress – by their very weakness and by their general appearance of permanently unfulfilled potential – serve to reflect the prevailing perspective of Congress as primarily an institution which has real meaning only in respect to its parts.

Individual variation

Another recurrent theme in Congressional commentaries is the assertion that the institution is fixed in nature and not susceptible to the sorts of changes experienced in the Presidency through the turnover in individual incumbents. In contrast to the Presidential office, the conventional view of Congress is one of consistency to the point of stultifying constancy. This view is derived primarily from the modern decline in the changes to the composition of Congress, and from the modern growth in the seniority rule, i.e. the reduction in horizontal mobility in and out of Congress and the reduction in vertical mobility within Congress. In the nineteenth century Congress experienced not only a much greater turnover of membership, but a much lower dependence upon extensive experience and long-standing service as a precondition of leadership. Before the Civil War, for example, the Congress was an altogether more fluid institution, with committee memberships changing regularly from Congress to Congress and even chairmanships rotating every two years. But after the war the Congress became a much more stable and professional body to which individuals, once elected, wanted to devote their career on a long-term basis.[105] Congress's domination of the federal government after the Civil War served to enhance its attraction to aspiring politicians. Furthermore, Congressional committees began to 'develop reputations for real expertise and became the primary units of Congress that made a substantive impression on legislation'.[106] This too led to an increase in the commitment of Congressmen to staying in Congress. Owing to the development of the party system and the consolidation of sectional divisions, the turnover in membership at elections began to decline during this period. It was not until the modern era, however, that the number of safe seats and long-term incumbency reached such exceptional levels. Even in 1900, for example, only 1 per cent of the House membership had served ten or more terms of office, but by 1971 the figure had increased to 20 per cent. In 1972, when the Ninety-second Congress had concluded and Congressmen faced their respective electorates, fully 93.6 per cent of those House incumbents seeking re-election were returned. This figure accounted for 365 members, or 83.9 per cent of the whole House membership. And there was nothing outstanding about the 1972 election. It was an example of what has become the modern norm. During the period 1979–84, for example, the average proportion of Congressmen seeking re-election who were successful was 92.7 per cent.[107] Furthermore, this feature of incumbency has been accompanied by a decline in the number of marginal seats, so that not only do a large proportion of Congressmen win re-election, but they do so by safe victory margins. These twin effects have led to a large amount of research into the relationship between the two. A wide variety of explanations have been presented to account for the electoral value of incumbency, ranging from advantageous redistricting[108] to careful constituency service,[109] and from the superior financial and media resources of the incumbents over their challengers[110] to the ability of incumbents to adopt visible political positions cutting across party lines and acting as voting cues to non-partisans and independents.[111] While the disputes as to why so many Congressmen retain their incumbency and why so many seats have become safe will no doubt remain a cause of controversy, what remains certain is that, so far as its membership is concerned, Congress does have every appearance of being a remarkably stable elective body.

The dimension of permanence is further strengthened by the organizational stability within Congress. This aspect of Congressional continuity has been due more than anything else to the committee system and, in particular, to its governing hierarchical principle of seniority. As part of the increasing professionalization of the Congress after the Civil War, the seniority factor in committee assignments and chairmanships graduated from being *a* criterion to *the* criterion of selection. Beginning first in the Senate during the 1880s and then in the House of Representatives over the 1911–25 period, seniority gradually became established as a working principle of committee hierarchy and as a defence against any arbitrariness from capricious party leaders or party caucuses.[112] The fluidity within the Congresses of the nineteenth century, when the turnover of committee memberships was high and when chairmanships had on occasions even been rotated, therefore, was severely reduced by the advent of the seniority rule. Individual Congressmen could dig themselves into committees by virtue of the length of their continuous service on those committees. Every two years they would graduate in power, irrespective of their voting record, their party loyalty, or their support for or opposition to the administration of the day. Furthermore, the seniority rule produced a dynamic all its own in so far as seniority became both a means and an end at one and the same time. It was a means to more seniority, which provided the essence of more power within the institution. This power raised the value of incumbency to the individual office holder still further and increased the potential of his electoral appeal over any challenger, who would by definition be devoid of seniority. In addition, increased seniority tended to generate increased respect for the rule amongst members of Congress and to heighten their appreciation of the whole infrastructure of committee privileges, decentralized decisions, insulated hierarchies, and reciprocal deference to one another's committee power stakes.

The seniority system may have prevented internecine strife in committees over promotion and it may have provided an incentive for long-term Congressional careers by committed legislators.[113] Nevertheless, it has also been referred to as an insidious principle which has crippled Congress as an institution by replacing fluidity with the predictability of immobilism. The effects of the lack of turnover in Congressional seats is said to be made even worse by the seniority rule, because it converts stability into a network of structural changelessness. The committee memberships change only marginally from Congress to Congress and then usually only at the lower end of the committee hierarchies. The senior sectors of the committees have normally been conspicuous by their persistent presence. They generally rise to their positions irrespective of their commitment to committee work, their representativeness, their party loyalty, their political obligations, their conflicts of interests, and their relationships with their colleagues on the committee. What is more, the committee leadership has, by virtue of the seniority principle, been relatively elderly and has tended to come from safe seats. This has served not only to 'strengthen the particularistic, centrifugal tendencies of Congress',[114] but also to increase Congress's reputation for being unresponsive and unrepresentative. In contrast to a century ago, when the average committee chairman was in his forties, the average age of committee chairmen by the early 1970s was sixty-seven. Thirty per cent of the committee chairmen in both houses from 1947 to 1967 were over seventy and nearly two-thirds were over sixty.[115] Because conservative southern Democrats from rural one-party states and districts accumulated such levels of seniority in the 1950s and 1960s, it became part of the folk wisdom of Congress that the institution was inextricably biased towards southern conservatism. As the south, which accounted for a quarter of the country's population, came to account for 59 per cent of the House chairmanships and for 60 per cent of the Senate chairmanships over the 1947–68 period,[116] so seniority along with Congress itself became equated not just with a disproportionate conservatism, but with an apparently implacable and intrinsic conservatism embedded in the very structure of the institution. This equation was widely and deeply felt, not least by freshman members, many of whom would no doubt have concurred with the radical black Congressman Ronald Dellums, who complained that 'there were too many old folks' in Congress and that what members got at the top was 'some dude who came to Congress thirty years ago from a swamp'.[117]

Far from being a mutable institution with a changing membership and a varying outlook, the Congress has commonly been presented as a fundamentally arthritic organization, incapable of real modification and locked into a constant posture and style by the insuperable forces of the members' deference to one another's institutional power bases. It is not so much that Congress has always been criticized in the modern era. What is significant is that it has always been criticized for the same things – namely the same type of structures and processes, always producing the same kind of results. For example, it is said that:

> Congress can and does thwart with impunity the wishes of the American electors.... By the working of the committee system and of the seniority rule in the committee system, effective power ... is in the hands of a group of elder statesmen who may be very unrepresentative of the general trend of public opinion.... It is intrinsically improbable that in an age so full of rapid and dangerous change as ours the United States can go on with the ideas and practices of a horse-and-buggy era. Yet a great part of the business of both houses is conducted, mechanically and spiritually, in the fashion of the horse-and-buggy era.[118]

This passage is typical of the customary indictment of Congress as an institution which conveys every appearance of being structurally impervious to substantial change. It is this traditional impression of Congress 'as a declining and hopelessly fragmented body' with an 'inefficient or unresponsive' structure and with rules that 'screen out the competent and stifle innovation'[119] which scholars have battled to dislodge from the public's imagination. Careful research has revealed that Congressional seniority does not consistently favour one region or ideology to the detriment of another;[120] that Congress's role in policy-making has been much more positive and active than popular opinion suggests;[121] that Congress has shown considerable sophistication and versatility in evaluating policies and in supervising the bureaucracy;[122] that the institution has been responsive to public opinion and social needs despite the lack of membership turnover;[123] that many of Congress's celebrated vehicles of minority obstruction (e.g. the Rules Committee, the filibuster) have not been as obstructive as first thought and whose use has often been condoned by majorities;[124] that Congress's rules and procedures do not in themselves produce the dilatoriness, prevarication, and even deadlock that tend to characterize the institution;[125] and that legislative impasses cannot be attributed primarily to Congress, for the institution 'reflects both the built-in difficulties of achieving decisive action from a constitutional system designed to prevent excessive governmental activity, and the close and indecisive ideological division of the country'.[126] Even the Senate, which was renowned in the 1950s and early 1960s as 'an institution insulated against social changes and political demands by a cocoon of self-perpetuating conservatism',[127] could be shown by the 1970s as having been susceptible to structural and ideological change.

And yet despite these many revisions to the old model of Congressional constancy, the imagery remains and the reputations continue.[128] In comparison with the Presidency, the Congress still appears to be a less changeable institution. This is merely because it is more of an institution than the Presidency, which, while being supposedly institutionalized, retains the appearance of being derived from the unity of the elected incumbent. The essence of the Presidency as an office is drawn from its highest and most concentrated level. And it is this level which is virtually reconstituted on every occasion when there is a change in the occupant of the Oval Office. Congress, on the other hand, is a collective body explicitly representing a highly diversified and pluralistic society. This has made it necessarily more structured in organization, more procedural in its operation, and altogether less susceptible to bold initiatives, unequivocal direction, or to radical innovations. Congress responds to the demands made upon it in the only way it knows how – i.e. on its own organizational terms. To this extent, Congress's reputation for being 'a legislature in which inertia seems a way of life'[129] is an accurate one, for it is necessarily bound by the inertial state of both its basic components and its general dynamics. It cannot help but be conservative in the institutional sense of retaining its traditions and rules, and in the relative sense of normally following in the political wake of the Presidency and acting as a lag upon both liberal and conservative administrations. It has been shown that Congress can change and has changed, but its changes and its capacity for change always appear minimal when set beside the Presidency, which is an office whose incumbents have forced public attention upon it by proclaiming the Presidency's own virtues of dynamism, speed, vitality, and flexibility. In the modern era, Presidents have succeeded in establishing precisely these attributes as the main criteria of political evaluation in the mind of the American public. As a result, Congress necessarily emerges as a body which, even when it is not acting as a laboriously immutable and machine-like entity, gives every appearance of being so in comparison with the Presidency's panoply of immediate and adaptive capabilities. It is precisely the President's reputation for being the 'greased pig' of American politics which keeps alive and fosters Congress's traditional reputation for being formal, predictable, pedestrian, and unspontaneously mechanistic in nature.[130]

Vitalism

It will be recalled that the Presidency's essential vitality was also reflected in the way it was studied. It was felt that the office was so lifelike that, like life itself, it could not be reduced to solid fact. Its ultimate nature was not discernible, for it was inherently a 'somewhat mysterious institution'.[131] In accounting for the extraordinary dearth of analyses of the Presidency, despite its obvious pre-eminence as the focal point of the political system, Emmet John Hughes proffers the following reason:

> The search of the 'scientist' of politics tends to be a quest for indisputable data, measurable forces, and provable judgements. This very demand for precision essentially explains his 'shyness' of the Presidency: the office refuses to qualify as an object of such fine scrutiny.... It defies neat analysis.... Each bar to its full understanding somehow gives a hint of its nature.[132]

Erwin Hargrove avoids allusions to mysticism, but draws attention to the general position of political scientists, who believe quantitative research techniques to be inappropriate to Presidential analysis and who remain sceptical as to whether 'any kind of generalisation described as theory about political regularities can be developed from the study of an institution that varies so much according to individual incumbents'.[133] Some of the problems in research on the Presidency are clearly related to the lack of systematic, continuous, and reliable information. Other problems are more fundamental and involve difficulties over conceptualization and operationalization. Addressing himself to executives in general, Anthony King discloses some of these problems in the following terms:

> It is hard to know what one's units of analysis should be. In the case of legislatures, the roll call vote is readily available as a behavioural datum.... But what is the comparable datum in the case of executives? The decision? The interaction? The initiative? .... Executives have been neglected because data are harder to come by, to be sure, but also because it has been less clear what the intellectual challenges are.[134]

These problems in coping with the lack of information and in comprehending what there is about the Presidency that needs to be explained have tended to leave the field free for the less rigorous and normative studies of the institution. In doing so, the Presidency almost by default has been left to wallow in its own unchallenged inscrutability.

What has been true of the Presidency, however, has most certainly not been true of the Congress. Those inhibitions, doubts, and anxieties that have plagued students of the Presidency have not been present to anywhere near the same extent in the buoyant and assertive ranks of Congressional scholars. In contrast to the shortage of works on the Presidency, the amount of research undertaken on the Congress has been prodigious, and it has led to an abundance of literature on the structure, operation, and behaviour of the institution. It is ironic that at the very time when Congress is reputed to have suffered a decline in its power and its importance as an institution, it has attracted so much greater attention from political scientists than its more illustrious partner.

A number of reasons can be advanced to account for this disparity. Among them are three which have particular relevance to this study. First, if analysis can be described as a general unpacking of the contents of a subject, then Congress undoubtedly possesses a great deal to be unloaded and examined. An institution which attends to over 10,000 Bills and resolutions in approximately 300 committees during the course of each year will also generate a high degree of interest from analysts, who will be attracted to the prospect of reducing the apparent muddle to some degree of order. A second reason for the abundance of Congressional research is that while the initial picture of Congress may be one of confusion and complexity, the institution is at least usefully packaged in identifiable units (e.g. parties, committees, informal associations, regional groups, voting blocs) operating in accordance with an identifiable format of rules and norms (e.g. seniority, specialization, reciprocity, legislative work, institutional loyalty, deference to committee decisions, party identification). Apart from giving some basic order to the institution, these units and processes provide a wealth of data on the underlying dynamics of the institution. Information on committee memberships or on roll-call voting, for example, yields data on certain structural and behavioural characteristics of Congress and Congressmen. This type of data provides anchorages for analysis through which Congress can be reduced to discernible components, which in turn can be examined for their relationships with one another and for their possible linkages to a whole host of additional variables derived from both inside and outside Congress.

A third reason for the extraordinary interest shown by political scientists in Congress comes from the subject's advanced potential for explanation. The ambiguity of the intellectual challenge, which Anthony King referred to in respect of the Presidency, is greatly reduced where Congress is concerned. Not only is the challenge a much clearer one, but there is far greater certainty that it can be met. In contrast to Presidential scholars, students of the Congress see as their challenge the need to explain how the institution works. While the Presidency serves to confuse and to confound those who would seek to attach general laws to such a mutable body, the institution of Congress offers the prospect of eliciting consistent patterns and timeless regularities from its diverse processes. Congress is regarded as a body altogether more amenable to a general understanding of its internal relationships and dynamics. Indeed, the premise which inspires so much of the prodigious research into Congress is the belief that the institution possesses a basically fixed nature, which makes an explanation of its working processes not merely the most appropriate objective, but one which is believed to be attainable. Congressional analysts proceed on the basis of this implicit trust in the existence of an unrevealed yet empirically accessible system beneath Congress's surface disorder. This promise of Congressional explanation was recognized by Woodrow Wilson a century ago. 'Its complicated forms and diversified structure confuse the vision and conceal the system which underlies its composition. It is too complex to be understood without an effort, and without a careful and systematic process of analysis.'[135] That effort and analysis have been proceeding at an ever greater pace in search of the keys to the central lock to Congress's nature. The search for the keys to an equivalent lock of Presidential explanation has barely begun and seems bound to falter, given the lack of conviction in the existence of such a lock.

Writing and research into Congress, therefore, have been characterized by a much greater confidence in their techniques of enquiry and in their capacity for producing more significant results than comparable commentaries on the Presidency. While books and articles on the chief executive tend to be eclectic, impressionistic, biographical, specific, and highly normative in tone, works on Congress tend to be notable for their empirical rigour, their behavioural approach, and their confidence in the inevitability of an eventual understanding of the institution. After experiencing the often self-imposed limitations of Presidential scholars, many of whom almost revel in the inscrutability of their subject, it comes as a noticeable change to hear Samuel C. Patterson assert boldly at the beginning of a review of Congress that 'there are questions for which very extensive answers are possible'.[136] This trust in the accessibility of knowledge which will decipher the code to Congress's highly complex secrets is notably deficient in studies of the Presidency. Even a scholar like Richard Pious, who deplores the mystique and 'anecdotalism'[137] in Presidential analysis and is in favour of a more rigorously empirical approach, feels forced to resign himself to the fact that 'no one model of the Presidency, no one notion of its "evolution" as an office, can explain how incumbents function or how the office works'. The most that can be hoped for are 'generalizations about the *probabilities* of power'.[138] Students of Congressional behaviour seem altogether less oppressed by their subject matter and less fatalistic over the reliability of the knowledge acquired. In his address to the American Political Science Association's Study of Congress Project, for example, Ralph K. Huitt reported that legislative research had sliced into the problem of Congress 'in enough ways to give us a notion of what is there'. Although Huitt went on to acknowledge that Congressional research still lacked a clear idea as to 'how Congress works', he was in no doubt that it was within the capability of a project like APSA's Study of Congress to provide a satisfactory account of 'how its principal parts do their jobs and how they are related to each other'.[139] This pointed disparity in the premises, methods, and objectives between Congressional research and Presidential analysis has in turn reinforced the widespread impression that the Presidency's real substance remains inherently incalculable, while Congress is ultimately reducible to ascertainable parts and processes.[140] Just as the unique vitalism of the Presidency with its 'singular mystique and almost magical qualities'[141] is retained, so Congress's property of explicability confirms its reputation as an entity 'that is incapable of magic'.[142]

Adaptation and evolution

Consistent with its reputation for being disaggregated and inorganic in nature, unvarying in personnel and structure, and ultimately comprehensible as a functioning institution, Congress is also seen as something that is incapable of adaptation and evolution. This is not to say that Congress cannot and has not changed. It is rather that its changes follow a unidirectional pattern which is governed less by outside forces and conditions than by the blind forces of its own internal dynamics. Instead of reacting to changed circumstances in the terms in which they present themselves, Congress is usually viewed as an institution which can accept only those changes which can be accommodated to its established structures, processes, and functions. It is accused of not adapting to the reality of the outside world, but of trying to make the world conform to the enclosed reality of its insulated state. While it is true that living things are motivated by the dual need to keep both their internal condition and their external environment stable, it is just as true that when the environment becomes unstable it is necessary for life to adapt for it to remain viable. The concern shown for Congress is born out of the belief that the political environment is in a constant state of change and that Congress has not revealed a capacity for genuine adaptation to that change. Congress's 'crisis', therefore, is widely defined as being an 'adaptation crisis'.[143]

Against a background of a requirement for change, Congress maintains its reputation for mechanistic non-adaptability by what is seen as its two primary reactions to the challenges and demands of contemporary American society. First, Congress is accused of attempting to maintain its central function of law-making and policy formulation in the face of conditions which make it a wholly unsuitable body to perform such tasks. In this light, Congress is regarded as an institution drifting remorselessly into decline to join the many other legislatures which have long since been merely vestiges of a lost past. The other reaction of which Congress is accused, and which is also viewed as not constituting a genuine adaptation, is the shift of emphasis towards the supervision and oversight of the executive branch. This function may be better tailored to Congress's decentralized and disaggregated organization, but it does not in itself represent anything qualitatively new to the institution. It is not a divergence from Congress's previous state or from its previous nature. The change represents a redistribution of the weighting given to Congress's pre-existing functions and, in this respect, it can be judged to be a technical adjustment rather than a change in nature; a rearrangement rather than an innovation; a case of modified continuity rather than a form of creative difference.

It is when Congress is set beside the professed vitality of the Presidency, however, that the legislature seems even more locked into a lifeless system of fixed quantities and static constraints. The main reason for this unfavourable comparison has been not merely Congress's delegation of decisional discretion to the Presidency, but its transfer of policy-making responsibilities and even formal law-making authority to the executive branch. In the field of domestic policy the Presidency, beginning in the 1930s and progressing at a steady pace since then, has successfully displaced Congress as the first provider of policies. Given the scale and urgency of the problems besetting America, the Presidency has developed into a factory of social investigation and 'a natural locus of policy leadership'.[144] Indeed, a modern President is now expected to have a programme – a set of innovatory and interrelated policies that will provide his administration with an overall rationale and identity, a general sense of purpose, and a standing agenda of prospective new laws. Strength and leadership in the Presidency, along with viability in the system at large, have become synonymous with the provision of Presidentially formulated and sponsored policies which are then presented to Congress. The process is characterized by the contemporary cliche that, contrary to constitutional norms, it is now the President who proposes and the Congress which disposes. It is the chief executive who draws up the legislation and the legislature that considers it in the terms in which it has been pre-set. As a consequence of this development, Congress, in the view of even its own members, has been reduced to 'little more than a glorified echo chamber for the executive branch of government – usually content to approve or disapprove, rarely willing to initiate';[145] to an institution which has given away 'a lot of its authority in domestic and fiscal matters';[146] and to a body which has permitted the constitution's policy-making procedure to deteriorate to a point where 'now, too often, the Executive both proposes and disposes, while the Congress reposes'.[147] In a spirit of realism, Congress may have deferred to the Presidency's organizational resources, to its specialist competence, to its functional effectiveness, and to its political direction, but in doing so it has also acknowledged that in modern conditions the legislature has been out-evolved by the Presidency. It has been out-adapted to the extent of being forced to relinquish its basic function of law-making and, thereby, experiencing a collapse in its formal rationale in the separation of powers framework.

The manner and the substance of Congress's altered position also cast doubt upon whether the institution's response to new conditions amounts in any way whatsoever to a form of adaptation and evolution. In respect to the causes of the change, the Congress's shift away from conventional law-making can be seen as being less a consciously initiated form of reactive innovation and more an unavoidable concomitant of the creative will and indigenous energy of the Presidency. The self-generating and inner-directed exertions of the executive's central and purposive nature has tended to give the Congress the appearance of being a passive and inert receptor to changes determined elsewhere and willed from without. As far as the substance of the changes in Congress's functional contribution as a legislature are concerned, this too can be regarded as substantiating its non-adaptability in the organic sense. This is because, in its modern role of a respondent to executive-initiated stimuli,

Congressional power has become more equated with obstruction and negativism than ever before. Congress may still be the world's most powerful legislature whose members 'have a level of independence and political influence beyond that of members of all other legislative bodies'.[148] Yet the hallmark of Congress's power is widely interpreted to be that of retarding progress and blocking change. This has invariably placed Congress in the dilemma of either responding favourably to Presidential requests and emasculating itself still further as a law-making body, or asserting itself by defying the Presidency and risking the charge of being a regressive anomaly in modern government.

> Thus, at the same time that it is an obstructive ogre to its enemies, Congress is also the declining despair of its friends.... Congress can defend its autonomy only by refusing to legislate, and it can legislate only by surrendering its autonomy.[149]

In his seminal article on Congressional responses to the twentieth century, Samuel P. Huntington argues that Congress's particular structure, processes, and inner motivations are best suited to the function of executive oversight and that, in the absence of fundamental reform, Congress ought finally to acknowledge the demise of its law-making role and to concentrate upon developing what is a more traditional function of legislative supervision of enacted programmes. Huntington's article is significant, for it not only records the reasons for Congress's decline (many of which are ultimately attributable to the executive), and describes the form of the decline (assessed mostly by comparison to the modern executive). It also shows that what might pass for Congressional adaptation is in essence really just a further accommodation on the part of Congress to the Presidency's own successful adaptation to modern conditions.[150]

This view of Congress as an institution embedded in its own passivity and immobilism is strengthened even further by the nature of the oversight function itself. In terms of general legislative development, this function represents a rudimentary and even primitive form of legislative activity. To the extent that it becomes performed to the exclusion of the law-making function, then it can be interpreted as not so much an institutional advance as a regression back to a rudimentary capability possessed by pre-modern representative assemblies. Congress's 'new' role in oversight, therefore, does not represent the conscious substitution of one function for another. It is more a consequence of an executive-inspired elimination of Congress's law-making role – leaving the legislature with the more basic and residual role of executive supervision. Thus, while the Presidency continues to give every impression of being active, adaptive, and forward-moving, the Congress, by its relative inaction and apparent immobility compared to the Presidency, is left giving the impression of going backwards – of suffering retrogression rather than grasping innovation.

The separation of paradigms

This comparison between the Presidency and the Congress has attempted to demonstrate the way that the two institutions have tended to attract different sets of descriptive terms and analytical concepts to themselves. The substance of what is perceived in the Presidency and what requires and constitutes an explanation of the office is widely regarded as being distinct from the way that Congress is viewed and analysed as an institution. Whereas the Presidency is generally seen as a living thing, it is widely believed that Congress possesses a mechanistic nature. However, it should be acknowledged that, just as the separation of powers principle fails to divorce the executive from the legislature, so the differentiation between organisms and machines is not an absolute one. Darwinism and Newtonianism are not mutually exclusive paradigms. The material parts of living processes are not immune to physical laws or to mechanical properties just because such matter is a constituent of an organism. As has already been mentioned, it is a subject of continuous debate as to whether biology can in the long term remain a separate and autonomous science, or whether it will collapse into physics to the point at which life can finally be shown to be reducible to purely physico-chemical properties. Given the potential reality of this advanced theoretical postulate, then artificial intelligence and genetic engineering may be seen as the early landmarks on the road to making biology and physics indistinguishable from one another. For the present, however, the distinctive idiosyncrasy of life and of its reactive condition within a changing environment has permitted biological terms of reference to retain their level of special meaning. So much so, in fact, that the intermixture of the life sciences with mechanics has been due as much to the application of biological concepts to machines (e.g. integrated circuits, central communications control, mechanical systems, environmental feedback) as it has to the reverse process of rendering life a construct of basic physical quantities. This lack of exclusivity in the meanings assigned to the nature of life and mechanics means that the Presidency's association with biology and the Congress's linkage with mechanics do not in themselves substantiate the existence of an absolute distinction between the institutions.

Another proviso and another source of confusion stem from the sheer range and power of Darwinism and Newtonianism as systems of explanation. Each one constitutes a totalistic scheme of perceiving the world and of organizing its specific parts into a generalized and intelligible order. Instead of regarding the subject matter of biology and physics as two coexisting frames of reference, it is perfectly possible to regard either one of them as the dominant point of perspective and as the overriding model of existence and meaning in the world. From this position of what the world consists of and how best it can be comprehended, it is then possible to reduce its forms, processes, and functions to those categories and criteria that are in accord with the system's conception of reality. Such systems of explanation not only determine the way in which the world is understood, but also perpetuate their scope and authority by necessarily reducing both the revealed and as yet unrevealed aspects of nature to their own foreclosed and monist frame of reference. The explanatory force of both Darwinism and Newtonianism has been sufficient to make the world conform to each of their universally applicable models of reality. What this means in relation to the Presidency and Congress is that if Congress can be seen as being mechanistic in nature, then there is nothing in this assumption that refutes or excludes the Presidency from being similarly regarded as mechanistic in form. It may even be thought to be the more plausible contention, in that if the Congress is understood in terms of a mechanical frame of reference, then it would be more consistent to accept the Presidency in the light of the same adopted paradigm. Such a perspective is by no means unknown in American politics. Indeed, the constitutional feature of checks and balances, in which institutions are expected and perceived to act as particulate units of matter interacting with one another in a timeless repetition of calculable impacts, represents one of the most central traditions of American political thought.

The same point is also true in respect to Darwinism. Again, if the Presidency can be absorbed into biological terms of reference, then this fact alone would imply that such terms would be applicable to Congress as well. This has occurred. Sometimes biological concepts are loosely attached to Congress more as a form of descriptive licence, or as a result of the use of everyday yet biologically derived terms of definition. Thus it is possible to be informed of 'the evolution of Congress'[151] – to be told that 'Congress is a living organism just as much as the Presidency';[152] that it is 'a functioning organism'[153] which has 'adapted itself well to a changing environment, its role having evolved to meet strenuous demands';[154] and that 'Congress changes, as all living things must change'.[155] Many of these sorts of remarks are often just verbal flourishes containing unexamined premises and unsupported assertions. They may show the extent of biology's penetration into the English language, but they are not intended as substantive statements of analysis. Other uses of biological terms in this context however, are conscious, deliberate, and systematic attempts to employ the concepts of the life sciences to the study of Congressional behaviour. Whether it is the nature of the legislative institution which suggests the use of biologically derived forms of analysis, or the prominence of biological instruments of enquiry within the analytical repertoire of modern political science, the fact remains that much of the empirical-behavioural research into Congress has depended upon biologically oriented forms of social investigation. The advanced studies into Congress are replete with such concepts as the political system, the governmental system, the legislative system, sub-systems, environments, structures, functions, processes, adaptation, exchange, mutual dependence, specialization, stability, integration, social organization, collective behaviour, systemic purposes, communication networks, inputs, outputs, external stress, internal control, feedback, boundaries, and interrelationships.[156] Research into Congress has become closely associated with systems theories, organization theories, and structu-

The separation of paradigms

ral-functional theories; and through them with the language, terms, and metaphors of biology. Using these tools of analysis, Congress can be presented in a dynamic, interactive, and organic guise for the purpose of explaining the legislature's organization and action, both in respect to itself and to the political system at large. As a result of these techniques of Congressional research, the institution can be more readily perceived as a coherent, responsive, and lifelike entity set in a wider political environment and integrated into an overall political system.

From these two provisos examined above, it is clear that there is nothing implicit in Congress's nature that makes it suitable only for those terms of reference which are unequivocally inorganic in content. The same can be said for the Presidency in respect to its affinity with the biological frame of reference. Neither the institutions nor the concepts popularly attached to them are mutually exclusive. Just as the emphasis given to mechanics in characterizations of Congress does not mean that the legislature cannot be empirically and conceptually treated as an organism, so the stress laid upon biological terms where the Presidency is concerned does not mean that the executive cannot be perceived as possessing basic mechanical properties. The point which does require to be underlined is that according to popular reputation and widespread impression the Presidency and the Congress are intrinsically distinct from one another. Their structures, their development, their modes of behaviour, their purposes, their political nature are seen as inherently different. What is significant is that these differences are conventionally denoted by, and rationalized according to, the differences between machines and living things. The references to mechanics and organisms may be made consciously or unconsciously, directly or indirectly, yet the pattern of designation is the same. The differences between the institutions are regarded as significant and this significance is expressed more often than not by the distinction between biology and physics. The general perspective, supported by the concepts and language employed in texts on American government and in the media's treatment of national politics, is that while the Presidency represents life, Congress amounts to a machine.

Whereas the Presidency attracts the imagery of vitality, the common impulse with Congress is to allude to it as if it were a machine. Sometimes the mechanistic metaphor is used to describe Congress's strengths as an institution (e.g. 'scholars have professed to see in the structure of Congress a marvelously coordinated machine';[157] 'the delaying mechanisms in the machinery of Congress'[158] being seen as an integral part of American constitutionalism). More often, it is employed to account for Congress's defects and to describe the reforms required in order to improve its legislative inefficiency. For example, Joseph Clark regards 'the rusty machinery ... of Congress' as a 'principal obstacle to the effective solution of modern problems'[159] and accordingly stresses the need to 'revamp its creaking machinery'.[160] Theodore White also refers to the 'antique machinery of Congress',[161] while Stephen Bailey warns that 'both houses need to improve their internal machinery'.[162] David Stockman declares that there is 'a breakdown in the Congressional machinery'.[163] Randall Ripley claims that at least 'the machinery of Congress is not inherently deficient'.[164] To Roger Davidson and Walter Oleszek, 'it is not decentralization itself that impairs Congressional policy making, but rather decentralization that is rigid, obsolete, and lacking in co-ordinating mechanisms'.[165] The same complaint is reiterated by Richard Fenno, who refers to 'the total absence of institutional machinery whereby the House (or, indeed, Congress) can make overall spending decisions';[166] by Lawrence Dodd, who deplores the fact that 'nowhere within a system of committee government is there a mechanism to ensure that decisions of authorization, appropriations, and revenue committees have some reasonable relationship to one another';[167] and by Ralph Huitt, who agrees that 'nowhere is there a handle with which to take hold of the whole of Congress'.[168] To James Sundquist, Congress is accordingly confronted by 'the mechanical problem of grafting a hierarchical authority on to the legislative structure'[169] to arrive at a 'central mechanism for developing solidarity and capacity to act within the Congressional majority'.[170] Leroy Rieselbach asks whether there are 'structural mechanisms that can permit Congress ... to exert policy influence'.[171] Whether the allusions are to the deficiencies of its machinery, or to the need for new forms of machinery, what remains significant is the underlying premise that Congress is mechanical in form and substance. It is the very fact that Congress is perceived to be, and to operate as, a machine that not only constitutes its chief distinguishing characteristic but accounts for its notoriety as an institution.

It is precisely because Congress is seen as a machine that it has come to be regarded as a problem not just to itself, but also to the political system as a whole. Congress is often portrayed as an institution with a dynamic all of its own, independent of external forces and even of the will of its own membership. It has been described as grinding remorselessly on at its own pace, acting in accordance with its rigidified processes, and remaining inherently incapable of departing from the set patterns of interaction between its component parts. One is informed that Congress is a 'house out of order'[172] with 'built-in weaknesses';[173] that it is a legislature that 'cannot legislate'[174] even when it wishes to; that 'Congress is, by disposition and structure, incapable of providing'[175] national leadership; that it is a 'Prometheus self-bound',[176] as it has 'shackled itself with ... archaic rules'.[177] 'Almost every year brings fresh evidence that Congress is unable to develop an internal leadership that can give direction and a modicum of discipline to our semi-anarchic legislature.'[178] Roger Davidson and Walter Oleszek's study of the House of Representatives' disappointing attempts at large-scale self-reform is significantly entitled *Congress against Itself*[179] – reflecting the belief that 'Congress ... can tinker with the machinery, but it cannot fundamentally reform or reorganize itself from within'.[180] These, along with many other similar references, reveal a basic assumption of the existence of an underlying mechanism to the legislature which accounts for 'the inability of Congress to control its own parts'[181] and for its 'weakness ... in trying to set its own course'.[182] Congress may possess a high level of institutional autonomy, and it may act of its own volition, but what this represents in real terms is usually seen as a predictably uniform pattern of relationships with a high level of immunity to both inside and outside disturbances. Just as Congress makes a major contribution to the regulatory framework of checks and balances within American government in general, so the Congress itself is regarded as possessing its own form of self-regulation by which the hidden hand of its structures, processes, and behaviour generates a mechanism of indigenous controls. Indeed, it can be said that Congress exemplifies the ethos and dynamics of the larger checks and balances framework in the American system. Thus, while 'the frequent gaps between public opinion polls and Congressional actions show the legislature is an independent force in the policy process',[183] the properties of this independence are more often than not interpreted as being mechanistic in nature rather than conscious and purposeful exertions of collective legislative will.

The differences between the Presidency and Congress, therefore, are by no means confined to those of function, or structure, or constituency. The contrast is starker and more vivid than that afforded by such formal attributes. The two institutions are differentiated from one another by the separate paradigms with which they have become associated. The conventional perspectives of the Presidency and the Congress have led to the two branches of government embodying two quite different conceptions of the nature and purpose of the American political system. The textbook view of the Presidency centres upon the organic qualities of life, adaptation, variation, and evolution. The themes, characteristics, and concepts related to the office revolve around the central feature of vitality (Figure 6).

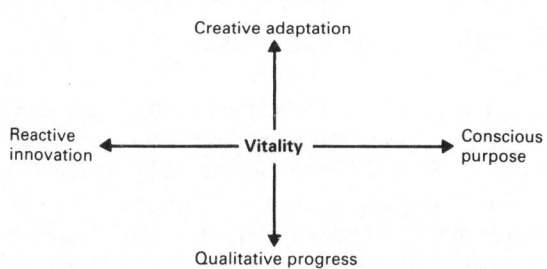

```
                    Creative adaptation
                            ↑
                            |
   Reactive    ←——————   Vitality   ——————→   Conscious
   innovation                                   purpose
                            |
                            ↓
                   Qualitative progress
```

The equivalent textbook model of the Congress is based upon the focal characteristics of mechanics (Figure 7). Mechanics seem to account so well for the way Congress structures and conducts itself. Its popular reputation is that of an agglomeration of discrete and independently motivated units acting either directly or unintentionally against each other in a state of decentralized disarray. Where Congress is concerned, mechanics often seem to be the only way of rationalizing such an apparently disorganized structure of blind forces and moving parts operating at a pace and in a direction all their own.

Laws, men and machines

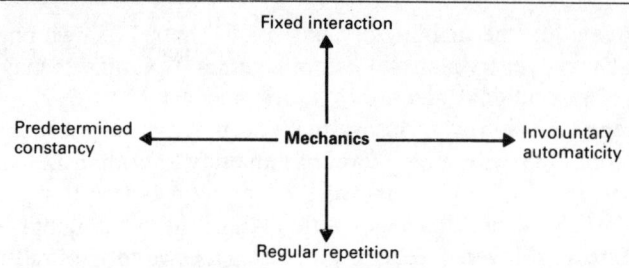

```
                    Fixed interaction
                           ↑
    Predetermined  ←—— Mechanics ——→  Involuntary
    constancy                          automaticity
                           ↓
                    Regular repetition
```

The association of the Congress with mechanics and the relationship of the Presidency to biology have been due in large part to the intrinsic characteristics and properties of the two institutions. Nevertheless, it is also true that an important, if not equally significant, source of the bio-mechanical dichotomy between the Presidency and Congress has been their formal proximity to one another in the policy-making process – a proximity that has generated a plethora of relativistic observations and assessments which have had the effect of dramatizing the differences between the two departments to one of deep and conspicuous contrast. Against a background of assumed constitutional comparability, institutional co-equality, and cultural comity, the disputes between the two branches over policy, power, procedures, and practices have led to an intensification of differences and to a widespread belief in the divergence of their respective natures. A form of inverted dialectical arrangement seems to characterize the relationship between the Presidency and Congress in so far as the more they are viewed in conjunction with one another the more they reveal themselves to be the opposite of one another. What ties them inextricably together as co-participants in the separation of powers system also serves to highlight their differentiation from one another and to magnify still further the imagery of mechanics and life already associated with the two institutions.

For example, Congress's dispersal of authority throws into sharp relief the conspicuous singularity of the Presidency. Likewise, the individual nature of the Presidential office makes Congress appear in comparison to be an irredeemably disunited collection of 535 members, who are incapable of organizing themselves into a coherent force. This sort of comparison may well be unfair and inaccurate. What may seem unresponsive obstructiveness may actually represent a high level of responsiveness. Aage Clausen reminds us that 'a deadlocked Congress, unable to form a majority in support of legislation to meet a well recognised problem, is a Congress that ... may be truly reflective of a national constituency that is badly splintered'.[184] On the other hand, it has to be acknowledged that one of Congress's best documented weaknesses has been its failure to co-ordinate its many parts into a central hierarchical authority, capable of invoking discipline from its specialized levels of decision-making and of forming lasting majorities in support of centrally determined policies. Despite recent reforms that have sought to break down some of the hardened centres of committee power and to build up the authority of the party caucus and party leadership positions, the possibility of any significant long-term change seems to be as remote as ever.[185] In some respects, the reforms may even have led to a further deterioration in central co-ordination and to an even greater dispersion of authority than before. The erosion of the committee chairmen's power, the proliferation of sub-committees, the increased participation amongst the general membership, and the decline in deference towards committee judgements by non-committee members have prompted commentators to conclude that 'the Congressional *modus operandi* is one of fragmentation'[186] and that 'a high degree of decentralization is probably the "natural" state of Congress'.[187] It may well be that Congress does suffer from an excess of legislative individualism. 'Perhaps the inevitable trend in Congress is toward ever greater delegation to its subgroups.'[188] The Congress may well be deficient in corporate consciousness, given the tendency of so many of its members to 'run *for* Congress by running *against* Congress... and by attacking the collective reputation of the Congress'.[189] Nevertheless, these traits do not in themselves secure the reputation of blind and particulate mechanics to Congress. On the contrary, many questions are begged on both sides. The Presidency may well be far more of an institutionalized office than the one which is normally portrayed. It may in reality be a hostage to bureaucratic inertia, structural continuities, agencies locked in jurisdictional conflict, established policies, and fragmented political constituencies. Behind the imagery of an organization fired by the concerted will of an individual, the Presidency can be seen as merely a figurehead, detached from 'the organizationally incoherent way in which many ... domestic programs are scattered throughout a crazy quilt of bureaus and divisions in the more than one hundred executive departments and agencies'.[190] Congress, on the other hand, might with closer inspection be seen to be a highly developed and sophisticated device, in which 'organization and procedure are woven into a seamless fabric'[191] to secure consensus support for policies from a multiplicity of diverse interests. These subtleties of distinction, however, are buried in the vivid imagery of opposites generated by the conjunction of the Presidency and Congress. The questions that are separately begged immediately become closed once the two institutions are placed in their customary juxtaposition. The interaction of the two appears to facilitate the final conversion of the Presidency into unified life and the Congress into an anonymous machine. The act of direct comparison seems to lead to more unequivocally divergent, and even exaggerated, conclusions than would be the case if the two institutions had been assessed apart from one another. In comparison with Congress, the Presidency and Presidential politics are made to seem altogether more oriented towards action, new programmes, conceptions of the future, clarified objectives, and conscious direction than would otherwise be the case. And when set against the Presidency, the 'bare machinery of Congress'[192] looks to be an altogether more disaggregated structure inherently inclined towards decisional stasis; its 'rusty, ante-bellum machinery ... declining into obsolescence'.[193] In this context of accustomed comparison, it is interesting to ask whether Charles Hardin, for example, would have made the same assertions concerning the Presidency and Congress if they had not been treated as a duality of fused opposites:

> Where the President is elected as the nonpareil, the father, the leader, the magic helper, the incarnation of the infallible goodness and wisdom of the people, Congressmen and Senators tend to be chosen as a means of assuring their constituents' shares of the national largesse.... Where the Presidency comes to life in the unification of power, Congress disperses power among a hundred leaders each with his own base in seniority and in sectional jurisdiction.[194]

Hardin's dichotomous judgements are not exceptional.[195] Placed together, the apparent contrast between the Presidency and the Congress is normally too stark to resist, and far too clear-cut to motivate the introduction of intrusive qualifications and reservations. In this way, the dialectical relationship between the two bodies leads each one to become the caricatured opposite of the other. The more the President presents the office through his own persona, the more Congress appears to be an impersonal set of disunited and directionless structures; and the more Congress seems irretrievably fixed in its multiple centres of power, so the Presidency appears to be even more reducible to the incontrovertible coherence and unity of the individual in the Oval Office.

The same process of mutual definition is discernible in other aspects of the Presidential–Congressional duality. The Congress is reputed to be an old, insular, and obstructive organization, which, when it is not excessively slow in responding to urgent social demands, is oppressed by its inner contradictions to the extent of complete immobilism. The Presidency, in contrast, is seen as a youthful office that constantly regenerates itself into a positive force for initiating innovation, prompting action, and inspiring change. Once again, popular impressions raise many awkward questions. For example, there may well be some substance to Congress's reputation for fixity and insularity. Congress has been accused of being controlled by a self-perpetuating oligarchy which is not only demographically unrepresentative of the major social and economic forces of contemporary America, but also unrepresentative of the rank-and-file membership of Congress itself. The level of continuity in Congress has been sufficient for it to have become 'institutionalized', with a stable membership acting through stable procedures. Before the early 1970s it was possible for Leroy Rieselbach to conclude that Congress's 'basic structures had undergone only modest alterations in the past half century' and that procedures had reached a point where 'change had tended to be marginal'.[196] Ernest Griffith went even further and asserted that the structure of Congress had remained 'substantially unaltered from the early days of the Republic'.[197] Nevertheless, this impression of Congressional fixity represents only one perspective. It is quite possible for Congress to be seen in a different and more dynamic light. For example, according to Barbara Hinkley, the underlying reality of Congressional stability is one of incessant change, and that to remain stable Congress requires the constant renewal of an indigenous balance of forces.[198] Gary Orfield complains that while the 'perceptions of Congress remain largely fixed',[199] the institution can change and has changed. It is not as pathologically unresponsive and inattentive as its 'obsolete images'[200] would have us believe. On the contrary, 'the Congressional process may be a good deal more responsive to certain kinds of social change than the executive branch'.[201] And, as far as its basic framework is concerned, the political changes and institutional reforms of recent years have been such that 'everyone recognises that much has changed in Congress ... ; its members are very different, its roles and internal organization have been restructured'.[202]

What is true of the Congress is just as true of the Presidency. The office can be seen as a rapidly evolving and highly variable entity that is effectively reconstituted with every incumbent and which is instrumental in orchestrating decisive changes in policy direction in accordance with the shifting pattern of preferences within the national electorate. But the office can also be viewed from quite a diffferent perspective. It can be depicted more as merely a symbol of coherence and destiny behind which lie the actuality of incoherence and fatalism. From this viewpoint, the President is less the master in his own house and more the hapless victim of gargantuan bureaucracies whose scale, complexity, and power make them formidable centres of resistance to any centrally exerted methods of control. The President may well be leader of the executive branch, but the separate constituents of that department of government have technical, political, and legal resources at their disposal to make the bureaucracy 'one of the principal sources of frustration'[203] confronting any chief executive. Much of the executive assumes the appearance of Congress – i.e. permanently established enclaves of power closely associated with the interests and welfare of their clientele groups and highly adept at defending their independence against external pressures. Within this context 'Presidential government' becomes a chimera, as the chief executive appears in reality to be beset by the undisciplined pluralism of departments and agencies, by his inability to organize and reform his own branch of government, by binding long-term budgetary and policy commitments, by the bureaucracy's established operational routines and standard procedures, and by the political forces brought to bear by the bureaucracy's social and economic constituents.[204] The executive can easily become confused with the legislature, as they both appear to be subject to a prevailing conservatism in which established policies and priorities are preserved and defended on a permanent basis by an entrenched and collaborative framework of legislative–executive inertia.

Once again, however, the variability of perspectives and interpretations of both the Congress and the Presidency seem to collapse the moment the two are considered in unison. As soon as they are placed next to one another, as they invariably are, the obscurity and ambiguity of their respective natures appear to be immediately reduced to a greatly simplified dichotomy. When considered jointly, 'legislators seem to travel the low road of "localism" while the President is associated with lofty qualities such as rationality, accountability and a commitment to the public interest'.[205] Taken together, 'the contrast' is that 'of the hierarchial, expert nature of the executive and the decentralized, generalist Congress'.[206] It is always in relation to the Presidency that the Congress is 'accused of being slow, inefficient, and haphazard, shot through with conflicts of interest [and with] its procedures stigmatized as undemocratic, irrational and obstructionist'.[207] It is because of the comparison with the Presidency that the Congress is seen, for example, as being the 'slow institution'.[208] Without the model of both the Presidency's co-equal status and its overtly contrasting characteristics, there would be no way of assessing whether Congress were slow or not. With it, however, the Presidency's relative swiftness of response and speed of action have the effect of rendering Congress a laborious and ponderous constitutional partner.

In contrast to Congress, the Presidency appears to be a dynamically adaptive office whose own growth and development have been integrally connected with the United States' own evolution as an economic and military superpower and with the growth in the federal government's role as a modern service state. From an earlier assumption of a structural constriction that would ensure a conformity to the office's formally designated role, the Presidency has shown itself to be the institution which has broken free most dramatically from its constitutional moorings. The Presidential office has quite literally grown. It has not only absorbed functions which it was not initially intended to perform, but it has also accommodated new responsibilities and roles in response to the changing requirements of government and leadership. Far from being just a formal chief executive, a ceremonial head of state, and an official commander-in-chief, the conditions surrounding the rise of the modern Presidency have led to Presidents becoming economic managers, bureaucratic controllers, budgetary directors, party leaders, legislative promoters, international statesmen, staff supervisors, mass-media figures, public educators, issue publicists, vote mobilizers, national security guardians, and tribunes of the American people. The revision of the Presidency's power and position amounts to a fundamental revision of the entire framework of institutional arrangements and relationships within the constitutional system. It also represents a basic change in public attitudes to and expectations of constitutional government. In this respect, the change in the role and status of the modern Presidency has coincided with, and mirrored, the contemporary change in public philosophy. Of all the factors and conditions that have contributed towards the rise of the Presidency, this one probably represents the most significant. So much so, in fact, that the evolution of the office can be seen as a direct consequence of the public's acceptance of the state assuming a progressively more central role in American society.

The separation of paradigms

This radical change in attitudes towards Presidential power may have been derived from a positive impulse to regard the Presidency as the 'formulator and symbol of the national purpose';[209] or as a vehicle of 'organic liberalism' facilitating the establishment of a 'modern service state ... to provide individuals with positive freedom';[210] or as the inspirational voice of American obligations, principles, and destiny in a world increasingly affected by American military and economic power. The change may, on the other hand, have been more the result of a fatalistic acquiescence to the unavoidable need for an enriched executive to discipline the bureaucracy, to make strategic interventions in the economy, to act decisively in national emergencies, and to take those critical decisions which cannot be effectively undertaken at any other level or safely delegated to any other sphere of government. Either way, the Presidency has come to signify that progression in public philosophy which has condoned the accelerated development of the bureaucratic service state in modern America. The office has been the prime political beneficiary of a modernizing process which has led to a vast expansion in the scope of governmental intervention and regulation. Presidential power, and even Presidential pre-eminence, have become progressively more acceptable in the modern era as the office has become closely identified with those ideas, demands, movements, and conditions that have motivated the rise of government to such a central position in society. The modern Presidency is seen as the institutional concomitant of the contemporary concept of social progress. It has become the most conspicuous example of political adaptation and evolution in a culture which has come to value efficiency and utility in the service of the public welfare and national interest over and above the principles of legal formality, constitutional protocol, and traditional process. The Presidency is celebrated as the 'common reference point for social effort'[211] in a society where effort, energy, and action have become valued functions. In the cause of action, the substance of Presidential power and the roots of executive hegemony have even been acknowledged to transcend the constitution. Executive force is seen as a vital energizing force; something which is not strictly in the constitution, or of it, or even accountable to it, but nevertheless integral to its maintenance and survival. The Presidency is afforded the licence and discretion of 'implied powers' to do 'anything that the needs of the nation demand'[212] in those cases which do not admit to defined and regular courses of formal treatment. In an increasingly precarious and crisis-prone world, this vitality of the Presidency's extra-constitutional authority is regarded not merely as a useful and tolerable component of government but as an indispensable necessity in its own right.

The Presidency, therefore, has come to be recognized as the touchstone of modernity. The modern Presidency is in essence the Presidential office in modern times – its power and status being symptomatic of the central-executive character of advanced industrialized society. An evolved and evolving Presidency is accepted as being implicit in the nature of modern national government, in the issues it has to confront, in the conditions with which it has to contend, and in the demands for action and services made upon it. So integral is the Presidency to the effective functioning of government as an organization that without its active and co-ordinative contribution the whole framework of policy and administration would be threatened with disarray and disintegration. Samuel Huntington notes that 'when the President is unable to exercise his authority, when he is unable to command the co-operation of key decision makers elsewhere in society and government, no one else has been able to supply comparable purpose and initiative'.[213] He continues:

> In the 20th century, whenever the American political system has moved systematically with respect to public policy, the direction and the initiative have come from the White House.... To the extent that the United States has been governed on a national basis, it has been governed by the President.[214]

Government has not only become dependent upon the assertive unity of the chief executive, it has come to be very largely synonymous with the office. So much so, in fact, that 'the President *is* the government for millions of Americans'[215] and a 'weakening of the Presidency is about as likely as the withering away of the state'.[216]

The Presidency's evident modernity as an office expanded and aggrandized in response to contemporary conditions casts Congress into the role of an institution of the past. Relative to the changeability of Presidential administrations, the Congress appears to be encumbered by only a very limited periodic turnover in membership, by the seniority system, and by 'organizational forms and procedures designed in a slower moving age and for a much less complex society'.[217] In the light of the Presidency's modern urban-industrial constituency with its demands for action, innovation, and regulation, Congress can often seem set in a previous age, with many of its members having the reputation of being small-town boys from main-street provincial America,[218] who are content to let their social conservatism be serviced by the immobilism of the legislative process. More normally, however, Congressional conservatism is seen as a function of the legislature's capacity to resist Presidentially inspired change by recourse to its ability to continue pre-existing trends and to preserve established priorities – irrespective of the ideologies of the executives involved. In Congress the 'forces promoting change and positive action find their path studded with procedural and organizational obstacles'.[219] Just as the executive's difficulties with Congress have tended to equate the Presidency with such innovative forces, be they conservative or liberal, so the legislature's reluctance to accede to such forces is made to seem like the involuntary reaction of an institution immobilized by the contradictory pressures inherent in its internal motivations and processes. The more the Congress is seen to be confronted by Presidents seeking action and urging change, the more the legislature attracts the imagery of structural and policy conservatism in which Congressional power becomes tantamount to negativism, obstruction, and an 'incapacity to adapt'.[220] Likewise, the more that Congress is 'considered antiquated'[221] and seems afflicted by the stasis and timelag induced by the apparently remorseless continuity of its inner workings, the more the Presidency appears with the heroic mantle of creative leadership and life-infusing energy. The result of this dynamic form of joint interpretation of the Presidency and the Congress is for each to be seen once again as the stylized antithesis of the other, with differences between them being largely characterized by reference to the distinction between biology and mechanics.

The Presidency and the Congress, therefore, are not merely two institutions. They embody and exemplify at the highest level of the political system two quite different paradigms of constitutional government. The Presidency has come to represent the concepts and values of organic development, while the Congress has come to represent the concepts and values of mechanical regulation. Although the two paradigms are not compatible with one another, they usually manage to coexist in the perceptions and interpretations of American politics without their contradictions becoming noticeably evident. Under normal conditions, the full potential for discord between them is not realized. This is mainly because one (i.e. the Presidency and organic development) is assumed to possess greater contemporary relevance and authority than the other. Furthermore, its superiority is also seen as gaining progressively in strength and significance with the passage of time. Congress and Congressional mechanics are clearly seen as the inferior party, irrevocably set on a course of decline and decay. While the Presidency is often quoted as being a substitute for, and even an antidote to, Congress, the reverse argument is never heard. The legislative branch is heavily associated with the fixity of its structures and organization, which, in a world that is acknowledged to be in constant flux, has the effect of assigning Congress's ethos and culture to the past. The consistent reliability of its checks and balances may have satisfied the Newtonian dispositions of the nineteenth century, but such legislative mechanics have become increasingly inconsistent with the Darwinian spirit and temper of the twentieth century. The Darwinian world view, which has done so much to cast Congress into the past as a static non-adaptive relic of the old Newtonian world view, has also been instrumental in promoting the Presidency to 'the pinnacle of our government' and in transforming the office into 'the most important single influence in our politics'.[222] The same perceptions and principles that have attended Congress's apparent passage into constitutional archaeology have facilitated the Presidency's metamorphosis from a purely executive functionary into an expression of national consciousness, community purpose, and superpower responsibility.

The Presidency and Congress in crisis conditions

The Presidency has become the outstanding example of institutional evolution in the American system. For an extensive period, it was thought that the normal and permanent condition of the American government was of Congress as 'the centre and source of all motive and of all regulative power'.[223] In *Congressional Government*, for example, Woodrow Wilson deplored the performance of the legislative branch and despaired of the Presidency, which he took to be quite incapable of counteracting the aggressive disharmony and divisiveness of Congress, or of representing the emergent interests and sentiments of nationhood. To Wilson, Congress's dominance and the Presidency's subordination to a purely nominal role seemed such an unwavering feature of American politics that it called into question whether the constitution would be able to 'adapt itself to the new conditions of an advancing society'.[224] During the course of the twentieth century, however, it was the Presidential office which intermittently yet inexorably accumulated sufficient power to relieve the system from the self-negating effects of its own divisions – divisions that had once seemed to condemn America to a terminally static government. It was the Presidency more than any other institution which was seen to redeem the system from its own immobilism by providing it with the stimulus to action. It is a commentary of the extent to which American government was believed to be incapable of change and mobility that such a basic attribute as that of 'action' was raised to the level of being a priority objective of government. The Presidency rose to pre-eminence on the grounds that it could provide action itself and could provoke action elsewhere in other sectors of the government. This came to be seen as a vital capability that would rescue government from the dead hand of its constitutional restraints and allow it to respond to the burgeoning social, economic, and international pressures that required increased governmental intervention. As the Presidency became alive to new needs and to new possibilities, so the governmental structure and the constitution came to be radically reinterpreted as dynamic and responsive entities. So much so, in fact, that the modern Presidency came to be seen as conclusive proof of the existence of a living system of government. Accordingly, the office 'was applauded as a necessary and desirable manifestation of the adaptability of American political institutions to meet the needs of the twentieth century'.[225]

The rise of the modern Presidency denoted the period during which the executive–Darwinian paradigm of American government became predominant. Individual incumbents succeeded in developing the focal centrality of the office to the point of rendering the progression of their own position compatible with the evolution of contemporary society. The meaning of Presidential dominance alluded to the success which Presidents had experienced in making the public's sense of realism correspond to their own Darwinian perspective of realism concerning the necessary nature and purposes of government. Nothing encapsulated and symbolized the shift away from Newtonian checks and balances to the primacy of adaptation and evolution with greater clarity than the Presidency's relationship with Congress. The formal structure of separate institutions and the established rationale of reciprocal controls had always made the adversarial rite of legislative–executive relations an important means by which Presidents could demonstrate their leadership qualities and political skills. In the modern era, however, the role of Congress became more that of an adjunct to a process of government in which the political initiative had become established in the executive as both domestic and foreign problems seemed to require a progressive orientation towards a form of centralized decision-making. In this climate of social precariousness, national threat, and ever deepening complexity, the Presidency entered an era in which chief executives were expected to prevail over Congress. The legislature had always been a proving ground to Presidents. It had enabled them, through a perpetual trial by ordeal, to pit their resources against those represented in the House and Senate and to arrive at accommodations which were seen as consequences of open institutional conflict between comparable forces. But beginning with Franklin Roosevelt's Presidency, and continuing at an increasing pace thereafter, the Congress came to be regarded as less of a force to be confronted and more of a base from which to depart in ways intrinsically distinctive to executive power – thereby enabling the Presidency largely to transcend Congress and to advance government to a form more evidently commensurate with its rapidly changing responsibilities and obligations.

It was during the period of the modern Presidency that the specialized capabilities of the office came to be regarded and valued as indispensable requirements to the government making imperative responses to what had become widely recognized as urgent foreign and domestic policy issues. The strong Presidency became integral to the post-World War II consensus. Unequivocal necessity not only concentrated convictions, it concentrated the means by which to come to terms with those elements which threatened to impinge themselves forcibly upon American society from both within and without. 'Historians, political scientists and journalists ... generally held that a strong Presidency was a necessity'[226] and 'essential to the future of this nation and the freedom of our people'.[227] Presidents were encouraged not merely to preserve their power sources, but to extend them and to maximize the scope of their power wherever and whenever they could in the interests of the nation and on behalf of the American people. Great Presidents became universally identified and culturally sanctified as powerful Presidents who engaged in a virtuous struggle against the adversity of conflict and discord, in order to project the nation further towards its historical destiny and to unify its separate parts into an enhanced order of national purpose and social progress. The aspiration of individual incumbents to become great Presidents was condoned as a minimal requirement. They might not succeed, but in attempting to fulfil the full potential of the position, they would at least have explored every possible avenue of advance and expended every effort to elevate government and society to a higher level of achievement in the process.[228]

The primary reason for the acceptance of this assumption, and the chief justification for the licence subsequently afforded to modern Presidents, was derived from the nature of the executive's two most fruitful sources of authority. The first lay with the executive's self-evident physical ability to act in accordance with those pressures which manifestly did not conform to the pace and style of the normal decision-making arrangements. Such pressures constituted 'crisis' that, by definition, required extraordinary action either to preserve society's equilibrium from the effects of serious internal disorder, or to defend society against those forces outside its immediate environment which threatened to compromise the integrity of American society to an unacceptably excessive degree. In a political system based upon the principle of divided and dispersed powers, and upon the practice of settled and predictable procedures, it was only the Presidency which proved itself capable of providing such extraordinary action. The very presence of such a contingent and highly valued capability within an otherwise explicitly constitutional context became the outward sign of the gravity of the needs which were believed to exist and which were expected to be serviced. The power possessed by the Presidency to supersede the ordinary forms and processes of political authority, therefore, was largely derived from the means of physical coercion and organized force made available to it and from the presence of those conditions necessitating its use.

The President's role and legitimacy within the system were, however, also dependent upon another factor which, during the modern era, became integral to the nature of both the office and the functions it was expected to perform. This second source of modern executive power was drawn from the Presidency's close association with both the abstract and the physical trappings of the 'public' and the 'nation'. The Presidency had always been notionally related to the concepts of the public and national interest, as witnessed by its acknowledged position as the ultimate guarantor and chief guardian of the republic *in extremis*. Nevertheless, during the modern era the Presidency came to co-opt the principles of popular will and national security to itself on such a scale that the office reached a position where it could claim almost exclusive proprietary rights to speak for, and act on behalf of, the public and the nation. Accordingly, the Presidency's identity as an office became strongly dependent upon the collective identity of the American nation and people, which in turn found its clearest and most effective focal expression in the form of the Presidency. It was not simply that the Presidency as an executive could exercise the traditional executive prerogative 'to make use of his power for the good of society'.[229] It was that the incontrovertible singularity of the office, in contrast to the heterogeneity and fragmentation surrounding it, made the Presidency's claim to be acting for the community's interests so much more plausible and convincing. Just as a unitary leadership presupposed the existence of a corporate consciousness and will, so it could be expected that whatever national sentiment and social solidarity existed it would register itself most faithfully through just such a medium as the Presidency.

Presidents in the past had sought to exploit the potential implicit in this relationship between the individuality of their office and the truism of a nation speaking with only one voice. But it was only in the modern period, when crisis conditions were conducive to a pronounced national consciousness and when new opportunities for the ceremonial and political cultivation of personalized popular leadership (e.g. White House staff, mass media, military pomp) were afforded to chief executives, that Presidents were able to establish an enduring link between the unity of the office and a wider and deeper social unity. In this way, the Presidency's unity became the chief cultural expression of an underlying organic unity of common interests, principles, and purposes within society. This collective–corporatist component of the modern Presidency became in turn integral to its other chief component of a recognized social need for governmental action. Both facets of Presidential power were dependent upon the other in that necessity was based upon a unanimity on what ranked as a necessity, while unity was chiefly expressed in terms of the needs that unified the nation and society. Taken together, they projected the Presidency emphatically into a biological paradigm of necessary organic adaptation to manifest environmental pressures. Echoing Abraham Lincoln's justification of his emergency expansion of Presidential power (namely, 'a popular demand and a public necessity'[230]), conventional opinion on the progressive enlargement of the modern Presidential sector concluded that the power of the office stemmed from the 'twin supports of democratic election and the necessities of a critical era'.[231]

In this context of executive dominance and of a prevailing biological paradigm that supported such dominance, the Presidency's traditional partner was seen to suffer an irrevocable decline. As Presidents sought to acquire the credentials of 'greatness', which included the 'ability to magnify their own department, and their own powers, at the expense of the other branches'.[232] Congress became increasingly seen as a fixed anachronism which Presidents felt obliged to derogate to a secondary and marginal role. Congress became the subject, or more accurately the target, of executive initiative and energy. The legislature was transformed into an adjunct of executive prerogative and Presidential superiority. It served both as a standing justification for the exercise of Presidential force, and as a register of the extent to which Presidents had succeeded in exerting power and developing their office. Presidential power largely became equated with legislative success, measured in quotient form by the percentage of victories over Congress. It was a period of legitimized 'greatness' in Presidents. A 'great Congress' was a misnomer or even a contradiction in terms as the legislature fell victim to the general conception of Congress exemplifying what the Presidency was required to confront for the system as a whole.

Presidents were far from unwilling accomplices in this process of reducing Congress to a position of necessary depreciation. They were able to exploit the contemporary conditions of public attitudes and material pressures and to dictate the terms of their confrontation with Congress. As Presidents adopted the role of relieving the unresponsiveness of the American system and of effecting its adaptation in an age of crisis, so they were able to present Congress's traditional opposition to executives in the guise of a structural and pathological opposition to modernity. The strategies employed and the outlooks adopted were varied. Sometimes a President would attempt to co-opt Congress and absorb it into a fused unity with the executive. President Johnson, for example, proceeded on the basis that the system was 'intended to function – not with Presidents and Congresses locked in battle with each other – but locked arm in arm instead battling for the people'[233] that they served together. And Franklin Roosevelt believed that while 'the letter of the Constitution wisely declared a separation, ... the impulse of common purpose declares a union'.[234] On other occasions, Presidents would allow their private misgivings and frustrations over Congress to determine a public posture of confrontation towards the legislative branch. President Truman railed against the Eightieth Congress and took the issue directly to the people in the 1948 election.[235] It was President Nixon, however, who probably allowed his personal disdain for Congress and his belief in the transcendent authority of his own office to reveal themselves to full effect in his public relationships with the Congress. From the transcriptions of the White House tapes, it is clear that the President entertained a very low opinion of the legislature. 'Congress is, of course, on its [inaudible]. And yet they are so enormously frustrated that they are exhausted ... they have become irrelevant because they are so damned irresponsible.'[236] His frustration with Congress was such that in 1972 he took it to task and lectured the American public on its behaviour:

> In the final months and weeks of 1970, ... the nation was presented with the spectacle of a legislative body that had seemingly lost the capacity to decide and the will to act.... In these times when the need to build confidence in government is so transparent, that was good neither for the Congress nor the country. Let us hope that it never takes place again.[237]

Ultimately, in his relations with Congress, President Nixon felt constrained to resort wherever possible to circumvention or evasion. Echoing F.D.R.'s private sentiment 'that the only way to do anything in the American government is to bypass the Senate',[238] Nixon regarded the avoidance of Congressional entanglements as a justifiable course of action and a thoroughly unexceptional extension of what previous Presidents had done to prevent the unity and development of government from being compromised by what they regarded as the regressive and outmoded agency of Congress.

Intrinsic to the whole notion of the modern Presidency, therefore, was the idea of an *un*modern Congress. Much of the Presidency's own role and identity was forged in the period by the projection of Congress as a mechanistic structure which was not only bound to the past, but also fixed to the constraints of its own blindly self-perpetuating forces. In relation to the Presidency's obvious unity and distinguishable individual will, Congress's multiplicity of complex moving parts came to be seen as a disembodied machine. Although reformers suggested various mechanical rearrangements in the firm belief that structural changes would automatically produce policy changes, most observers either despaired of ever seeing Congress modify itself or else concluded that any modifications would only ever be marginal and temporary in character. Congress appeared to be inextricably locked into a mechanistic identity and, with it, into the machine age of the late nineteenth and early twentieth centuries when the constitution was widely believed to be an immutably fixed charter of government in which clearly discernible units were thought to occupy exclusive spheres of responsibility and to interact with one another according to a predetermined pattern of movement. This was an era during which American government was more often than not dominated by Congress. It was an era which ultimately became characterized as one of government failure. The notion of Congress and Congressional government, therefore, became discredited not just because of its actual deficiencies but because it was part of an age which had been superseded by another age whose respect for change was demonstrated to maximum effect by the advent of Presidential government. Congressional obstruction, or immobilism, or negativism came to be seen as such because the institution was believed to be, more than anything else, mechanical in nature and, therefore, mechanically attached to the past. These may have been inaccurate and unwarranted assumptions, but in the modern era of Presidential government, with its attendant emphases upon such Darwinian credentials as responsiveness, variability, mobility, innovation, and development, the impulse to deduce outmoded Congressional mechanics from legislative unresponsiveness to the Presidency was almost irresistible. Congress's legislative inefficiency suggested mechanical efficiency. Congress's major characteristics were regarded as defects, which in turn were seen to be directly attributable to Congress's chief problem – namely, that it possessed a demonstrably mechanistic nature in a manifestly non-mechanical environment.

The ascription of mechanics to Congress and its subsequent derogation as an institution were part of that larger and broader biological conception of government which Presidents had succeeded so much in embodying and in exploiting for their own purposes. The worth and status of modern Presidents became attached not so much to the simple accumulation of power, but to the cultivation of a qualitatively distinct and overarching form of corporate power which drew its strength and inspiration from the country's increased levels of social integration and national solidarity. It was not that the Presidency had engaged in a straight take-over of powers that had once been regarded as Congressional in nature – even though some of the office's new responsibilities could be construed in this light (e.g. the President as chief legislator). It was more that the Presidency became the most distinctive element and the most conspicuous emblem of a deep-seated change in American society and in its position in respect to the rest of the world. Congress was not displaced. It was eclipsed by an institution that operated in a different dimension and on a different plane to that of the legislature. The Presidency's position and responsibilities were seen as exceptional, imperative, even mysterious and magical. Its power was implicit in the functions it was expected to perform, which in turn were dependent upon contemporary conditions and needs that were not amenable to treatment through the normal channels of defined institutional arrangements and formal constitutional processes. The Presidency became the equivalent of a tacit admission that American government had evolved beyond its customary forms and that the separation of powers structure had 'undergone a radical and enfeebling transformation'[239] in the face of overriding pressures. Just as the imagery and force of Presidential power signified the presence of change and vitality, so Congress's mechanistic overtones and declining status completed the picture of a new condition of government that was no longer reducible to comparable components and compatible powers. In this altered context, Congress became a point of reference demarcating the extent to which the Presidency had departed from the previous norms and practices, and confirming the reality of a governing process in change. Moreover, as Congress slipped increasingly into a recidivist syndrome of unresponsiveness, myopia, and stasis, then the more it seemed to reaffirm the existence of a linear and irreversible progression of government into Presidential government. In accordance with the prevailing biological paradigm, it was assumed that historical and social forces would lead inexorably to an intensification and to an ever greater validation of the Presidency's already pre-eminent position. Nothing seemed capable of disturbing the certainty of such an assumption, or of challenging the attitudes and conditions which underlay it. Implicit in the adaptive and evolutionary conception of Presidential power was the belief that a disruption of current trends was not merely improbable but actually implausible.

It was in this context of assured executive expansionism that the crisis over what became termed the 'imperial Presidency' occurred in the late 1960s and early 1970s. At the very time when all the supportive elements of Presidential power seemed at their most impregnable, the evolutionary process surrounding the Presidency was suddenly subjected to an unanticipated and unprecedented challenge. The confrontation was more than a simple intensification of the adversarial condition that had traditionally characterized the relationship between the Presidency and Congress. It was also a confrontation whose significance and repercussions went far beyond matters of policy, or party, or personalities. The outcry over the Presidency represented a much deeper malaise, for among its many dimensions was a revealing reappraisal of the nature and value of executive power, together with a vigorous resurgence of interest in the original purposes and contemporary effectiveness of the constitution's formal structure of institutional dynamics. Ultimately, the disquiet surrounding the Presidential office turned into a general reaction against the ethos and scale of executive power – and with it a challenge to the previously accepted notions of historical progress, institutional evolution, unilinear advance, and the whole biological paradigm of political development.

Crises and scandals are, of course, interesting in their own right. But they are also interesting in what they disclose about the way a society defines, interprets, analyses, and evaluates them. The crisis over the American Presidency embraced a 'series of constitutional crises more serious than any since the Civil War'[240] and culminated in the Watergate scandal, which, according to Arthur Schlesinger, 'brought to the surface, symbolized and made politically accessible the great question ... of Presidential power'.[241] The first point raised by this controversy is the question of how and why the Presidency came to be perceived and accepted as a problem by the American public. There can be little doubt that the office was seen as controversial, because it was recognized as having become a much more powerful office than it had been before. It had grown to the point where it was widely believed to have become a centre of not merely increasing power but of excessive power. Such assertions immediately beg the question as to how it was possible to determine whether the office had graduated to the point of possessing more power than it should. At the climax of the crisis there was a strong conviction amongst the public that the severe problems confronting American society were at root attributable to the Presidency and, in particular, to the Presidency's excess of power. But how were these conclusions arrived at? Why was so much distrust and scepticism directed to an office which not long before had been celebrated as heroic and beneficial? What led Americans to be so sure of their calculations of Presidential power that they were prepared to allow and to encourage other elements in the governmental process to precipitate a prolonged and fundamental constitutional crisis?

Answers to these sorts of questions are legion. They range from actual examples of unchecked Presidential power such as the indiscretions and misdemeanours of individual incumbents to partisan critiques of administration policies couched for political effect in the inflammatory terms of excessive power; and from the distaste and distrust shown on the part of some sectors of the American public for the personalities of such Presidents as Lyndon Johnson and Richard Nixon to the anguished cries of Caesarism from a Congress 'inclined to translate its internal failings into crusades against Presidential usurpation of power'.[242] One cannot deny the significance of any one of these answers, but in an important way they remain incomplete without taking into account an underlying substructure of perception and explanation to which such answers, and others like them, are variously attached. It is this substructure which was instrumental in activating much of the disquiet shown towards the Presidential office and in rationalizing that concern in terms of its own principles and axioms. The presence and use of this perceptual framework became quite evident during the crisis over the Presidency and revealed a widespread intellectual dependence upon concepts and values which were long since thought to have become largely redundant in contemporary

American politics.

The framework in question came to be used as a sort of structural theorem that made sense of the world by relating those phenomena to be explained back to certain basic principles which were conceptualized primarily in terms of structures and of the physical relationships between them. These central principles – from which so many propositions could be logically inferred and so many observations could be satisfactorily comprehended – were those most closely associated with the Founders and with the philosophy that lay behind their design of the constitution and their arrangement of its constituent institutions.

The first principle was the belief in man's flawed nature. While individuals were capable of laudable actions and virtuous works, they were more motivated by an unquenchable appetite for self-advancement at the expense of others. The Founding Fathers derived little comfort from the idea of entrusting any man or group of men with power over their contemporaries, even if this was derived from the republican principle of popular consent. To them, the fusion of man with power was a combination which aroused the deepest possible suspicion and upon which any constitution would necessarily have to be based. The Founders' most illustrious contemporary, Thomas Jefferson, was quite unequivocal on this need for vigilance:

> It would be a dangerous delusion were a confidence in the men of our choice to silence our fears for the safety of our rights: Confidence is everywhere the parent of despotism – free government is founded in jealousy, and not in confidence.... In questions of power, let no more be heard of confidence in man, but bind him down from mischief by the chains of the Constitution.[243]

It was man's nature which had generated the need for government, so government itself could not depend upon human self-restraint in order to despatch its responsibilities. To preserve liberty, it was necessary to depend upon incessant distrust and upon the means of translating that distrust into a force capable of constraining power with power.

The second principle follows from the first. It is the assurance that power will be confronted by the only restraint known to be effective in checking it – namely, an established and comparable counter-force. This is the clear rationale behind the Founders' separation of powers scheme. According to James Madison, their objective was to 'secure the public good and private rights against the danger of ... faction ... and its ruling passion'.[244] The Founding Fathers' way of achieving this objective was a governmental framework organized to ensure that man's appetite for power would be played off against itself through the device of checks and balances between mutually external bodies. These three branches lent an evocative symmetry to the conceptual qualities of the government. The symmetry, however, was not confined simply to the arrangement and mechanics of the three inter-balancing departments.

By relating the physical structure of government together with its planned dynamics to the central objective of efficient yet limited government, the Founding Fathers also succeeded in establishing a symmetry between liberty and the configuration of the government – i.e. between a quality and a quantity; between a major value and a key design feature of the constitution. Given, as Madison had asserted, that 'the accumulation of all powers, legislative, executive, and judiciary, in the same hands ... may justly be pronounced the very definition of tyranny'[245] and given that nearly every American citizen is presented with this declaration as an empirical fact and as an irrefutable doctrine of government, then it is understandable that the interrelationship between the three institutions is viewed as a physico-mechanical expression of the central value of liberty. According to the professed mechanics of the system, in the same way that a convergence in the position of the three can be equated with a decline in liberty and a corresponding increase in tyranny, so a resurgence in liberty can be detected and affirmed by the appearance of its structural analogue (i.e. a wider distribution of powers between the three branches) in accordance with the terms provided by the political system. In this way, the conspicuous emphasis given to institutional dynamics within the constitution not only provides a device for securing liberty from arbitrary and oppressive government, but also affords a mechanical register by which to determine the system's degree of success in achieving its objective.

The shifting topography of interrelated institutions is certainly in theory a way of observing political developments and of acquiring a normative response to them. The question remains, however, as to whether it is actually used as an instrument of perception and evaluation. Prior to this crisis over the Presidency, it would have been difficult to make a very convincing case that the separation of powers format had remained in the forefront of the American political mind as a conceptual and analytical device. As has already been acknowledged, there were many indications during the rise of the modern Presidency that the ethos of checks and balances was gradually being displaced by a supposedly more realistic approach to the exigencies of modern governmental requirements and responsibilities. Nevertheless, with the onset of the severe criticism lodged against the Presidency, it became quite clear that the traditional mechanistic paradigm of a regulatory interplay of institutions had by no means been eroded away under the pressure of Presidential government. On the contrary, the crisis revealed, in a quite exceptional manner, the extent to which the American public remained dependent upon the Founding Fathers' structural theorem concerning the geometrical and physical properties of power within the terms of definition established in the constitution. The organization and rationale of the constitutional system offered not only a defined meaning as to what the crisis consisted of, but also an explanation of how and why it had occurred, and what needed to be done to resolve it. The remarkable feature of the crisis was that what the system had to offer in this way was grasped with such alacrity by so many people.

It will be recalled that the challenge to the Presidency in the late 1960s and early 1970s was set in a political context of dissidence, anxiety, and frustration.[246] The combination of inflation, street crime, pornography, violent demonstrations, campus revolts, drug abuse, assassinations, racial tension, radical social critiques, and the excruciatingly inconclusive war in South East Asia produced a severe dislocation of American society. Expectations of progress were challenged. The customary consensus was fractured. Political authority came under assault. Things had gone seriously wrong. Mismanagement had occurred; misjudgements had been made; misadventures had taken place. Liberal programmes were seen as 'failures'. The Vietnam war was regarded as a 'mistake'. The economy was in 'disarray'. Given the government's central and focal position in modern American society, assertions that things had gone wrong was the same as saying that the government had gone wrong. This was a profound and disquieting conclusion in a political system that was specifically designed to regulate itself. The principle underlying the system was that the dynamics of its institutional arrangements would generate a self-stabilizing equilibrium which would preclude the possibility of a serious malfunction. By the same token, if a serious malfunction occurred, then, as a matter of course, it could be accounted for only by a failure in the system – namely, a departure from its normal equilibrium into the instability of imbalance. This concept of imbalance came to characterize the nature of the crisis just as much as any of the more immediate effects that were reputedly derived from the imbalance.

In so far as an imbalance of power was assumed to exist, then in the context of the modern era there was never any doubt as to the identity of the source and beneficiary of that imbalance. Since the rise of the Presidency to such a position of prominence in the traditional triumvirate of government branches, the office might have established itself as 'the embodiment of American mass democracy'[247] and 'the focal point of national life',[248] but, in doing so, it also established itself as the force most likely to disturb the stability of the constitution. Bearing in mind that the commonly accepted objective of the constitution is the control of positively exerted power, then the modern Presidency's reputation for escaping from restraints, and for embodying that part of government so aptly suited to governing, resulted in the office being recognized as the chief suspect in any case involving an imbalance of power. In other words, given that modern conditions boosted Presidential power, and given that such power was usually characterized as the ability to overcome constitutional restraints, then the potential always existed for a *prima facie* case against the Presidency even in normal conditions. In abnormal conditions, when attention turned towards the concept of an imbalance in government, interest immediately focused upon just that agency with the acknowledged capacity to change the weights in the scales.

In the imperial Presidency crisis, pre-existing suspicions were capitalized upon and converted into hard accusation and subsequent condemnation. Misgivings turned into a crusade against Presidential government. The process was assisted by two factors in particular. The first was what could be termed 'nominal accountability'. This refers to the general principle of the President's responsibility, as the elected chief executive, for the political and administrative performance of the federal government. It is this principle which has been used to justify the attempts made by Presidents to exert forms of putative central control over the government. This assumed obligation on the part of Presidents, combined with the massive personalization of their office into a highly visible embodiment of government policy, led to an implosion of accountability within the system. Strong Presidents and a powerful Presidency drew unto them public assumptions of responsibility. This development could sometimes be politically beneficial to the office holder and serve to enhance the status of the Presidency still further. Nevertheless, its effect could be double-edged. Presidents could find themselves being held responsible for any mismanagement or policy disappointment occurring during their administration – irrespective of their actual culpability. Both President Johnson and President Nixon suffered from this phenomenon of general Presidential blameworthiness. It helped to create the atmosphere of open distrust and scepticism towards executive power that came to mark their administrations and to accompany the political failures and excesses associated with them.[249]

The second factor was that of 'substantive accountability'. This refers to those incidents of mismanagement and abuse of power that were directly and explicitly attributable to the chief executives themselves, or to their immediate circle of advisers and assistants. The decisions and actions for which President Johnson and President Nixon were directly held responsible have been well documented and need no repetition here. In addition to their notoriety as inflammatory abuses or provocative mistakes, however, these singular failures had a broader and more general significance. They gave the issue of Presidential power a clarity of focus which allowed it to develop out of the generalized disquiet formed from the Presidency's 'nominal accountability' for social and economic disarray, and graduate into a full-scale constitutional crisis. President Johnson, but more especially President Nixon, were confronted with the double effects of these two forms of accountability and, as a result, their office was subjected to an unprecedented assault. The zeal with which it was attacked was born out of the firm conviction that the agency responsible for society's dislocation had been correctly located. Just as attention turned increasingly towards the Presidency, so there was a corresponding rise in interest in Congress's formal role as the political countervailing power to the executive branch. Congress became associated with the assault upon the Presidency to such an extent that the crisis quickly became characterized as a *bona fide* confrontation between two constitutional partners, in strict accordance with the traditional mechanics of the Founders' checks and balances system.

It should be recalled at this point that Congress has had a history of incessant complaint over the power of the Presidency; that there has always existed a rich potential for open conflict between the two institutions; that in the pluralist mainstream of American politics the Presidency and Congress have traditionally been expected to clash, owing to the probability that different permutations of economic and social interests would be represented in the two institutions; and that 'waving the bloody shirt' of Liberty in the face of the leviathan executive state has become an accustomed ideological impulse and well worn political tactic by which to oppose suggested policy changes. What has to be appreciated about the imperial Presidency issue was the extraordinary degree to which it largely transcended these normal features of American politics and became a genuinely constitutional issue, i.e. one fought out according to the constitution's own terms and concepts. The issue represented something substantially more than merely exaggerated partisanship, simple pluralism, or customary institutional rivalry. The forces implicit in these loyalties and motivations may indeed have served to fuel the crisis, but they could not be said to have determined the perceived nature of the crisis. The way in which the American public responded to the issue could not be satisfactorily explained purely in these terms. What was so striking about the issue was the manner in which the myriad allegiances, attitudes, and opinions related to the issue were rationalized and clarified by reference not merely to the traditional American anxiety over power *per se*, but to the Founding Fathers' distinctively mechanistic conception of power and to the significance of the constitution's formal institutional arrangements in elucidating that conception.

The mechanistic character of the crisis was nowhere more evident than in the way the relationship between the Presidency and Congress was elevated to a position of priority where it served to define the problem with which the republic was confronted, and to determine the remedies available to the American people. During the imperial Presidency crisis, there arose an extraordinary revival of popular interest in the relationship between the two institutions and, in particular, the purpose that this association was meant to serve according to traditional precepts. Attention shifted to the old assumptions concerning the professed dynamics of the executive and legislative branches and the concepts of power upon which such dynamics were based. As the crisis progressed, it became clear that interest was mixed with belief and that concern over misrule and the abuse of power aroused a conviction over the actuality of the system's formal machinery. Furthermore, the nature of the anxiety expressed over the Presidency revealed not just a conviction of the system's mechanistic properties as an explanation of the crisis but a profound appreciation of the significance and value of such properties.

During the rise of the modern Presidency there arose a strong belief in the existence of a close relationship between executive expansion and legislative contraction; between Presidential aggrandisement and a corresponding decline in Congressional power. For much of the time, however, this relationship was ill defined and imprecise. It was perceived in a variety of different guises. For example, Congress was occasionally viewed as an institution which had necessarily submitted to Presidential leadership because of the executive's distinctive abilities in leadership, decision-making, and administration. On other occasions, Congress was seen as a stable entity which had remained static while the Presidency had assumed new attributes and had, as a result, diverged from Congress along a separate developmental path. Sometimes Congress was cast in the role of a hapless victim of circumstances that had conspired to render the institution inappropriate to modern conditions. At other times, Congress was seen as a body in decline, but also as a body in control of its decline in so far as it was actively responsible for delegating its functions to the executive branch. According to another perspective, the change in Congress's role was attributed to its decision to vacate an area of joint responsibility and grant it to the executive by default. There were claims that Congress had ceded powers through conscious self-restraint, through a lack of political willpower, through structural weaknesses, through an understanding of the realities of modern government, and through a mature appreciation of its own deficiencies. But there were also claims that Congress had remained a highly potent legislative institution which had retained its independence and used it to great effect by adapting itself to the modern role of executive oversight and supervision. The nature of the executive's influence upon the Congress, therefore, was manifold and not easily reducible to a unidimensional conception of interchangeable power. Neither was there any general incentive or impulse to see the relationship between the Presidency and Congress as one of opposing forces, or of standardized counterweights, or of a necessary balance of power. For much of the period of the modern Presidency, the atmosphere was one of an informed acquiescence in, or a reluctant acceptance of, both the need for and the value of changes in the nature of government which served to enhance the executive branch. Whatever additional power accrued to the Presidency as a result was seen as almost incidental to the process. If there was criticism, then, more often than not, it was that an insufficient amount of attention was being given to the Presidency's lack of power and to the office's inability to discharge the responsibilities and obligations that were increasingly placed upon it. In conceptual terms, Presidential power in relation to other branches of government was of secondary importance. Power was seen as being dependent upon the qualitative distinctiveness of the office rather than as a unit in a mechanistic framework of cause and effect. In this era, the Presidency's special attributes offered the prospect of governmental action at a time when there was a strong public demand for positive government even if it meant a change in the traditional relationships between the government's constituent elements. What was important was the uses and purposes of a particular kind of power, rather than the amounts and allotments of an undifferentiated power.

The modern Presidency and the public reaction to its power were the epitome of that biological paradigm of politics and society which, by the mid-1960s, had become almost a conventional perspective of the nature of American government. The Presidency was celebrated as an evocative child of nature – responding to impulses, searching out new experiences, innovating skills, developing its inner potential, and relishing the self-renewal and emancipation proffered by nature's open system. And yet, at the height of its power, and at the very moment when the belief in its organic and irreversible development seemed at its most intact, the Presidency suffered from a reversion to mechanistic models of analysis and evaluation. After such a sustained period of viewing the Presidency as a qualitatively idiosyncratic entity, it was unexpectedly subjected to criticism on the basis of mechanistic precepts concerning quantities of power, proportions of weight, and relativities of size. The anxiety and disquiet aroused from numerous sources and for numerous reasons became translated into a starkly mechanical conception of government which featured checks and balances as its primary vision of reality and as its primary systemic value. Just how marked the restored mechanistic paradigm was, and just how intense the attachment to it, could be gauged by the accounts given of the relationship between the Presidency and the Congress. Before the crisis, the relationship had not been regarded as being crucially significant to the polity. Furthermore, the interaction of the two institutions had been difficult to conceptualize in any rigorous and consistent pattern. This was because the Presidency and the Congress were largely seen as possessing different roles both of which were valuable to the system and both of which were difficult to conceive as being merely two portions of the same material force. The notion of a balance of power did not really fit the model, for, in an avowedly open system, the Presidency could gain weight of his own accord and in his own way irrespective of Congress. Furthermore, the legislature might lose weight and energy to the environment, thereby precluding any necessary and automatic acquisition of power on the part of the Presidency. The picture could be made even more complicated by claiming, as many did, that by being an open system it was made quite possible for both the Presidency and the Congress to increase in power simultaneously. Theodore Lowi, for example, thought it incorrect 'to say that the power of Congress had declined [for] as an instrument of national government Congress was more powerful than ever'.[250] Taking account of both the institutional and historical perspectives, it might be said that 'Congress had ... both lost and acquired power'.[251] In response to the balance of powers principle, therefore, it was possible under these conditions either to accept the existence of an imbalance with equanimity, knowing that the two institutions had different natures and fulfilled different roles; or essentially to fudge the issue by claiming that the Presidency and the Congress were both growing in their separate and distinctive ways. While Congressmen may have complained about executive usurpation and about the prominence given to the Presidential office, very few of them would have regarded the idea of Congress resuming its old responsibilities in the name of a restored balance as being a very plausible, or relevant, or even a very desirable proposition.

The separation of paradigms

By the late 1960s, however, the picture had dramatically changed. The middle of that decade had witnessed as great a flowering of the positive and heroic qualities of the Presidency as had been experienced since the 1930s. And yet, in just a few years, the general outlook on the office had altered so drastically that it precipitated a sudden revival of interest in the origin, form, and value of America's traditional constitutional structure. Condoned discretion turned to a search for categorical definition; accustomed trust turned to axiomatic distrust; passive fatalism turned to stern inquisition; and an unquestioning allegiance to the needs of power and powerful Presidents turned to a passionate concern over the nature and limits of such power. The energies of the executive had, of course, always represented a challenge to the principle of constitutionalism and to its legal framework of hard definitions, clear boundaries, set relationships, and predictable processes. The intellectual and political problems posed by the nature of executive power had always been ones of whether it was in essence compatible with the structure and purpose of constitutional government. For most of the modern era, this conundrum was not regarded as particularly significant. People accepted an ambiguity which worked. By the late 1960s and early 1970s, however, attitudes had changed. The American public became absorbed in constitutional doctrines and in the precepts underlying those doctrines. 'The words of the Founding Fathers were once again in fashion – and ... the words of our Constitution ... achieved a renewed nobility.'[252] In particular, there developed a revived awareness of the existence of the three branches of government and of their declared function of checking one another. Implicit within this design was the great conceptual leveller of physical force which rendered the branches readily compatible with one another through, and only through, this material dimension. This was the indispensable basis to the Founding Fathers' balance of powers. This principle of equilibrium denoted much more than just mutual influence or even interdependence. It concerned a real and direct interaction of bodies – bodies which, in the American constitution, had been deliberately created and specifically positioned to produce a self-balancing effect. Taken together, the institutions represented a dynamic system of units whose behaviour was to be determined by and registered through the position of each unit in relation to the others. According to this conception of the constitution, power was necessarily reduced to the physical exchange of a fixed amount of force between a fixed number of institutional centres. During the crisis over Presidential power, it became clear that it was this mechanical conception which proved to be paramount in the way that Americans tended to perceive the nature of the problem, to analyse the reasons for its presence, and to define what would constitute a solution.

This dependence upon mechanics can be shown in a number of ways. First, the crisis over the Presidency came increasingly to be seen specifically as one of constitutional imbalance. As has already been acknowledged, the malaise and anxiety of the period generated a profound introspection amongst Americans into their system of government. It appeared that the system had malfunctioned in the only way that it could, according to its own properties – i.e. by becoming unbalanced. The imbalance was characterized by an excess of Presidential power. Initially the imbalance tended to be viewed in a diffuse and generalized manner. This ambiguity was due to a mixture of conceptions surrounding the Presidency. For years the office had been seen and valued as the 'living Presidency'[253] or the 'evolving Presidency',[254] but this conception sat very uncomfortably amidst the conception of lifeless weights and balances. As the public's consciousness of Presidential power as a problem grew, however, the biological paradigm was progressively disrupted by the mechanistic paradigm, with the result that the relationship between the Presidency and the Supreme Court and Congress was increasingly seen to be that of an exact physical connection. Presidential power became equated with such properties as size, speed, movement, concentration, acceleration, and scale. As a result, there was a renewed emphasis upon the Supreme Court and, in particular, upon the Congress, which gave effect to such properties. Presidential power, therefore, was no longer simply a case of observing the expansion of the executive branch in isolation, but of taking into account a correlated reduction in the power of the other two branches – much in the way portrayed in the cartoon, Figure 8. In a system that was being increasingly seen as one whose rationale was that of a balanced interchange of forces, it was meaningless to refer to a growth in Presidential power without envisaging a corresponding

Figure 8 From *Time*, 15 January 1973, by courtesy of Don Wright, *Miami News*.

decline in the status of the remaining two branches. Just as the gravitational pull of the sun could be gauged by the behaviour of the planets in the solar system, so, according to this way of seeing things, the magnitude of Presidential power could be determined through the movement and position of the Congress and Supreme Court.

Instead of the Presidency being viewed as an evolving entity growing through its own processes and assimilating new capabilities and forms in response to environmental forces, the office came to be seen far more as a uniform weight in a set of scales. Formally, the scales were a three-way device representing the three branches in the separation of powers scheme. In practice, however, the notion of balance was progressively simplified by recourse to a two-way equilibrium in which the counterweight to the Presidency was reduced to that of Congress. This was a reflection, first, of the judiciary's noted reluctance to engage itself in the political disputes surrounding the lines of demarcation between the two representational branches of government; and, second, of Congress's position as an institution whose political and electoral credentials were comparable to those of the Presidency and sufficient to allow the legislature to be identified as the executive's chief institutional adversary and potential counterweight. With this conception of legislative–executive relations, Congress could no longer be regarded as somehow developing in tandem with the Presidency, or of retaining its position while the Presidency advanced in its own right and through its own means. On the contrary, Presidential power became reduced to the conceptually manageable form of a physical force within a closed system, so that for every accretion of executive weight there was thought to be a directly related diminution of Congressional weight on a direct one-to-one basis. So far as the 'imperial Presidency' was concerned, it was not simply that it embodied a 'shift in the constitutional balance – with ... the appropriation by the Presidency ... of powers reserved by the constitution and by long historical practice to Congress'.[255] It was that 'the central premise of the theory' underlying the confrontation between the Presidency and Congress was 'that the relationship was of a balance scale or zero-sum character, and ... that a strong President must mean a weak Congress and vice versa'.[256] The constitutional system may have been in an unbalanced condition, therefore, but at least the exact nature of that imbalance was thought to be known.

The second point follows on from the assumed zero-sum character of the linkage between the Presidency and the Congress. Given that the political system's malfunctions and misrule were largely attributed to the existence of an imbalance between the two institutions, it followed that such an imbalance must have developed from a condition of balance or something approximating to such a condition. The conception of balance, therefore, could be used not only to account in general terms for the phenomena but also to provide clear reasons for their presence. In the case of the 'imperial Presidency', there was little inhibition in drawing upon the idea of balance to produce what were,

Figure 9 From the *Congressional Quarterly Guide to Current American Government*, fall 1978 (Washington, D.C., Congressional Quarterly Press, 1978), p. 75; by courtesy of Congressional Quarterly Press.

within the logic of the idea, the direct and explicit causes of excessive Presidential power.

It is significant that public attention turned primarily towards Congress during the crisis over the Presidency. This was not simply because of party, or political, or organizational reasons. An important element in its increased salience was the way the legislature became the chief patron and advocate of the issue of unbalanced government. Congress had had long experience of Presidential power. It had become accustomed to its force. It had experienced a decline in stature and prestige as a result of modern conditions, which favoured the functional capacities and executive privileges of the Presidential office. Congress, in other words, was in a perfect position to claim that it had been on the receiving end of Presidential power and that it, more than any other body, could sense and assess when that power had become sufficiently great to constitute an imbalance. In accordance with the concept of balanced powers, it was Congress which one would have expected to have been most keenly aware of changes in the weight of executive power and most determined to criticize and draw public attention to such a challenge to the equilibrium. This may have been true in theory but, for most of the era of the modern Presidency, these expectations were not fulfilled. Government was not seen or valued as a balance between comparable units. It might well have been in Congress's interests to adopt a rigorous checks and balances perspective but more often than not the inclination was absent. Presidential power was not a public issue and, as a result, the ethos of checks and balances became a jaded philosophy. By the beginning of President Nixon's first administration, however, public interest had shifted towards the theme of power, its distribution in the political system, and the mechanisms available for its control. Congress reflected that change in attitudes but it also reinforced it by exploiting to the full its newly rediscovered role as a register of Presidential power and the embodiment of one side of a constitutional balance. In becoming the recognized focus of opposition to Presidential power, Congress succeeded in reviving public interest in the constitutional doctrine of balance, in regenerating a political vocabulary of mechanical terms, and in resurrecting a general belief in the plausibility of perceiving America's problems in the light of balanced government. In doing so, Congress succeeded in renovating itself as an institution. It had long been established as the epitome of checks and balances in so far as its own organization was concerned, but in the early 1970s it was instrumental in changing the public's conception of the system at large to match the legislature's own structures and orientations. The emphasis had become that of countervailing power. As a result, Congress's rationale as an institution was clarified in purpose and raised in value.

The significance of the Presidency and Congress being seen as the two sides of a single balance lay in the way that it provided a causal explanation of the expansion of Presidential power. Having accepted that the 'constitution was out of balance';[257] that 'the balance had moved sharply in the President's favor since the Second World War';[258] and that the Presidency and Congress constituted a dynamic relationship in which 'one had been expanding and the other eroding in a way that had thrown the American system fundamentally and dangerously out of balance'[259] – then it was possible to deduce the source of the executive's enlarged powers. The mechanical properties of balancing institutions determined that the expansion in executive power could have been derived only from Congress. In other words, the clear implication from the renewed emphasis upon balanced government was that the Presidency's celebrated evolutionary development was in reality reducible to a straight conversion of Congressional energy into executive energy: i.e. that the constituent parts of the Presidency's excess weight had once belonged to and had existed within Congress.

It is evident from the assertions made and from the arguments employed at the time that the Presidency came increasingly to be seen as possessing a physical superiority to Congress because of powers that had been achieved at the direct expense of the legislature. Some laid stress upon the Presidency having usurped powers from Congress. Senator J. William Fulbright, for example, believed constitutional democracy in America to be in danger of 'degenerating into an imperial dictatorship' because of the appetite for power shown by modern Presidents. He drew attention in particular to 'executive incursions upon Congress's foreign policy powers' and to the 'takeover by the executive of the war and treaty powers of Congress'.[260] Such Presidents as

Franklin Roosevelt, Harry Truman, and Lyndon Johnson had 'subverted the Congress' and had subordinated the constitutional process to political expediency, 'resulting in each case in an expansion of Presidential power at the expense of Congress'.[261] A more common interpretation, however, laid the blame on Congress itself. It was thought that the legislature had been generous to a fault and had delegated away too many of its powers and privileges to the executive branch. James Sundquist's comments typify this widespread suspicion of legislative abdication:

> The accretion of Presidential power was all done with the consent, and often with the leadership of Congress. The Congress took its powers and handed them over to the President.... The modern aggrandisement of the Presidency was the product of considered legislative decisions.[262]

In Sundquist's view, it was the Congress which had created the imperial Presidency by tossing power 'over a barrier ... into alien territory – out of direct control, out of easy reach, even out of sight'.[263] Whether it was Congressional abdication or Presidential usurpation, the implication behind the process of executive aggrandisement was the same on both counts – namely, that the rise of the modern Presidency was attributable exclusively to what Congress had afforded to the executive either by design, or by force, or by neglect. The common assumption was that of a 'transfer of power'[264] whereby 'power tended to flow from Congress to the Presidency'.[265] The suggestion underlying this general imagery of legislative–executive relations was that, just as Congress had given power away, so it possessed the potential to take it back. In other words, there could be 'ebbs and flows of executive–legislative relations'.[266] Congressional weakness, therefore, was something of a paradox. If executive supremacy was born out of legislative licence, then the solution to Presidential power lay in Congress's own hands. Legislative self-effacement was double-edged, for, while the Congress was seen as having been the immediate cause of executive excess, so it also offered the best prospect of resolving the problem.

This leads to the third way in which the imperial Presidency crisis revealed a deep attachment to mechanical principles of government within American political culture. This third point alludes to Congress's position as a remedy of first resort. Far from being merely an abstract or theoretical source of countervailing power, it became a matter of habit for Congress to be recognized as the genuine source of an executive counter-force. In the past, 'power flowed to Presidents'.[267] 'The pull of executive leadership was ... seen as inevitable and irreversible'.[268] During the crisis, however, the inevitability and irreversibility of the transfer of power were openly challenged, not least by members of Congress themselves. 'We can take the power back if we want',[269] asserted Senator Robert Packwood. And Senator Mark Hatfield thought that 'the arrogance of power so evident in the Watergate case illustrated ... the need to reverse the flow of power before ... a greater constitutional crisis'[270] presented itself.

The belief in the existence of a balance determined the nature and identity of the solution. In response to such issues as to whether 'the autonomous Presidency [could] be effectively constrained', or whether it could 'become more responsive to democratic norms, ... attention turned to Congress as the alternative political branch'.[271] To Alexander Bickel, for example, it was a self-evident fact that 'the way to control Presidential power was for Congress to strengthen itself'.[272] F. G. Hutchins agreed and asserted that 'the balance of power between legislative and executive branches should be redressed more favorably to Congress'.[273] On the basis of constitutional doctrine and mechanistic suppositions, the Congress was looked to intuitively as the remedial element capable of matching executive force with legislative force and of restoring the 'classic balance of powers'.[274] It was remarkable enough that the Presidency's accumulated growth should suddenly be regarded as reversible – especially since the prevailing view prior to the crisis was that the office had been the subject of a necessarily progressive and historically ineluctable process of evolution. It was even more remarkable that the full weight of public expectations concerning this retrogression should have fallen upon the Congress, which had been the very institution whose weaknesses modern Presidents had sought to alleviate by enhancing their own position. Furthermore, such expectations over Congress's capability and purpose had to be set against what had been the conventionally accepted view of the legislature as having been 'overwhelmed by the Presidency, with its expertise, its reports, its commission studies and its near monopoly on information and evaluation'.[275] Despite the customary misgivings over Congress's contemporary competence and relevance, commentators, journalists, analysts, and political participants rushed to allocate to Congress the fundamental responsibility of satisfying the logical requirements of a political system which had by then come increasingly to be seen as a mechanical construct. Having characterized the problem as being one of governmental imbalance, the natural rejoinder was that of rebalance. This was not to be a new condition, but a return to a past one through the activation of the system's capacity to arrest the imbalance and to right itself through the deployment of a counterweight. Congress was readily identified as the available and appropriate balance – irrespective of the legislature's ability and willingness to provide the authentic check to executive power. The doubts and reservations that had previously coloured attitudes towards Congress were largely dismissed. They were eclipsed by the exuberant revival of faith in checks and balances that led to the uninhibited expressions of trust in Congress's capacity to restore the required equilibrium.

Probably the best illustration of this instinctive and often extravagant belief in Congress's capacity to check executive power came in the field of foreign and military policy. It will be recalled that it was precisely in this area that the Presidency's distinctively executive attributes had been recognized as being appropriate to the nature of international relations and to the successful conduct of foreign policy. During the prolonged crisis of the Cold War, these attributes of expertise, subtlety, secrecy, action, direction, command, adroitness, foresight, authority, responsiveness, discretion, and hierarchy were accepted as the indispensable requirements not merely to an effective diplomacy but to the very survival of the republic. The biological paradigm was at its most compulsive within this function of government activity. It was not so much that the Presidency was the most suitable means by which the system could respond to the international environment, it was more that the forces implicit in that environment were thought to determine, and to determine absolutely, the manner by which the system could adapt to and come to terms with the stringencies of the outside world. This was not a matter of interpretation. It was not even a matter of choice. It was an imperative imposed upon the structures and processes of American government by conditions which challenged their continued viability. In this way, Presidential pre-eminence in foreign and defence policy was publicly condoned and constitutionally sanctioned as a systemic necessity that overrode the formalities and prescriptions of internal autonomy. 'Without question, the overwhelming consensus of the intellectual community in this century has accepted the legitimacy of executive dominance in foreign affairs.... Executive dominance was, until Watergate, a fact of life.'[276]

The Presidency became so closely identified with the disciplines and demands of foreign policy and national security that its own power and position came to be seen as an expression of the extent to which the republic was in jeopardy and in need of the extra-constitutional protection afforded by the life force of the executive's basic energies. If it was true, as President Nixon claimed, that the United States needed a President only for foreign policy,[277] then it was also true that the country required the sort of coherent and effective foreign policy which could only be provided by just such an agency as the Presidency. What was thought to be the inherent appropriateness of the executive in the foreign-policy field was corroborated and reinforced by what was seen as the inherent inappropriateness of Congress in the same area. 'Congress could not ignore or overturn the complicated world,' nor render it amenable to America's indigenous processes – 'nor could it be, nor should it be, a substitute for the President in foreign affairs'.[278] Given the nature of foreign policy and its critical urgency, then Congress had necessarily to defer to Presidential domination, which was based firmly upon the executive's functional utility in a policy area that placed a premium value upon central decision-making and concerted action.

What was true for foreign policy was seen as doubly so where national security and war powers were concerned. All the functional arguments and rationalizations applicable to the normal conduct of foreign policy were magnified and enriched whenever international tension threatened to deteriorate into armed conflict involving American forces. In such cases, Congress became a caricature of the functional incapacity and unsuitability of legislatures in the whole field of foreign affairs. If war represented the furthest point on a continuum of what foreign policy in general required in the way of government structures and processes, then it was to be expected that Congress's role in the conduct of the Vietnam War would be minimal. Before the imperial Presidency episode, Congress's participation in the management of the war was indeed negligible. War still remained the classic case of what the Supreme Court had once described as a state of affairs that 'the President was bound to meet in the shape it presented itself without waiting for Congress to baptize it with a name'. The President was 'bound to resist force by force [and] bound to accept the challenge without waiting for any special legislative authority'.[279] Initially, the Vietnam War proved to be no exception to this general rule. Like previous wars, it mercilessly exposed Congress's organizational weaknesses in the sphere of military policy-making within a theatre of action where the commander-in-chief retained supreme authority. Accordingly, after having issued an extraordinarily escapist authorization of Presidential war-making (i.e. the Gulf of Tonkin resolution), Congress relapsed into a state of semi-hibernation in deference first to its self-acknowledged disability to do otherwise in such an executive-oriented field, and second to the strictures of the Cold War consensus which overlaid natural legislative handicap with a blanket of conformism to executive security judgement.

Just as Congressional acquiescence had exemplified the Cold War consensus, so the disruption of that consensus occasioned by the Vietnam engagement was marked by the increased use of Congress as a centre for criticism of the war. Political forces opposed to the war found expression in the Congressional arena – mostly because they could not find effective expression inside the administration. Important elements in Congress became a sort of institutionalized opposition to the administration in that most sensitive and ostensibly un-Congressional field of foreign and military affairs. Active criticism of the war and of the commander-in-chief's conduct of the war would have been almost tantamount to un-American activities in the 1950s. In the late 1960s, however, such criticism began to be heard with increasing urgency and intensity on Capitol Hill. Congress began to threaten the Presidency's prerogative of moulding public opinion in this area. In response, President Johnson and President Nixon became more secretive and defensive, certain in the knowledge that they knew the nation's interests better than any other agency and had the means to achieve whatever objectives were deemed necessary. Both Presidents continued to maintain and to exploit the privileges and power which they had been conditioned to expect during the era of the heroic Presidency. Nevertheless, the Congress, and the Senate in particular, continued to intrude into this previously sacrosanct area. Legislative efforts to participate in military policy-making even reached the point where Congress tried to exert its influence on the tactical movement of combat troops in the battle zone. What transpired was a titanic confrontation between two branches of government in which the capability and position of the legislature in the conduct of foreign policy was closely re-examined and re-evaluated.

Fired with the theory of constitutional balance and with the renewed public interest in institutional checks, Congress began to challenge the Presidency by trying to redefine its nature and function according to strictly mechanistic principles and, in doing so, to make it more vulnerable to legislative restraint. As the remedy of first resort, Congress was increasingly seen as the political counter-force to the executive, which had reputedly deranged the constitution to produce an aberrational war. Members of Congress moved to satisfy public expectations and to salvage the esteem of an institution that had been devalued by a rampant executive in the past. In one of the most controversial challenges to Presidential authority at the time – the Senate's passage of the Cooper–Church Amendment to the Foreign Military Sales Act in 1970 – it was clear that legislators were employing explicitly mechanistic concepts to substantiate their position. As the following extracts from the debate show, Senators were motivated by a belief in the validity and effectiveness of legislative checks upon the commander-in-chief in a theatre of war:[280]

> The Senate's adoption of the Church–Cooper amendment will be a significant step toward restoring the health of our constitutional system of checks and balances.... The amendment is directed against those very activities which led to our entrapment in Vietnam. Its adoption would erect a legal barrier against further penetration of American forces into the jungles of Southeast Asia.
>
> (Sen. J. William Fulbright[281])

> Are we going to permit our Government to slide relentlessly toward all power being concentrated in the hands of one Chief Executive? Are we going to permit our Government to become a Caesardom, or are we going to reassert the authority that the Constitution placed in Congress?... This debate should be focused, not on whether this proposal ties the President's hands – it does not – but on whether it will help untie the knots by which Congress has shackled its own powers. The Cooper–Church amendment is a step in righting the imbalance in our system.
>
> (Sen. Frank Church[282])

> The genius of our system is that we have co-ordinate, co-equal branches of government, with checks and balances one upon the others and the others upon the one. The warmaking powers are vested in the legislative and the executive. A war cannot be waged except with the support of both.
>
> (Sen. Albert Gore[283])

> If a reassertion of a constitutional obligation by the Senate prevents expedient decisions by the executive branch in the future that is precisely its intent.... I believe that the cross-checks and safeguards of the constitutional processes in matters of war and peace must be accepted by the Senate if we are to retain free constitutional government in this nation.
>
> (Sen. Mike Mansfield[284])

The issue of the war in Vietnam has become so vital and significant to America in the last ten days that references to the intent of the Founding Fathers in granting Congress the power to fund and declare war have become more than patriotic sloganeering. At stake is the separation of powers upon which our experiment in democratic government is based.
(Sen. Alan Cranston[285])

The vote shall test whether the checks and balances of our governmental system are to remain asleep or whether they shall be revived to double-check and oversee and, if necessary, refrain the President from committing our Nation to a war of any scope, against any adversary and for any duration.
(Sen. Joseph Tydings[286])

The Constitution tells us that the power to declare war and to appropriate funds for the waging of war is reserved to Congress. The Constitution also provides that the President ... has the power to respond quickly to an immediate threat to ensure national safety or the safety of our troops. The two principles are not inconsistent; the Constitution dictates that they be balanced. But a proper balance will result only if both Congress and the President are aware of their separate responsibilities and are prepared to act to fulfil them.... Today I am sorry to state that the balance has tipped heavily to one side. This tipping is not solely the fault of the present President. It is a process that has been going on for years.... It is fitting that we begin the process of reasserting our responsibilities by addressing the most recent example of executive arrogation ... ; namely the venture in Cambodia.... The President's unilateral decision must be balanced, and balanced immediately by a firm and clear expression of the will of Congress.
(Sen. Stuart Symington[287])

What needs to be defined is how the Congress is to exercise its policymaking power with respect to war.... This is a power granted to the Congress under the system of checks and balances in the Constitution.... In the current debate we are writing a legislative record which history may deem as second in importance only to the deliberations of the Constitutional Convention itself.... The Constitution divides and balances power. It deliberately tries to keep the power to get the Nation into war in the hands of Congress, and away from the arbitrary exercise of Executive power.
(Sen. Jacob Javits[288])

Although the Cooper–Church amendment was passed by the Senate and was subsequently hailed as a classic piece of legislative insurgency, the measure was probably more notable for the way it revealed many of the inherent, and arguably insuperable, problems that Congress faced in trying to become an active partner in foreign and military policy-making. It is true that the Senate had in effect censured President Nixon for his invasion of Cambodia. It is also true that it marked the first occasion in American history when the Senate had restricted the expenditure of funds for a specific military purpose while the nation was engaged in war. The amendment's supporters had prevailed over the objections of the President's supporters, who had warned that the Senate's attempt to 'advise and consent on operational decisions'[289] would send negative or conflicting signals of American intentions, offer aid and comfort to the enemy, and represent the 'greatest resurgence of classic isolationism ... seen in this country for nearly half a century'.[290] Despite the appearance of a triumph, however, the amendment was not the Congressional success it appeared to be. The measure had not only been watered down by concessions and provisos to the point where the Nixon administration claimed it faithfully represented the President's own position, but had been filibustered for so long on the floor of the Senate by the administration's supporters that American troops were already departing from Cambodia when the amendment finally gained Senate approval. The amendment faced many other additional problems.[291] For example, the House of Representatives rejected it and effectively nullified its content.[292] But the measure would not have been secure even if it had been passed by both Houses. The President might well have vetoed the entire Foreign Military Sales Act and then relied upon a third of the Congress to sustain the veto. And even if the amendment had survived all this pressure, the administration might well have either financed the continuation of the venture by various Pentagon contingency funds, or created a public reaction against the law by keeping the troops in the field without pay or proper provisions. It might be said that, in the very act of attempting to restrict the Presidency's control of a battlefield military decision, the Congress had run the risk of making a bad situation worse in that it revealed the extent to which a President could deflect, circumvent, or elude statutory control, while, at the same time, benefiting from the vagaries of legislative draftsmanship which could unwittingly afford the executive a renewed affirmation of his authority.[293]

The Cooper–Church amendment, in effect, revealed less of Congress's strength and more of its difficulties in controlling an executive in the full flow of its discretionary prerogatives in the field of foreign and military policy. The same problems arose and the same arguments were expounded on many other occasions when the Congress had attempted to raise itself from a sleeping partner in foreign policy to the position of a senior consultant – and even to that of an active policy-maker. While members of Congress, lawyers, and academics engaged in exhaustive studies of the respective constitutional roles of the Congress and the Presidency as sanctioned by the Founding Fathers, the President stood as the living contradiction of such legal fundamentalism and strove to protect what history, precedent, and evolution had established to be the necessary power of the Presidency. The Congressional spirit to check the executive and to rebalance the constitution may well have been present, but in practice it was constantly confronted by the difficulty of making military decisions susceptible to legislative influence and by President Nixon's implacable opposition to being placed on Congress's Procrustean bed of checks and balances. Congress was encumbered by the slow process of devising legal resolutions and abstract formulas while still having to leave room for the President to exercise executive discretion, in order to ensure the safety and protection of troops in the field, and to preserve and maximize any tactical military advantages open to American forces. This left Congress with the function either of critical retrospection or of legalistic prescription, both of which were of questionable utility in wartime when the President, as commander-in-chief, had the capacity to alter conditions and to control information that could render legislative decisions not only ill informed but totally irrelevant.

Congress's attempted incursions into the executive's previously exclusive preserve of military policy exposed the variegated nature of Presidential authority and the dexterity with which an incumbent could exploit it. Executive adroitness in avoiding legislative checks was perhaps most conspicuous during the Congressional campaign to legislate an end to America's military engagement in Indochina. For example, when Congress repealed the Gulf of Tonkin resolution in 1970 in an attempt to qualify the President's authority in the management of the war, it had little or no effect on the administration's position. Although the resolution had been used explicitly by his predecessor as authorizing a combat commitment to South Vietnam and had been employed by President Nixon himself as a basis to the continued American presence in the area, the Nixon administration declared that its repeal would not alter the position at all.[294] According to the White House, the Gulf of Tonkin resolution was significant only in building up American forces – not in scaling them down, which was the official Nixon policy position. The basis of the President's authority, therefore, had melted away from the readily accessible Tonkin measure to the far more ambiguous and elusive legitimacy derived from the executive's prerogative as commander-in-chief, which included the general obligation to protect and defend American forces. Congress discovered that while it could authorize an initial American commitment, it could not terminate it by a simple cancellation of the original mandate. As commander-in-chief the President was constitutionally responsible for creating the safest conditions in which to carry out a planned troop withdrawal. The nature of these conditions was defined, of course, by the commander-in-chief, who reasoned that he could even extend the scope of the war in order to facilitate a phased reduction of military support.

Similar difficulties arose in March 1973 when the administration resumed the heavy bombing of Cambodia.[295] This highly controversial action was ordered two months after the Paris Peace accord had formally ended the involvement of American ground forces in Indochina. The administration regarded the operation as simply a continuation of its established strategy of aerial offensives against Vietcong supply routes and sanctuaries within Cambodia and against the Khmer Rouge forces, which were threatening the Lon Nol regime in Phnom Penh. Cambodia remained the conspicuous exception to the general condition of a cease-fire in the area and, as such, was regarded as a dangerously destabilizing force that could threaten the Vietnamese peace agreement and the United States' disengagement from South East Asia. What may have seemed to the administration like a consistent posture of support for the non-communist government in Cambodia was denounced in Congress as another example of the arrogance of executive power. Reflecting the public disquiet and frustration in the country at large, Congress attacked the saturation bombing of Cambodia on three main fronts. First, it regarded the action as a rash and provocatively foolhardy resumption of a war from which the United States had taken eight years to extricate itself. The risk of even further American casualties or the capture of US aircrew by communist forces would reopen the entire question of prisoners-of-war once again and threaten to embroil American forces in another open-ended commitment to defend part of South East Asia from communist guerilla forces. Second, the administration had been financing the aerial war over Cambodia by discreetly transferring funds from other allocations in the Pentagon budget.[296] This accounting device of reprogramming normally requires the prior approval of the House and Senate Appropriations Committees, but in this case the Nixon administration had offended Congressional protocol by bombing first and requesting permission later. This was regarded as not only discourteous but grossly provocative, as it had occurred in relation to such a controversial issue and at a time when Congressional attitudes towards executive power were already at their most sensitive. Third, Congress challenged the President's authority in ordering such an action. President Nixon could no longer claim that, as commander-in-chief, he was protecting American troops, because all the combat forces had departed. Furthermore, Congress had assumed that the repeal of the Gulf of Tonkin resolution would at the very least have made it impossible for a President to renew America's commitment to the area without explicit legislative authorization. Congress had made it known to the White House since 1971 that it urged an end to the war at the earliest possible date,[297] but the Nixon administration seemed oblivious to Congress's assertions and pleas. Although Cambodia had disclaimed any protection from the United States under the South East Asia Treaty Organization, had not received any American combat forces since 1970, and had clearly been recognized by Congress as a country whose American aid could not be 'construed as a commitment by the United States ... for its defense',[298] it was, nevertheless, termed an 'ally' by the administration and treated as such to the point of an American offensive to save its government. Congress railed against the substance of the policy, the technical means used to support it, and the authority by which the policy was made.

Matters came to a head in March 1973 during the consideration of a Supplemental Appropriations Bill for the Defense Department. This measure contained a request to transfer $750 million from one category to another

The separation of paradigms

with the understanding that the Cambodian bombing campaign might be dependent upon the approval of the transfer.[299] This was the second time that the administration had been guilty of 'credit bombing' and on this occasion the Congress was opposed to allowing any transfer for the purposes of conducting what was regarded as an unauthorized war. The administration's basis of authority for the bombing had now switched to Article 20 of the Paris peace agreement, which referred to the obligation of foreign countries to end all military activities in Cambodia and Laos.[300] Since the administration interpreted this as the equivalent of a cease-fire condition, the Khmer Rouge's continuation of the civil war with the Lon Nol government prompted the United States to try and impose a cease-fire from the air. It was highly debatable whether Article 20 represented any such thing, especially since the Cambodians and Laotians had not been signatories to the Paris agreement. It seemed even more contentious for the President to assume the power to enforce his view of Article 20, as there had been no enforcement measures considered or included in that part of the agreement. Certainly no unilateral enforcement powers had been accepted by the signatories as far as the peace accord in general was concerned. Members of Congress strongly objected to what was seen as war-making on credit by the President's distorted reading of an agreement which was not a treaty and which had never been formally presented to the Senate. Once again, the Congress denied the President the authority to bomb Cambodia whilst squadrons of B52s and F111s pounded the Cambodian countryside. Nixon's strategy became more accessible to legislative influence only when through lack of funds he was forced to approach Congress for new transfer authority. But even on such occasions as these, when the President seemed more like a supplicant, the White House still seemed to possess several inherent advantages which could make Congress a subordinate partner. The Secretary of Defense, Eliot Richardson, announced that the administration requested additional funds for the Cambodian operation but that if such funds were rejected then the government would continue the bombing by using funds appropriated in other parts of the budget. To add a further twist to the conundrum, the administration made it known that should Congress approve the transfer of funds, this would be cited as legal sanction for the United States' operations in Cambodia. Richardson was quoted in the *Washington Post* as saying, 'If an amendment were offered to specifically restrict the use of any of those funds for air support in Cambodia and it was defeated ... we would be justified in regarding that vote to at least acquiesce in that activity.'[301] The only way Congress could have any effect whatsoever was to cut off all funds absolutely, including funds from every other source of prior appropriations. This was indeed what Congress did through the Eagleton amendment, which provided that none of the funds appropriated in the Act 'or heretofore appropriated under any other act may be expended to support directly or indirectly combat activities in, over or from off the shores of Cambodia or in or over Laos by United States forces'.[302] Yet even this unambiguous declaration of legislative intent was thwarted by the executive, for although the amended Bill was passed by Congress, it was subsequently vetoed by President Nixon. A large majority of the House of Representatives opposed the veto, but the administration's opponents failed to reach the necessary two-thirds majority to overturn it. The veto was, therefore, sustained and the policy endorsed.

It is true that the Congress managed eventually to impose its will upon an administration whose resistance had become drastically weakened by the Watergate crisis. But even against a gravely depleted Presidency, the Congress's deletion of funds for Cambodian air operations was notable for its accommodation of the administration's position to the extent of fitting the cut-off into a timetable acceptable to the President. The Cambodian episode, which was portrayed as a stunning example of Congressional assertiveness and a vindication of the checks and balances system, was in reality an illustration of the problems endemic to Congress's attempts to participate seriously and effectively in foreign policy-making. It not only revealed the stark fact that the 'secret air war' represented a gross failure of oversight on the part of Congress, but once the operation had become a matter of grave public concern the Congress found itself tied up in procedural and constitutional knots to such an extent that, ultimately, the only way it could effectively exert any influence at all was to resort to the blunt instrument of a total financial ban. This was a crudely effective device, but it was also one born out of Congress's intense frustration over its previous ineffectiveness in gaining entry to the subtle and discreet world of foreign policy. In many ways the cutting off of funds could be seen as a mark of Congress's inherent inability to integrate itself into the culture of diplomacy and international relations sufficiently well to act as a genuine check upon the executive. Instead of dispelling doubts, the legislative history of the Cambodian air strikes actually served to deepen them. The issue raised more questions than it answered concerning the role of a legislature in such an area. In this respect, the Cambodian controversy was no different from the Cooper–Church amendment or the repeal of the Gulf of Tonkin resolution. Amidst the rhetoric of checks and balances and the declared faith in constitutional mechanics, Congress found itself plagued with restraints, inhibitions, and disabilities. Congress may have been effective as a general barometer of public attitudes and political tolerance, but as an authentic challenger for the control of foreign policy appearance served to belie the reality of an institution often out of its environment and out of its depth. Despite the imagery of a decisively assertive Congress defeating the Nixon administration on the Cambodian bombing strategy, a case history of the record reveals that Congress for the most part found even a mortally wounded President almost impossible to cope with where foreign and military policy was concerned. Appearances notwithstanding, the legislature's incursions into the international arena raised profound doubts as to what a Congressional check consisted of; whether such a check was feasible; and, if it was, whether or not it was controllable in its effects. It was a measure of the doctrinal fundamentalism of the period, however, that the empirical misgivings were barely acknowledged, let alone seriously considered. At the very time when Congress's record as a check upon the executive in the past together with its potential as a restraint upon the Presidency in the future might justifiably have been subjected to more scrutiny and scepticism than ever before, the legislature continued to be identified as the self-evident counter-balance to executive power.

The same instinctive trust in balanced government and in the feasibility and necessity of Congress restoring an equilibrium lost to executive power was also apparent in the controversy over the Central Intelligence Agency, which arose in the aftermath of the Watergate crisis. In this case the issue centred upon the even more nebulous and elusive executive attribute of secrecy. A secret organization secretly engaged in secret work raised a host of logical and operational problems in subjecting it to control. There appeared to be something in the very essence of a secret service that rendered it, by definition, inconsistent with the normal standards and procedures of democratic supervision. To many both inside and outside the intelligence community, the CIA, by the nature of the function it was expected to perform, was simply not amenable to the customary norms of democratic control and direction – especially if these principles were regarded as being confined solely to formal institutional arrangements of open scrutiny. Problems like these were further compounded by the fact that the CIA was formally under Presidential direction and represented one of the fullest expressions of his obligation to preserve, protect, and defend both the security and the interests of the United States. The existence of such an organization seemed to bear witness to the critical threat facing America and its Western allies, and to the need to resort to extraordinary, and even extra-constitutional, means to meet it. Whether it was possible to impose democratic standards of control and accountability on the CIA, therefore, became bound up with whether it was consistent with the national good even to attempt to do so. The feasibility of control became obscured by the Cold War consensus that resolved all such problems in favour of allowing the CIA to evade external constraints and for the American public to place their trust in the self-restraint of honourable men. Reflecting the biological paradigm that was predominant at the time, the CIA was seen as analogous to a small but invaluable antibody instinctively responding to anything from the 'brutal world'[303] outside that threatened the health and survival of the American system at large.

By the mid 1970s, however, perceptions had changed, and from being a heroic adjunct of national destiny and American purpose the CIA was derided as the 'action arm of the imperial Presidency'.[304] Instead of being a necessary means by which to respond to the world and its complex and dangerous pressures, the agency was seen as 'Frankenstein's monster'.[305] It stood accused of large-scale surveillance of US citizens, unauthorized domestic intelligence-gathering, drug experimentation, intelligence operations against political dissidents, wire-tapping, break-ins, mail opening, clandestine military engagements abroad, destabilizing foreign governments, and, most controversially of all, attempting to assassinate or being implicated in the assassination of foreign political leaders.[306] In the 1950s such matters might well have been viewed fatalistically as examples of 'the ways of the world'. But such equanimity was absent in the 1970s. The CIA's activities were seen as being motivated more by considerations of executive power at home than by the power of the country's adversaries – more on behalf of the Presidency's interests than the long-term interests of the United States. The agency's behaviour was seen as the inevitable consequence of an excessive concentration of power within the government. It was not that the CIA had simply been found guilty of excessive and unacceptable exertions of power, it was that as an instrument of the executive the agency stood revealed as symptomatic of 'the larger problem of the modern Presidency, of the dramatic accretion and distortion of Presidential power'. It was misguided to expect the President to control the CIA, as 'it was his own means of escaping control, ... of making policy in total secrecy',[307] of evading constitutional processes, and of promoting policies by clandestine methods in the name of national security.

It was a measure of the extent to which the American political mind had returned to the concepts of balanced government that the CIA, of all agencies, was expected to be accommodated within the traditional structure of mechanical cause and effect. The CIA was probably the body that most nearly conformed to the notion of a government function and organization idiosyncratically and exclusively executive in nature. It seemed to have evolved from the demands placed upon it and to have become an incomparably specialized and legitimately privileged unit. Its very immunity from the customary format of American government seemed to confirm the presence of conditions requiring the agency's existence and position. It was, in effect, the most mysterious component of the modern Presidency's mystique. And yet, once President Nixon had 'undermined the consensus of trust in Washington which was a truer source of the agency's strength than its legal charter',[308] and once the revelations of the CIA's activities had been made, then the agency's special status was quickly dispelled. Along with the evaporation of the Presidency's own mystique came that of the CIA's. The agency itself began to be seen as a subversive threat to American society and government. As a consequence, the CIA became reclassified for the purposes of public analysis and evaluation as simply another part of the executive branch. The familiar 'structural theorem' of the Founding Fathers took over and the CIA, which for a generation had been regarded as so totally ill fitted to the framework of checks and balances that it transcended it altogether, was suddenly projected into the world of tangibly distributed powers and measurable allocations of force. The one centre of government which had depended most upon the public trust showed that such trust was as misplaced as Jefferson and Madison had always warned that it would be. Even a former director of the agency admitted that the CIA 'got a bit overextended in the past in terms of covert action'.[309] Once again, abuses of power had been shown to come from excessive concentrations of power. According to one experienced observer, 'such abuses were the inevitable consequence of great power, essentially unchecked, cloaked in the mystique of national security and authorised to operate in secrecy'.[310] This being so, the cause of the abuses was attributable less to those directly involved and more to those responsible for the breakdown of the mechanism designed to offset the opportunities for abuse that come from a malapportionment of power. The solace of a known cause was provided by Congress.

According to the tenets of checks and balances, Congress was identified as the reason for the initial imbalance and for its subsequent perpetuation. Attention was drawn to the Act of Congress which had originally established the agency's organization and powers. While it would seem that the Congress had intended the CIA to be exclusively concerned with intelligence, the National Security Act of 1947 was notable for the flexibility built into the agency's charter. Congress later came under heavy criticism for Section 102 in particular, which afforded the agency great potential to evade statutory control and to resort to activities outside its remit of intelligence-gathering and co-ordination. By authorizing the agency to 'perform such other functions and duties related to intelligence affecting the national security as the National Security Council may from time to time direct',[311] this section was thought to have prompted the CIA's capacity for covert military operations and clandestine political destabilization. Additional proof of Congressional culpability for what later transpired was provided by the Central Intelligence Agency Act of 1949, which further removed the agency from the normal processes of the constitution. This Act formally endowed the CIA with the privilege of a secret budget, which exempted the agency from statutory spending limitations, waived the customary constitutional requirement to disclose details of its organization, functions, and personnel, and allowed its funds to be concealed in other agencies' accounts and for them to be transferred secretly by private arrangements between the agency, the Office of Management and Budget, and the chairmen of the House and Senate Appropriations Committees.[312] This arrangement made it 'unnecessary for the CIA to defend, or even present, a budget to Congress' and in so doing gave the legislature 'no basis whatever for reviewing the policy, or judging the performance, of the Agency'.[313] As a result, the CIA was left 'largely unsupervised,[314] by Congress. Although Congress maintained four intelligence sub-committees'[315] their record in monitoring and overseeing the activities of the agency was so minimal that it amounted to the legislature being co-opted by the agency. William Colby, Director of the CIA from 1973 to 1976, describes the relationship in the following terms:

> The traditional concept was that intelligence was the sole business of the President, a business to be conducted in total secrecy, a business, moreover,

with which Congress shouldn't concern itself.... The President and his CIA chief could not only get away with stonewalling the Congress, they were in a sense obliged to – and could count on the leaders of Congress to support them.[316]

It was not just that the members involved suffered from a lack of information and staff resources; it was that the Cold War consensus suffused the whole relationship between the Congress and the agency with a lack of motivation to engage in criticism or investigation. There were no political benefits to be derived from subjecting the agency to publicized review. Moreover, there was very little interest amongst members in becoming embroiled in the discreet and unsung obligations of keeping a tight private rein on the agency through painstaking oversight. As a result, Congressional supervision assumed the reputation of being 'non-existent'.[317] It fell between the two stools of a lack of information and interest on the part of the general membership, and a 'rejection of responsibility on the part of the Congressional monitors'[318] who had access to information but who were either unprepared to use the information available against the agency, or loath even to request the provision of information owed to them. It was with this record of Congressional control in mind that the Rockefeller Commission, in its 300 page *Report on CIA Activities*, felt able to dismiss its review of the legislature's oversight of the agency since 1947 in five lines. It dryly acknowledged that the four intelligence subcommittees had historically been 'composed of members of Congress with many other demands on their time'. It concluded that the CIA had 'not as a general rule received detailed scrutiny by the Congress'.[319]

In spite of a general acceptance that Congress had, in the past, 'failed for two decades to exercise its constitutional obligation to oversee the activities of the intelligence agencies',[320] this did not inhibit the recognition of Congress as the remedy to the most controversial of those agencies. Sometimes the call was for Congress to use its ultimate power and to achieve a 'total solution' by eliminating the CIA altogether and taking its considerable weight completely out of the scales of balanced government.[321] More often the calls were for Congress to exert its potential weight in the area, in order to provide a check to the agency that would ensure proper behaviour by dissipating its power. Even though Congress's oversight record had been so poor in the past, and even though the logical and operational problems involved in subjecting such an organization and function to legislative scrutiny were prodigious – if not insuperable – nevertheless, the underlying premise of the CIA being checked by Congress was never seriously challenged. The norm of an attainable balance between the CIA and the Congress remained the basis to most of the proposed solutions to the CIA. It is true that new mechanisms of internal executive control, improved freedom of information, and a greater public awareness of the agency's activities were recognized as important potential restraints. But the general thrust of the various responses to the problem conformed remarkably closely to the conventional framework of constitutional prescription. Instinctively, the solution to the CIA was seen as that of a check and, just as instinctively, the source of that check was identified as Congress. The enthusiasm for such a solution may well have varied a good deal but, despite the attendant reservations, the general orientation towards Congress as the only available long-term answer to the problem remained unmistakably clear. The sheer availability of Congress, together with the orthodox doctrine of checks and balances, served to simplify the issues and to arouse faith in the system's capacity to respond to the problem and to resolve it on the constitution's own terms as a matter of course. This attitude was evident even amongst those who were most aware of the scale and complexity of the CIA's challenge to American government. Journalists, academics, and members of Congress, who possessed first-hand knowledge of the CIA and the ways by which it had so adroitly eluded accountability in the past, would nevertheless often conclude their appraisals by calling upon the doctrinal purity of checks and balances to relieve the pessimism and fatalism that normally shrouded the issue of the CIA's secretive power:

> Intelligence agencies do need privacy, but our system requires that they be ultimately accountable to a detached scrutineer, which is Congress.... The safety of liberty in this country rests on respect for the separation of powers – on Congress as a balance to the growth of Presidential power.
> (Anthony Lewis[322])

> The more important necessity, without which oversight is likely to be futile, is for Congress to rewrite and sharply restrict the missions of the security agencies to clearly defined activities.
> (Tom Wicker[323])

> It is clear that the existing system of controls over the intelligence agencies in the United States is inadequate. It is also clear that measures to correct the situation must take the form of legislation.
> (Thomas Emerson[324])

> The question of secrecy and the right of Congress to deal with classified information are basically questions that must be resolved if we are to preserve our constitutional form of government. That establishes the Congress as a separate but equal and independent branch.
> (Sen. Frank Church[325])

> Existing laws have repeatedly been broken.... CIA covert operations from rigging elections abroad to overthrowing governments and instituting political assassinations should be specifically barred by law in peacetime.
> (David Wise[326])

> The first need then is to have Congress maintain an oversight system with responsible Congressional leaders who can be consulted on very sensitive

information ... without running the risk of surfacing the information, the source, or the means by which the intelligence was provided.

(Ray Cline[327])

The Congress ... has the constitutional power and, indeed, the responsibility to monitor the CIA.... If there is to be any real, meaningful change in the intelligence community, it must come from Congress ... Congress should take action to limit the agency to the role originally set out for it.

(Victor Marchetti and John D. Marks[328])

Intelligence [knowledge] is power, and since power corrupts, it must be counterbalanced. And that is the role of Congress.

(Harry H. Ransom[329])

These opinions are illustrative of the reliance placed upon the assumed mechanics of the constitution, not merely in suggesting an answer to the problem, but in assuring its provision. Adherence to constitutional dogma dictated the solution. Whether it was a case of responsibility being placed upon Congress by outside parties or of Congress actively assuming responsibility itself, the result was the same. Congress was thought of as being the natural and self-evident counter-force to the executive – not in spite of its past failures but because of them. Just as the imbalance had been due to Congress relinquishing power to the Presidency, so a restoration of balance had to be possible through the simple device of Congress asserting itself as a legislature.[330] The prospect of such an attainable and lucid solution automatically made Congress the remedy of first resort.

The fourth way in which the 'imperial Presidency' crisis served to highlight the mechanistic assumptions that lay beneath American politics was the manner in which balanced government was used as a rationalization of positions, events, and decisions. Whereas the third point alluded to balanced government in the prescriptive sense of a plausible, appropriate, and necessary solution, this point refers to the concept of checks and balances in the guise of a solution having already been accomplished. Just as there was a willingness to regard checks and balances as the remedy of first resort, irrespective of the logical and practical problems involved, so, in like manner, was there a tendency to assume that a solution to unbalanced government had been achieved by the mere presence of forces activated against the Presidency. In other words, there was an accentuated willingness to accept the appearance of a solution as being real because of its approximation to a mechanical response to a mechanical problem. From a mechanical perspective, it is certainly true that the irrefutable precondition of a restored balance is the introduction of an additional material force exerted against whichever body possesses the excessive weight. When such mechanical principles are applied to the interaction between political institutions, however, much of their clarity and precision is lost. Even if the problem within government is accepted as that of an imbalance and that the remedy is, thereby, a restored balance, it is difficult to distinguish between appearance and substance; between the mere existence of a potential counterweight and its actual capability as a checking force; between the exertion of force upon Presidential power and a forceful restraint of such power; and between the devices created to produce balance and the degree to which balance is actually achieved or not. These are fine but profound distinctions. Such was the mechanistic fervour of the reactions to Presidential power that the prodigious empirical and conceptual complexities associated with balanced government were overlooked. The apparent simplicity and accessibility of a mechanical solution were sufficient to distract attention from the problematic, and even unfathomable, nature of a balance in this context.

This presumption of a Congressional counterbalance to executive power was evident, for example, in the passage of the War Powers Resolution in 1973. The legislation was presented and considered as an attempt by Congress to regain its lost authority in military policy-making. And once the resolution had passed into law, it was immediately hailed as a reversal of Presidential power and, thereupon, acknowledged to be a genuine expression of balanced government. 'Dynamic tension', 'division of powers', and 'constitutional checks' were the types of terms used to rationalize and to acclaim the legislation.[331] It was denounced by the White House as unconstitutional for precisely the same reasons. It was seen as a serious assault upon the chief executive by relocating power within the system in such a way as to divest him of 'authorities which the President had properly exercised under the constitution for almost two hundred years'.[332] And yet, despite these declarations of a fundamental redistribution of power by the resolution's supporters and opponents alike, the war powers legislation can be seen as being by no means the solution to Presidential aggrandisement that it has often been reputed to be. For example, the resolution has never been formally accepted by any President as binding upon the office; it has never been invoked in practice during hostilities; it fails to define the President's emergency powers, which could be used to circumvent the resolution's provisions; and it employs a legislative veto through a concurrent resolution which can always be challenged as unconstitutional. Furthermore, it is said to have failed in its objective by actually surrendering Congressional authority over declaring war through passing the power to initiate hostilities to the Presidency for a period of sixty days.[333] During that time the President could not only determine the basic nature of the military engagement, but also establish sufficient public support for his position to make any Congressional veto politically improbable. Far from exerting its power to the full by formally prescribing its own participation in any initial decision to engage in hostilities, Congress drew back to a position where its members had the 'option to exercise power, but ... would not force them to do so if that exercise might prove costly in political terms'.[334]

The same intuitive assumption of a rebalance was even evident with the case of the CIA. The agency had stood revealed as having exceeded its powers, abused its authority, and exploited its secretive organization to avoid control and escape accountability for its actions. Because of the nature of its function and its power, the CIA posed prodigious problems to all those who wished to see it subjected to a form of public control. Not the least of these were the practical difficulties of acquiring information on and about an agency that was inherently secretive in nature; the extent to which it was possible to know what 'control' consisted of in this context and when it had been achieved; and whether such 'control' might or might not be self-defeating in so far as it could lead to the CIA becoming either even more secretive than before, or dangerously compromised as an intelligence agency. Confronted by such problems, it was possible to remain sceptical about the feasibility of the CIA ever being adequately supervised. Garry Wills, for example, believed that control over the CIA would always be illusory, as the agency was 'born on principle, out of control ... [and] formed expressly to escape accountability'.[335] Conventional opinion, however, rallied to the ethos of checks and balances. Prompted by revelations of the CIA's past activities by two Congressional committees,[336] attention and faith lodged with the legislature and its ability to accommodate this most modernistic of governmental instruments to the traditional structure of constitutional balance. Even William Colby, who was the Director of the CIA at the time, had no doubt that the agency could and should be made 'an integral part of our democratic process, subject to our system of checks and balances'[337] by 'Congressional consultation and responsibility in American decisions about intelligence operations called for by the constitution'.[338] Congress certainly responded to the public's call for supervision with new committees, new procedures, new restrictions, and a new awareness of the CIA as a Congressional responsibility. These legislative endeavours were subsequently acknowledged as having constituted a direct check to the offending agency and, by doing so, had inaugurated a beneficial state of balance between it and the Congress. The legislative action, regarded in principle as being the necessary prerequisite of resolving the problem, was widely perceived to have occurred and, as such, to have been sufficient to transform the relative weightings of the CIA and the Congress. As one study concluded, 'no more dramatic example of the new Congressional assertiveness with respect to foreign policy was to be found than in the *changed relationship* between Congress and the intelligence community'.[339]

Despite such assertions, it was by no means clear whether Congress's exertions in this area did constitute a real check to the CIA.[340] The availability and reliability of evidence supporting such a contention must always remain questionable. It is extremely difficult to determine, in such an elusive and nebulous field as this, whether Congress has really managed to supervise the CIA. Much depends on how one defines Congress. The need for security within specialist committees, for example, might lead to its members being better informed and having a greater role in intelligence decision-making, but it might also

The separation of paradigms

make them captives of their own discretion and separate from Congress by the need to keep secret what they have been informed about. Much will also depend on whether legislative restrictions upon an agency like the CIA are used and assessed as positive devices for monitoring and supervision, or as instruments of an assault by a Congress intent upon rendering the agency susceptible to checks and balances and, thereupon, to a redistribution of power. These distinctions remain a matter of conjecture. What cannot be doubted was the inflated belief that Congress had immediately and almost effortlessly 'tamed the intelligence community'[341] once it had chosen to exercise its legislative prerogatives. It is true that Congress statutorily required the agency to keep the legislature informed on even its most sensitive activities. It is also true that the personnel and resources assigned to the CIA's most controversial sector of covert operations were sharply reduced by Congress. It is doubtful that such measures as these were sufficient to have been responsible for what was later seen as the disabling of the CIA. Nevertheless, following the logic of checks and balances, Congress's mere activity in this sensitive field quickly became translated into a substantive cause of such intelligence failures as the Soviet invasion of Afghanistan (1979) and the Iranian revolution (1979). By the late 1970s Congress was being blamed for much of the disarray in American foreign policy. So pronounced was the belief in the reality of checks and balances that the decline which the United States experienced in the world at that time was widely attributed to Congress having gone too far and having been too effective in restricting the CIA. By the 1980s the presumption of an excessive Congressional counterbalance was so well established that it led to the introduction of several proposals designed to relax many of those limitations on the CIA which the Congress had only recently invoked.[342]

Once the problem of the Presidency and executive power became defined as one of an imbalance, the issue immediately lent itself to the prospect of a clear and accessible solution in the form of a restored equilibrium. In reality, this solution was far from being precise or even comprehensible. Its complexity, however, was largely ignored in the general rush to depict Presidential power as being susceptible to a material reduction through the imposition of checks and balances. The appeal of the concept of equilibrium was so prevalent at the time that even President Nixon was forced to defend himself in terms of preserving the existing constitutional balance. During the 'imperial Presidency' crisis, Congress made strenuous efforts to render the Presidency containable by shifting the conventional perspective of the chief executive from an organic, mutable, and adaptive entity with certain intrinsic and unpredictable properties to a composite of known material quantities capable of being countered by comparable units of force. President Nixon, in particular, resisted this attempted shift in the conception of his office. He was keenly aware of the need to preserve the Presidency's idiosyncratic qualities and privileges, which had developed in response to the republic's history. This attitude was, of course, not unaffected by personal self-interest. Nevertheless, it should be stressed that in protecting himself President Nixon resorted to those very arguments and assertions that his predecessors had habitually employed in defending the Presidency from previous attacks by the corrosive agents of constitutional reductionism. While the interests of the Presidency determined that the White House would wish to emphasize the specialist qualities of the separation of powers, so Congressional interests ensured that Capitol Hill would acknowledge the pre-eminence of checks and balances.[343] It always seemed that the Nixon Presidency was better able to withstand Congressional assault by standing upon the special status afforded to it by the separation of powers framework, in which the executive was recognized as being necessarily different from the legislature. It was a sign of President Nixon's increasingly precarious position, therefore, when he began to defend the office less from a perspective of a historical bequest held in trust for future generations and more on the grounds of maintaining an existing balance. For example, in his letter responding to the House Judiciary Committee's subpoenas for Presidential tape-recordings and documents, President Nixon concluded his case by stating his determination 'to do nothing which, by the precedents it set, would render the Executive branch henceforth and for evermore subservient to the Legislative branch, and would thereby destroy the Constitutional balance'.[344]

Bearing in mind the success that Congress had in securing public acceptance of its assertion of an imbalance within government, President Nixon's defence was doomed almost from the start. By subscribing to Congress's own terms of reference the President automatically became more vulnerable to attack. Implicit in the President's own admission that balance was the key issue lay the premise that the Presidency's nature was reducible to physical properties and mechanical terms. Being forced to confront the crisis in the terms adopted by his adversaries, the President's defence served only to underline the pervasive attraction of the mechanical paradigm at the time. Such was the intensity of the belief in the value and feasibility of checks and balances that the principle of countervailing power not only suggested the manner by which the crisis could be resolved but, in many ways, seemed to predetermine the acquisition of that very solution. By becoming the predominant criterion of popular constitutional argument and political analysis at the time, the concept of balance instilled an expectation of an achieved equilibrium once the decisions had been made and the measures had been taken to obtain one. A spirit of self-fulfilling prophecy suffused Congress's assertiveness against the Presidency. Once the forces had been released and the dynamics had been operationalized, the consequences of redistributed power and revised relationships seemed to be taken as read. Even in the field of foreign policy, where the Presidency's position had previously been unassailable and where Congressional subordination had seemed a reflection of an inborn deficiency, dogmatic mechanics replaced experience, custom, and even realism. Congress's incursions into this almost alien area were zealously hailed as a turning of the tide and a reversal of history occasioned by a swing of the balance back to the Congress. After a generation of ingrained and intuitively accepted executive predominance, the renewed cult of constitutional mechanics prompted the impetuous conclusion that the United States had embarked 'clearly upon a period of Congressional ascendancy'[345] – 'reversing at least three-quarters of a century'[346] of legislative–executive relations. Congress had 'reaffirmed and reinforced its authority to take command of foreign policy'[347] to such an extent that it constituted a 'Congressional revolution', producing an 'exponential growth in foreign policy by legislation and a commensurate shrinkage in unfettered Presidential discretion to conduct foreign policy'.[348] There could be no more explicit testament to the American faith in the reality of checks and balances.

The fifth and final point concerning the 'imperial Presidency' issue and the nature of the response to it relates to the belief in the existence of a dynamic and autonomous equilibrium underlying the relationship between the President and the Congress. It was one thing to claim that 'some rebalancing was needed',[349] or that 'the balance between the executive and the legislative branches had to be restored',[350] or even that it had been successfully regained and the 'trend of a hundred years ... dramatically reversed'.[351] It was quite another to treat the revival of Congress's position as a direct material consequence of a historically and constitutionally generated balance wheel that revealed itself through 'alternating periods of executive and legislative hegemony'.[352] The notion of a dynamic balance between the Presidency and the Congress is a well established one in American politics. Sometimes it is referred to as 'a shifting balance of power',[353] in which the imagery is that of a 'ceaseless seesaw of powers'.[354] Sometimes it is seen as a historical cycle in which one branch's acquisition of power prompts the other in time to develop its institutional resources to a point where it can retrieve its previous pre-eminence. According to Lawrence Dodd, for example, 'the inherent tension between personal power and institutional power in the twentieth century Congress generates an explosive dynamic ... between Congress and the President ... which is cyclical in nature, and follows a relatively clear long term pattern'.[355] On other occasions, the relationship between the executive and legislative branches is seen as being governed by 'the law of ebb and flow'.[356] Most commonly, the balance between the President and the Congress is conceived of as a pendulum. 'This oscillation [is seen as having] characterised Presidential–Congressional relations through American history',[357] in which the 'pattern has been one of rivalry and pendulum swings of popularity from one branch to another'.[358] The pendulum is not only the most mechanically regular and predictable of images; it is the most deterministic, as the alternating periods of Presidential and Congressional dominance are interpreted as being derived from the mechanical properties of a swinging balance and not from any human and institutional agency. These varied conceptions of a balance have long been a traditional feature of American constitutional thought. Although they had become largely submerged during the Cold War era of executive ascendancy, the imperial Presidency crisis suddenly revealed the depth of both the public's regard for the principle of balanced government and its belief in the existence of an automatic balance at work within the institutional structure.

The onset of a more active and assertive Congress came to be seen as a resurgence of power; a revival of the past; and a return to a previous state. The regeneration of Congress coincided with a renewed attachment to the forms and processes of institutional checks. Nowhere was this attachment more evident than in the popular perception of the changing relationship of the Congress to the Presidency. The Congressional movement against the executive was widely seen as being the outward manifestation of a set of underlying physical forces that were always bound at some time or another to arrest the expansion of the Presidency and to enlarge the power of the legislature. In this ultimate reaffirmation of a closed zero-sum universe, the President and Congress were presented as the institutional constructs of an historical and mechanical process that – irrespective of incumbents and conditions – subjects the two branches to directly connected and inversely proportional positions of power. It was not just that the apparent changes in the relationship between the Presidency and the Congress lent themselves to such an interpretation. To many commentators, the two bodies were the expression of a shifting material equilibrium that physically determined alternating swings of institutional power. The fatalism of this mechanistic perspective is clearly discernible in the outlook of John Johannes, for example, who, on the basis of the Watergate crisis, concluded that 'the pendulum may be swinging – or may have already swung back toward the Congress'.[359] This view of institutions as passive registers of external forces led inevitably to the question of where destiny would lead – 'how far can and will the pendulum swing?'[360] A point reiterated by Thomas Cronin, who likewise saw that the only uncertainty lay in the characteristics of the swing and not in the swing's existence or in its mechanical properties – 'the pendulum has already swung back in the other direction, although how far it will swing and what consequences will follow cannot yet be determined'.[361]

In reactivating the conception of checks and balances, the imperial Presidency crisis also regenerated the theme of an institutional balance as an explanatory and predictive device. It was not simply that a restored balance was a plausible proposition to consider, or that it was a desirable condition to work towards. It was the belief that the balance would be restored as a matter of course, with or without any purposeful intervention by those involved. By referring to 'institutional conflict that results from the pendulum of power in national affairs swinging back from the gross imbalance'[362] of recent decades or to the institutional 'dialectic once again assert[ing] itself',[363] the clear implication is that there was something more to the demise of the Nixon

The separation of paradigms

Presidency than a simple change in the distribution of power. The assumption was that the redistribution did not just occur through the vagaries of events, conditions, and personalities, but was always bound to happen as a result of a dynamic within the system that preordained the provision and direction of the change which took place. This was the equivalent of balanced government as a *deus ex machina* within the political system in so far as it could be relied upon to impose itself once the need arose. In doing so, it could correct malfunctions, redirect developments, and retrieve lost stability. It was essentially a mechanistic conclusion to mechanistic premises.

This sense of institutional mechanics as a *deus ex machina* was particularly evident in many of the discussions and commentaries on the subject of President Nixon's prospective impeachment. The issue was often referred to as if it were an autonomous mechanical process which, once set in motion, moved inexorably towards its predetermined end. In his resignation address, for example, President Nixon described the plight in which he found himself as a constitutional 'process',[364] which he would have preferred to see through to its conclusion. The President, who had always treated the Watergate crisis as a mystifying event, appeared at the climax of the drama to be as stunned by his ill fortune as ever and to be observing the unfolding of events as a detached witness. This attitude was prevalent amongst his supporters and his detractors, both of whom wished to see the final outcome of the procedures set in motion by the President's behaviour. As a result, Richard Nixon's resignation and subsequent pardon introduced a note of disquieting ambiguity amongst the parties to the dispute. The manner of Nixon's departure raised doubts over what had become the central issue, namely, the reliability of the constitution's control mechanisms in resisting the development of excessive executive power. It could be argued that the President, in introducing an element of human agency, had not only deranged the processes but also compromised their autonomy. Even without impeachment and a trial in the Senate, however, there were many who believed that the President's resignation was itself a vindication of the constitution and a demonstration of the effectiveness of its system of checks and balances. Commentators sought to overcome any damaging doubts and to compensate for any residual uncertainty with emphatic reassurances to the public that the system had performed according to its mechanical specifications. 'It was customary to say, during the two years when Richard Nixon was being driven from power, that "the American system worked".'[365] 'We heard a lot at the end of August [1974] that the "system worked".'[366] 'In the months after the exposure, Americans tended to preen themselves on the virtues of the American form of government: "the system worked".'[367] Certainly, there were no doubts on the matter from Emmet John Hughes: 'we have just watched our balance of federal powers work with almost wondrous rectitude and effect';[368] or from Louis Koenig: 'this errant Presidency was checked and eventually terminated by mechanisms the Founding Fathers provided for such an extremity'.[369] Henry Steele Commager was emphatic that while the crisis had 'challenged the basic assumptions of our constitutional system itself, and the basic processes and mechanisms through which it worked'[370] and while the Nixon administration 'called into question both the beauty of her motion and the skill of her builders, ... almost miraculously, the system worked'.[371] *The New York Times* was similarly unequivocal in its editorial on the day of the resignation:

> A mammoth task of self-cleansing has been carried out under principles and procedures established by the Founding Fathers almost two centuries ago. The checks and balances of a tripartite system, strained by the abuses of an aberrant Chief Executive, have proven adequate to restore faith in the integrity and responsibility of that system.[372]

And it was significant that, on assuming the Presidency, Gerald Ford felt obliged to reiterate the same theme. 'Our long national nightmare is over. Our constitution works. Our great republic is a government of laws and not of men.'[373] President Ford did not give emphasis to the change in administration or to the orderly transfer, or even to President Nixon's downfall as a result of popular pressure and democratic sanctions. Instead, he sought to offer reassurance to the American people primarily by reaffirming that the system had worked – that it had shown it could be relied upon to regulate itself and that it warranted being perceived as a piece of imperturbably predictable machinery. President Ford's declaration was designed to rehabilitate the American public's trust in government in the most effective way. This was achieved by assuring the American people that its governmental system was a mechanical system which could accurately be described as having worked because it could be seen as having worked like a machine.

From the commentaries and analyses at the time, one might be forgiven for thinking that the 'government of laws' President Ford referred to was in effect a government of Newton's laws. In this deepest of all constitutional crises in twentieth-century American history, when the American political mind was exposed to an unprecedented extent in the modern era, both the instinctive impulse and the reasoned argument were clearly directed to mechanistic interpretations and solutions. These were not limited to what was hoped would happen or to what should be done. They were based upon a firm conviction that the processes of institutional interaction would inevitably take their course in strict accordance with the material properties which they were assumed to possess. The interpretation, definition, comprehension, and analysis of the crisis over the Presidency became conspicuously dependent upon the exclusively physical components of the institution's respective natures. As a result, the relationship between the Presidency and the Congress lent itself to the application of general physical principles. This was evident in the concerted emphasis given to cyclical patterns, oscillations, seesaws, and pendulums. Underlying this imagery, however, was an even deeper attachment to the mechanics. Namely, the acknowledgement and acceptance that the relationship between the legislature and executive was determined by Newton's fundamental laws of motion.

The incorporation of the Presidency and Congress into the timeless universalism of Newton's material world took various forms and was variously expressed. In some instances, the usages of Newtonian principles were implicit, yet nevertheless unmistakable. It should be recalled that Newton's third law states that whenever a force acts on an object an equal and opposite force acts on the agent producing the original force. Bearing this in mind, it is clear that there was an implicit evocation of Newtonianism in many of the observations and assertions made regarding the nature of the legislative–executive relationship. For example, in their description of the dynamics of the pendulum swings between the Presidency and the Congress in American history, Thomas Franck and Edward Weisband stated categorically that 'each swing contains within itself the excesses that generate the counter-force for the next swing'.[374] The same Newtonian overtones were also evident in the following generalization provided by the *Congressional Quarterly*: 'during times of great crisis, the executive usually becomes predominant ... but there is always a reaction, and when the crisis atmosphere passes, a resurgence of Congressional power usually occurs'.[375] And a similar assurance in the mechanics of American political institutions was provided by James Sundquist's conclusion that 'an extraordinary abuse of Presidential power triggered a counteraction equally extraordinary, and the ponderous processes of institutional change were expedited'.[376] Other allusions to Newtonianism were more explicit and drew consciously on the laws of mechanics as an explanatory frame of reference for the interaction of political institutions:

> According to Isaac Newton's first law, the law of inertia, an object once in motion will continue in motion unless acted upon by outside forces. Newton's law enables us to distinguish between two key elements for analyzing the future of the American Presidency. First, the constitutional creation of a Presidency with the capacity and flexibility to grow in power set in motion an 'object' – namely Presidential power – which accelerated in momentum during the twentieth century.... Second, the Presidency of Richard Nixon ... used the power in a manner that caused outside forces to check his exercise of Presidential power.
>
> (C. W. Dunn[377])

In the case of Watergate particularly, the capacity of the system to cope with stress was vividly demonstrated. Until I began looking back over those events, I had always thought of the phrase 'checks and balances' in essentially static terms: dome, pediment, and pillars frozen forever in a symmetrical equilibrium.... What I had not grasped is that the checks and balances were not designed simply to maintain equilibrium but when necessary to *restore* it. At the time when the framers constructed the Constitution, the scientific discoveries of Sir Isaac Newton loomed large on the intellectual

> horizon. Newton's Third Law of Motion declares that to every action there is an equal and opposite reaction. Being keenly aware of the propensity of human nature for 'vice', the framers took it for granted that greed, ambition, and the love of power would be powerful motivating forces. These forces had to be controlled in order to prevent any person or any part of government from gaining excessive advantage. What better way of accomplishing this than to use the thrust of one person's self-interest to generate an equal and opposite reaction from someone else's self-interest? The influence of this principle on the design of the checks and balances seems to me inescapable.... The United States government works best when the branches of government behave in accordance with the assumptions underlying the construction of these ingenious checks and balances. In the case of Watergate, the Congress and the Judiciary dealt with the excesses of the executive branch by asserting to the full the roles that the framers envisioned for them.
>
> (Elliot Richardson[378])

Whether the allusions to Newton were implicit or explicit, the significance of them lay in the fact that they were made at all. They illustrate the extent to which the forms and characteristics of government had come to be thought of as disaggregated entities moving and exchanging force in accordance with the general laws of physics. Institutions were seen as blocs of matter with mechanical properties of their own which, during the imperial Presidency crisis, produced a mechanically defined and a mechanically attainable solution in the form of a renewed equilibrium. It was not so much that action was taken with balance in mind or that actions were motivated by the need or desire to secure a balance. It was the belief that the required actions were themselves triggered automatically by, and in strict proportion to, those forces that had caused the original imbalance. Mechanics had become the most relevant, the most reliable, and the most authoritative model of political explanation and prediction available to opinion leaders during this critical time.

The most significant aspect of the whole imperial Presidency episode was the way in which it revealed the continuing salience of the mechanistic paradigm within the American political tradition. What was important was not the degree to which the concept of balanced government was or was not achieved; nor the extent to which the concept of balanced government represented an ascertainable physical condition in the world of institutional conflict; nor whether there existed an original and definitive balance that could be used as a frame of reference against which succeeding states of balance could be measured. What was important was the way that arguments were formulated, debates conducted, and analyses made as if balance within government was a fully recognizable and precisely delineated feature of political relationships. During this period, developments at the highest and most prominent levels of

The separation of paradigms

American government were perceived and interpreted, more than anything else, in terms of particulate units interacting with one another in accordance with the principles of mechanics. The physical properties of institutions, that were assumed to be in motion and in contact with one another, became the paramount instruments of observation and evaluation. As a result, the issue of Presidential power became one of weight and velocity within an enclosed system of material cause and effect, in which the behaviour of any of the constituent units was strictly and solely determined by the behaviour of the others.

The apprehension surrounding the Presidency and the subsequent assault upon the office demonstrated that the mechanistic schema of interpretation was not as outmoded and as anachronistic as it was reputed to have become during the halcyon era of the modern chief executive. In the battle over how the issue would be perceived and appraised, the more traditionalist and static framework of checks and balances successfully confronted the modernist conception of Presidential government. The rise of the Presidency had coincided with the increased acceptance of government as an entity existing within an open system and growing more integrated and systemic in nature as it evolved purposefully in response to changing conditions and differing pressures. The chief executive had been both the vanguard and symbol of this transformation. The office's vitality bore testimony to the system's own vitality and to its adaptive and mutable qualities, which for the most part were either celebrated as positive benefits or accepted as simple necessities. And yet, notwithstanding this 'realism' towards an ever larger and more centralized state whose capacity and output had become more important than its constituent structure, the old doctrines of institutional atomization, internal mechanics, and constitutional self-limitation suddenly reimposed their authority. The imperial Presidency crisis showed the zeal with which Americans sought to comprehend and assess their predicament by reference to explicitly mechanistic concepts. While President Nixon defended his office by warning that the attacks upon it would jeopardize the existing harmony of the constitution's balance, his detractors claimed that the government was already dangerously out of balance and in need of new restrictive measures to restore its equilibrium. Issues revolved around the notion of balance; points were argued in terms of balance; and conflicts were translated into differing conceptions of balance. It was a time when most Americans turned into amateur observational scientists confident that the forces present could be precisely demarcated as tangible institutional solids whose courses could be accurately plotted with a view to explaining causes, predicting effects, and regulating behaviour. It was a time when all energies seemed directed to the 'constitutional theology of the separation of powers'[379] and to a tireless search for what was assumed to be the underlying reality of a material matrix of discrete bodies colliding with one another according to their physical characteristics.

All this was a far cry from even the recent past. Then the maximum emphasis had been given to the logic of the separation of powers, in which the distribution of power had been of far less significance than the utility derived from the functional and qualitative differentiation of powers. In the terms 'executive power' and 'legislative power' the stress was laid on the adjectives rather than on the nouns. Just as executive power represented the power implicit to executives by virtue of their being executives, so legislative power was power idiosyncratically and exclusively derived from the legislature's function as a law-making institution. In an open system envisaged like this, it was possible for both the executive and the legislature to grow in strength and stature concurrently. The question of relative power was not a matter of major concern, partly because of the difficulties of measuring two qualitatively distinct attributes and partly because it was thought to be a basically irrelevant question. Whatever power the President possessed was seen as accruing to him because of the nature of the office. Likewise, the power of Congress was power particular to Congress simply because it was Congress. The dismay engendered by the Vietnam War and the Watergate scandal, however, ushered in a reversal of attitudes in which the stress was laid upon power and its distribution within the system. The logic of checks and balances was revived and, as a result, Congressional and Presidential powers were reduced to allotments of an elemental and undifferentiated force that was fixed in quantity and interchangeable in character. As power was reduced to a standardized material commodity, institutions became compatible with one another as repositories of the same universal component. Institutions came to be seen as embodiments of physical properties and registers of physical forces. Together they provided an absolute frame of reference in which the apportionment of power within the system might be gauged and redistributed where necessary. In this way, the renewal of interest in the theme of checks and balances, which had been prompted by the public's concern over governmental power, allowed the problem of power to be viewed in a form most appropriate to the provision of a satisfactory outcome, i.e. as a mechanical malfunction susceptible to corrective action.

Although the constitution had seemed to foster an organic conception of government and political development during much of the modern era, the imperial Presidency crisis gave graphic illustration of the latent potential within the constitution of a quite different perspective of the nature of the political system. The controversy surrounding the office showed that, contrary to existing trends and established expectations, Americans had not after all abandoned their more formalistic and mechanistic criteria of political understanding in favour of the contemporary fatalism of irrepressible evolutionary change. Considering the allegiance which had previously been devoted to such concepts as overriding necessity, unavoidable centralization, executive prerogative, and irreversible adaptation, the resurgence of faith in the existence of an autonomous system of internal checks represented not merely a disjunction but a deeply paradoxical disjunction. The acceptance of a mechanistic paradigm as comparable to, and even exceeding, the science and validity of an organic paradigm, after a prolonged period when a greater emphasis had been given to the latter, represented something far more significant than the acknowledgement of simply another perspective. It constituted a paradox in that it revealed an organic paradigm to be coexisting with a paradigm based upon mechanical principles that were not only inconsistent with organic principles but which, in the evolutionary terms of the previously dominant organic framework, were not supposed even to have existed any longer as a serious strategy of political explanation. By rights, the static and in-grown formalism of rigorous checks and balances should have remained an anachronistic and largely moribund piece of constitutional archaeology. Nevertheless, against the tide of historical progression and systemic adaptivity, the theme of constitutional mechanics re-emerged as a highly plausible and much subscribed-to frame of reference. It would be rash to assert that this mechanical perspective was the paramount conception of American politics or the predominant criterion of American political argument. What can be claimed, however, is that the mechanistic paradigm demonstrated that it had retained its position as a major distinguishing characteristic of American constitutionalism. At the beginning of the century Woodrow Wilson had impressed upon his countrymen the need to see government not as a machine but as a living thing, 'accountable to Darwin, not to Newton'.[380] The demise of the Nixon administration revealed this Newtonian disposition to be still lodged in the American consciousness and still strong enough in the third quarter of the century to warrant precisely the same admonishment that if the constitution had been 'composed in the spirit of Newton, it had to be construed in the spirit of Darwin'.[381]

Chapter five

A government of laws, men and machines

This study was prompted by the numerous references to Isaac Newton and to Newtonian mechanics in general that can be found in the literature on American government and politics. So central is this Newtonian presence thought to be that it becomes mundane and controversial at the same time. Mundane in that Newtonianism has become a descriptive term commonly attached to American government and widely accepted as a valid characterization of its nature; and controversial in so far as the government's Newtonian properties are regarded as being so real that they are often thought to constitute a continuing crisis of adaptation in a political system threatened from within by the mechanical fixity of its own structures and processes. The American practice of enlisting the support of Newtonian science in the categorization of its government, therefore, is seen as a matter not merely of historical interest but also of contemporary social concern. And yet, notwithstanding the ready invocation of Newton's name and the habitual usage of Newtonian principles in connection with the values and practice of American government, the nature of the relationship remains obscure. It cannot be denied that Newtonian mechanics occupy a prominent position in American discourse on government and politics, and that they do so in such a way as to contribute powerfully to America's reputation of exceptionalism in relation to other Western democratic cultures. What requires clarification, however, is the precise meaning of Newtonian mechanics in the context of the American political experience and the level of significance that can be attributed to the existence of such a term in the conventional perspective of the American political system. The variety of references and allusions to the Newtonian legacy in the literature on American constitutional history and political analysis may well represent a distinguishing feature of American government, but it is one plagued with incoherence and ambiguity. So much so, in fact, that the impression left by much of what is written on Newtonianism in this field is that it is so ubiquitous, familiar, and self-evident as to require little or no explanation. As a result, it is left as a presence which is sensed rather than known, experienced rather than understood, and recognized rather than discovered.

It was in response to this ambiguity that the current study was undertaken. Its objective has been to submit the assertion of a linkage between the principles of Newtonian mechanics and the principles of American government to close inspection and critical examination. In its quest for a clearer understanding of the nature of the relationship and a better estimation of its substance, the study sought answers to the following types of basic question. By what means has the contention of a linkage been generally supported? How did such an assertion come about and how has it been sustained? What is it about the content of Newtonian mechanics that makes them seem so especially appropriate a term of description for American government? And conversely, what is there about the nature of the American governmental process that makes it so susceptible to Newtonian terms of reference? In examining the merits of the case made for Newton in this field, the study took as its acid test the principle of balanced government, which, in the American system, embraces the themes of both separated powers and checks and balances. The feature of balanced government was selected for two principal reasons. First, it is generally recognized to be one of the most fundamental elements of American government and one which is reputed to distinguish the structural and normative framework of the American system. Second, balanced government has been more often associated and more closely identified with Newtonian mechanics than any other feature of the American political process. If a genuine case for a Newtonian presence in the American system were to exist, therefore, there could be no more appropriate subject in which to look for its influence and no better basis on which to test the system's Newtonian credentials.

The study addressed itself to the most obvious linkage between mechanics and the American constitutional principle of balanced government. Namely, that, either directly or indirectly, the Newtonian element in American government was established at the outset and that, as a result, it can be effectively understood only as a historical legacy of extraordinary tenacity. What lends weight to such a proposition, and thereby strengthens the association of Newton with the basis of American government, is the character of the intellectual and cultural environment from which the constitution arose. By accepting that Newtonianism constituted an integral feature of the eighteenth century's Enlightenment culture, and by further accepting that American society was a part of such a culture, then a case for a Newtonian influence upon the design and working principles of the American constitution can be made.

When examined in detail, however, this historically logical case for Newtonianism's influence upon the Founding Fathers proved to be far from straightforward. There were strong grounds for including Newtonian mechanics as a seminal influence upon the basic outlook and principles of that sector of society from which the Framers were drawn. Not the least of these was the implausibility of *excluding* the spirit of Newtonian dynamics, which was so pervasive at the time. While the circumstantial evidence is strong, and while it would be very difficult to imagine Newtonian principles not being an intellectual force to have been used or at the very least to have been reckoned with by the Founders, no *conclusive* evidence is available to prove the existence of Newton's direct effect upon the organization of American government. The popularly perceived impression of the Newtonian nature of the government's design, therefore, remains one that seems noticeably out of proportion with the historical evidence supporting it.

This riddle provided the lead to a much more substantial source of Newtonian connection in American politics. It threw into high relief the existence of a different and far more revealing dimension to the issue; a dimension altogether separate from the historical-causative linkage which stresses the role of Newtonianism in the origins and creation of the constitution. Although it has a subsequent bearing on the historical aspects of Newton's contribution and can serve to explain the strength of belief in the Founders' Newtonian credentials, the dimension in question represents a quite separate vein of argument in support of Newton's name being connected with American government. It refers to the widely supported contention that the operational dynamics of the federal government's three institutions can legitimately be described in terms of Newtonian mechanics. This is not regarded as a matter of mere descriptive licence. It is seen as a conclusion justified by the patterns of physical cause and effect that appear to characterize the relationship between the three institutions. Far from being a loosely drawn analogy to mechanics, or an outmoded remnant from a previous conception of government, the prodigious and persistent application of mechanical terms of reference to the political system reveals a deeply rooted conviction in the mechanistic reality of American constitutional processes. It is this conviction, coupled with the belief that institutional mechanics are integral to the constitution's purposes, which leads to Newtonianism being employed as a substantive term of descriptive characterization and as a principle of normative value. The Newtonianism imputed to the constitution in this respect, therefore, does not relate to the intellectual conditioning of the Founding Fathers, or to the structural formalism incorporated in their institutional arrangements, or to the prescriptive foundations underlying the constitution's design. It relates instead to the presence of a mechanistic paradigm in contemporary American constitutionalism. This is instinctively defined by recourse to the name of Newton, which is still so closely identified with the science of mechanics as to be synonymous with it. In contrast to the historical criterion of the constitution's Newtonianism, this contemporary criterion depends upon the content of the constitution and upon the observed behaviour of its institutional components. This more empirical and operational dimension should not be seen as simply a continuation of a historical legacy into a contemporary context. It is separate and independent from the sources and origins of the constitution's structure. It employs Newtonianism as an analytical measure warranted by the perceived nature of the constitution's dynamics. As such, it draws on a different category of material, uses different criteria for evidence, ascribes a different meaning to Newtonianism, evinces a different significance from the subject, and generates an altogether different perspective from that of the historical-causal approach.

Chapter 3 examined the general scale and depth of belief in the Newtonian nature of the separation of powers scheme in operation at the federal level of government. It drew attention to the modern American disposition towards conceptualizing and depicting the interrelationship of political institutions in terms of a closed material framework of discrete units in physical contact with one another. It noted the way that changes in the power of one institution were accounted for through changes in the position and form of the others. Likewise, the restoration of equilibrium would be assured by a redistribution of power activated by the self-same forces that had caused the original imbalance. This portrayal of an autonomous process of physical interplay between organizational solids within a fixed universe of available and interchangeable power was recognized to be both a conventional conception of institutional dynamics and a normative principle of constitutional government. Institutions behaving in strict accordance with their mechanical properties and changing only in respect to, and in direct proportion with, those forces exerted by other institutions were revealed to be a remarkably potent instrument of political understanding and evaluation.

In much the same way as the historical account of the constitution's link with Newton has come under assault, so the contention of a Newtonian dimension to the constitution has been subjected to critical appraisal. It has been claimed that, behind the formal edifice of the separation of powers, the system has experienced a large-scale shift of effective power away from Congress to the other two branches, and, in particular, to the burgeoning executive department. Whether this redistribution has been due more to Presidential and judicial usurpation or to legislative abdication, the net effect has been to transform the governmental process from the static fixture of the past into an altogether more adaptive entity responding to the obligations of an advanced service state and to the requirements of a major international power. According to this view, the separation of powers system – together with its corollaries of institutional tripartism, organizational co-equality, and self-regulating equilibrium – have become anachronisms or even shibboleths in an age when constitutional formality has necessarily had to recede in the face of the centralizing, nationalizing, and bureaucratizing forces of modern American society. With the advent of Presidential policy-making, 'iron triangles', multifunctional commissions, executive–legislative liaison, permanent 'sub-governments', White House staffs, executive privilege, judicial activism, delegated legislation, administrative discretionary authority, and the press, the military, and the bureaucracy variously hailed as 'fourth branches of government', both the symmetry and the inclusiveness of the separation of powers have been eroded away into a remnant of tradition. Although 'we still have the forms of a tripartite government', Philip Kurland, for example, believes that as a result of contemporary developments 'the division of powers contemplated by the Founders has long since disappeared' and that 'the ancient concept of separation of powers and checks and balances has been reduced to a slogan'.[1]

In this respect, modern conditions can be seen as having finally exposed the conceptual and logical flaws that had always been implicit in the separation of powers format. The Supreme Court had long recognized that the structure of separated powers was not, and never could be, as definitively precise and calculable as its appearance suggested. The Founding Fathers may have 'viewed the principle of the separation of powers as a vital check against tyranny', but, according to the Court, they saw that 'a hermetic sealing off of the three branches of government would preclude the establishment of a Nation capable of governing itself effectively'.[2] In other decisions, the Court had made it plain that such a 'hermetic sealing off' of the constituent departments of government was not merely impracticable or undesirable, but conceptually implausible and empirically unsubstantiated. It was impossible to differentiate clearly the three functions attributed to the system and, as such, it was equally impossible to demarcate institutional boundaries on the basis of such functions. Both the functions and the institutions confounded abstract delineation by invariably merging into and interacting with one another in such a way as to remove the qualities of solidity and exactitude from the framework, and to infuse the system with a fluidity by which it could contravene its own organizational logic and meet the requirements of the times. It was during the modern period that these requirements appeared to have finally led to an acknowledgement of the misplaced mechanical exactitude that had previously surrounded the separation of powers and to a recognition that the structure had been superseded by the *realpolitik* of executive hegemony and the modern regulatory state.

And yet, in spite of what could be seen as a period in which there had never been more conspicuous or more conclusive evidence of the separation of powers' demise, and in which the public's consciousness of the scheme's indeterminacy and mutability might be expected to have reached unprecedented heights, the salience of separated powers has nevertheless remained undiminished. The separation of powers has continued to be an object of widespread allegiance and veneration. Even in the face of its own contradictions and its apparently outmoded nature, the presence and value of separated powers have not been dislodged as an article of faith in the American political ethos. This almost instinctive attachment to a formality of constitutional organization represents the other side of the separation of powers' status in contemporary American politics. On the one hand, the scheme is criticized and condemned for falsely representing the real configuration of power within government and for having failed to perform its intended function of preventing concentrations of power. On the other hand, it is recognized that the separation of powers doctrine 'has continued to have a hold on the minds if not the deeds of the American people'.[3] Despite the controversy surrounding its relevance and effectiveness, therefore, the separation of powers seems to have retained its position not just as a compulsively popular portrayal of institutional relationships, but also as a tangible and dependable device for redressing the abuses of power that arise from a disequilibrium between the institutions.

Few cases better illustrate the depth of belief in the empirical reality of the separation of powers system and in the value attached to it as an active mechanism of political control than the issue of the 'imperial Presidency'. From the analysis presented in Chapter 4, it is clear that the American public had retained an instinctive dependence upon the mechanistic logic underlying the separation of powers in identifying the existence of a disorder in government, in analysing the nature of that disorder, and in discerning the means by which such a disorder could be satisfactorily remedied. The Presidency had succeeded in triggering off a public reaction to the scale and concentration of executive power in terms which revealed the existence of a fundamentalist attachment to the premises and axioms of formal constitutional dynamics. What made the use of mechanical criteria so remarkable was that such observational and evaluative principles were widely thought to have been superseded by the prevailing impression of an organically constituted and systemically evolving form of government. Furthermore, the primary embodiment of the modernist conception of government as a living and adaptive entity was the Presidency itself. It was the Presidency which had not only been instrumental in diverting the character of American government away from the immobilism of the old enclosed system of constitutional limitation to the activist ethos of a more open creative and responsive system, but had also become the most conspicuous expression of a more integrated and purposive government servicing the systemic requirements of the public and national interest.

And yet, just when this executive-biological paradigm seemed most secure and the Presidency's growth appeared to be an integral and necessary feature of a continuous and irreversible evolutionary development, both the organic conception of government and the Presidency were suddenly subjected to forms of analysis that had previously been regarded as semi-redundant. What before had been seen as an office qualitatively and even mystically distinct from any other institution, and possessing an intrinsically indeterminate but life-giving character to the rest of the government, was redefined according to the precepts of separated powers and, thereby, processed back into the mechanistic matrix of checks and balances. The reputed magic of the Presidency that had previously confounded analysis and distracted interest away from executive power was abruptly dispelled by the desire to render the Presidency determinate and, thereby, controllable. The idiosyncrasies of the executive function and the authority of the office were duly reformulated into a measurable unit of material with the capability of being countered by the physico-mechanical properties of other comparable units of institutional material. So pronounced was the drive to accommodate the Presidency into the precisely delineated structure of balanced government that the cry went up for the office to be 'secularized' and 'demythologized'. Encouraged by Congressional politicians that 'what we needed was balance'[4] and assured by experienced analysts that 'each of the virtues of the executive ... has a reciprocal and checking counterpart among Congressional attributes',[5] the popular image of the Presidency was made to conform increasingly to the requirements of a mechanical solution to what had by now come to be perceived as a mechanical problem. Under the auspices of traditional checks and balances, therefore, the evolutionary progression of Presidential power was effectively transmuted into an institutional disequilibrium. This could not only be reversed but would inevitably be reversed by way of the irresistible dynamics of organizations interacting with one another as uniform material entities within a closed zero-sum system of physical cause and effect.

What was so extraordinary about the imperial Presidency episode was the way it exhibited a profound commitment on the part of the American public to mechanical principles in understanding and coping with the crisis. Events were discussed, issues debated, causes identified, and solutions determined in terms that were explicitly and conspicuously mechanistic in nature. The vocabulary of political debate was replete with references to collisions, impacts, weights, counterweights, dynamics, pendulums, inertia, forces, imbalances, equilibria, action and reaction, and self-regulatory processes. These were no mere platitudes or figures of speech. They were used and acted upon in a way that betrayed a deep-seated conviction in the mechanistic nature of government. Whether it was through instinctive impulse or reasoned insight, mechanics became a primary conceptual device for appraising political developments and for applying remedial measures with the expectation of assured effectiveness that comes from a belief in the presence of geometrically regular solids. Far from being an outmoded conception of political relationships, therefore, the public anxiety over the Presidency revealed an established faith in the value of balanced government and in the existence of the means by which it could be secured and maintained. Such was the level of trust in the mechanical efficiency of the checks and balances scheme that, despite the previously acknowledged problem of whether the most uninstitutionalized and non-mechanical element of government could ever be accommodated within the scheme's framework, the Presidency was none the less accepted as having been brought under control through the activation of corrective counterweights. All the theoretical objections and practical barriers which before had defeated even the idea of genuine Presidential constraint were swept aside in the fervour with which the issue was reduced to rigorously mechanistic categories and criteria. The system was applauded as having worked. It had worked properly quite simply because it had satisfied the mechanical criteria assigned to it.

The uninhibited use of, and conceptual dependence upon, such a mechanistic paradigm by both political observers and politicians alike led understandably to a renewed application of Newtonian terminology to the processes of government. Whether it involved implicit references to the laws of classical mechanics, or explicit allusions to Newton and Newtonianism, it served to reveal an underlying belief both in the mechanical properties of institutions and in the mechanistic character of their relationships. The use of Newtonian categories and the conviction with which they were held also served to prompt a reappraisal of the sources of, and reasons for, this mechanistic outlook. Rather like the historical-causal dimension, this contemporary-empirical perspective of the role of Newtonianism in American politics can be accounted for by a variety of explanatory interpretations. Taking the central example of the Presidency and Congress, these explanations would include the physical presence of the institutions; the differences in their functions, constituencies, memberships, and tenures; a history of constitutional confrontations and disputes, present-day organizational and political rivalries; separate coalitions of pluralistic interests, different political priorities and policy dispositions; and the existence of '*two* popular majorities – the Congressional and the Presidential'.[6] These types of explanation may be well founded and lend material weight to the idea of separate and interactive institutions. Nevertheless, they do not in themselves account for the initial idea, or for the public's receptivity to having the idea corroborated and substantiated. According to these interpretations, the Presidency and the Congress are conceived as being different from one another primarily because of evidence to show that they are institutionally and politically separate, and set in conflict with each other. But a no less relevant and, arguably, a more plausible and convincing explanation of the belief in the inherent tension between the legislature and the executive is suggested by the status afforded to the idea of separated powers and by the way in which that idea is first conveyed to and subsequently assimilated by the individual citizen.

From the analysis of textbook descriptions of the separation of powers contained in Chapter 3, it is clear that the scheme is presented as a self-evident and incontrovertible feature of American government. It is portrayed as a characteristic so elemental that it obviates the need for anything much in the way of description or analysis. The textbook accounts proceed on the basis of what is assumed to be an already accepted and thoroughly familiar axiom of political observation. Nothing in their introductory portrayals is aimed at dislodging or challenging the presupposed reality of tripartism. On the contrary, the content and style of both their initial descriptions and their subsequently abbreviated analyses serve to conform, to strengthen, to perpetuate, and, furthermore, to exaggerate the imagery of the separation of powers' symmetrical solidity. So ingrained does the notion of separated powers appear to be that the textbooks merely affirm what is already assumed and further consolidate the predisposition towards seeing the institutions as separate entities. Instead of regarding the Presidency and the Congress as separate because of their organizational and political differences, it is probably more accurate to say that they are seen to be organizationally and politically different from each other primarily because they are preconceived to be separate from each other.

It is claimed, most notably by Gordon Wood,[7] that the constitution marked the end of the classical conception of politics in the United States. This was because the Federalists had succeeded in divorcing the notion of a balance of government functions from that of a balance of social estates. In doing so, they had 'destroyed the age-old conception of mixed government'[8] in which the differentiated elements of society's hierarchy were not only embodied formally in government but were the determinants of its structure, its powers, and its stability. According to Wood, this integrated, ordered, and changeless ideal of a 'static equilibrium'[9] among permanent classes was revolutionized in America by the introduction of a 'balance of governmental functionaries without social connections'.[10] Wood concludes that the separation of powers allowed institutional politics to become 'abstracted in a curious way from its former associations with the society'[11] and permitted political power to become 'disembodied' and 'essentially homogeneous'.[12] While it was some years before most men 'rid themselves entirely of a residual tendency to associate the branches of the new government with democracy, aristocracy and monarchy',[13] even Woods's critics agree that the constitution's ratification 'assured the gradual rejection of the ancient habit of thinking in terms of a governmental balance of social estates'.[14] An ancient habit was displaced by what became a newly established convention of treating the components of government as functionally differentiated units. This may well be considered to be the critical change in outlook that signifies the modernization of American politics. Nevertheless, from an analysis of the separation of powers, Woods's conclusions can be challenged as incomplete. On the evidence of the rigour and stringency with which mechanical precepts have been attached to the scheme of separated powers during the modern era, it would appear that the transformation of balanced government wrought by the Founding Fathers was not as final or as conclusive as it is often reputed to be. Since the constitution's acceptance, there has occurred another and no less profound progression in the conception of balanced government. The contention is that if the Founding Fathers arranged for the 'disembodiment of government from society ... [by] divesting the various parts of government of their social constituents',[15] subsequent constitutional development has largely divested even the functional framework of government of its qualitative distinctions. While a residual tendency to associate the components of government with the executive, legislative, and judicial functions still exists, the basic perspective of balanced government has shifted decisively towards the reductionism of checks and balances. The three branches are no longer seen as different bodies that happen to check each other. In the modern era, they are primarily regarded as checking bodies that happen to be different from one another.

The doctrine of separated powers, together with the principles of mixed and balanced government to which it became attached in the eighteenth century, was the product of a long and complex historical development. As a result, the doctrine embraced a rich variety of theoretical constructs, empirical propositions, social connotations, diverse origins, past experiences, disputed meanings, and traditional roots. The variegated legacy of classical mixed government was severely narrowed by the reconstitution of governmental balance in the shape of institutions separated in accordance with functional differentiation. Yet this loss was slight compared with the near total collapse of historical and conceptual perspective which has accompanied the development of the separation of powers since the Founding Fathers, and in particular during the course of this century. The separation of powers has retained its exalted position as the primary structural characteristic of American government and as the foremost prerequisite to the constitution's central principle of limited government. Nevertheless, the separation of powers has been drained of its multifarious historical linkages and of its wealth of conceptual allusions. The colour and history of balanced government have been reduced to a timeless monochrome of mechanical properties as the separation of powers becomes increasingly understandable only in terms of the face value of its co-equal and standardized entities whose rationale is necessarily that of physical interaction and reciprocal restraint. 'The widely known but little understood doctrine of the separation of governmental powers'[16] has become the victim of its own 'superficial clarity'.[17] It is that apparent clarity which has served to perpetuate the scheme's salience as a conception of government by making the separation of powers one of the most easily perceived and readily assimilable summations of a political system in existence. Its compulsive symmetry belies its internal complexity, but it is that symmetry which makes the scheme so attractive and enduring as a popular depiction of government.

From an early age the citizen is presented with the separation of powers in a thoroughly ahistorical and predigested form. Knowledge of the three institutions and of their respective functions is conveyed as an axiomatic frame of reference generated *de novo* by the Founding Fathers at a given point in time. This celebrated act of collective creation may have ended classical politics in America, but it also conditioned subsequent generations of Americans to a reductionist perspective of the three departments as comparable in origin, in power, and, ultimately, in purpose. As long as the three functions retained something of their ancient legacies and social associations, and as long as the scale of government remained relatively static, then this reductionist perspective could be inhibited by the sense of qualitative distinction inherent in the trinity of institutions. With the passage of time and the Founding Fathers' raw materials for balance receding ever further into constitutional prehistory, the old historical and social supports to a qualitative differentiation of the branches became progressively displaced by the separation of powers' own increasingly homogenized continuity. Furthermore, with the onset of large-scale government, together with ever increasing social pressure for more governmental services and a corresponding growth in anxiety over governmental power, the three branches have been further denuded of their separate identities. The acknowledged and sanctioned fluidity of functions has witnessed the President becoming 'chief legislator', the Congress turning into a counter-bureaucracy, and the Supreme Court acting as a 'superlegislature to decide whether the legislation that comes under its scrutiny would have been worthy of its support at the enactment stage'.[18] The modern pressures for governmental action have further promoted the conception of separated departments into an aggregate framework of political power centres and policy-making agencies – with each one complementing, or compensating for, the others. This in turn has served to accommodate still further the mechanics of checks and balances as the preponderant principle of institutional organization and dynamics in both the positive sense of functional licence and the negative sense of atomizing and inhibiting political authority. Modern government, therefore, has succeeded in affirming, rather than repudiating, the initial imagery of three co-equal and interactive powers. Indeed, with the progressive abstraction of the three powers into a unidimensional medium of interchangeable roles and physical weightings, the mechanical imagery has been enhanced and the socialization of the political system as a mechanical system has been intensified. In this respect, the salience of Newton to American government can be seen as being less a matter of historical legacy or conceptual tradition and more one of contemporary perception and justified descriptive licence. In other words, the American balance of power – 'latterly called the Newtonian theory of government'[19] – has, with time and constitutional development, become increasingly Newtonian in the mechanization of the structure and operation of its processes.

From the way the arguments in support of the Newtonian element within American government devolve into two distinct categories, it is apparent that the Newtonian connection is not a singular, static, and continuous tradition in American politics, but a variable convention of conceptualization. The natural impulse when confronted first with the common assertion that the constitution was based on the 'premise that for every political action there is an equal and opposite political reaction (*à la* Newton)',[20] and second with the general characterization of American government as a functioning constitutional mechanism, is to draw the two observations together into one unified tradition in which past structures physically determine present arrangements. This impulse is more pronounced given the continuity of the constitution as an eighteenth-century artefact and its association with Newtonianism, which admits only physical causes and effects to its scheme of explanation. Together, they suggest an interdependent combination of permanent constitutional processes and fixed mechanical principles. The progression of the constitution throughout its history, therefore, can be seen as a unilinear succession of similar states, with each one a derivative of the physical properties of the preceding one. Any development could occur only within the fixed confines of the original closed system of constitutional objects and forces, and in strict accordance with the mechanical relationships of its constituent parts. As a result, the present-day political system, whose formal framework bears a remarkably close resemblance to the original model, can appear to be the direct product of a mechanistic process of self-perpetuation.

In reality, history can be just as much the product of the present as it is its determinant. It may be true that the Founding Fathers consciously or inadvertently designed a political system which possessed genuinely mechanical properties. It may also be true that the Founders and their contemporaries were inspired, or at least strongly influenced, by Newton in their conception of how the constitution should and would work. The exact extent of this dependence on Newtonianism both in the 'soft' sense of a generalized model of explanation and in the 'hard' sense of a universally applicable mechanical construct remains an open question. What is more certain, however, is the way in which the historical perspective becomes conditioned by contemporary convictions to the extent of recasting the Framers' design in the image of the political system's modern characteristics. Far from being simply a uniform continuity proceeding from the Founders to the present day, the Newtonian tradition is as much, if not more, a product of retrospective extrapolation – stylizing, abstracting, and homogenizing the sources and substance of American balanced government in the past in precisely the same terms that it is experienced in the United States today. The mechanical uniformity of the present is projected on to the notional similarity of past structures and powers, with the result that the constitution is increasingly accommodated into a historical base compatible with the unidimensional view of what succeeded its acceptance.

If the nineteenth century saw the 'declassicizing' of American politics, then the twentieth century has witnessed the separation of powers being not merely 'dehistoricized' but 'defunctionalized' and replaced by increasingly standardized institutional agencies interacting with one another by way of their mechanical properties. With this came a pronounced predisposition towards viewing the American experience of separated powers in the same form which it had come to assume in the present. Because the scheme's design is the most easily assimilable structural abbreviation of American government and because its basic format has remained the same, in appearances at least, a rich potential for standardizing the history and nature of American institutions inheres in the mere presence of the three institutions. That potential has been largely fulfilled by the contemporary perception of American institutions as enmeshed in a mechanical matrix of collisions and balances. Implicit to mechanics, and integral to the belief in the presence of mechanics, is the existence of a static and timeless frame of reference within which objects move and forces are exchanged and registered. Part and parcel of envisaging the present political system in mechanical terms, therefore, is the backward projection of the present arrangements in such a way as to allow the separation of powers to appear anchored in the supposedly Newtonian credentials of the Founders. In having insinuated this mechanical fixity on to the past, the Founding Fathers appear increasingly as a group of premeditated system builders, having achieved a feat of engineering that has rolled onwards through time by virtue of its mechanical properties. At this point the Newtonianism of history, ideas, and causes becomes conjoined to the Newtonianism of modernity of practice and effects. The result is a self-reinforcing, and ultimately circular, relationship between the past and the present that satisfies the conceptual requirements of an increasingly non-historical attachment to, and understanding of, an increasingly non-historical governmental framework.

While the historical and observational dimensions of Newtonianism retain a separate and discrete explanatory identity, contemporary experience has shown that one can nevertheless be encompassed and redirected by the other to the extent of appearing to be a concomitant feature of the other. The capacity of the modern mechanistic conception of separated powers to reorientate, and even to displace, historical perspective opens up the question of the scale and depth of the repercussive effects of such a conception. Given the centrality of the separation of powers to American constitutionalism and given the salience of Newtonianism to the separation of powers, then does the penetration of mechanical principles to this level suggest a wider and more general characterization of American political perspectives drawn from the separation of powers as a first principle of both constitutional government and governmental mechanics? In other words, is it to be assumed that the mechanistic imagery attached to the framework of separated powers, and checks and balances, is in itself a generative force which radiates outwards and disposes other elements of the system to being seen and treated in the same manner?

Before examining this broader but justifiable question, it is important to acknowledge the self-imposed limitation of the present study in answering it. It has not been, nor is it, the aim of this study to allow the theoretical totality of Newtonianism as a scheme of universal comprehension and explanation to incorporate American politics into its framework by deductive fiat. It may well be that between the microscopic dimension of sub-atomic particles, quantum mechanics, and the 'principle of indeterminacy', on the one hand, and the cosmological sphere of high-velocity motion, energy–mass equivalence, and relativity physics on the other lies a world of ordinary experience and common mental outlook that remains ultimately conformable to a clockwork-like mechanism. It is quite possible that Newtonian mechanics are 'embodied in the present structure of the average human intellect or in what is usually called "common sense" ',[21] and that they are 'based on deeply ingrained habits of imagination and thought whose strength is far greater than we are generally willing to concede'.[22] It may be reasonable to suppose that the corpuscular-kinetic format of the immediate world of human experience is duplicated in the nature of human organization – thereby giving rise to a Newtonian sociology reducing 'society to a cluster of human atoms, complete and self-contained each in itself and only mutually attracting and repelling each other'.[23] Furthermore, it may be a defensible proposition to argue that the most Newtonian of societies are liberal societies because of their 'adherence to a political, economic and social Newtonianism in which the stability and movement of society depend upon its constituent parts remaining in balanced relationships'.[24] Following on from the 'similarity between the symbolic form of liberalism and the Newtonian cosmology',[25] it can be claimed that the exceptionalism of America's liberal consensus makes the United States the most Newtonian society of all and firmly establishes it as 'an atomistic and egalitarian construct following the findings of Newton in the physical world'.[26]

Using these foundations, it is possible to venture all manner of assertions concerning the nature of American society and politics. The framework of constitutional checks and balances, for example, might be adequately represented and accounted for in terms of a broader social reality comprising a 'Newtonian pattern of order arising automatically from the interaction of isolated and self-contained atoms'.[27] The nature and distribution of political power in the American system might actually be reducible to a configuration of observable objects moving solely in accordance with Newton's laws of motion and force, with the power of each object physically determinable through changes in the positions and velocities of the other constituent objects in the system. And the recent rise and decline in Presidential power may be explained as another example of the temporary and local reversal of entropy produced by living matter before the order and structure of its sustained energy level inevitably slides back into the universe's overriding thermodynamic trend of dissipated energy and increasing disorder.[28] While such propositions may be well founded and sensitively argued, they nevertheless remain speculations devoid of conclusive evidence in their favour. They may be plausible portrayals of an underlying reality but they do not determine the existence of that reality. As stated earlier, it is not the purpose of this study to ride on the back of grand Newtonian designs. Such designs are unverified and, arguably, unverifiable. Accordingly, the analysis is not geared to assessing the merits or demerits of Newtonian systems in accounting for political or social phenomena. It is not an appraisal of the extent to which American government approximates to some selected Newtonian model. And neither is it an enquiry as to whether the use of Newtonian terms of reference in connection with institutional and organizational politics is warranted, appropriate, or literally correct. Instead the focus of interest lies in the significance of the popular belief in the existence of Newtonian mechanics operating at the centre of American government, and in the influence and effects of such a mechanical outlook upon what is widely regarded as the most conspicuously distinctive and most highly valued characteristic of the American system.

From a close scrutiny of the premises adopted, the vocabulary employed, the ideas advanced, the suppositions made, the problems identified, the causes established, the effects expected, the dynamics assumed, the explanations presented, and the conclusions reached in connection with the Presidency and the Congress, it is evident that the mechanical outlook is by no means confined to legislative–executive relations. While the Presidency and Congress may provide the most well known, well established, and dramatically conclusive expressions of institutional dynamics, the same pattern of mechanistic perception and comprehension is discernible in other areas of government. Perhaps the most remarkable and revealing example of this conceptual transference is provided by the role and authority afforded to the judiciary in the political system.

The judicial department is formally part of the separation of powers scheme. It thereby possesses a notionally co-equal and co-ordinate status with the other two branches. Despite its formal prominence, the judiciary has often been thought to be 'the weakest of the three branches',[29] as it has neither the power of the sword or the purse, nor the authority derived from the normal electoral channels of political representation. Furthermore, the power of judicial review was not expressly provided for in the constitution, but had to be inferred from Article III and subsequently developed into a working practice by the courts themselves and, in particular, by the Supreme Court. Eventually the judiciary acquired a position in which it successfully claimed the right to determine the constitutionality not just of state legislation and administrative action but, far more controversially, of statutes passed by Congress and of actions undertaken by the President. In a society where 'scarcely any question arises ... which does not become, sooner or later, a subject of judicial debate'[30] and where a written constitution emphasizes the importance of correctly allocated and distributed powers, the Supreme Court's role of constitutional interpretation has allowed it to become the final judge as to the limits within which government can act as well as the ultimate arbiter as to what powers properly belong to which level or unit of government in the system. The Court's power to pronounce public laws and governmental actions void and to invalidate the authority upon which duly elected legislatures and executives make their decisions, amounts to a conspicuous anomaly in a system based upon popular consent and organized according to the principles of representative government. Thomas Jefferson, for example, believed that the Court had contravened its only rationale as an adjudicator in cases arising from enacted laws and, by doing so, had compromised the separation of powers principle and destabilized the system of checks and balances.[31] In prescribing the rules by which the other branches of government were to conduct themselves, Jefferson believed the Court to be a regressive departure from republican government and a return to the forms and practices of non-elective and unrepresentative authority. Ever since Jefferson's condemnation of judges as political guardians, the Court has continued to arouse anxieties about the centrality of its role and the scale of its power. It has never been devoid of controversy and, periodically, it has been subjected to such intense criticism as to lead to demands for its jurisdiction to be reduced and occasionally for its chief justices to be impeached.

Many of the objections and criticisms surrounding the Court have been countered by assurances that seek to accommodate the judiciary more into the democratic mainstream of the system as a whole. Reference is made to the judges as Presidential appointees, to the deterrent of impeachment, to Congress's power to organize the courts, to the process of constitutional amendment, to the courts' freedom from binding precedent, to its tradition of self-restraint, and to its customary avoidance of explicitly 'political questions'. Furthermore, it is claimed that the Court is so conscious of its tenuous position that its interpretation of the constitution cannot long withstand the direction of dominant opinion and that the Court's authority is ultimately dependent upon its congruence with contemporary public philosophy.[32] Far from constituting a threat to the republic, the Supreme Court's responsiveness and passivity can be portrayed as a positive benefit to the governing process and one quite consistent with its main principles. The Court can be seen as affording expression to commonly held values and beliefs that may not be given proper consideration in other decision-making centres. It serves to legitimize the actions of the elective elements of government by assuring the public that such actions do not violate constitutional limitation and are, thereby, validated as within constitutionally granted powers. The Court is also thought to provide a central reference point and a necessary source of final settlement to the many political and jurisdictional disputes that are generated by a written constitution. And, finally, the Court can be seen as an institution which is only able to sustain itself, if not by unqualified public consent, then at least by public acquiescence in its existence and in the socially accepted framework of limited government within which the Court has fulfilled a major role.

Despite this reassuring reconstitution of the Supreme Court into either a withdrawn and inhibited inferior to the 'political' branches of government, or else a responsive participant in the democratic process, the Court remains a conspicuously unorthodox branch of government that sits uncomfortably in the representative matrix of the American system. Belying its ostensible weakness lies a potential power that has occasionally burst forth to precipitate some of the republic's gravest constitutional crises. More often than not, these periods of judicial activism have been marked by the Court conforming to its conventional rationale as a check upon the impulsiveness of popular majorities and, thereupon, as a restriction upon the scope of government. During the recent past, however, the judiciary has been active in the positive sense of 'projecting affirmative policy, ordering that certain things be done, commanding actions and expenditures ... in order to achieve legislative effects that have been rejected by the legislatures themselves'.[33] Instead of being a negative force periodically frustrating democratic majorities and obstructing policy initiatives, the Court over the last thirty years has developed into such a consistently active part of the governing process that it has become 'a major domestic policy maker in the United States'.[34] It has been this willingness to abandon its tradition of self-restraint in favour of initiating constitutional construction that has led to charges of a judicial hegemony, or even an imperial judiciary, existing in the United States. The Court's development of judicial review into a regular process of statute reconstruction has earnt it the title of the United States' third legislative chamber. To its critics, this intrusion into policy innovation and statute supervision on the part of the federal court system has allowed the courts to become 'far more powerful than ever before' in the way that they 'reach into the lives of the people, against the will of the people, deeper than they ever have in American history'.[35] These recent developments are significant for the way they throw into stark relief the intrinsic power of the courts in America and the complex issues of law and politics, constitutionalism and popular sovereignty, judgement and will that are attached to their role. But they are also significant for another reason. They reveal the remarkable extent to which the problematic nature of these issues is simplified, or rather satisfactorily suspended, by the mechanistic suppositions underpinning the American scheme of separated powers.

In the separation of powers triumvirate, the Supreme Court is at first sight conspicuously different and even alien from the other two branches. The Court reacts to the other two departments of government, adjudicates between them, and depends on them to carry out its decisions and conform to the spirit of the law. The Presidency and Congress are distinguishable as the political departments – a term made relevant only by the Supreme Court's presence as the third party. The representative credentials of the legislature and executive grant them a *prima facie* right to check and balance one another that the Court does not appear to possess on any political basis. But once the separation of powers perspective is adopted and the principle of limited government is employed as the overriding criterion, then the Court's position becomes legitimized as a weight, a check, a counter-force – in essence a materialized function set in a world of physical properties. It is a tribute to the sweep and scale of the separation of powers doctrine and to its hold on American political perception that the power of the Supreme Court can be satisfactorily accommodated within it – even to the extent of facilitating an acceptance of the Court's power as being not merely compatible, but co-equal, with the power held by each of the other two branches. The effect of this reductionism is plain to see in the literature on the Court and, particularly, in the way that mechanistic axioms displace interest in, or concern for, the many problematic intricacies involved in the legitimacy and significance of the Court's role in American government.

The power of the Supreme Court is rendered intelligible and defensible through the agency of equilibrium. The history and nature of the Court are projected into a rich variety of regulatory balances that serve, first, to rationalize the institution as an integral part of a generalized system of checks and balances; and, second, to justify the Court as a necessary counterweight to the other constituent forces of the system. When the Court adopts what might be termed its conventional power of invalidating laws and actions, this is couched as 'a kind of brake or negative "balance"',[36] to the instability threatened by unrestrained majoritarian government. When, on the other hand, the Court engages in the more modern practice of positive intervention, then this too receives the sanction of equilibrium. Judicial activism is seen as a way in which the system compensates for the insufficiency of some of the other policy-making centres. Whereas the

> 'old' judicial review, especially after 1890, lagged behind Congress, the President, and state governments, the 'new' judicial review has been far ahead of each and has had a substantial influence in stimulating the political branches of government to catch up as well as to work considerable changes in public opinion.[37]

Even the policy content of the Court's decisions is reduced to a discernible pattern of balance through time – a fact so self-evident that it is taken as read in the following routine *Congressional Quarterly* report on the Supreme Court in 1982:

> Historically, the Court has served as a balance wheel within the federal system. The Court has moved to the 'conservative' side of issues when Congress or the President veered sharply to the left, as in the early New Deal days. And the rulings of the term that ended July 2, 1981, indicated the Court might be taking a more liberal stance on certain issues now that the Reagan administration and the 97th Congress are moving to the right.[38]

Whether the Court is liberal or conservative, new or old, activist or negative, the rationalization follows the same formula of equilibrium in which the Court is recognized as a political institution participating fully in the policy-making process and, by doing so, contributing to its internal harmony. Justice Robert H. Jackson both acknowledges and applauds the arrangement:

> The political function which the Supreme Court, more or less effectively, may be called upon to perform comes to this: In a society in which rapid changes tend to upset all equilibrium, the Court, without exceeding its own limited powers, must strive to maintain the great system of balances upon which our free government is based.[39]

And whether the Court is perceived as just one of a number of weights in the scales, or the critical regulative weight 'to break the impasses which are inherent in any structure of balanced powers',[40] its power is nevertheless legitimized primarily in terms of mechanics. 'So the limits on court power in government are not set by either constitutional theory or discoverable law, but rather by the tolerance of the countervailing powers.'[41] In accordance with the principle of a balanced mechanism, that tolerance has remained intact, for, despite the many criticisms of the Court and the periodic reform drives to reduce its power, the very notion of an intentionally weaker judiciary is inimical to the ethos of balanced government. The judiciary's defence is not simply that 'courts, like all institutions of government in the United States, are limited in their power by being part of the checks and balances scheme'.[42] It is rather the instability that would presumably arise from a diminution of its power, and the fear generated by the unknown effects of a withdrawal of one of the links in a system noted for its interconnected parts. 'Who can say how the delicate mechanisms of power in Congress, or in our federal union, will adjust themselves, if the political departments operate without the consciousness of a possible check by the Court?'[43] To Charles L. Black, merely to ask such a question is tantamount to providing the answer.

The same observational and judgemental apparatus is also employed in respect to federalism. This other great structural characteristic of American government began as a pragmatic and imprecise arrangement for acquiring the advantages of an authoritative central government whilst retaining the benefits of state sovereignty and local autonomy. It was in no sense a rationally conceived plan of governmental organization. On the contrary, it was a hybrid construct produced through compromise and bargaining by negotiating parties who required nothing other than a workable settlement. The result was a compact amongst the states by which they relinquished some of their sovereignty, in order to form a separate and collective tier of national government that would perform those functions thought to require a broad-based authority (e.g. defence, foreign relations, currency, interstate commerce, the postal service). While these two levels or spheres of government offered the prospect of a clear and explicit rationale to the federal structure, the meaning of American federalism has, nevertheless, always remained elusive. The differentiation of government and sovereignty into two forms has continued to pose profound definitional and conceptual problems. Of these, two are of particular significance.

The first is the difficulty of establishing a criterion that would satisfactorily determine, or account for, the division between the federal and state spheres of responsibility. The most common response to this problem is to assume that the central government supervises those functions that are national, general, or common in nature, while the state governments are appropriately confined to local or particular matters. But as Rufus Davies explains:

> What one must note is that this 'inescapable federal principle of distributing functions' is only a meaningful directive if there is a mode of knowing what is a 'national', 'common', 'local', or 'particular' matter.... What is the differentiating property of ... activities which characterises them as 'national' or 'local'? Is it in the nature of the need or the purpose they are intended to satisfy; the nature of the organisation required to

administer these needs, or is the identification of 'national' or 'local' matters a purely subjective preference for centralised or decentralised government in one field of activity or another? There is nowhere a clear answer.[44]

And because there is not a clear answer, then not only does the division between the federal and state levels remain unclear, but the identity and solidity of the governments themselves fall prey to continuous dispute and uncertainty. And following on from the issue of differentiation is the problem of the relationship between the two levels. The dual spheres of government can be seen as separate and exclusive, or conjoined and inclusive; competitive and hostile, or concurrent and co-operative; only partially overlapping in jurisdiction, or unavoidably and inherently overlapping. 'Local functions' can merge into 'national functions'. National responsibilities may permit the federal government to pre-empt an area of formal, but unexercised, state authority. State responsibilities, on the other hand, may preclude the assumption of local obligation by the national authority. Again there are no clear answers to these questions from the concepts and structure of American federalism.

The disputes and debates surrounding the issue of the differentiating characteristics of the two levels of government and the subsequent relationships between them bears a very close resemblance to the problem encountered in the separation of powers. Namely, the need to square the functional integrity and qualitative differentiation supporting the separateness of the branches with the empirical reality of their functional interlinkage and interdependence. Just as he was forced to admit that 'no skill in government had yet been able to discriminate and define, with sufficient clarity, its three great provinces – the legislature, executive and judiciary',[45] so James Madison felt similarly impelled to acknowledge the ambiguity of the federal–state partnership:

> Here, then, are three sources of vague and incorrect definitions: indistinctness of the object, imperfection of the organ of conception, inadequateness of the vehicle of ideas. Any one of these must produce a certain degree of obscurity. The convention, in delineating the boundary between the federal and State jurisdictions, must have experienced the full effect of them all.[46]

He concluded that the constitution was 'in strictness neither a national nor a federal constitution, but a composition of both'.[47] This unavoidable mixture allowed Madison to tread the same path as he had done with the separation of powers and to render the federal arrangement intelligible and purposeful by recasting it as another device for reciprocal power management. Madison's equation of 'partial agency' with 'control'[48] had the effect of transforming the intermixture of the legislative, executive, and judicial branches into points of contact, thereby confirming simultaneously both their physical differentiation and their physical interaction. The ambiguity of the jurisdictional and functional boundaries within the federal–state relationship served to enmesh the federal organization in a system of vertical checks and balances, in the same way as he had sought to reduce the separation of powers into a matrix of horizontal checks and balances. Moreover, he regarded the two systems as not merely compatible with one another, but reducible to a single overall framework of governmental limitation:

> In the compound republic of America, the power surrendered by the people is first divided between two distinct governments, and then the portion allotted to each subdivided among distinct and separate departments. Hence a double security arises to the rights of the people. The different governments will control each other, at the same time that each will be controlled by itself.[49]

In this way it was shown that the definitional and conceptual difficulties endemic to federalism could be simplified by the transference of those mechanical categories more normally associated with the separation of powers directly to the relationships and purposes of federalism.

Initially such a new and untried arrangement as the federal compact could not be expected to be seen and treated in this mechanically coherent manner. But by the end of the nineteenth century the Supreme Court had guided the development of the relationship between the federal and state governments into one of separation, check, and balance. The doctrine of 'dual federalism' proceeded on the premise of the theoretical existence of two separate spheres of responsibility and power.[50] The Court sought to substantiate this dichotomy by imposing a rigidly defined line of demarcation between the federal and state jurisdiction. As a result, the notion of the federal and state governments possessing some intrinsically irreducible qualities or separate functional attributes that distinguished them from one another was progressively displaced by the mechanistic construct of a physical division of power occasioned by the desire to account for the weighting of each level and to assure that an appropriate equilibrium between them could exist. Rather than two distinctive powers, the federal and state sectors became recognized and accepted as two allotments of power. Accordingly, the federal system became schematized along Madisonian lines into an explicit arrangement of power management in which the centripetal force of the federal government was thought to check and to balance the centrifugal forces of the state governments, and vice versa. The federal and state governments, therefore, were seen as coexisting, yet wedged apart into virtual independence in order to satisfy the joint demands for organizational clarity and political control.

Later, with the emergence of the federal government's revenue-gathering superiority, the onset of grants-in-aid, and the renewed awareness of federalism as a 'separation of governments sharing power', the principle of dual federalism was seen as an excessively rigid and static formalism. In retrospect, it was regarded as having failed to provide an accurate portrayal of the federal system in the nineteenth century,[51] and of being quite unable to accommodate the pragmatic and fluid reality of federal–state relationships in the second third of the twentieth century. The old federal dogma was duly criticized as a 'billiard ball concept'[52] based upon the tacit if crude assumption that 'the total amount of power was constant and, therefore, any increase in federal power diminished the power of the states',[53] and vice versa. Implicit in this conception of federalism was the notion of an ever-present equilibrium that would ensure a 'relationship of co-ordinate equality between the states and the central government'.[54] The new-style federalism, by contrast, was ostensibly quite different. It became 'hardly possible to think any longer of a federal equilibrium, if we mean by that an equal balance of opposing forces in the usual physical sense'.[55] It was recognized that 'state and national power was not a seesaw in which one side has to be up and the other down'.[56] According to this altered perspective, national and state governments could expand their spheres of responsibility concurrently with one another; they could influence, bargain with, and persuade one another; they could redevise relationships, experiment in partnerships, and engage in pragmatic forms of co-operation; and they could combine in varying degrees of amalgamation to 'respond to needs and problems that transcend state boundaries in an increasingly closely-knit economic and social community'.[57] The emphasis was switched from separation and independence to interpenetration and interdependence. Instead of the prescriptive order of legal distinctions and the imposed clarity of mechanized relationships, the new federalism was characterized more by the actual disorder, incoherence, and mutability of the federal union; by a concern for positive and affirmative government action almost irrespective of jurisdictional barriers and formalized divisions; and by the 'marble-cake'[58] structure of the diversified finances, policies, and administration of what had by then become known as 'intergovernmental relations'.[59] Even the very meaning of the federal idea became dissipated and open to doubt. It seemed to have lost the anchorage of its earlier connection with divided powers, 'each, within a sphere, co-ordinate and independent'.[60] Under assault from the more empirically based studies of how federal relationships actually worked in practice, and in reaction to the legalistic style of earlier studies, the conceptual analysis of federalism, according to one noted commentator, reached 'the point where the definitions that were offered were almost totally vacuous'.[61]

Despite the adoption of this more realistic perspective, the underlying ethos of the mechanistic conception of federalism has remained remarkably intact. The much heralded emancipation from the old perceptual and evaluative strictures was in actuality far more apparent than real. The new realism may well have led to a greater recognition of the responsiveness and adaptability of the federal system. But it also led to a more acute realization that the 'sharing of functions is, in fact, the sharing of power'[62] and that the constitutional configuration of federal relations is strongly moulded by political forces with interests at stake in the distribution of governmental powers. This in turn fostered a renewed suspicion of federalism as a Trojan horse of political integration – i.e. as a disguised progression towards a national and centralized structure of policy-making and administration, to the inevitable detriment of states' rights and local autonomy. As a result, the values, principles, and traditions associated with decentralization were once again perceived to be dependent upon, and secured by, the ability of the states to counteract and balance the unifying forces of the federal government. Likewise, the advantages and benefits of centralism were similarly recognized as being a function of decentralization and of the equilibrium between the physical properties of the two opposing forces. Even the generic definitions of federalism began to show signs of reverting to a more mechanistic basis (e.g. 'the study of federalism becomes the study of all those techniques ... which serve to maintain, or to erode, the balance between mutual independence and interdependence between levels of government';[63] 'federalism, conceived as anything other than a "weak" ideology of balance, is not very satisfactory'[64]). As for the condition of American federalism, this too showed the extent to which observers, analysts, and politicians continued to draw instinctively upon the premises, principles, and vocabulary of mechanics, in order to describe and explain the contemporary nature of the federal–state relationship. In the face of the 'secular drift towards the concentration of power',[65] in which the national government appeared as the chief instigator of redistributing power within the federal system, the concept of balance has, nevertheless, retained its popular appeal – both as a depiction of fact and as a statement of value. Despite the massive changes wrought in the federal system since the New Deal and the periodic reports of the 'death of federalism' reflecting the latter stages of the United States' final transformation into a unitary state,[66] the American federal structure is still conventionally described in terms of balances acquired or balances to be acquired.

The references to federalism continue to be dominated, first, by the concept of tension:

> There is a real dilemma when it comes to the issue of centralisation versus decentralisation – when one argues over federal power versus states' rights.... Tension between the two principles is almost automatic.[67]

> A continual process of give-and-take goes on between the national and state governments.[68]

Second, by the contribution of local and state governments as counterweights to national action:

> By providing numerous more or less independent or autonomous centers of power throughout the system, they reinforce the principles of balanced authority and political pluralism.[69]

By using their power to strengthen their own governments and those of their subdivisions, the states can relieve much of the pressure for, and generate a strong counterpressure against, improper expansion of national action.[70]

Third, by the need to secure or retain a balanced relationship between the federal and state sectors:

Almost all agree, however they differ on particular issues, that a country the size of the United States needs strong and active state governments and that a major problem of federalism is how to maintain a balance between national and state governments.[71]

What is needed is an intricate balance between national dominance, where the national interest is primary, and local discretion, where the local opinions are more important than national ones.... The centrifugal force of domestic politics needs to be balanced by the centripetal force of strong Presidential leadership. Simultaneous strength at center and periphery exhibits the American system at its best.[72]

And fourth, by the assumption of an existing, if changeable, balance within the federal system.

The balance between the national government and the state governments is ... in a constant state of flux.[73]

Federalism ... is an effective balance between fractionalisation into many small nations and the centralisation that destroys local autonomy.[74]

Our federal idea is complex and subtle. It involves a balance of strengths.[75]

No single index can measure the complex and interactive balance of power in the federal system.... The American federal system has never been static. It has changed radically over the years, as tides of centralisation and decentralisation have altered the balance of power.[76]

Another great balance is that which lies at the heart of federalism – the balance between national action and state and local vitality.[77]

The concepts and vocabulary of interaction and equilibrium have not been as readily dispensable as some commentators may have supposed or even wished. The susceptibility to mechanical categories for the purposes of explanation and prescription has remained, even to the extent of rationalizing the proposed reversal of historical trends in the 'New Federalism' of general revenue-sharing. Much in the same way as the power of the modern Presidency was thought to be a unilinear and irresistible evolutionary progression until the mechanistic paradigm was reinvoked, so the transition from an 'unfinished nation' into an integrated national community, under the aegis of an evolving and centralizing federalism, was seen to be similarly frustrated by President Nixon's insistence that historical directions not only could be, but should be, reversed. Nixon made it quite clear that his New Federalism programme was intended 'to introduce a new and more creative balance' to the approach to government by reversing 'the flow of power and resources from the states and communities to Washington and start power and resources flowing back from Washington to the states and communities'.[78] The plausibility and general acceptability of this plan were not based merely upon a political 'reaction against the use of federal money to impose national priorities and standards on state and local government',[79] or upon the self-interested motives of state bureaucracies in increasing their discretion to gear federal programmes to their own needs and priorities. It was also a 'testament to the enduring political strength of the states and localities and the tradition of decentralization in American politics',[80] which possessed no clearer or more emphatic expression than that of their contribution to the actual or potential balance within the federal system.[81]

What holds true for the federal system and the Supreme Court also holds true for any other distinguishable power centre that enters the field of political vision. The same modes of perception and principles of evaluation are applied, resulting in the same framework of responses and rationalizations. The emergence of a large, permanent, and professional federal bureaucracy, for example, has tended to be received and treated as a new and separate locus of force in the governmental system. The bureaucracy's organizational and functional nature can be seen as idiosyncratically different from the system's other institutions and distinguishable, in particular, from the conventional understanding of the executive role more normally associated with the Presidency. Nevertheless, the power and position of the bureaucracy are almost effortlessly accommodated into the traditional structure of the governmental system by the simple extension of the separation of powers principle to include an additional partner – or, as it is widely known, the 'fourth branch of government'. The novelty of the bureaucracy's scale and influence as an institution is, thereby, reduced instinctively to a common mechanistic frame of reference within which the institution can acquire a legitimacy as one element amongst others contributing its weight and force to an overall system of dynamic action and reaction. This not only leads to an acceptance, and even to an expectation, of the bureaucracy behaving as a politicized body, but generates analyses of the bureaucracy in terms of discoverable balances and of prescribed equilibria to which the institution might be made to approximate.

The best known and most cited case of balance in this field is that between the Presidency and the remainder of the executive branch. Despite being the nominal chief executive of a nominally hierarchical structure, Presidents have had to acknowledge that the bureaucracy's accumulation of administrative law and delegated legislative discretion, combined with its specialist expertise, its rules and regulatory procedures, its policy experience and programme attachments, its continuity of personnel and practices, its indigenous communication networks, and its cultivation of clientele constituencies have together afforded the bureaucracy such a level of influence as to make 'the task of getting the bureaucracy to follow his leadership ... a formidable assignment for any President'.[82] The bureaucracy 'becomes in many instances the most powerful single limitation upon the Presidency'[83] and, as such, it is recognized that 'one of the most crucial of Presidential responsibilities is to gain control over the existing bureaucracies and make them work with and for the White House'.[84] Far from constituting an enhancement of Presidential power, therefore, the federal bureaucracy represents 'a semi-autonomous branch of government ... exercising strong influence on the President',[85] and making 'Presidential government ... by no stretch of the imagination a pyramid-like structure with a single pinnacle'.[86] This view of the bureaucracy as an influential element of government in its own right has led to charges of organizational indiscipline, insufficient democratic control, and reduced political accountability. More often than not, these complaints are transformed into declarations of an imbalance between democratic and bureaucratic forces. Such anxieties have been used to justify the accelerated development of the Executive Office of the Presidency, in order to redress the balance and to allow the chief executive to exert a greater degree of control over the policy-making and management activities of the executive branch. This, in turn, has led to charges of a concentrated and insular Presidency, 'isolated from traditional, constitutional checks and balances',[87] and to fears of the chief executive unbalancing the power relationship between his office and the bureaucracy.

It is a testament to the centrality of checks and balances in American constitutionalism that such an imbalance is seen as being just as reprehensible as the one affording superior weight and advantage to the bureaucracy. The Presidency is expected to check the bureaucracy, but not to the extent of domineering it. This is not just because the bureaucracy has a representative and democratic authority of its own that to its apologists has permitted it to become 'a far more sensitive register of changing currents of opinions than ... Congress'.[88] It is more because the bureaucracy provides an additional and more contemporary counterweight to the forces of concentrated power and centralized control. Its negative characteristics of delay, obstruction, fragmentation, complexity, and incoherence provide it with an independence which is taken as making a positive contribution to a constitutional system dedicated to the division of power and the dispersal of authority. Bureaucracy's compatibility with constitutionalism by way of power mechanics is clearly discernible in the following passage from an article by Peter Woll and Rochelle Jones celebrating the bureaucracy's role in curbing the excesses of President Nixon:

> Under the Nixon Administration the bureaucracy is turning into a vital although little noticed safeguard of the democratic system.... In a system marked by a weak Congress and a Supreme Court that is increasingly taking its directions from Nixon appointees, the bureaucracy is turning into a crucial check on Presidential power.... Perhaps, in the final analysis, we are saved from tyranny by the pluralism of our system and even its inefficiency. The pluralistic and independent bureaucracy, although often inefficient and yielding to special-interest group pressure, helps to preserve the balance of powers among the branches of government that is necessary for the preservation of our system of constitutional democracy.[89]

It is ironic that the bureaucracy, which has the reputation of being the least accountable of institutions, should be presented as a crucial element in maintaining constitutional government. Such is the emphasis on power and on its distribution, however, that almost any body that can be seen to be draining power from a locus threatening to draw an excess of power to itself is considered worthy of constitutional sanction. It is precisely because the bureaucracy is thought to possess these mechanical properties within a system which stresses the efficacy and validity of checks and balances that commentators like Norton Long are led to refer uninhibitedly to the need of American constitutional theory to 'recognise and understand the working and the potential of our great fourth branch of government, taking a rightful place beside President, Congress and Courts'.[90]

Working on the same principles and with the same methods, there emerge other contenders for the title of the fourth branch of government. The first is the military establishment, whose massive size and penetrating influence on American society and government generate concern over the degree of control imposed upon it. To some commentators, the military's power is adequately circumscribed by the conventional apparatus of civilian control of the policy-making and budgetary processes. 'The really remarkable thing' to Stephen Ambrose, for example, 'is that America has managed to create an institution of such staggering size without being swallowed up by it. For important as the military is, it does not dominate our lives, establish values, or dictate our foreign and domestic policies.'[91] Others disagree and claim that the military's exceptional role and status as the guardian of national security at a time of sustained international tension, combined with its traditionally secretive and enclosed organization, its mastery of its own complex and technically demanding subject matter, and its political and economic leverage as the largest purchaser of goods and services in the United States, have allowed the military to assume a position of virtual autonomy.[92] Because of this:

> the relationship between the executive branch and the military is a complex matter, often more like that between two branches of government than a straight-line chain-of-command. Each uses its own power bases with

Congress, pursues its own interests in the political arena and jockeys with the other for advantage or accommodation.[93]

Once again, the presence of a distinguishable separate unit of government is confirmed by its material effect on the other units in its proximity. Critics conclude that 'the constitutional framework of separation of powers has proved insufficient in itself to check and control the powerful military establishment which has emerged since the Second World War'.[94] And, in accordance with the mechanical logic of checks and balances, the blame for what can only be diagnosed as an imbalance of power is attributed to a failure of the countervailing powers to exercise a restraining influence upon the military. The Congress has been accused of being overwhelmed by the military's technical expertise and political influence. The civilian policy-makers in the executive branch are accused of submitting to the military establishment in the formulation of foreign policy 'despite periods of vacillation and sporadic attempts at applying civilian checks and balances'.[95] But it is the Presidency in particular to which responsibility for the military's asserted power is assigned. According to Adam Yarmolinsky, this is because 'the military is at no time more powerful than the President of the United States – the Commander in Chief of the Armed Forces – is prepared to allow it to be'.[96]

Taken together, it is the apparent inadequacy of these counterweights that has allowed the military to become, in the words of J. William Fulbright, 'a monster bureaucracy that can grind beneath its wheels the other bureaucracies, whatever their prescribed roles in the process of government and their legitimate needs'.[97] While some observers find solace in the intense rivalry between the services which is seen as providing the fragmentation necessary for an internal and self-regulating equilibrium,[98] most critics regard this as an unreliable and unsatisfactory method of achieving control. The solution to a problem posed by an imbalance is generally recognized to be a redress of the unbalanced state, with power pitted to counter power. Even if it is no longer possible to achieve the 'restoration of the old balance of civil–military relations which had prevailed until World War II',[99] it is taken as read that a greater degree of balance is not only possible but necessary in order 'to get the military power under firm civilian control'.[100] The measures suggested for achieving this objective have included 'electing a President on this issue' of military control;[101] improving the procedures by which the President acquires information and implements decisions; reactivating Congress's constitutional responsibility to subject the Pentagon's structure and budget to rigorous legislative scrutiny; and by enhancing the chances of an effective counterweight through the development of additional checks like J. K. Galbraith's suggestion of a Military Audit Commission composed of highly qualified scientists and citizens whose 'function would be to advise the Congress and inform the public on military programs and negotiations'.[102]

The last noteworthy candidacy for the fourth branch of government is the press, or more latterly the media. The same disposition of analysis through balance is as conspicuous in this field as it is in the bureaucratic and military spheres. Perhaps the assimilation of the press into the structure of checks and balances is a more outstanding example of the applicability of constitutional mechanisms, as the news organizations are not ostensibly part of either the formal system of representation or the apparatus of a government founded upon popular consent. In spite of their external position to government, the press and the media in general have become crucially important to the governmental process by performing the role of intermediary between the public and its political representatives in a mass society where communications have become not just a major industry but a cultural preoccupation. As responsibility for political leadership, policy direction, and administrative management normally devolves upon the Presidency, it is the media's relationship with the White House that is usually portrayed as constituting the essence of the media's role and position in respect to the government. A very familiar theme emerges from this relationship – namely, that the press and the Presidency are seen as interdependent. Both represent a source, and a limitation of power, to the other. While the media require information about, and access to, the White House in order to satisfy their audience's almost inexhaustible appetite for news about the Presidency, the chief executive himself needs the media to educate and mobilize the public support necessary to develop his leadership and to secure his objectives in a system in which his authority always remains tenuous and provisional. It is precisely because the President's reputation and leverage within the government are so dependent upon the perceptions of popular support and approval he receives outside Washington that the stock of an entire administration can hinge upon the successful presentation of the President to his political constituency.[103] But because the priorities and interpretations afforded to the President's policies and actions by the media may not correspond to the priorities and interpretations of the White House, tensions invariably arise.

The relationship between the new organizations and the Presidency can easily fluctuate from co-operation, through the acknowledgement of mutual need, to conflict and the creation of an adversarial format in which the media come to 'regard themselves as surrogates for the public'[104] and seek to perform a critical and inquisitorial function on behalf of the people. It was during the Vietnam and Watergate era that relations between the White House and the media deteriorated to a level of basic hostility. While the media concerned themselves increasingly with the alleged abuses of executive power, the White House accused the media of bias, distortion, and political motivation, it harassed news organizations by threatening anti-trust actions and licence renewal reviews, and it even went so far as to subject individual reporters to surveillance through the illegal use of wire-taps.

The conduct and effect of this adversarial relationship prompted a widespread debate and analysis of both the role and the power of the American press. Ultimately, the Nixon administration brought to a head the manner by which the influence of the press could be satisfactorily accounted for in the American system. It revealed the general criteria against which the media could be assessed as a political force. The pattern that emerged was the familiar one of balance. With few exceptions, the subtleties and complexities of the Presidency–media relationship were either confined at the outset or reduced by way of conclusion to that of a material equilibrium of comparable but opposing units of power:

> The relationship of the press to a President is, and necessarily must be, one of tension.... The President must try to shape the news, and journalists, covering him, must resist. There is a built-in conflict in this situation.[105]

> Watergate ... raised basic constitutional questions concerning the interrelationship among all our political institutions, including of course the press.... Many of the abuses symbolised by Watergate ... were in fact directed at the press as part of the administration's campaign to make the news media less critical. If these efforts had been successful, they would have reduced press freedom and altered the balance between government and the press in favor of the former.[106]

> There must be checks on the President if the government is to be kept in balance, as contemplated by the constitution. The responsibility devolves on Congress, the courts and the press.[107]

> It could be said, I suppose, that the runaway Presidency had been checked by the recalcitrance of institutions – the independent judiciary, the free press, the investigative power of Congress.[108]

> The media do provide the public with protection against abuses of power by the White House.... The media have served as valuable checks on those in the White House who took it for granted that they could use their position for personal gain or to remain immune from the ordinary legal processes governing citizens and officials, or who abused their power in the pursuit of political goals for themselves or for the President.[109]

> But there are problems ... that together have been working to reverse the old balance of power between the Presidency and the press. It is the thesis here that, if this balance should tip too far in the direction of the press, our capacity for effective democratic government will be seriously and dangerously weakened.[110]

From this selection of illustrative passages, it is clear that the media's power was afforded the mantle of constitutionality as a further restraint on the exercise of power and as an additional agency of political fragmentation that would help to prevent an excessive concentration of power. Perspectives of the 'relative position of the two institutions in the constitutional system'[111] might range from Tom Wicker's claim that it is impossible for the press to undermine or ruin a President, because 'any President has far too big a lead to start with',[112] to Robert Entman's proclamation of an 'imperial media' in which the question for a President 'has not been *whether* the media would obstruct the leadership, but *when* and *how*'.[113] Nevertheless, the central assumptions of the media, as an assimilable power within the traditional political structure and, thereby, as an active, integral, and even necessary participant in its institutional dynamics, remain intact. Reminiscent of Newton's third law of mechanics, the media are recognized as having 'become one of the principal forces on the national political scene, influencing the other major forces – the President, Congress, the bureaucracy, the parties, and the pressure groups – and in turn being influenced by them'.[114]

The relationship between and amongst the three branches of government and the twin levels of the federal system, together with the bureaucracy, the military, and the media, do not by any means exhaust the use of balance to describe the structure and operation of the political system. The major institutions may be the most prominent subjects to which the mechanics of equilibrium are applied, but there are so many others that it can appear that no political form or process is immune to characterization by balance. It is claimed, for example, that the House of Representatives and the Senate act as counterweights to each other; that the White House staff checks the Cabinet; that the President's national security advisers balance the State Department, even to the extent of generating two foreign-policy structures and occasionally two foreign policies; that the army, navy, air force, and marines provide a creative tension within the Pentagon; that the states interact not only with one another but also with local governments to set up a series of reciprocal restraints; that the Office of Management and Budget confronts and exerts a corrective balance upon the federal bureaucracy; that the Democratic and Republican parties provide the essential constituents of a dynamic two-party system; and that through the competitive interplay of pluralistic interest groups a self-regulating equilibrium of political forces is maintained.

Balances can be large-scale or small-scale. They can be composed of two components, or of a profusion of interacting parts. And they can be static and immobile, or dynamic and alternating in character. They can range, therefore, from Walter D. Burnham's reference to the 'constitution's clever clockwork mechanisms'[115] to Theodore Lowi's claim that Congress's internal fragmentation in itself gives the American system 'several hundred "checks and balances"',[116] and to Burns and Peltason's allusion to a grand 'political pendulum',[117] by which 'Republicans and Democrats have alternated in power with a fair degree of regularity'.[118] From the concepts, outlook, and vocabulary used in the conventional literature on American government and politics, it is apparent that there exists a quite uninhibited disposition towards the use of mechanical principles to describe and to account for the nature of political relationships. References to dynamics, characterizations of balance, rationalizations by means of equipoise, and recognition of problems and solutions in terms of material cause and effect pervade the texts on American government. Just as there appears to be no limit to the extent to which many analysts will seek to project a mechanical mode of explanation upon their subject matter, so also there seem no lengths that other analysts will not go to in order to derive a mechanistically based interpretation to their observations. Sometimes these efforts are ingenious and convincing. On other occasions they can reflect a complacent deference to formalism and convention. Either way, the general tone and substance of much of the literature reveal a fundamental orientation towards the structures and values of mechanics in the quest to provide satisfactory portrayals of the character of American government.

The United States' exceptional predilection towards the principle of balance in its political system, however, is not confined merely to the level of material institutions, or to the identifiable tiers of government, or to the other discrete and tangible entities that are invariably associated with the varied states of equilibrium in American politics. The assertions of multiple balances within the political system are noteworthy and significant in their own right. But they are also important for what they reveal about the underlying psychology of a political culture so attached to mechanical forms and relationships. In particular, they serve to exemplify an orientation towards a mechanistic paradigm that is deeper and more far-reaching than is normally appreciated. Indeed, it can be argued that mechanics have penetrated American political culture to such an extent that Newtonian principles heavily circumscribe not only the conventions of political observation and interpretation but also the logic of political argument and even the nature of political value structures.

Before going any further, it would be appropriate at this stage to make a number of basic observations on the meaning and nature of equilibrium. First, the notion of balance is dependent upon the existence of at the very least two entities which, though connected to one another, remain separate and discrete. Second, because a balance is an intrinsically physical condition, the two entities (i.e. x and y) must necessarily be two material entities whose solidity is thereafter confirmed by the existence of the balance between them, registering the differential or equivalence in their relative weights. The two entities may be qualitatively different from one another, yet, by virtue of the balance, they are shown to possess a basic common property by which a relationship between them is established. According to the logic of an equilibrium, the differentiation becomes a spatial differentiation which allows the common property of weight to determine the relationship in terms of a material configuration of forces (Figure 10). Third, the balance reveals that the relationship between x and y is a direct zero-sum interaction, in which any change in the position of one will immediately lead to an equal, but opposite, change is the position of the other. Furthermore, the changes are seen as occurring within a closed system of cause and effect in which a change in the weight and, therefore, the position of x unequivocally determines a proportionate change in the relative weight and position of y (Figure 11). Fourth, an inequitable

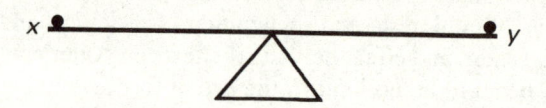

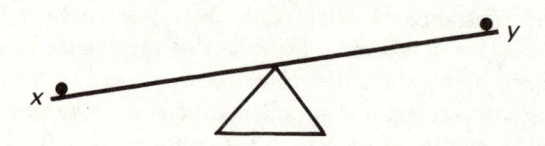

configuration of force and position is a graphic departure from balance. It is an imbalance. This condition is only definable and discernible through the reliability of information concerning what a balance consists of and looks like. Only by accepting that a horizontal line between x and y represents a balance is it possible to conclude that x now possesses excess weight while y has too little. The condition suggests its own solution: namely, a redistribution of weight that will rectify the imbalance by virtue of both x and y's own physical properties. Fifth, while the mechanics of the balance might be described as negative in so far as they are based on x offsetting y, the effect is normally given a positive value. This is not just because a structure of weight and counterweight offers a vision of disharmony and discordance when out of balance, it is also because a balance strongly suggests a composite of the positive elements within x and y held together by the dynamics of a stable equilibrium. The balance itself, therefore, does not represent a fusion of x and y into a new entity. On the contrary, it suggests an aggregate of the two original units, which remain mutually exclusive and, thereby, in occupation of opposite ends of the scale, but none the less dependent on one another for perpetuating the balance and securing for each other its own balance ($+$) between 'too much' ($-$) and 'too little' ($-$) (Figure 12).

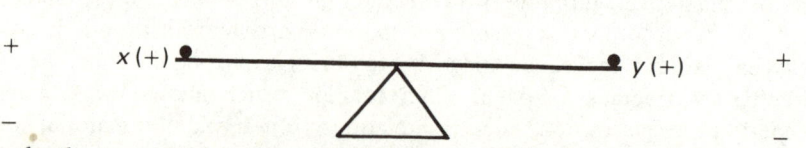

Lastly, the terms of definition and description attached to balances are inherently tautologous in that they are dependent upon one another for their meaning and measurement. For example, a balance consists of a state of equilibrium between two opposites, which are known to be opposites because they are evenly held in balance. These opposites are compatible with one another because they can be balanced, and they can be balanced because they are compatible. And, finally, an imbalance is caused by an excess of weight on one side. The excess is determinable only by the loss on the other side, just as the loss itself is calculable only by the increase at the opposite end of the balance.

With these characteristics of balance in mind, it is noticeable how so much of the literature on American politics becomes encircled and, consequently, entrapped by the closed system of description and explanation produced by the prevailing attention given to equilibria. Premises become confused with conclusions, observations merge with deductions, and forms and features fall prey to circular definitions in terms of one another. Balances are presupposed to exist between two entities, while the latter are predetermined to constitute an interactive duality through the presence of an actual or potential balance between them. Shifts in the position of one or other sides of a balance become defined purely in terms of a cause–effect relationship occurring exclusively within the confines of the balance. And since balances automatically imply checks and mutual restraint, checks of any nature are sanctioned as facilitating balances irrespective of the negativism and immobilism they may produce.

Most, if not all, of these problems are generated by the closed nature of a system seen to be given over so much to checks and balances. Such a system offers the appearance of clearly delineated relationships between readily identifiable and interconnected solids behaving in strict accordance with calculable laws of mechanics. The reality of such a system, however, is quite different. It is plagued not only with tautologies, but with relativism, and with all the arguments, uncertainty, and ambiguity associated with it. What remains absent in this political environment of stated equilibria and professed harmonies is an absolute and fixed frame of reference by which 'checks' can be confirmed as checks, and 'balances' can be assured of being balances. While it is true that a ' "balance of power" implies equality of power, and equality of power seems wholly fair and even honorable', owing to the lack of an absolute framework by which to ascertain balance, it is just as true that 'what is one man's honorable balance is often another's unfair imbalance'.[119] An activist Supreme Court, for example, can be interpreted as 'encroaching on the powers and prerogatives of other branches of our government, thereby upsetting our constitutional system of checks and balances'.[120] This might well be seen as a 'fortunate imbalance', reviving 'old concepts of justice and fair play' and encouraging 'Congress ... to take progressive action'.[121] Nevertheless, it remains an imbalance. From another perspective, however, an interventionist judicial body like the Warren Court can be seen as providing a legitimate compensating balance to the negativism of the other branches and acting as 'an instrument of national moral values that had not been able to find other governmental expression'.[122] Both positions can be considered defensible through reasoned argument and careful evaluation. But neither of the positions can be verified in the terms in which they are primarily presented, i.e. neither can be proved correct in respect to the physical properties of balance and imbalance by which each seeks to establish its validity. The existence or not of a balance remains a matter of perspective, conjecture, interpretation, and argument. Conclusive proof remains elusive, for, without a settled and definitive reference point, balance is fated to be both a relative term and a mutable condition.

In spite of the empirical uncertainties of such an apparently determinable and calculable condition, analysts have continued to proceed on the assumption that balances can not only be observed in the past and present, but also acquired in the future. As matter of habit and tradition, references to and usages of equilibria continue to permeate the language of political description, to shape the methods of political enquiry, and to mould the perceived nature of political problems and solutions. Such is the dependence upon the conceptual apparatus of checks and balances that John Lehman, for one, has been prompted to take his fellow scholars to task on the matter. Alluding to the relationship between the Presidency and Congress in the field of foreign policy, Lehman remains staunchly fatalistic:

> There are, in short, no frameworks, no cookbooks, no valid models, and no 'golden ages' of administrations past to which we might refer in judging a 'proper' distribution of powers or even 'constitutional' relationship between branches. The student of these affairs must therefore resign himself to continuing paradox, to insoluble contradiction, even to an element of sustained mystery.[123]

Lehman goes on to apply the same scepticism to the notion of prospective balances. He disapproves of the way that 'all too often scholars and commentators seem to assume that some ideal constitutional balance exists ... which, if discovered and enacted into law, will forever guarantee the formulation and conduct of wise and just foreign policy'.[124] Despite such censures and admonitions, the academic and journalistic communities show few signs of even wishing to extricate themselves from the all-enveloping embrace of constitutional mechanics. The literature remains replete with the self-fulfilling circularity and determinism of balances perceived and deduced at the same time. To the average reader of texts on American government, it is well nigh impossible to avoid repeatedly stumbling over assertions of 'self-evident' balances and subsequently falling into pits walled with mirrors so that each image reflects back the reverse impressions of itself.

For example, because Congress acted against the Presidency by passing the War Powers Act (1973), it was thought to have achieved a new balance of powers. And assuming this to be the achievement, then motivations tended to be recast in terms of the end result – leading Thomas Cronin, for example, to claim that the Congress had been prompted into passing the Act 'in an attempt to redress the imbalance'.[125] To take another example, just as a policy produced by the joint efforts of the Presidency and Congress may be described as an incidence of balanced government, so the policy itself tends to become transmuted by definition into a balanced or moderate policy. In referring to the accommodation between President Reagan and the Ninety-eighth Congress over social security legislation in 1983, Norman Ornstein declared that 'the best features of checks and balances are in play ... ; we are arriving at a set of centrist and sensible policies'.[126] The same implication is present in Samuel Huntington's description of the changes in civilian–military relations as a result of the Cold War. The high level of defence activities 'intensified the impact of the separation of powers on civilian–military relations ... by enhancing the role of Congress'[127] in military policy. Since the rivalry of the Presidency and Congress 'required each to distinguish itself from the other by advancing its own contribution to national policy', if only to 'assert itself as at least a co-equal in running the government',[128] the net effect in this newly significant area of public policy was that 'it tended to produce a pluralistic or balanced national military strategy'.[129] Another example of the myopic determinism induced by checks and balances is provided by Max Lerner. By accepting the assumption that the federal system is characterized by an integral and indispensable balance between the federal government and the state governments, any change in the relationship is necessarily predetermined to be a balance of a different order or in a different guise. There is no other way of comprehending Lerner's unsupported yet avowedly self-evident proposition 'that after each extension of the federal power, a new equilibrium is struck at the higher level'.[130] Lerner is by no means exceptional. A more recent occupant of the same reflective pit has been Peter Woll, with his statement that 'the original constitutional scheme represented a delicate balance between national and state interests, which is continually changing as the national government and the states struggle for political power'.[131] These cases are by no means exceptional. They are the norm. Commentators and scholars are so immured by the mechanics of equilibria that only the most attentive and circumspect can avoid succumbing to the beguiling appeal of balance – a fact that ought perhaps to be appreciated more by John Lehman than by many others, for, after having criticized his colleagues for their futile preoccupation with the search for balances, he concluded the passage quoted above with the following ironic statement: 'The present balance is there, well-developed and functioning. It is to that reality that analytic attention should be addressed.'[132]

A still more revealing illustration of the penetrative qualities of mechanical precepts in American government is provided by the way in which intangible attributes and principles become aligned with institutions and organizations to the extent that they not only become closely identified with them, but come to assume many of the material properties which those institutions or organizations are assumed to possess. In this way the mechanical interactions that are thought to characterize institutional relationships are extended, consciously or unconsciously, to embrace those roles, values, or norms that are commonly thought to distinguish institutions from one another. As a result, institutional traits and principles become part of the mechanistic framework in their own right and are treated accordingly.

This process was very much in evidence in the debate over secrecy in government during the mid-1970s. Much of the controversy revolved around the CIA and Congress's past neglect and future intentions. The problems generated by the CIA were interpreted at the time in terms of institutional and organizational imbalance. Proposals were therefore advanced that sought to resolve the issue by redressing the imbalance and establishing a set of balanced relationships between the agencies, committees, and institutions involved.[133] What was also noticeable, however, was the way the two principles central to the controversy – namely, secrecy and democracy – became habitually reified from abstract terms into material elements that were discussed and analysed as if they possessed real physical properties in their own right. So much so, in fact, that the most commonly accepted premise of the debate was that there existed a direct and mechanistic relationship between them analogous to the mechanics that have traditionally characterized the connection between the executive and legislative branches of American government.

This was not an uncontested premise. Some commentators were insistent that government secrecy of the magnitude revealed by the CIA's activities posed an insuperable problem to any democratic state. It was claimed that secrecy was fundamentally incompatible with democracy and that it could not be tolerated without compromising those principles of openness, participation, consent, accountability, and self-government that a democratic state purported to embody. On the other hand, secrecy was not always seen as a 'source of illegitimate power ... unjust, morally wrong ... evil ... and in direct conflict with democratic principles'[134] and thereby requiring the abolition of bodies like the CIA.[135] State secrecy could be defended as an integral and indispensable requirement of a democratically elected government intent upon ruling on behalf of, and in the interests of, the people. Ultimately, neither of these approaches or solutions to the issue was adopted or, for that matter, seriously considered. The accepted solution was not acquired through any choice of principles or positions so much as by acquiescing in the only solution that presented itself in response to what was believed to be the nature of the problem.

As the CIA was perceived to be only out of balance with its restraining influences, it could be safely assumed that secrecy and democracy were compatible with one another for the purposes of balance. The objective, thereupon, became a matter of how 'a workable balance between necessary secrecy on the one hand and oversight on the other'[136] could best be achieved. Whether secrecy and democracy were taken as being reconcilable because of balance, or were held to be in some form of direct contact because they were regarded as compatible with one another, is impossible to unravel. Either way, the end result was the same, i.e. the conversion of secrecy and democracy into a mechanical duality in which only balance ranked as a solution and in which the only conceivable solution was that of balance. It might be said that such a device represented not so much a solution to the riddle of secrecy and democracy as a way of effectively suspending it. This is because the solution was not a co-option of one by the other, or an introduction of a third principle, or even a genuine synthesis between secrecy and democracy. It was a mechanical solution by which secrecy and democracy were juxtaposed with one another to form an aggregate. This was a way of having both at the same time, with balance interposed to determine the appropriate quantities and to rationalize the arrangement. Implicit in the logic of such a solution was the recognition that each element in isolation would be unbalanced and incomplete without the other. Only together would they determine and secure one another's positive values through a process of reciprocal definition and mutual restraint. In this way, secrecy and democracy were held to be amenable to a balanced solution in which each would be rendered beneficially free from excess by the physical presence of the other. With the reactivation of organizational dynamics between the executive and legislative branches, and between different elements of the executive, the generally accepted criterion for a solution was satisfied and public attention consequently shifted to other matters – secure in the knowledge that what had been achieved was the institutional affirmation of a balance between secrecy and democracy.

The way that secrecy and democracy were assumed to possess the physical features necessary to be understood as an interactive duality capable of balance is characteristic of a widespread disposition to perceive conditions and values in terms of mechanics. In American political debate and analysis it is common for quantities to become compounded with qualities, for just as values are given mechanical expressions, so the mechanics of the political system become value-loaded. Sometimes it appears that the process begins with quantities and moves to qualities. For example, much of the literature on federal–state relations begins with the physical characteristics of the two-tier structure and then proceeds to relate different values to its separate levels. The federal government tends to become attached to equality of opportunity, social integration, efficiency, uniformity, nationalism, majority rule, and central power. State governments, on the other hand, are regularly associated with liberty, diversity, self-government, local autonomy, participation, disunity, inefficiency, responsiveness, inequity, minority rights, and traditionalism. While the evaluative connotations attached to the two levels of government may vary with changes in conditions and issues, the habit of insinuating a condition comparable to the federal balance into relationships between opposite traits and principles remains constant.

On other occasions the process seems to be reversed, with qualities as the point of departure and quantities coming in their wake, giving representational form to otherwise intangible balances. The 'tension between conservatism and liberalism'[137] for example, has often been invested with a mechanistic nature by way of institutional associations. While liberalism has tended to be ascribed to the Presidency, conservatism has usually been projected on to the Congress. Thus 'the stronger the exertion of Presidential power, the more liberal and internationalist it will be because of the make-up and dynamics of the Presidential party', but the 'stronger the exertion of Congressional power, the more conservative and isolationist will be our national policy because of the structure of Congressional forces'.[138] It is the internal structures and forces of the institutions that have led to their distinctive susceptibilities to differing ideologies. Congress has traditionally embodied the ethos of minority rights and governmental restraint through its fragmented organization, elaborate procedures, coalitional politics, and multiple veto points. The Presidency, by contrast, has aroused the hopes of social reformers through the office's capacity to generate the centralized power and directional leadership necessary to secure changes through concerted governmental action. It is because the Presidency has the capacity to become the 'strong Presidency' and to gear the system towards activism and innovation through a concentration of executive power that the office 'in the liberal view, is uniquely equipped to authorize and give legitimacy to political and social programs which are of urgent importance but which can be counted on to meet opposition or be hamstrung if left to the inherently obstructionist procedures of the national legislature'.[139] In the same way that Congress used to be seen as inherently conservative because of its ability to prevent action, so Presidential activism came to be so closely associated with the liberal expansion of the positive state that, according to Erwin Hargrove, 'the quiet crisis in our beliefs about the Presidency' may have been 'one manifestation of the larger dilemma of American liberalism'.[140] These conflicting attitudes reflect the way in which the composition and dynamics of American government can become identified with the political prerequisites of ideological programmes to such an extent that not only does the governmental system become an issue in its own right, but the formal checks and balances that exist between the Presidency and Congress can come to characterize the relationship between liberalism and conservatism.

Whether the sequences of interpretation are inductive or deductive, the net effect has been to infuse organizational dynamics into ideologies, principles, values, characteristics, and traits in a quite unique way. References to such intangible equilibria are legion. Potential or actual balances are claimed to exist between 'administrative autonomy and political control';[141] between 'clear command ... and popular support';[142] between 'civil liberties and the demands of national security';[143] between 'the needs ... of the policy-making establishment [and] the rights of the press and people to information';[144] between 'ideals and self-interest';[145] between 'constitution and statute law', 'the sphere of law and the sphere of individual freedom', 'pluralism and unity', and 'partisanship and independence';[146] and even between 'cynicism and suspicion on the one hand and faith and trust on the other'.[147] Attention is drawn to the need for the system of checks and balances to 'be strong enough for effective leadership, while dispersing power enough to insure liberty'. And because such a 'balance is delicate, ... rebalancing efforts such as the Congressional reassertion of the 1970s will often be necessary'.[148] There is speculation on 'how best to effect an equilibrium between Presidential power, on the one hand, and democracy on the other'.[149] Another commentator refers to 'the inconsistency between representation and government, or synonymously, participation and decision' and regards the need to achieve a 'balance between these two *forces*'[150] as the basic problem confronting American institutions. The device of checks and balances is projected into the most fundamental issues of American political theory and into the very core of American values. According to Clinton Rossiter, for example, when an American 'proclaims his devotion to political democracy, he is thinking of democracy in which power is diffused by a written constitution and the wielders of power are held in check by the rule of law'. Because of this 'check', there is to the American 'no incompatibility between democracy and constitutionalism'.[151] It is balances like these – between democracy and constitutionalism, 'between liberty and authority',[152] 'between power and liberty',[153] 'between freedom and order',[154] 'between authority, be it state or nation, and the liberty of the citizen', and 'between the rule of the majority and the rights of the individual' – which to Justice Robert H. Jackson constitute 'the great system of balances upon which our free government is based'.[155]

In many respects, the mechanics of equilibrium represent not merely a distinguishing feature of the American system, but its most distinctive and persuasive characteristic. So prevalent is the dependence upon mechanistic categories for comprehending and analysing political developments and so ubiquitous is the use of mechanistic definitions and terms of reference in political observation that mechanics can be regarded as the predominant and guiding conceptualization of American government. This conventionally received impression of the American system approximates to a genuine paradigm in the way that it both confines enquiry according to certain pre-selected criteria and determines the intelligibility and legitimacy of information on government in so far as it conforms to the accepted framework of what requires explanation and what ranks as explanation. If John Adams was well known in the eighteenth century for his habit of trying to balance everything, his fellow countrymen today are made equally conspicuous by their habit of seeing balances everywhere. No one seems completely immune to the disposition and no subject appears to be resistant to mechanical categorization. There seems no limit to the phenomena that can be brought together or wedged apart into physically interdependent and balanced dualities by which each element acts as a beneficial antidote to the other. It is not simply that institutions and organizations are persuasively declared to be in balance; or that values are perceived to check and hold one another in equilibrium; or that 'most political issues ... are matters of balance and proportion'.[156] It is, in addition, that the concept of balance has been elevated in the United States to an unequivocal value in its own right – or rather to the central, all-embracing, self-affirming, and preponderant value in American politics. Balance in these conditions is not merely a solution. It is not even that it is the only satisfactory solution. It is that balance is the only conceivable solution in a system that defines malfunctions and failures as imbalances. If, as has been claimed, divided and balanced government represents 'a unique contribution of Americans to political science',[157] then balance in government for its own sake and as an end in itself is quintessentially American. It is the distinguishing tradition of American politics, stretching from the eighteenth century and an individual like Thomas Jefferson, who regarded divided government as 'the first principle of good government',[158] to the present day and an individual like Aaron Wildavsky, who not only positively 'likes checks and balances ... the separation of powers ... [and] conflicts',[159] but, like Jefferson, deems them to be the hallmark of good government:

> Our safety lies not in individual morality but in systemic virtue.... The test of good government ... is not the absence of error but the ability to correct errors when they occur. How well have American institutions passed this test ...? Have the checks checked and the balances balanced in the American system?[160]

It might be thought that the mechanistic paradigm present in the study of American government and politics is a derivative of another and altogether more fundamental impulse or ethos. For example, it can be claimed that the preoccupation with balance comes from a broad and long-established commitment to liberalism and to its assumption of progress through the dynamics of freely circulating ideas and resources, and through the conflicting interplay of diverse and individual interests. It can also be plausibly argued that the concern for balance is attributable to a basic cultural conservatism which has always stressed the importance of restraints and divisions in popular government, in order to retain the community's stability and integration. The attention given to balance may on the other hand be seen as an outgrowth of conditions. To C. Wright Mills the image of government as 'a sort of automatic machine, regulated by the balancing of competing interests ... is simply a carry-over from the official image of the economy'.[161] Max Lerner roots the concern for balance in 'the heterogeneous quality of American society and the talent for equilibrium it has shown'.[162] Lerner, along with most of the pluralist school, interprets the institutional features of separated powers and checks and balances as nothing other than the governmental expression of society's own diversity. It may well be the case that balanced government represents an integral feature of other ideas, or is consistent with the nature of social conditions. It is not within the remit of this study to engage in a reductionist attribution of causes or to assess whether the usage of terms is justified by the actuality of circumstances. It is not concerned with why things are, but with how things are seen as they are and with how things come to be seen as they do. In this respect, the perception of mechanics within American government is no doubt assisted by philosophies, ideologies, and traditions, and by various constructions of socio-economic reality.

But what must not be overlooked is the governmental system's own contribution to the orthodox portrayal of itself as a mechanical system. Those who dismiss institutions and institutional relationships as the mere epiphenomena of underlying social or economic *fundamenta* run the risk of missing what institutions can serve to signify and what they can reveal by way of 'habits magnified'.[163] Those who underestimate the American system of institutions, in particular, do so at their own peril, for the American organization of government is probably more responsible than anything else for its own mechanistic image. Far from being the passive recipient of extrapolated ideas and determining conditions in an institutional guise, the structure and dynamics of American government actively generate forms and meanings so strongly suggestive of mechanics that they can hardly be imagined in alternative ways – even in spite of the changes in social and economic perspectives that may have occurred elsewhere. This is not to say that the American system is a self-contained and autonomous entity solely responsible for its own association with balanced government. But it is to claim that the system is far more of an active agent in determining its unique identity, and in propagating that identity outwards into the broader hinterland of ideas and impressions, than is normally appreciated.

The inability or unwillingness to acknowledge the contribution that institutions make to the perspectives of government and beyond is due not so much to any clinical rejection of superstructures, as to a failure to see the wood for the trees. This is an understandable failure in as much as it is attributable to a basic resistance towards ascribing great significance to anything so elementary, basic, and even prosaic as the separation of powers. What appears as a self-evident simplicity belies a concealed or dismissed complexity. The sheer familiarity of the separation of powers is such that it normally diverts attention from the profundity that lays within. It probably takes a newcomer, or a stranger, or a foreign observer unaccustomed to the ethos of balanced government, to sense the full impact of the separation of powers upon the cognitive processes of an individual in the formative stages of a political education. Both inside and outside the United States, it is the scheme of separated powers which almost invariably represents the first received impression of the basic nature of American government. Its simple geometrical symmetry and its basic dynamics possess a compulsive appeal that allow the separation of powers to become quickly assimilated not only as the first principle of government, but also as the first instrument of political perception and conceptualization. The separation of powers establishes at the very outset that American government is a pattern that can be discerned; a framework whose regularities can be elicited; and a system with moving parts, points of contact, and convincing images of material cause and effect. As a 'prime characteristic',[164] 'central tenet',[165] and 'essence of the American system of government',[166] the separation of powers fixes the sights and aligns the imagination in such a way that institutions become timeless and homogenized units with the optical and tactile qualities of a mechanical device. It would be difficult to conceive of any system more assured of being perceived in Newtonian terms, or better able to provoke a mechanistic disposition towards the nature of government. In addition to the enclosure of the system through the declaration of three, and only three, governmental branches constituting the full universe of the system's content, the checks and balances between the three units seal the character of the package and ensure that it will be looked upon as a material structure whose role is exclusively kinetic in purpose.

The centrality of the separation of powers as the first fact and empirical generalization of American government, combined with its distinction as the primary value of the American system, makes it a focal point of observation and evaluation by which the *form* of balance becomes fused with the *value* of balance. With such an explicitly schematic device for mechanical self-regulation placed in the position of being such an elementary object of socialized fact and value, it is difficult to imagine that the separation of powers has not exerted a generative force of images, assessments, and judgements upon the minds of American citizens. It might be argued that, had it not been for the American tradition of checks and balances, the judiciary's power over the Congress and Presidency would never have been tolerated and accepted to the extent that it has been. Because the judiciary's independence and its restraining force of judicial review fitted into the logic of separated powers, it was afforded a legitimacy that might otherwise have been absent. What could be extended to accommodate the judiciary in a partnership of co-equality with the Presidency and Congress was also applied in time to the bureaucracy, the military, and the media. Instead of these new power centres threatening the rationale or integrity of the constitutional framework, they acquired an acceptability through the direct application of the separation of powers' original mechanical principles. The balance of powers overrode other considerations and, in accordance with the nature of a mechanical system, the emergence of new structures of power necessarily affected and were affected by existing institutions. To claim otherwise would be the equivalent of saying that while some planets in the solar system were subject to gravitation, others were not. In this way, once a mechanical system becomes established as a generalized impression of the political framework, then it tends to lead to a self-completing process of mechanization from first principles and from the first institutions embodying those principles. For example, once it is fixed in one's mind that 'whenever any branch of government acquires a new technique which enhances its power in relation to other branches, that technique will soon be adopted by those other branches as well',[167] or that when the 'branches of government have been out of balance ... and the Presidency, or the Congress, or the courts become too powerful – power has a way of shifting and a modicum of balance is restored',[168] then it is but a small step to the belief that the American system as a whole 'contains within it corrective elements that are set in motion by its disturbance'.[169] Such belief in the existence of a 'self-correcting mechanism'[170] by which the Presidency and Congress 'like tuning forks, when struck trigger complementary vibrations and reverberations'[171] leads on to more generalized conclusions. Namely, that 'the logic of checks and balances is that every form of political power must be subject to some constraint';[172] that 'in politics, every force must have a counter-force';[173] that 'power creates its own resistance';[174] and that 'in politics as in physics for every action there is a reaction',[175] for 'politics is like physics, action begets reaction'.[176] This being so, the prospect of a new source of power poses few problems to the system's integrity, as Peter Woll discovered with the rise of the federal bureaucracy:

> The precepts of constitutional democracy ... had a chance to become firmly embedded as part of the American political tradition before the administrative branch began to take shape as a significant force threatening the governmental balance of powers. This tradition has been a permanent influence shaping old and new political institutions into its own distinctive pattern, and the bureaucracy has not been an exception.[177]

Moreover, this process of mechanistic incorporation is not confined to the macro level of major power blocs but radiates down into the micro level of internal compartmentalization and control. There seems to be no point at which the conceptual inspiration of the separation of powers can be said to confront the upward translation of social and economic pluralism into political form. They both intermingle and merge imperceptibly into one another, with neither prevailing over or contradicting the other. Instead of being inferior to, or dependent upon, exterior and underlying political interests, the separation of powers stands revealed as a potent source of pluralist ideas and a major agent in developing the American susceptibility to pluralism as a plausible explanation of socio-political relations.

The separation of powers has been of major importance in the development of mechanics as the predominant conception of American politics. The elevated and dramatized examples of the Presidency confronting the Congress, or the Supreme Court reviewing executive and legislative actions, have succeeded in generating an imagery so evocative of weights and counterweights that the pattern has become a fixed, internalized feature of perception that can be dislodged only temporarily under pressure of circumstances. The rise of the modern Presidency into the 'imperial Presidency', for example, was in retrospect adjudged to be a classical imbalance rather than the emergence of a more biologically and organically oriented paradigm. What before had been seen as an evolutionary trend towards adaptive and irreversible centralization was quite suddenly discarded in an instinctive reversion to first principles and old axioms.[178] Faith in leadership was denigrated; trust in power was seen as futile; self-restraint was refuted as a principle unknown in physics; and the concentration of power and abuse of power were once again recognized as interchangeable terms. The broken trust and abuse of power represented not simply a mechanical failure of the system, but also a failure to see and use and value the system as a machine. This led to a new and heightened awareness of the mechanical potential of the system and to an increased interest in the mechanistic utility of the constitution's design and operation. The 'imperial Presidency' episode prompted a renewed profession of faith in the mechanistic paradigm and a rededication to its principles. As causes, effects, problems, and solutions received a mechanistic construction, and the Presidency was duly transformed from a 'ghost in the machine' to one of its component parts, the analysts and apologists of executive power were left with the discomfiture of squaring their previous observations and judgements with the renewed orthodoxy. Sometimes this led to conundrum-like mixtures of biological and mechanistic paradigms. For example, Arthur Schlesinger maintained a strong Presidency to be 'both a greater necessity than ever before and a greater risk' and, thereby, arrived at the conclusion that the 'nation required both a strong Presidency for leadership and the separation of powers for liberty'.[179] And while Theodore Sorensen thought that 'the role of Congress should be strengthened to restore constitutional balance', he insisted that this 'could not be accompanied by weakening the executive'.[180] On other occasions, it led to assurances that the historical and evolutionary trend towards executive hegemony had remained intact and would inevitably continue in the future. What compromised such assurances was the mechanistically loaded forms of expression used to make them. The assertions that 'the power in the American order was bound to flow back to the Presidency',[181] or the claim that 'the pendulum had already swung back in the other direction',[182] only served to reveal the captivating force of mechanistic concepts even to those most intent upon avoiding them on those occasions when allusions to evolutionary continuity ought to have precluded any mention of them.

The same predilection towards mechanics was also discernible amongst those analysts and commentators who doubted whether the system had responded adequately to quell doubts that had arisen over its efficiency. Far from being a celebration of the system's potential for mutual restraint and reciprocal control, many thought that the traditional structure of checks and balances had barely managed to cope with the strains exerted upon it. As a result, a wide variety of structural reforms were recommended which were aimed either at reducing the power of the Presidency, or maintaining it in a responsible manner by making it more politically accountable. Typical of the suggestions were the introduction of some elements of parliamentary government (e.g. vote of censure, right of dissolution) that might increase executive power but would also ensure a greater counter-force against it whenever political conditions warranted it; the further revival of Congress as an independent and assertive institution which would act as a permanent constraint upon Presidential aggrandisement; and the invigoration of the party system by electoral, organizational, and institutional means which would enable the Presidency to exercise forceful leadership, but only within the constraints of party consent.[183] What is significant about many of these reformist ideas was their recognition of the value of mechanical relationships between political and governmental agencies. It was as if the reforms were themselves based upon the traditional premises of checks and balances, and their objectives were to improve the ways by which the Newtonian law of action and reaction could be harnessed to government. The proposed changes sought to allow the assumed existence of a potential counter-force to executive power to present itself more positively than before and to communicate its power through better lines of transmission than before. The laws of mechanics were not questioned so much as reiterated and reaffirmed.

Epilogue

The 'imperial Presidency' episode may have been the most dramatic and conspicuous example of the use of mechanical categories in political appraisal, but it was in no way an exceptional mode of interpretation or an unorthodox method of constitutional construction. On the contrary, it exemplified the depth of public attachment to, and dependence upon, a mechanistic paradigm whose principles and criteria could be extended from the separation of powers to embrace any or all additional loci of perceptible power. It is this intuitive adherence to mechanics, coupled with the inherent capacity of mechanics to reduce everything to its own terms, that has not only given American government its distinctive character, but fostered an association with Newton and Newtonianism that is quite exceptional amongst political systems. Allusions to Newton or to his classical laws of mechanics are looked upon as normal and commonplace in the United States, whereas elsewhere they would be regarded as unfounded, misguided, or quite simply incongruous. In these contexts what would be regarded as significant would be not so much the extent to which Newton and Newtonian mechanics are used in political commentary, but rather the fact that they are used at all. In the American example, on the other hand, significance is afforded to Newtonianism by virtue of the high incidence of mechanical references and by the sheer scale of what Newtonianism is called upon to account for. In no way can Newtonian terminology be lightly dismissed as insubstantial alliteration or colourful rhetoric. In the American political system, the Newtonian connection denotes real meanings and evokes high feelings. It is seen as salient, substantive, and significant. It is alluded to as a central constitutional tradition; it is employed as a mainstream technique of political observation and assessment; and it is instinctively drawn upon to account for political developments and to explain the nature of American government. But, most of all, the Newtonian terminology is a reflection of the belief in the existence of a machine within American government.

It is not simply that comparisons are drawn between the governmental system and a mechanical system. Neither is it a matter of looking upon the government as if it were like a machine. It is the genuine belief that the government possesses an authentically mechanistic nature which fully warrants its Newtonian mode of definition. Whether the sources of this outlook are seen as being primarily historical in the form of the reputedly Newtonian methods, objectives, and achievements of the Founding Fathers, or empirical in so far as the government appears to possess mechanical properties and to operate according to mechanical laws, or, as this study has concluded, a mixture of the two in a retrospective and self-perpetuating process of psychological conditioning to the static imagery of institutional checks and balances, the end result remains the same. Namely, a working conviction that the machinery is there and functioning or malfunctioning as a machine. For the most part, its presence is accepted, if somewhat fatalistically, and valued, if somewhat equivocally. It is looked upon more as a force of nature to come to terms with, in that Americans seem governed by it just as much, and in the same way, as the force and laws of mechanics govern their physical existence. Accordingly, while political will may be exerted and innovations proposed, such changes are seen as being conditional upon the mechanical properties of the system and, therefore, in turn ultimately determined by them. More often than not, however, institutional and organizational mechanics are seen as disallowing the passage of change – rendering the United States 'unique among the world's democracies in the extent to which the institutional system is weighted on the side of restraint regardless of the mandate of the people'.[1] Its uniqueness extends even further than this in that such restraint by procedures and instrumentalities is not only tolerated but accepted as legitimate. It would be a mistaken assumption simply to dismiss such acquiescence as nothing other than a necessary condition of pluralist democracy in which groups agree to disagree and accept the obstructionist consequences until and unless they can coalesce into extraordinarily large and durable majorities. A material support to division and constraint is not the same as an autonomous conception of governmental balance in its own right and on its own terms. It is the latter which characterizes the fundamental American approach to government far more than the pluralist account. Conceptually the notion of balance in American government is primarily a 'top down' rather than a 'bottom up' construction. It applies initially to institutions but, thereafter, it embraces values, attributes, and conditions that come to be seen either as balances transposed from institutions, or as equilibria expressed through institutions. As a result, 'it is remarkable how much of the American system can be explained in these terms of balance and equilibrium'.[2] By definition, balance refers to a balance of power between phenomena which much necessarily be material in nature and, therefore, with physical properties inherent to them that afford the potential for equilibrium. In this way, the American cult of balance can and does provide a common frame of reference by which everything derives meaning and value from the way it is physically related to everything else. Whether the balance is between the Presidency and Congress, or between nationalism and localism, or between liberalism and conservatism, the Newtonian ethos is the same – i.e. a state of physical interdependence by which each material element relies on the other not only to retain its position but also to preserve it from the excesses of both itself and its partner in balance.

The analysis and philosophy of American government are replete with such balances but there is one which more than any other expresses the magnitude and significance of the American disposition towards governmental mechanics. This is the reputed balance between constitutionalism and democratic government. The importance attached to this balance is twofold. First, it shows that, once introduced into a subject, a total philosophical system like Newtonian mechanics knows no bounds and does not readily submit to being selectively confined to partial or marginal explanations. This is reflected in the extension of mechanical principles even into an area as fundamental and theoretical as the source and nature of political authority. Second, the balance between constitutionalism and democracy – or, as it is variously known, between fundamental law and political will, or between *jurisdictio* and *gubernaculum*[3] – is seen in the United States as being secured by and embodied in the constitutional mechanisms of checks and balances. In other words, the nature, condition, and identity of the relationship between legal authority and political authority are reduced in the American context to a form not merely consistent with checks and balances, but determined in actuality by them. The mechanization of values and concepts combined with the elevation of mechanics to a value in its own right has had the effect of making constitutional dynamics the material form of the relationship between constitutionalism and democracy. Checks and balances, in effect, collectively define and provide the central check and the central balance in the system. In doing so, checks and balances become the ultimate expression of the mechanization of American government. They reveal the American conception of constitutional and democratic authority as actually corresponding to a physical balance and one, moreover, produced automatically through the interplay of their physical properties in a medium of material contact, cause, and effect.

This conception of institutional dynamics as the necessary interface, amalgam, and controlling balance to constitutionalism and democracy is many-sided and has wide and lengthy repercussions throughout the American system. For example, it has had the effect of intermingling constitutionalism and democracy within a single mechanized framework. Just as the force of democracy is exerted and felt through the channels of checks and balances, so the force of constitutionalism is similarly expressed and experienced through the same channels. Likewise, it is the system of checks and balances which registers and embodies the confrontation between constitutional authority and public authority – confrontations which are seen to be resolved by way of, and in terms of, the normal processes of checks and balances.

On the other hand, it is also in the nature of balances to separate and compartmentalize the constituent weights. The central balancing function of institutional checks and balances has, therefore, served to exaggerate the differentiation between constitutionalism and democracy to such an extent that the two principles are intuitively regarded as mechanical adversaries set in a zero-sum world of one-to-one profit and loss. The interposition of mechanics as a mediating structure between constitutionalism and democracy has been instrumental in denuding American constitutionalism of such traditional concepts as political order and community and, in the process, leaving the theme of governmental limitation in conspicuous isolation as the prevailing characteristic of the American constitution.[4] This divestiture has in turn made constitutionalism altogether more compatible with mechanical arrangements because it has had the effect of placing constitutionalism and democracy in an explicitly dichotomous relationship requiring balance so that each can offset the deleterious effects of the other's excess. This has strengthened to the point of mechanical rigidity the American trait of defining and measuring constitutional liberty in terms of freedom from governmental power, while conversely using the scale of governmental power to arrive at a mechanical value of the degree of liberty left in society. If the habit of divorcing government from individual liberty and community purposes is an American tradition, then that tradition has been massively reinforced and irretrievably fixed by the logic of balance in wedging constitutionalism and democracy apart into mutually exclusive yet interactive spheres – whereby governmental authority is seen to be exerted against constitutional authority and liberty, while constitutional authority is seen to be invoked to limit governmental authority in order to preserve or extend liberty. With this mechanical conception of power and freedom, the American republic has never been infected either with the 'belief that a republic, being a people's thing, could be magnified only to the public's advantage',[5] or with the notion that political power might embody a collective need, a social purpose, or a corporate will that could serve to secure and enhance liberty. On the contrary, the United States has maintained a distinctively prejudicial outlook towards government as a threatening, mischievous, untrustworthy, wilful, and alien force in human affairs: a force requiring constitutional restraint which is seen and accepted as being embodied by the scheme of constitutional checks and balances. This makes the confrontation between constitutional authority and democratic government intelligible as a form of mechanical action and reaction, whereby government is checked and balanced by the constitution, which, in the process, is reduced to a physically immobilizing and disaggregative counter-force, whose power is negatively inclined but positively valued for its mechanical quality.

The final noteworthy repercussion arising from the prominence and status accorded to institutional dynamics within the American system is the way that checks and balances have come to assume much of the identity of both constitutionalism and democracy. In accordance with the nature of balances, a state of equilibrium is considered to be an amalgam of the elements being balanced. The American scheme of checks and balances is no exception. As the balance wheel between the two great forces in American government, the checks and balances framework is seen as being both constitutional and democratic at one and the same time. It is not simply that the system of institutional dynamics provides the means by which two intensive and apparently exclusive traditions of sovereignty can coexist with so little indication of contradiction or conflict. It is that in accounting for, and embodying, the balance between these two sovereignties, the checks and balances structure succeeds in accommodating them to the extent of assuming for itself the consequent form of mixed sovereignty.

This is reflected in a doubly exceptional trait of American politics. First is the extraordinarily strong belief in the existence of a fully operational governmental machine; and second is the extraordinarily high level of tolerance afforded to it, even on those occasions when it is seen to be frustrating majority opinion. The separation of powers, together with its associated checks and balances, excites remarkably little interest in such a self-consciously democratic culture. As a result, it has generated conspicuously little criticism as a structure and process of government. It is quite true that critics condemn American government for its mechanical autonomy and for what they regard as its derivatives: namely, its built-in tensions, its structural constraints, its self-administered immobilization, its blindly unresponsive inertia, and its insuperable resistance to change – in short, the feeling that 'Americans have lost control of the government and that government has lost the capacity to act, to respond, to move on the challenges that confront the nation'.[6] Such complaints are commonplace and customarily lead to proposals designed to eliminate what are seen as the growing disjunction between the organizational realities of American society and the structural conservatism of American political institutions. Nevertheless, what is also true is that the critics and reformers constitute only a very small minority and that they advance their schemes for change secure in the knowledge that none of them will ever be brought to fruition. The sceptics' anguished helplessness at the futility of their reforms is in itself a reflection of that solid consensus of settled belief in the machinery of American government – belief both in the factual sense of a conviction in its existence and in the normative sense of an acceptance of its processes. Such a belief cannot simply be written off as merely an attachment to tradition, or as an intellectual concomitant to pluralism, or even as an affirmation of the instrumental value of institutional relationships. The mechanical conception of government represents something far deeper and more significant than this. It represents nothing less than an expression of sovereignty in the American republic. Namely, the implicit acceptance of government as a mechanically autonomous device. In the main, this sovereignty has remained unrecognized, unacknowledged, and unsung. Against the background of constitutional sovereignty and popular sovereignty that together have traditionally dominated American government, this third sovereignty tends to be sensed rather than expressed, to be familiarly apparent without being intellectually evident. Although it fosters ubiquitous and habitual references to mechanical principles and processes, and intuitive, if fitful, connections with Newton, the significance of these compulsive associations is too often not only overlooked, but also not understood even by those who make them. Hopefully, the present study will have succeeded in rectifying this omission by making explicit why it is that mechanical categories seem so peculiarly appropriate and salient to American government and why it is that the name of Newton is regularly called upon as a substantive term of political description.

Notes

Chapter 1. Newtonian mechanics and American constitutionalism

1. M. Lerner, *America as a Civilization: Life and Thought in the United States Today* (Jonathan Cape, London, 1958), p. 258. See also L. Mumford, *Technics and Civilisation* (Harcourt Brace, New York, 1934).
2. L. Marx, *The Machine in the Garden: Technology and the Pastoral Idea in America* (Oxford University Press, London, 1964), p. 343.
3. G. M. Ostrander, *American Civilization in the First Machine Age: 1840–1940* (Harper & Row, New York, 1970), p. 228.
4. W. B. Munro, *The Makers of the Unwritten Constitution* (Macmillan, New York, 1930), p. 119.
5. R. D. Mosier, *The American Temper: Patterns of our Intellectual Heritage* (University of California Press, Berkeley, 1952), pp. 120, 131.
6. M. Landau, 'Redundancy, rationality and the problem of duplication and overlap', in F. E. Rourke (ed.), *Bureaucratic Power in National Politics*, 3rd edn (Little Brown, Boston, Mass., 1978), p. 431.
7. L. Morrow, 'The ark of America', *Time*, 6 July 1987.
8. H. S. Commager, *The American Mind: an Interpretation of American Thought and Character since the 1880s* (Bantam, New York, 1970), p. 319.
9. R. S. Westfall, *Never at Rest: a Biography of Isaac Newton* (Cambridge University Press, Cambridge, 1980), p. 483.
10. The edition used in this study was I. Newton, *The Mechanical Principles of Natural Philosophy*, trans. Andrew Motte, intro. I. B. Cohen (Dawsons of Pall Mall, London, 1968), vols I and II. The works upon which the following description and appraisal of Newton's work in mechanics are based are as follows: J. Bronowski, *The Common Sense of Science* (Heinemann, London, 1951), pp. 26–40; G. Burnistan Brown, *Science: its Method and its Philosophy* (Allen & Unwin, London, 1951), pp. 83–108; H. Butterfield, *The Origins of Modern Science, 1300–1800*, rev. edn (G. Bell, London, 1957), pp. 139–58; I. B. Cohen, *The Birth of a New Physics* (Heinemann, London, 1960), pp. 152–90; Cohen, *Introduction to Newton's Principia* (Cambridge University Press, Cambridge, 1971); Cohen, *The Newtonian Revolution: with Illustrations of the Transformation of Scientific Ideas* (Cambridge University Press, Cambridge, 1980); E. J. Dijksterhuis, *The Mechanization of the World Picture* (Oxford University Press, London, 1961), pp. 463–91; A. Rupert Hall, *From Galileo to Newton, 1630–1720* (Collins, London, 1963), pp. 36–131, 216–43, 276–328; Hall, *The Scientific Revolution: the Formation of the Modern Scientific Attitude* (Longman, London, 1954), pp. 244–74; J. Herivel, *The Background to Newton's 'Principia'* (Oxford University Press, London, 1965); A. Koyre, *Newtonian Studies* (Chapman & Hall, London, 1965); F. E. Manuel, *A Portrait of Isaac Newton* (Harvard University Press, Cambridge, Mass., 1968); F. E. Manuel, 'Newton as autocrat of science', in F. E. Manuel (ed.), *Freedom from History and other Untimely Essays* (University of London Press, London, 1972); J. D. North, *Isaac Newton* (Oxford University Press, London, 1967); R. Palter (ed.), *The 'Annus Mirabilis' of Sir Isaac Newton, 1666–1966* (MIT Press, Cambridge, Mass., 1970); M. Perl, 'Newton's justification of the laws of motion', *Journal of the History of Ideas* 27, 4 (October–December 1966), pp. 385–92; S. Toulmin and J. Good-

field, *The Fabric of the Heavens* (Hutchinson, London, 1961), pp. 228–49; R. S. Westfall, *The Construction of Modern Science: Mechanisms and Mechanics* (Cambridge University Press, Cambridge, 1977); Westfall, *Never at Rest*, Westfall, 'Newton's scientific personality', *Journal of the History of Ideas* 28, 4 (October–December 1987), pp. 551–70.
11 For Copernicus, see A. Koestler, *The Sleepwalkers: a History of Man's Changing Views of the Universe* (Penguin, Harmondsworth, 1964), pp. 121–222; Toulmin and Goodfield, *The Fabric of the Heavens*, pp. 153–81. For Kepler, see Koestler, *The Sleepwalkers*, pp. 227–427; Cohen, *The Birth of a New Physics*, ch. 6. For Galileo, see A. Koyre, *Galileo Studies* (Harvester, Hassocks, 1978), pp. 65–109, 154–209; Koyre, 'Galileo and the scientific revolution of the seventeenth century', in Koyre (ed.), *Metaphysics and Measurement: Essays in the Scientific Revolution* (Chapman & Hall, London, 1968) pp. 1–15; S. Drake, 'Galileo's new science of motion', in M. L. Rightini and W. R. Shea (eds), *Reason, Experiment and Mysticism in the Scientific Revolution* (Macmillan, London, 1975); Drake, *Galileo* (Oxford University Press, Oxford, 1980); P. Tannery, 'Galileo and the principles of dynamics', in E. McMullin (ed.), *Galileo: Man of Science* (Basic Books, New York, 1967), pp. 163–77; W. Hartner, 'Galileo's contribution to astronomy', in McMullin (ed.), *Galileo*.
12 *Law 1*: every body continues in its state of rest, or of uniform motion in a right line, unless it is compelled to change that state by forces impressed upon it. *Law 2*: the change of motion is proportional to the motive force impressed; and it is made in the direction of the right line in which that force is impressed. *Law 3*: the mutual actions of two bodies upon each other are always equal, and directed to contrary parts.
13 See Cohen, *The Birth of a New Physics*, pp. 90–129, 158–63; Cohen, 'Newton's second law and the concept of force in the *Principia*', in Palter (ed.), *The 'Annus Mirabilis' of Sir Isaac Newton*, pp. 143–85; D. Shapere, 'The philosophical significance of Newton's science', in Palter (ed.), *The 'Annus Mirabilis' of Sir Isaac Newton*, pp. 285–99; J. Nicholas, 'Newton's extremal second law', *Centaurus* 22 (1978), pp. 108–30.
14 A. N. Whitehead, *Science in the Modern World* (Penguin, Harmondsworth, 1938), p. 61.
15 For descriptions of the Aristotelian orthodoxy prior to the scientific revolution, see Dijksterhuis, *The Mechanization of the World Picture*, pp. 32–6; J. Lossee, *A Historical Introduction to the Philosophy of Science* (Oxford University Press, London, 1972), pp. 5–15; B. Russell, *History of Western Philosophy and its Connection with Political and Social Circumstances from the Earliest Times to the Present Day* (Allen & Unwin, London, 1946), pp. 226–30; Toulmin and Goodfield, *The Fabric of the Heavens*, pp. 90–114.
16 See Shapere, 'The philosophical significance of Newton's science', in Palter (ed.), *The 'Annus Mirabilis' of Sir Isaac Newton*, p. 299.
17 Butterfield, *The Origins of Modern Science*, rev. edn, pp. 65, 140.
18 See Westfall, *The Construction of Modern Science*, pp. 25–9; Butterfield, *The Origins of Modern Science*, rev. edn, pp. 141–9.
19 See A. Koyre, 'Newton and Descartes', in Koyre (ed.), *Newtonian Studies*, pp. 53–114; A. Kenny, *Descartes: a Study of his Philosophy* (Random House, New York, 1968), pp. 200–15.
20 See Cohen, 'Newton's second law and the concept of force in the *Principia*', in Palter (ed.), *The 'Annus Mirabilis' of Sir Isaac Newton*, pp. 143–86.
21 Quoted in Koyre, 'Concept and experience in Newton's scientific thought', in Koyre (ed.), *Newtonian Studies*, p. 51.
22 Newton, *The Mathematical Principles of Natural Philosophy*, vol. II, p. 392.
23 Koyre, 'The significance of the Newtonian synthesis', in Koyre (ed.), *Newtonian Studies*, p. 17; Koyre, 'Gravity an essential property of matter', in Koyre (ed.), *Newtonian Studies*, p. 163.
24 Westfall, *The Construction of Modern Science*, p. 143.
25 Dijksterhuis, *The Mechanization of the World Picture*, p. 490.
26 Whitehead, *Science and the Modern World*, p. 63.
27 Koyre, 'The significance of the Newtonian synthesis', in Koyre (ed.), *Newtonian Studies*, p. 15.
28 Dijksterhuis, *The Mechanization of the World Picture*, p. 495.
29 Bronowski, *The Common Sense of Science*, pp. 44, 45. For an examination of the ways in which Newton's mechanics were extrapolated into other fields such as biology and psychology, see H. Guerlac, 'Stephen Hales: a Newtonian physiologist', in H. Guerlac, *Essays and Papers in the History of Modern Science* (Johns Hopkins University Press, Baltimore, 1977),

pp. 170–92; W. Coleman, 'Mechanical philosophy and hypothetical physiology', in Palter (ed.), *The 'Annus Mirabilis' of Sir Isaac Newton*, pp. 322–32; Westfall, *The Construction of Modern Science*, pp. 82–104; T. M. Brown, 'Medicine in the shadow of the *Principia*', *Journal of the History of Ideas* 48, 4 (1987), pp. 629–48.
30 I. Berlin, 'The Age of the Enlightenment', in I. Berlin, H. D. Aiken, and M. White, *The Great Ages of Philosophy* (Houghton Mifflin, Boston, Mass., 1962), p. 6.
31 Quoted in R. Grimsley, 'Introduction', in Grimsley (ed.), *The Age of the Enlightenment, 1715–1789* (Penguin, Harmondsworth, 1979), p. 11.
32 Pope's epitaph for Sir Isaac Newton was as follows:

> Nature and Nature's Laws lay hid in night;
> God said, Let Newton be – And all was light.

33 Quoted in N. Hampson, *The Enlightenment* (Penguin, Harmondsworth, 1979), p. 109.
34 D. Hume, 'Enquiry concerning human understanding', in *Enquiries concerning Human Understanding and concerning the Principles of Morals*, 3rd edn, rev. P. H. Nidditch (Clarendon, Oxford, 1975), pp. 1–165. Hume, 'That politics may be reduced to a science', in T. H. Green and T. H. Grose (eds), *Essays: Moral, Political and Literary* (Longman, London, 1875), pp. 98–109; D. Forbes, *Hume's Philosophical Politics* (Cambridge University Press, Cambridge, 1975), pp. 102–21, 224–30.
35 P. Hazard, *European Thought in the Eighteenth Century* (Penguin, Harmondsworth, 1965), p. 7.
36 B. Bailyn, 'Political experience and Enlightenment ideas in eighteenth-century America', *American Historical Review* 67, 2 (1962), p. 339.
37 P. Gay, 'The applied Enlightenment?' in E. M. Adams (ed.), *The Idea of America: a Reassessment of the American Experiment* (Ballinger, Cambridge, Mass., 1977), p. 12.
38 H. S. Commager, *The Empire of Reason: how Europe Imagined and America Realized the Enlightenment* (Weidenfeld & Nicolson, London, 1978), p. ix. See also G. Wills's remark that America was 'a product of the Enlightenment' (*Inventing America: Jefferson's Declaration of Independence*, Doubleday, Garden City, N.Y., 1978, p. 99); P. Gay's characterization of America as 'the Enlightenment in practice' (*The Enlightenment: an Interpretation*, vol. II, *The Science of Freedom*, Weidenfeld & Nicolson, London, 1970, p. 558); and Ralph Dahrendorff's claim that America was 'the Enlightenment applied' (quoted in Gay, 'The applied Enlightenment?', in Adams, ed., *The Idea of America*, p. 11). For the general theme of the American Enlightenment, see also H. F. May, *The Enlightenment in America* (Oxford University Press, London, 1976); M. Curti, *The Growth of American Thought* (Harper, New York, 1943), pp. 103–26; C. Becker, *The Declaration of Independence: a Study in the History of Political Ideas* (Harcourt Brace, New York, 1922), pp. 24–79; A. Koch (ed.), *The American Enlightenment* (G. Braziller, New York, 1965); H. Wish, *Society and Thought in early America: a Social and Intellectual History of the American People through 1865* (Longman, New York, 1950), pp. 143–83; S. Persons, *American Minds: a History of Ideas* (Holt Rinehart & Winston, New York, 1958), pp. 71–143; Mosier, *The American Temper*, pp. 85–155; J. R. Pole, 'The Enlightenment and the politics of American nature', in R. Porter and M. Teich (eds), *The Enlightenment in National Context* (Cambridge University Press, Cambridge, 1981), pp. 192–214; D. Adair, '"That politics may be reduced to a science": David Hume, James Madison, and the tenth *Federalist*', *Huntington Library Quarterly* 20, 4 (August 1957), pp. 343–60; G. Wills, *Explaining America: the Federalist* (Athlone, London, 1981); D. H. Meyer, 'The uniqueness of the American Enlightenment', *American Quarterly* 28, 2 (summer 1976), pp. 165–86; J. Ellis, 'Habits of mind and an American Enlightenment', *American Quarterly*, 28, 2 (summer 1976), pp. 150–64.
39 For the status and role of science in eighteenth-century America see B. Hindle, *The Pursuit of Science in Revolutionary America, 1735–1789* (University of North Carolina Press, Chapel Hill, 1956); Hindle (ed.), *Early American Science* (Science History Publications, New York, 1976); F. E. Brasch, 'The Newtonian epoch in the American colonies', *American Antiquarian Society Proceedings* 49 (1939), pp. 314–32; Brasch, 'Newton's first critical disciple in the American colonies – John Winthrop', in *Sir Isaac Newton, 1727–1927: a Bicentenary Evaluation of his Work* (Baltimore, 1928), pp. 301–28; I. B. Cohen, 'Science and the growth of the American republic', *Review of Politics* 38, 3 (July 1976), pp. 359–98; Cohen, *Franklin and Newton: an Inquiry into Speculative Newtonian Experimental Science and Franklin's Work in*

Electricity as an Example Thereof (American Philosophical Society, Philadelphia, 1956); S. E. Morison, *The Intellectual Life of Colonial New England* (New York University Press, New York, 1956), pp. 241–75; M. Savelle, *Seeds of Liberty: the Genesis of the American Mind* (University of Washington Press, Seattle, 1965), pp. 84–150; Commager, *The Empire of Reason*, pp. 15–39; C. Rossiter, *Seedtime of the Republic: the Origin of the American Tradition of Political Liberty* (Harcourt Brace, New York, 1965), pp. 130–4; P. Miller, *The New England Mind from Colony to Province* (Harvard University Press, Cambridge, Mass., 1953), pp. 437–46; F. Kilgour, 'The rise of scientific activity in colonial New England', *Yale Journal of Biology and Medicine* 22 (1949), pp. 123–30; C. Bush, *The Dream of Reason: American Consciousness and Cultural Achievement from Independence to the Civil War* (Edward Arnold, London, 1977), pp. 9–14, 60–78, 127–37, 195–7; R. Stearns, *Science in the British Colonies of America* (University of Illinois Press, Urbana, 1970); Hindle, 'Witherspoon, Rittenhouse, and Sir Isaac Newton', *William and Mary Quarterly* 15, 3 (July 1958), pp. 365–71; Hindle, 'Cadwallader Colden's extension of the Newtonian principles', *William and Mary Quarterly* 13, 4 (October 1956), pp. 459–75; H. Woolf, *The Transits of Venus: a Study of Eighteenth Century Science* (Princeton University Press, Princeton, 1959); R. S. Klein, *Science and Society in early America: Essays in Honor of Whitfield J. Bell, Jr.* (American Philosophical Society, Independence, 1986).

For the specific link between science and politics, see A. Ranney, '"The divine science": political engineering in American culture', *American Political Science Review* 70, 1 (March 1976), pp. 140–8; Gay, *The Enlightenment*, vol. II, *The Science of Freedom*, pp. 555–68; Commager, *The Empire of Reason*, pp. 176–235; Wills, *Explaining America*, pp. 95–264; A. J. Beitzinger, *A History of American Political Thought* (Dodd Mead, New York, 1972), pp. 202–44; Adair, '"That politics may be reduced to a science": David Hume, James Madison, and the tenth *Federalist*', *Huntington Library Quarterly* 20, 4 (August 1957), pp. 343–60; Adair, '"Experience must be our only guide": history, democratic theory, and the United States constitution', in T. Colbourn (ed.), *Fame and the Founding Fathers* (W. W. Norton, New York, 1974), pp. 107–23.

40 Cohen, 'Science and the growth of the American republic', *Review of Politics* 38, 3 (July 1976), p. 365.
41 I. B. Cohen, 'Science in America: the nineteenth century', in A. M. Schlesinger, Jr (ed.), *Paths of American Thought* (Houghton Mifflin, Boston, Mass., 1970), p. 170.
42 C. M. Walsh, *The Political Science of John Adams: a Study in the Theory of Mixed Government and the Bicameral System* (Knickerbocker Press, New York, 1915), p. 256.
43 Cohen, 'Science and the growth of the American republic', *Review of Politics* 38, 3 (July 1976), p. 365.
44 R. Hofstadter, *The American Political Tradition* (Jonathan Cape, London, 1967), p. 8.
45 Rossiter, *Seedtime of the Republic*, p. 134.
46 F. Gilbert, 'The English background of American isolation in the eighteenth century', *William and Mary Quarterly* 1, 2 (April 1944), p. 157.
47 M. Landau, *Political Theory and Political Science: Studies in the Methodology of Political Inquiry* (repr. Humanities Press, Atlantic Highlands, 1979), pp. 84, 87.
48 Mosier, *The American Temper*, p. 126.
49 Mosier, *The American Temper*, p. 129.
50 S. Pargellis, 'The theory of balanced government', in C. Read (ed.), *The Constitution Reconsidered* (Columbia University Press, New York, 1938), p. 46.
51 Pargellis, 'The theory of balanced government', in Read (ed.), *The Constitution Reconsidered*, pp. 38–9.
52 W. U. Solberg (ed.), *The Federal Convention and the Formation of the Union of the United States* (Bobbs-Merrill, Indianapolis, 1958), p. xcvi.
53 W. Wilson, *Constitutional Government in the United States* (Columbia University Press, New York, 1911), p. 57.
54 Wilson, *The New Freedom: a Call for the Emancipation of the Generous Energies of a People*, intro. and notes, W. E. Leuchtenburg (Prentice-Hall, Englewood Cliffs, 1961), p. 41.
55 Wilson, *Constitutional Government in the United States*, pp. 55–6.
56 L. H. Tribe, *The Constitutional Structure of American Government: the Separation and Division of Powers* (Foundation, Mineola, 1978), p. 15.
57 Pole, 'Enlightenment and the politics of American nature', in Porter and Teich (eds), *The*

Enlightenment in National Context, p. 195.
58 W. Lippmann, *A Preface to Politics* (University of Michigan Press, Ann Arbor, 1962), pp. 16–17.
59 M. Kammen, *A Machine that would Go of Itself: the Constitution in American Culture* (Knopf, New York, 1986), pp. 17, 189.
60 A. M. Schlesinger, Jr, *The Imperial Presidency* (André Deutsch, London, 1974), p. vii.
61 T. L. Hankins, *Science and the Enlightenment* (Cambridge University Press, Cambridge, 1985), p. 9.
62 J. Appleby, 'Republicanism in old and new contexts', *William and Mary Quarterly* 43, 1 (January 1986), p. 33.
63 J. Ellis, 'Habits of mind and an American Enlightenment', *American Quarterly* 28, 2 (summer 1976), p. 164.

Chapter 2. The death of constitutional Newtonianism?

1 A. M. Schlesinger, Jr, *The Politics of Hope* (Eyre & Spottiswoode, London, 1964), p. 63.
2 A. de Tocqueville, *Democracy in America*, trans. H. Reeve, intro. H. S. Commager (ed.) (Oxford University Press, London, 1946), p. 370.
3 L. Hartz, *The Liberal Tradition in America: an Interpretation of American Political Thought since the Revolution* (Harcourt Brace Jovanovich, New York, 1955).
4 Hartz, *The Liberal Tradition in America*, p. 10.
5 Hartz, *The Liberal Tradition in America*, p. 6.
6 Hartz, *The Liberal Tradition in America*, p. 55.
7 D. J. Boorstin, *The Genius of American Politics* (University of Chicago Press, Chicago, 1953).
8 Boorstin, *The Genius of American Politics*, p. 161.
9 Boorstin, *The Genius of American Politics*, p. 9.
10 It used to be customary for American and European historians to 'downplay the religious dimensions of eighteenth century thought and present it as a celebration of science and scepticism' (J. T. Kloppenberg, 'The virtues of liberalism: Christianity, republicanism, and ethics in early American discourse', *Journal of American History* 74, 1, 1987, p. 12). More recent work has, however, challenged this assumption from two points of view. First, it has drawn attention to the enduring attachment to superstition, astrology, alchemy, witchcraft, and ritual magic shown in many sectors of eighteenth-century American society. Even in the colonial colleges, such old Renaissance orthodoxies as geocentrism, the four 'humours', and the four basic elements of the world were able to withstand the buffeting of Bacon, Locke, and Newton for a much longer period than would have been expected had the Enlightenment been as assiduously embraced as it was reputed to have been (cf. H. Leventhall, *In the Shadow of the Enlightenment: Occultism and Renaissance Science in Eighteenth Century America* New York University Press, New York, 1976). Second, the Enlightenment's supposed agnosticism has been revised by work showing the 'persistence of either explicit or implicit religious ideals in the enlightenment ... and especially on the corrosive effect of religious enthusiasm on prevailing patterns of deference' (Kloppenberg, 'The virtues of liberalism', p. 12), leading to a confluence of evangelical nonconformism and radical political dissent – cf. the bibliography of recent work in Kloppenberg, 'The virtues of liberalism', pp. 12–13. This ambiguity between religious zeal and Enlightenment emancipation also characterized the relationship between religious devotion and the authority of scientific knowledge. More often than not, the religious tradition of Puritanism, for example, has been seen as implacably opposed to the pretensions of Newtonian science, which proffered the heresy of nature being a self-contained and autonomous construction capable only of conforming to its own processes. The Puritans possessed a dogmatic belief in the pervasive and all-encompassing presence of God in the world, and in the absolute sovereignty of God's mind in providing the form and purpose of everything within the world. The 'enmity of reason to faith' was derived from the belief in one ultimate superiority of faith over reason. To the Puritan, 'faith demands the acceptance of things above reason ... grace fills men with the power to believe the impossible.... Even when reason is legitimately employed, its conclusions must always be tested by the propositions of faith, and whatever reason turns up to the contrary must be at

once discarded' (P. Miller, *The New England Mind: the Seventeenth Century*, Macmillan, New York, 1939, p. 32). And yet, in another sense, Puritanism can be portrayed as a genuine precursor of the Enlightenment because of the emphasis Puritanism laid upon the individual's inner faculty for acquiring religious knowledge and, thereby, upon his capacity for free enquiry, personal experimentation, and release from Scholastic doctrines. This intellectual duality could produce a figure like Cotton Mather, who 'would praise Francis Bacon, revere Robert Boyle, admire Isaac Newton' but also 'write about devils, angels, and witches as phenomena no less real than men and the force of gravity' (D. Levin, *Cotton Mather: the Young Life of the Lord's Remembrancer, 1663–1703*, Harvard University Press, Cambridge, Mass., 1978, pp. 26–7). Nevertheless, while it is normally the emphasis upon human sin and depravity within a God-centred world of revelation which is seen as being characteristically Puritan, the other more enquiring dimension of Puritanism is just as important. Natural philosophy was acceptable to, and even encouraged by, the Puritans; but it was an enquiry that had to be correctly motivated. 'If the visible world [was] seen correctly as the map and shadow of the spiritual estate of the beholder, as a means of divine communication with the devout, then the understanding of its law and workings [became] an essential part of Christian knowledge' (P. Miller and T. H. Johnson, eds, *The Puritans: a Sourcebook of their Writings*, vol. II, Harper & Row, New York, 1963, pp. 730–1). The rationalistic implications of Puritan theology, together with its stress upon the experiential and the practical, can serve to make Puritanism not merely consistent with the scientific revolution, but an integral part of the intellectual transformation from which it was derived. See Miller, *The New England Mind*, pp. 437–46; Morison, *The Intellectual Life of Colonial New England*, pp. 241–75; R. L. Greaves, 'Puritanism and science: the anatomy of a controversy', *Journal of the History of Ideas* 30, 3 (1969), pp. 345–68.

11 For example, see R. Hofstadter, *The American Political Tradition* (Jonathan Cape, London, 1967), pp. 3–17; M. Farrand, *The Framing of the Constitution of the United States* (Yale University Press, New Haven, 1963), pp. 196–210: H. J. Storing, 'The Federal Convention of 1787: politics, principles and statesmanship', in R.A. Rossum and G.L. McDowell (eds), *The American Founding: Politics, Statesmanship, and the Constitution* (Kennikat, Port Washington, 1981), pp. 12–28.

12 J. P. Roche, 'The Founding Fathers: a reform caucus in action', in J. P. Roche (ed.), *Shadow and Substance: Essays on the Theory and Structure of Politics* (Collier-Macmillan, London, 1964), p. 109.

13 Roche, 'The Founding Fathers', in Roche (ed.), *Shadow and Substance*, p. 109.

14 Roche, 'The Founding Fathers', in Roche (ed.), *Shadow and Substance*, pp. 119–20.

15 The classic exposition of just this type of personal and material motivation is still Charles Beard's iconoclastic *An Economic Interpretation of the Constitution of the United States* (Macmillan, New York, 1913). By challenging the previously benevolent portrayal of the Founders' olympian detachment in drawing up the constitution, Beard not only impugned the intellectual and political integrity of the Framers, but also compromised the constitution's status as a derivative of an exercise in genuine reasoning applied to the universal problems of government.

16 C. M. Kenyon, 'Men of little faith: the anti-federalists on the nature of representative government', in J. P. Greene (ed.), *The Reinterpretation of the American Revolution, 1763–1789* (Harper & Row, New York, 1968), p. 530.

17 J. Coniff, 'The Enlightenment and American political thought: a study of the origins of Madison's *Federalist* no. 10', *Political Theory* 8, 3 (1980), p. 398.

18 See M. J. C. Vile, *Constitutionalism and the Separation of Powers* (Oxford University Press, London, 1967), pp. 98–118: W. B. Gwyn, *The Meaning of the Separation of Powers: an Analysis of the Doctrine from its Origin to the Adoption of the United States Constitution* (Tulane University Press, New Orleans, 1965), pp. 82–128; S. Pargellis, 'The theory of balanced government', in C. Read (ed.), *The Constitution Reconsidered* (Columbia University Press, New York, 1938), pp. 37–49; C. Weston, *English Constitutional Theory and the House of Lords, 1556–1832* (Routledge, London, 1965), pp. 123–37; F. D. Wormuth, *The Origins of Modern Constitutionalism* (Harper, New York, 1949), pp. 169–83; J. B. Owen, *The Eighteenth Century, 1714–1815* (Nelson, London, 1974), pp. 94–122; B. Bailyn, *The Ideological Origins of the American Revolution* (Belknap Press, Cambridge, Mass., 1967), pp. 70–7.

19 See C. L. de S. Montesquieu, *The Spirit of the Laws*, trans. T. Nugent, intro. F. Neumann

(Hafner, New York, 1949), pp. li–lix, 149–82; R. Aron, *Main Currents in Sociological Thought*, vol. I, trans R. Howard and H. Weaver (Penguin, Harmondsworth, 1968), pp. 30–5; Vile, *Constitutionalism and the Separation of Powers*, pp. 76–97.
20 *Commentaries on the Laws of England* (London, 1765). See E. Barker, 'Blackstone on the British constitution', in E. Barker (ed.), *Essays on Government*, 2nd edn (Clarendon, Oxford, 1951), pp. 120–53; H. J. Storing, 'William Blackstone', in L. Strauss and J. Cropsey (eds), *History of Political Philosophy*, 2nd edn (Rand McNally, Chicago, 1972), pp. 594–606; Weston, *English Constitutional Theory and the House of Lords*, pp. 126–8.
21 *The Principles of Moral and Political Philosophy* (London, 1785). See Barker, 'Paley and his political philosophy', in Barker (ed.), *Traditions of Civility: Eight Essays* (Cambridge University Press, Cambridge, 1948); Weston, *English Constitutional Theory and the House of Lords*, pp. 130–2.
22 *The Constitution of England* (London, 1775). See Vile, *Constitutionalism and the Separation of Powers*, pp. 105–6; Weston, *English Constitutional Theory and the House of Lords*, pp. 128–30.
23 Gwyn, *The Meaning of the Separation of Powers*, pp. 91–6; I. Kramnick, *Bolingbroke and his Circle: the Politics of Nostalgia in the Age of Walpole* (Harvard University Press, Cambridge, Mass., 1968), pp. 137–87; J. H. Burns, 'Bolingbroke and the concept of constitutional government', *Political Studies* 10, 4 (1962), pp. 264–76; R. Shackleton, 'Montesquieu, Bolingbroke and the separation of powers', *French Studies* 3, 1 (1949), pp. 25–38.
24 Bailyn, *The Ideological Origins of the American Revolution*, p. 71.
25 Quoted in Bailyn, *The Ideological Origins of the American Revolution*, p. 67.
26 Bailyn, *The Ideological Origins of the American Revolution*, pp. 75–6.
27 G. S. Wood, *The Creation of the American Republic, 1776–1787* (University of North Carolina Press, Chapel Hill, 1969), pp. 197–255; Bailyn, *The Ideological Origins of the American Revolution*, pp. 272–301; C. M. Walsh, *The Political Science of John Adams: a Study in the Theory of Mixed Government and the Bicameral System* (Knickerbocker Press, New York, 1915), pp. 37–59, 74–9.
28 The federal constitution was sufficiently reminiscent of the format of contending powers associated with the tradition of mixed government that it led such overseas celebrants of the American revolution as Turgot, Rochefoucald, and Condorcet to bemoan the timidity of American republicanism in failing to prevent itself from reverting to British constitutional principles. Condorcet, for example, regarded the formulation of the federal constitution as 'something arresting and majestic' because it was a 'new structure, framed deliberately ... ; something which had not grown, but was planned ... [and] put together mechanically'. Even so, he felt compelled to criticize the separation of the three powers of government. 'Why ... is the simplicity of these constitutions [federal and state] disfigured by the system of the balance [separation] of powers?' To Condorcet it was one thing to have been bequeathed three separate powers from history and to seek ways of combining them, but quite another to set out intentionally to establish three powers, 'in order to have the pleasure of setting them against one another' (J. S. Schapiro, *Condorcet and the Rise of Liberalism*, Harcourt Brace, New York, 1934, pp. 223–4). The division and separation of powers in the constitution were to critics like Condorcet not so much a progressive and enlightened construction of government as a ratification of the past and a confirmation of America's lack of immunity to the historical continuity of political ideas and constitutional forms. See also C. M. Kenyon, 'Men of little faith: the anti-federalists on the nature of representative government', in Greene (ed.), *The Reinterpretation of the American Revolution, 1763–1789*, pp. 526–66; M. Lienesch, 'In defense of the anti-federalists', *History of Political Thought* 4, 1 (1983), pp. 65–88; W. Nicgorski, 'The anti-federalists: collected and interpreted', *Review of Politics* 46, 1 (1984), pp. 113–26; H. J. Storing, *What the Anti-federalists were for: the Political Thought of the Opponents of the Constitution* (University of Chicago Press, Chicago, 1981).
29 Plato, *The Laws*, trans. and intro. T. J. Saunders, rev. edn (Penguin, Harmondsworth, 1976), pp. 118–56; see also R. F. Stalley, *An Introduction to Plato's Laws* (Blackwell, Oxford, 1983), pp. 74–9, 115–22; E. Barker, *Greek Political Theory: Plato and his Predecessors*, 5th edn (Methuen, London, 1960), pp. 343–5; L. Strauss, *The Argument and the Action of Plato's Laws* (University of Chicago Press, Chicago, 1975), pp. 38–53.
30 Aristotle, *The Politics*, trans. and intro. T. A. Sinclair (Penguin, Harmondsworth, 1962), pp. 235–54. See also J. B. Morrall, *Aristotle* (Allen & Unwin, London, 1977), pp. 86–103; G. H.

Sabine and T. L. Thorson, *A History of Political Theory*, 4th edn (Dryden, Hinsdale, 1973), pp. 113–17; K. Von Fritz, *The Theory of the Mixed Constitution in Antiquity: a Critical Analysis of Polybius' Political Ideas* (Columbia University Press, New York, 1954), pp. 81–2.

31 According to Plato, the cycle of corruption might well be retarded by a mixed state that managed to combine the intelligent, virtuous, and lawful features of monarchy with the democratic principles of liberty and civic participation. This practical ideal of stability was not a vehicle for facilitating a dynamic balance between contending social forms so much as an aggregate of values derived from different sources within the state. The same classical predilection towards conceiving a constitution as a systemic structure embodying the corporative and purposive nature of the whole *polis* was also evident in Aristotle's advocacy of mixed government. In coming to a conclusion concerning the better types of constitution that were feasible in the real world, Aristotle largely dismissed the ideal, and therefore improbable, types like kingship and aristocracy in favour of a polity which was a mixture of oligarchy and democracy – the two most common forms of constitution. The mixture would represent primarily an amalgam of principles and institutions related to the two constituent forms. However, while there were obvious implications concerning social class in such a compound, it is apparent that Aristotle did not regard the polity as a mechanism for balancing the rich and the poor. Rather, it was a device which permitted the midle class to predominate in the name of moderation and stability. There may have been an incidental balance between the polar extremities of rich and poor through the central stabilizing weight of the middle class, but the polity was not interpreted by Aristotle as a means by which to achieve a co-ordinated mixture of the three constituent classes in society. What political balance existed was pre-established by a large middle class which in turn facilitated the mixture of forms.

32 L. Homo, *Roman Political Institutions: from City to State* (Routledge, London, 1962) pp. 113–18; M. I. Finley, *The Greek Historians: the Essence of Herodotus, Thucydides, Xenophon, Polybius* (Chatto & Windus, London, 1959), pp. 473–501; F. W. Walbank, *Polybius* (University of California Press, Berkeley, 1972), pp. 302–52.

33 Sabine and Thorson, *A History of Political Thought*, 4th edn pp. 151–3.

34 Von Fritz, *The Theory of the Mixed Constitution in Antiquity*, pp. 60–95, 184–219, 306–52.

35 N. Machiavelli, *The Discourses*, trans. L. J. Walker, intro. B. Crick (ed.) (Penguin, Harmondsworth, 1983), pp. 100–31, 249–57, 430–2; Q. Skinner, *Machiavelli* (Oxford University Press, Oxford, 1981), pp. 64–71; S. Anglo, *Machiavelli: a Dissection* (Gollancz, London, 1969), pp. 97–103.

36 Von Fritz, *The Theory of the Mixed Constitution in Antiquity*, p. v.

37 Gwyn, *The Meaning of the Separation of Powers*; Vile, *Constitutionalism and the Separation of Powers*.

38 Gwyn, *The Meaning of the Separation of Powers*, pp. 11–27, 37–81; Vile, *Constitutionalism and the Separation of Powers*, pp. 37–75; D. W. Hanson, *From Kingdom to Commonwealth: the Development of Civic Consciousness in English Political Thought* (Harvard University Press, Cambridge, Mass., 1970), pp. 240–55; Weston, *English Constitutional Theory and the House of Lords*, pp. 23–123; Z. Fink, *The Classical Republicans* (Northwestern University Press, Evanston, 1945); Wormuth, *The Origins of Modern Constitutionalism*, pp. 50–72.

39 See C. Robbins, *The Eighteenth-century Commonwealthman: Studies in the Transmission, Development and Circumstance of English Liberal Thought from the Restoration of Charles II until the War with the Thirteen Colonies* (Harvard University Press, Cambridge, Mass., 1959), pp. 88–133; Gwyn, *The Meaning of the Separation of Powers*, pp. 11–27, 82–99; J. G. A. Pocock, 'Machiavelli, Harrington, and English political ideologies in the eighteenth century', *William and Mary Quarterly* 22, 4 (1965), pp. 549–83.

40 C. Hill, *Puritanism and Revolution:Studies in the Interpretation of the English Revolution of the Seventeenth Century* (Secker & Warburg, London, 1958), pp. 58–125.

41 See Bailyn, *The Ideological Origins of the American Revolution*; Wood, *The Creation of the American Republic*; Pocock, *The Machiavellian Moment: Florentine Political Thought and the Atlantic Republican Tradition* (Princeton University Press, Princeton, 1975); R. E. Shalhope, 'Toward a republican synthesis: the emergence of an understanding of republicanism in American historiography', *William and Mary Quarterly* 29, 1 (1972), pp. 49–80. The 'classical republican thesis' in American historiography has attracted considerable interest and has generated an extensive body of scholarship seeking to refine or to revise the main components of the original assertion of a preponderant republican ethos based upon civic virtue,

moral fervour, and the ideal of community. See Shalhope, 'Republicanism and early American historiography', *William and Mary Quarterly* 39, 2 (1982), pp. 334–56; I. Kramnick, 'Republican revisionism revisited', *American Historical Review* 87, 3 (1982), pp. 629–64; J. Appleby, 'Republicanism and ideology', *American Quarterly* 37, 4 (1985), pp. 461–73; Appleby, 'Republicanism in old and new contexts', *William and Mary Quarterly* 43, 1 (1986), pp. 20–34; L. Banning, 'Republican ideology and the triumph of the constitution, 1789–1793', *William and Mary Quarterly* 31, 2 (1974), pp. 167–88; Banning, 'Jeffersonian ideology revisited: liberal and classical ideas in the new American republic', *William and Mary Quarterly* 53, 1 (1986), pp. 3–19; J. P. Diggins, *The Lost Soul of American Politics: Virtue, Self-interest and the Foundation of Liberalism* (Basic Books, New York, 1984); J. H. Hutson, 'Country, court and the constitution: antifederalism and the historians', *William and Mary Quarterly* 38, 3 (1981), pp. 337–68.

42 Pocock, 'Machiavelli, Harrington, and English political ideologies in the eighteenth century', *William and Mary Quarterly* 22, 4 (1965), p. 568.

43 Pocock, 'Machiavelli, Harrington, and English political ideologies in the eighteenth century', p. 572.

44 Pocock, 'Machiavelli, Harrington, and English political ideologies in the eighteenth century', p. 573.

45 H. Arendt, 'Constitutio libertas', in Greene (ed.), *The Reinterpretation of the American Revolution*, p. 589.

46 H. Wheeler, 'Constitutionalism', in F. I. Greenstein and N. W. Polsby (eds), *Handbook of Political Science*, vol. 5, *Government Institutions and Processes* (Addison-Wesley, Reading, Mass., 1975), pp. 1–91.

47 N. C. Thomas, review of Greenstein and Polsby (eds), *Handbook of Political Science*, vol. 5, *Government Institutions and Processes*, in *American Political Science Review* 71, 4 (1977), pp. 1629–30.

48 See R. Barber, *The American Corporation: its Power, its Money, its Politics* (Macgibbon & Key, London, 1970); P. A. Baran and P. M. Sweezy, *Monopoly Capitalism: an Essay on the American Economic and Social Order* (Penguin, Harmondsworth, 1968); M. Zeitlin (ed.), *American Society, Inc.: Studies of the Social Structure and Political Economy of the United States* (Rand McNally, Chicago, 1977), pp. 1–60; T. R. Dye, *Who's Running America? The Carter Years*, 2nd edn (Prentice-Hall, Englewood Cliffs, 1979), pp. 19–51; I. Katznelson and M. Kesselman, *The Politics of Power: a Critical Introduction to American Government* (Harcourt Brace Jovanovich, New York, 1975), pp. 35–150; D. Bell, 'Modernity and mass society: on the varieties of cultural experience', in A. M. Schlesinger, Jr and M. White (eds), *Paths of American Thought* (Houghton Mifflin, Boston, Mass., 1970), pp. 411–31.

49 See T. Lowi and A. Stone (eds), *Nationalizing Government* (Sage, Beverly Hills, 1978); E. E. Schattschneider, *The Semisovereign People: a Realist's View of Democracy in America* (Holt Rinehart & Winston, New York, 1960), pp. 76–94; D. E. Stokes, 'Parties and the nationalization of electoral forces', in R. G. Niemi and H. F. Weisberg (eds), *Controversies in American Voting Behaviour* (W. H. Freeman, San Francisco, 1976), pp. 514–31.

50 I. McLean, *Dealing in Votes: Interactions between Politicians and Voters in Britain and the USA* (Martin Robertson, Oxford, 1982), p. 50.

51 See L. M. Seagull, *Southern Republicanism* (Wiley, New York, 1975), pp. 1–21, 147–58; N. V. Bartley and H. D. Graham, *Southern Politics and the Second Reconstruction* (Johns Hopkins University Press, Baltimore, 1975).

52 F. J. Sorauf, *Political Parties in the American System* (Little Brown, Boston, Mass., 1964), pp. 36–7.

53 W. D. Burnham, 'American politics in the 1970s: beyond party?' in J. Fishel (ed.), *Parties and Elections in an Anti-party Age: American Politics and the Crisis of Confidence* (Indiana University Press, Bloomington, 1978), p. 338.

54 See Burnham, 'American politics in the 1970s', in J. Fishel (ed.), *Parties and Elections in an Anti-party Age*, pp. 333–41; Burnham, 'The changing shape of the American political universe', in Niemi and Weisberg (eds), *Controversies in American Voting Behaviour*, pp. 451–83; N. H. Nie, S. Verba, and J. R. Petrocik, *The Changing American Voter* (Harvard University Press, Cambridge, Mass., 1976), pp. 43–95, 156–73, 243–69, 289–306; H. Asher, *Presidential Elections and American Politics: Voters, Candidates, and Campaigns since 1952* (Dorsey, Homewood, 1976), pp. 49–85; McLean, *Dealing in Votes*, pp. 44–67; J. Clubb, W.

H. Flanigan, and N. H. Zingale, *Partisan Realignment: Voters, Parties and Government in American History* (Sage, Beverly Hills, 1980), pp. 122–34; E. C. Ladd, Jr, and C. D. Hadley, *Transformations of the American Party System: Political Coalitions from the New Deal to the 1970s* (W. W. Norton, New York, 1975), pp. 181–331; D. S. Broder, *The Party's Over* (Harper & Row, New York, 1972); G. Pomper, 'The decline of partisan politics', in L. Maisel and J. Cooper (eds), *The Impact of the Electoral Process* (Sage, Beverly Hills, 1977), pp. 13–38; W. Crotty, *American Parties in Decline*, 2nd edn (Little Brown, Boston, Mass., 1984), pp. 4–58, 75–186; M. Wattenberg, *The Decline of American Political Parties, 1952–1980* (Harvard University Press, Cambridge, Mass., 1984).

55 Nie, Verba, and Petrocik, *The Changing American Voter*, pp. 348, 352.

56 J. L. Sundquist with D. W. Davis, *Making Federalism Work: a Study of Program Co-ordination at the Community Level* (Brookings Institution, Washington, D.C., 1969), pp. 1–32; M. D. Reagan, *The New Federalism* (Oxford University Press, New York, 1972), pp. 54–72; L. D. Epstein, 'The old states in a new system', in A. King (ed.), *The New American Political System* (American Enterprise Institute for Public Policy Research, Washington, D.C., 1978), pp. 338–42; G. E. Hale and M. Palley, *The Politics of Federal Grants* (Congressional Quarterly Press, Washington, D.C., 1981).

57 Reagan *The New Federalism*, pp. 145–68.

58 M. Grodzins, 'The federal system', in A. Wildavsky (ed.), *American Federalism in Perspective* (Little Brown, Boston, Mass., 1967), p. 276.

59 M. J C. Vile, 'Federal theory and the "new federalism"', *Politics: Journal of the Australasian Political Science Association*, 12, 2 (1977), p. 8.

60 A. K. Weinberg, *Manifest Destiny: a Study of Nationalist Expansion in American History* (Peter Smith, Gloucester, 1958), pp. 160–323; A. Ekirch, Jr, *Ideas, Ideals, and American Diplomacy: a History of their Growth and Interaction* (Appleton-Century-Crofts, New York, 1966), pp. 22–60; R. W. Van Alstyne, *The Rising American Empire* (Blackwell, Oxford, 1960), pp. 100–23; H. Kohn, *American Nationalism: an Interpretive Essay* (Macmillan, New York, 1957), pp. 181–94; H. N. Smith, *Virgin Land: the American West as Symbol and Myth* (Vintage, York, 1950), pp. 20–46, 165–77.

61 See E. May, *Imperial Democracy* (Harcourt Brace Jovanovich, New York, 1961); Kohn, *American Nationalism*, pp. 171–228; S. E. Ambrose, *Rise to Globalism: American Foreign Policy, 1938–1980* (Penguin, Harmondsworth, 1980).

62 D. J. Devine, *The Political Culture of the United States: the Influence of Member Values on Regime Maintenance* (Little Brown, Boston, Mass., 1972), pp. 94–5. The countries used in the poll were the United States, Norway, Mexico, France, Australia, Italy, West Germany, and the Netherlands. In another poll measuring national pride and patriotism in the United States, Great Britain, Spain, Italy, France, and West Germany, it was revealed that Americans were far more willing to fight for their country (79 per cent) and had far more national pride (80 per cent) than any of the other nationalities. (Poll findings quoted in J. Q. Wilson, *American Government: Institutions and Policies*, 3rd edn, D. C. Heath, Lexington, 1986, p. 82.)

63 The philosophical basis for the transition from *laissez-faire* to a more concerted community consciousness in America has been attributed to a wide variety of influences. Included amongst them would be (i) the new science of social psychology, which not only adopted society rather than individuals as the base unit of evolution, but recognized that societies were changed from within by the active assertion of the collective will; (ii) the barely suppressed Hegelianism of writers like Josiah Royce and Herbert Croly, who sought to redefine the individual in terms of a communal ideal; (iii) the force of the pragmatist school, which preached the importance of knowledge as an instrumental value to be used experimentally to ameliorate immediate social problems in a spirit of openness and lack of finality which refused to see man as part of any closed, determined, or rational order; (iv) the popular appeal of the utopian genre of writers such as Henry George and Edward Bellamy; (v) the revival of Christian social ethics nurtured by the Social Gospel movement; (vi) the rise in respectability of sociological jurisprudence, which sought to release the law from its anchorage of fixed principles, predetermined design, and mechanistic nature into the open sea of public experience, public choice, and public welfare; (vii) and finally the less articulate and more intuitive general demand for the status and moral substance of America's more traditional social ideals to be revived. See H. S. Commager, *The American Mind: an Interpretation*

of American Thought and Character since the 1880s (Bantam, New York, 1970), pp. 92–109, 203–30, 344–400; C. B. Forcey, *The Crossroads of Liberalism: Croly, Weyl, Lippman and the Progressive Era, 1900–25* (Oxford University Press, New York, 1961); H. W. Schneider, *A History of American Philosophy* (Liberal Arts Press, New York, 1957), pp. 197–352; R. H. Gabriel, *The Course of American Democratic Thought: an Intellectual History since 1815*, 2nd edn (Ronald Press, New York, 1956), pp. 198–215, 237–68, 280–9, 331–8; S. Persons, *American Minds: a History of Ideas* (Holt Rinehart & Winston, New York, 1958), pp. 349–451; M. J. Skidmore, *American Political Thought* (St Martin's Press, New York, 1978), pp. 166–95; D. E. Price, 'Community and control: critical democratic theory in the Progressive period', *American Political Science Review* 68, 4 (1974), pp. 1663–78.

64 See Hofstadter, *The American Political Tradition*, pp. 311–47; Hofstadter, *The Age of Reform: from Bryan to F.D.R.* (Jonathan Cape, London, 1962), pp. 300–26; E. Goldman, *Rendezvous with Destiny* (Knopf, New York, 1972), pp. 346–73; H. H. Humphrey, *The Political Philosophy of the New Deal* (Louisiana State University Press, Baton Rouge, 1970), pp. 80–121; W. E. Leuchtenburg, *Franklin Roosevelt and the New Deal, 1932–1940* (Harper & Row, New York, 1963), pp. 118–42, 340–8.

65 *West Coast Hotel* v. *Parrish* 300 U.S. 379 (1937).

66 Cf. 'Attitudes toward welfare', Harris Survey, February 1976, quoted in Wilson, *American Government*, 3rd edn, p. 490; Yankelovich, Skelly, and White, survey in *Public Opinion*, June–July 1985, quoted in J. L. Sundquist, 'Has America lost its social conscience – and how will it get it back?' *Political Science Quarterly* 101, 4 (1986–7), p. 521.

67 S. H. Beer, 'Liberalism and the national idea', in R. A. Goldwin (ed.), *Left, Right and Center: Essays on Liberalism and Conservatism in the United States* (Rand McNally, Chicago, 1967), p. 169.

68 Beer, 'Liberalism and the national idea', in Goldwin (ed.), *Left, Right and Center*, pp. 164, 168, 160.

69 Vile, *Constitutionalism and the Separation of Powers*, pp. 1–20; R. A. Dahl, *A Preface to Democratic Theory* (University of Chicago Press, Chicago, 1956), pp. 4–33; H. Finer, *The Theory and Practice of Modern Government* (Holt Rinehart & Winston, New York, 1949), pp. 94–108; A. King, 'Executives', in F. I. Greenstein and N. W. Polsby (eds), *Handbook of Political Science*, vol. 5, *Governmental Institutions and Processes* (Addison-Wesley, Reading, Mass., 1975), pp. 175–82.

70 Dahl, *A Preface to Democratic Theory*, p. 6.

71 Dahl, *A Preface to Democratic Theory*, p. 22.

72 E. S. Corwin, *The President: Office and Powers, 1787–1948: History and Analysis of Practice and Opinion*, 3rd edn, rev. (New York University Press, New York, 1948), p. 38.

73 W. Wilson, *Constitutional Government in the United States* (Columbia University Press, New York, 1911), p. 70.

74 *U.S.* v. *Curtiss-Wright Export Corporation* 299 U.S. 304 (1936).

75 S. P. Huntington, 'Congressional responses to the twentieth century', in D. B. Truman (ed.), *The Congress and America's Future* (Prentice-Hall, Englewood Cliffs, 1965), p. 6.

76 E. S. Corwin, 'The aggrandizement of presidential power', in R. S. Hirschfield (ed.), *The Power of the Presidency: Concepts and Controversy* (Atherton, New York, 1968), p. 27.

77 Quoted in D. B. Kearns, *Lyndon Johnson and the American Dream* (Harper & Row, New York, 1976), p. 221.

78 *Time*, 3 July 1983.

79 N. E. Long, 'Bureaucracy and constitutionalism', *American Political Science Review* 46, 3 (1952), pp. 818, 817.

80 *Springer* v. *Government of the Philippine Islands* 277 U.S. 189, 211 (1928).

Chapter 3. The perpetuation of constitutional mechanics

1 F. Engels, 'Ludwig Fauerbach and the end of classical philosophy', *Karl Marx and Frederick Engels: Selected Works* (Lawrence & Wishart, London, 1968), p. 603.

2 See R. M. Gummere, 'The classical ancestry of the United States constitution', *American Quarterly* 14 (1962), pp. 3–18; G. Chinard, 'Polybius and the American constitution', *Journal of the History of Ideas* 1, 1 (1940), pp. 38–58.

3 J. A. Robinson, 'Newtonianism and the constitution', *Midwest Journal of Political Science* 1, 3 (1957), pp. 252–66.
4 M. Landau, *Political Theory and Political Science: Studies in the Methodology of Political Inquiry* (repr. Humanities Press, Atlantic Highlands, 1972), pp. 103–21.
5 Robinson, 'Newtonianism and the constitution', *Midwest Journal of Political Science* 1, 3 (1987), p. 254.
6 Robinson, 'Newtonianism and the constitution', p. 259.
7 Robinson, 'Newtonianism and the constitution', p. 262.
8 Robinson, 'Newtonianism and the constitution', p. 265.
9 Robinson, 'Newtonianism and the constitution', p. 259.
10 Landau, *Political Theory and Political Science*, p. 87.
11 Landau, *Political Theory and Political Science*, p. 84.
12 Landau, *Political Theory and Political Science*, pp. 83–4.
13 Landau, *Political Theory and Political Science*, p. 87
14 Landau, *Political Theory and Political Science*, p. 87.
15 See J. G. A. Pocock, 'Languages and their implications: the transformation of the study of political thought', in Pocock (ed.), *Politics, Language and Time: Essays on Political Thought and History* (Methuen, London, 1972), pp. 3–41. For a review of the growing literature on the relationship between political metaphors and the sources of political knowledge, see E. F. Miller, 'Metaphor and political knowledge', *American Political Science Review* 73, 1 (1979), pp. 155–70; J. Rayner, 'Between meaning and event: an historical approach to political metaphor', *Political Studies* 32, 4 (1984), pp. 537–50.
16 M. D. Irish and J. W. Prothro, *The Politics of American Democracy*, 4th edn (Prentice-Hall, Englewood Cliffs, 1968), p. 311.
17 'High Court re-examines separation of powers', *Congressional Quarterly Guide to Current American Government*, fall 1986 (Congressional Quarterly Press, Washington, D.C., 1986), p. 84.
18 R. E. Neustadt, *Presidential Power: the Politics of Leadership* (Wiley, New York, 1960), p. 33.
19 The thirty textbooks selected were as follows: S. K. Bailey, H. D. Samuel, and S. Baldwin, *Government in America* (Holt Rinehart & Winston, New York, 1957); J. M. Burns and J. W. Peltason, *Government by the People: the Dynamics of American National, State and Local Government*, 3rd edn (Prentice-Hall, Englewood Cliffs, 1957); A. de Grazia, *The American Way of Government: National, State and Local Edition* (Wiley, New York, 1957); R. White with H. L. Imel, *American Government: Democracy at Work*, 2nd edn (Van Nostrand, Princeton, 1963); E. S. Redford, D. B. Truman, A. Hacker, A. F. Westin, and R. C. Wood, *Politics and Government in the United States: National Edition* (Harcourt Brace & World, New York, 1965); W. C. Havard, *The Government and Politics of the United States* (Hutchinson, London, 1965); R. K. Carr, M. H. Bernstein, and W. F. Murphy, *American Democracy in Theory and Practice: Essentials of National, State and Local Government*, 3rd edn (Holt Rinehart & Winston, New York, 1965); J. C. Livingston and R. G. Thompson, *The Consent of the Governed*, 2nd edn (Macmillan, New York, 1966); W. H. Young, *Ogg and Ray's Introduction to American Government*, 13th edn (Appleton-Century-Crofts, New York, 1966); J. H. Ferguson and D. E. McHenry, *The American System of Government*, 10th edn (McGraw-Hill, New York, 1969); P. H. Odegard with H. H. Baerwald and W. C. Havard, *The American Republic: its Government and Politics*, 2nd edn (Harper & Row, New York, 1969); C. R. Adrian and C. Press, *The American Political Process*, 2nd edn (McGraw-Hill, New York, 1969); M. C. Cummings, Jr, and D. Wise, *Democracy under Pressure: an Introduction to the American Political Process* (Harcourt Brace Jovanovich, New York, 1971); P. Woll and R. Binstock, *America's Political System* (Random House, New York, 1972); K. Prewitt and S. Verba, *Principles of American Government* (Harper & Row, New York, 1975); E. L. Levine and E. E. Cornwell, Jr, *An Introduction to American Government*, 3rd edn (Macmillan, New York, 1975); R. A. Watson, *Promise and Performance of American Democracy*, 2nd edn (Wiley, New York, 1975); D. J. Olson and P. Meyer, *To Keep the Republic: Governing the United States in its Third Century* (McGraw-Hill, New York, 1975); R. E. Wolfinger, M. Shapiro, and F. I. Greenstein, *Dynamics of American Politics* (Prentice-Hall, Englewood Cliffs, 1976); M. Krasner, S. G. Chaberski, and D. K. Jones, *American Government: Structure and Process* (Macmillan, New York, 1977); R. Sherrill with J. D. Barber, B. I. Page, and V. W. Joyner, *Governing America: an Introduction* (Harcourt Brace Jovanovich, New York, 1978); K. Pre-

witt and S. Verba, *An Introduction to American Government*, 3rd edn (Harper & Row, New York, 1979); S. C. Patterson, R. H. Davidson, and R. B. Ripley, *A More Perfect Union: Introduction to American Government* (Dorsey, Homewood, 1979); P. Woll, *Constitutional Democracy: Policies and Politics* (Little Brown, Boston, Mass., 1982); A. B. Saye, J. F. Allums, and M. B. Pound, *Principles of American Government*, 9th edn (Prentice-Hall, Englewood Cliffs, 1982); W. D. Burnham, *Democracy in the Making: American Government and Politics* (Prentice-Hall, Englewood Cliffs, 1983); R. Hilsman, *The Politics of Governing* (Prentice-Hall, Englewood Cliffs, 1985); J. Q. Wilson, *American Government: Institutions and Policies*, 3rd edn (D. C. Heath, Lexington, 1986); L. Lipsitz, *American Democracy* (St Martin's Press, New York, 1986); K. Janda, J. M. Berry, and J. Goldman, *The Challenge of Democracy* (Houghton Mifflin, Boston, Mass., 1987).

20 For example, see Wolfinger, Shapiro, and Greenstein, *Dynamics of American Politics* (total pp. 650); Adrian and Press, *The American Political Process*, 2nd edn (total pp. 869); Cummings and Wise, *Democracy under Pressure* (total pp. 718); Patterson, Davidson, and Ripley, *A More Perfect Union* (total pp. 766); Burnham, *Democracy in the Making* (total pp. 654); Janda, Berry, and Goldman, *The Challenge of Democracy* (total pp. 718). It is true that a few works give an extended examination of the separation of powers principle – most notably Levine and Cornwell, *An Introduction to American Government*, 3rd edn; Livingston and Thompson, *The Consent of the Governed*, 2nd edn; Odegard, Baerwald, and Havard, *The American Republic*, 2nd edn But they remain the conspicuous exceptions and are heavily outweighed by those works which make only passing reference to the separation of powers in their text, and by those which do not even list the separation of powers in their index (e.g. Burns and Peltason, *Government by the People*, 3rd edn (total pp. 990); Young, *Ogg and Ray's Introduction to American Government*, 13th edn (total pp. 979); Olson and Meyer, *To Keep the Republic* (total pp. 588); Sherrill with Barber, Page, and Joyner, *Governing America* (total pp. 654); Hilsman, *The Politics of Governing* (total pp. 484); Wilson, *American Government* (total pp. 642).

21 B. Bailyn, *The Ideological Origins of the American Revolution* (Belknap Press, Cambridge, Mass., 1967), pp. 66–93, 272–301.

22 W. B. Gwyn, *The Meaning of the Separation of Powers: an Analysis of the Doctrine from its Origin to the Adoption of the United States Constitution* (Tulane University Press, New Orleans, 1965).

23 G. S. Wood, *The Creation of the American Republic, 1776–1787* (University of North Carolina Press, Chapel Hill, 1969), pp. 197–255, 430–67, 519–64, 593–615.

24 M. J. C. Vile, *Constitutionalism and the Separation of Powers* (Oxford University Press, London, 1967), pp. 119–75.

25 Prewitt and Verba, *An Introduction tro American Government*, 3rd edn, p. 37.

26 De Grazia, *The American Way of Government*, p. 89.

27 Sherrill with Barber, Page, and Joyner, *Governing America*, p. 48.

28 Burns and Peltason, *Government by the People*, 3rd edn, pp. 64–5.

29 Woll and Binstock, *America's Political System*, p. 65.

30 Cummings and Wise, *Democracy under Pressure*, pp. 58–9.

31 Vile, *Constitutionalism and the Separation of Powers*, p. 122.

32 Vile, *Constitutionalism and the Separation of Powers*, pp. 151, 157.

33 Quoted in L. Fisher, 'A political context for legislative vetoes', *Political Science Quarterly* 93, 2 (1978), p. 228.

34 J. Madison, 'Federalist Paper no. 37', in A. Hamilton, J. Madison, and J. Jay, *The Federalist Papers*, intro. C. Rossiter (Mentor, New York, 1961), p. 228.

35 Madison, 'Federalist Paper no. 47', in Hamilton, Madison, and Jay, *The Federalist Papers*, intro. Rossiter, p. 302.

36 Madison, 'Federalist Paper no. 47', in Hamilton, Madison, and Jay, *The Federalist Papers*, intro. Rossiter, p. 301.

37 Carr, Bernstein, and Murphy, *American Democracy in Theory and Practice*, 3rd edn, pp. 60–1.

38 Wolfinger, Shapiro, and Greenstein, *Dynamics of American Politics*, p. 46.

39 Sherrill with Barber, Page, and Joyner, *Governing America*, p. 48.

40 De Grazia, *The American Way of Government*, p. 91.

41 Livingston and Thompson, *The Consent of the Governed*, 2nd edn, p. 144.

42 Levine and Cornwell, *An Introduction to American Government*, p. 47.
43 Lipsitz, *American Democracy*, p. 49.
44 Patterson, Davidson, and Ripley, *A More Perfect Union*, p. 47.
45 Hilsman, *The Politics of Governing*, p. 45.
46 Ferguson and McHenry, *The American System of Government*, 10th edn, p. 32.
47 Janda, Berry, and Goldman, *The Challenge of Democracy*, p. 85.
48 Prewitt and Verba, *Principles of American Government*, p. 184.
49 Watson, *Promise and Performance of American Democracy*, 2nd edn, pp. 45–6.
50 Burns and Peltason, *Government by the People*, 3rd edn, pp. 65, 67.
51 Adrian and Press, *The American Political Process*, 2nd edn, pp. 111–12.
52 Olson and Meyer, *To Keep the Republic*, p. 32.
53 Odegard with Baerwald and Havard, *The American Republic*, 2nd edn, p. 139.
54 Havard, *The Government and Politics of the United States*, pp. 31–3.
55 Madison, 'Federalist Paper no. 47', in Hamilton, Madison, and Jay, *The Federalist Paper*, intro. Rossiter, p. 302.
56 E. S. Griffith, *The American System of Government*, 2nd edn (Methuen, London, 1966), p. 4.
57 J. M. Burns, *The Deadlock of Democracy: Four-party Politics in America* (Calder, London, 1963), p. 20.
58 Redford, Truman, Hacker, Westin, and Wood, *Politics and Government in the United States*, p. 79
59 Woll and Binstock, *America's Political System*, p. 81.
60 N. W. Polsby, *Congress and the Presidency*, 2nd edn (Prentice-Hall, Englewood Cliffs, 1971), p. 147.
61 D. S. Broder, 'The case for responsible party government', in J. Fishel (ed.), *Parties and Elections in an Anti-party Age: American Politics and the Crisis of Confidence* (Indiana University Press, Bloomington, 1978), p. 22.
62 J. L. Sundquist, *Politics and Policy: the Eisenhower, Kennedy and Johnson Years* (Brookings Institution, Washington, D.C., 1968), pp. 510–11.
63 Burns, *The Deadlock of Democracy*, pp. 6, 205–6, 324.
64 L. N. Cutler, 'To form a government', *Foreign Affairs* 59, 1 (1980), pp. 126–7, 128, 139, 143.
65 T.R.B., 'Turbulence ahead', *New Republic*, 20 July 1974.
66 A. S. Miller, 'Separation of powers: an ancient doctrine under modern challenge', *Administrative Law Review* 28, 3 (1976), pp. 324–5.
67 J. W. Gardner, *In Common Cause* (W. W. Norton, New York, 1972), pp. 16, 17, 18.
68 F. Lewis, 'The parts and the whole', *Herald Tribune*, 3 October 1980.
69 C. M. Hardin, *Presidential Power and Accountability: toward a new Constitution* (University of Chicago Press, Chicago, 1974), p. 2.
70 A. Tofler, *The Third Wave* (Pan Books, London, 1981), pp. 402–3, 424.
71 A. Fortas, 'Strengthening government to cope with the future', *New Republic*, 9 November 1974.
72 K. P. Phillips, 'Our obsolete system', *Newsweek*, 28 April 1973.
73 H. Wheeler, 'Constitutionalism', in Greenstein and Polsby (eds), *Handbook of Political Science*, vol. 5, *Governmental Institutions and Processes*, p. 77.
74 Excerpt from President Carter's televized address to the nation on 15 July 1979. *Congressional Quarterly Almanac, 96th Congress, 1st Session, 1979* (Congressional Quarterly Press, Washington, D.C., 1980), p. 46E.
75 H. M. Barger, *The Impossible Presidency: Illusions and Realities of Executive Power* (Scott Foresman, Glenview, 1984), pp. 396, 139.
76 L. LeLoup, *Politics in America: the Ability to Govern* (West Publishing, St Paul, 1986), pp. 13–14.
77 Woll and Binstock, *America's Political System*, p. 255.
78 H. S. Commager, 'The shame of the republic', in R. E. Pynn (ed.) *Watergate and the American Political Process* (Praeger, New York, 1975), p. 9.
79 J. M. Burns, 'The power to lead', in D. L. Robinson (ed.), *Reforming American Government: the Bicentennial Papers of the Committee on the Constitutional System* (Westview, Boulder, 1985), p. 160.
80 L. Berman, *The New American Presidency* (Little Brown, Boston, Mass., 1987), pp. 1–2.
81 J. Allen Smith, *The Spirit of American Government* (Macmillan, New York, 1907); C. A.

Beard, *An Economic Interpretation of the Constitution of the United States* (Macmillan, New York, 1913); V. L. Parrington, *Main Currents in American Thought* (Harcourt Brace, New York, 1927), vol. 1, pp. 267–307; Vile, *Constitutionalism and the Separation of Powers*, pp. 263–93.

82 M. Stanton Evans, *Clear and Present Dangers: a Conservative View of America's Government* (Harcourt Brace Jovanovich, New York, 1975), p. 23.

Chapter 4. The Presidency, the Congress and the separation of paradigms

1 W. Wilson, *The New Freedom: a Call for the Emancipation of the Generous Energies of a People*, intro. W. E. Leuctenburg (Prentice-Hall, Englewood Cliffs, 1961), pp. 19, 25, 26, 21.
2 Wilson, *Constitutional Government in the United States* (Columbia University Press, New York, 1911), p. 56.
3 These functional categories pertain to the widely used physiological definition of life. There are, however, other definitional formats that attempt to isolate and to extract the irreducible characteristics of life. They include a *metabolic* definition (i.e. a system exchanging materials with its environment whilst retaining a basic continuity in form and constituent properties); a *biochemical* definition (i.e. a system containing reproducible hereditary material in complex self-replicating molecules); a genetic definition (i.e. a system dependent upon having been, and continuing to be, evolved into higher states of complexity by natural selection working through mutation and environmental pressures); a *thermodynamic* definition (i.e. a system providing a localized and temporary reversal of entropy through its ability to build up a complex structure of order, pattern, and harmony in an open system of interaction, as opposed to the closed and isolated system of the universe as a whole).
4 See F. J. Ayala, 'Biology as an autonomous science', *American Scientist* 53, 3 (1968), pp. 207–21.
5 See R. S. Westfall, *The Construction of Modern Science: Mechanisms and Mechanics* (Cambridge University Press, Cambridge, 1977), pp. 82–104; H. Butterfield, *The Origins of Modern Science, 1300–1800*, rev. edn (G. Bell, London, 1957), pp. 117–26; A. C. Crombie, *Augustine to Galileo*, vol. II, *Science in the Later Middle Ages and Early Modern Times, 13th to 17th Centuries* (Heinemann, London, 1959), pp. 242–9; M. D. Grmek, 'A survey of the mechanical interpretations of life from Greek atomists to the followers of Descartes', in A. Beck and W. Yourgram (eds), *Biology, History and Natural Philosophy* (Plenum Press, New York, 1972), pp. 181–96.
6 D. L. Hull, *Philosophy of Biological Science* (Prentice-Hall, Englewood Cliffs, 1974), p. 142.
7 J. Huxley, *Evolution in Action* (Penguin, Harmondsworth, 1963), p. 37.
8 Huxley, *Evolution in Action*, p. 15.
9 C. Patterson, *Evolution* (Routledge, London, 1978), pp. 26–37; G. L. Stebbins, *Darwinism to DNA: Molecules to Humanity* (W. H. Freeman, San Francisco, 1982), pp. 30–7.
10 B. Silcock, 'Master of the gene machine', *Sunday Times*, 19 October 1980.
11 A. N. Whitehead, *Science and the Modern World* (Penguin, Harmondsworth, 1938), pp. 94–8.
12 Whitehead, *Science and the Modern World*, p. 98.
13 Hull, *Philosophy of Biological Science*, pp. 127–9; J. Monod, *Chance and Necessity: an Essay on the National Philosophy of Modern Biology* (Fontana, London, 1974), pp. 15–50; R. Sheldrake, *A New Science of Life: the Hypothesis of Formative Causation* (Blond & Briggs, London, 1981). For the debate on whether organisms are reducible to mechanical properties, see M. A. Simon, *The Matter of Life: Philosophical Problems of Biology* (Yale University Press, New Haven, 1971), pp. 144–67; A. Koestler and J. R. Smythies (eds), *Beyond Reductionism: New Perspectives in the Life Sciences* (Hutchinson, London, 1969); Hull, *Philosophy of Biological Science*, pp. 125–41; M. Grene (ed.), *Interpretations of Life and Mind: Essays around the Problem of Reductionism* (Routledge, London, 1971); J. O. Wisdom, 'Must a machine be an automaton?', in Beck and Yourgram (eds), *Biology, History and Natural Philosophy*, pp. 291–8; K. W. Deutsch, 'Mechanism, organism and society', *Philosophy of Science* 18 (1951), pp. 230–52; M. Gardner, *Mathematical Circus* (Penguin, Harmondsworth, 1981), pp. 102–110; 'Why can't a computer be more like a man?', *Economist*, 9 January 1982.
14 Simon, *The Matter of Life*, p. 147.
15 S. Black, *The Nature of Living Things: an Essay in Theoretical Biology* (Secker & War-

burg/Heinemann, London, 1972), pp. 11–12.
16 R. C. Lewontin, 'The corpse in the elevator', *New York Review of Books*, 20 January 1983.
17 Lewontin, 'The corpse in the elevator'.
18 P. J. Bowler, *Evolution: the History of an Idea* (University of California Press, Berkeley, 1984), pp. 142–75; P. J. Vozimmer, *Charles Darwin: the Years of Controversy: The Origin of Species and its Critics, 1859–1862* (University of London Press, London, 1972), pp. 3–96; R. C. Olby, *Charles Darwin* (Oxford University Press, London, 1967), pp. 32–59; M. Ruse, *Darwinism Defended: a Guide to the Evolution Controversies* (Addison-Wesley, Reading, Mass., 1982), pp. 3–29; M. T. Ghiselin, 'Darwin's route to his finest idea', *New Scientist* 94 (1982), pp. 156–9.
19 Bowler, *Evolution*, pp. 206–32; D. Ospovat, *The Development of Darwin's Theory: Natural History, Natural Theology, and Natural Selection, 1838–1859* (Cambridge University Press, Cambridge, 1981), pp. 146–228; D. R. Oldroyd, *Darwinian Impacts: an Introduction to the Darwinian Revolution* (Open University Press, Milton Keynes, 1980), chs. 6–11; J. Howard, *Darwin* (Oxford University Press, Oxford, 1982), pp. 20–61; I. M. Lerner, *Heredity, Evolution and Society* (W. H. Freeman, San Francisco, 1968), pp. 26–39; Ruse, *Darwinism Defended*, pp. 30–60.
20 J. Bronowski, *The Ascent of Man* (British Broadcasting Corporation, London, 1973), p. 309.
21 For example, see R. Hofstadter, *Social Darwinism in American Thought*, rev. edn (Beacon, Boston, Mass., 1955); C. E. Russett, *Darwin in America: the Intellectual Response, 1865–1912* (W. H. Freeman, San Francisco, 1976).
22 Wilson, *Constitutional Government in the United States*, p. 57.
23 Wilson, *Constitutional Government in the United States*, p. 60.
24 Wilson, *Constitutional Government in the United States*, p. 60.
25 Wilson, *Constitutional Government in the United States*, p. 68.
26 Wilson, *Constitutional Government in the United States*, p. 68.
27 Wilson, *Constitutional Government in the United States*, p. 69.
28 Wilson, *Constitutional Government in the United States*, p. 73.
29 Wilson, *Constitutional Government in the United States*, p. 70.
30 For example, see A. King's review of R. Reeves, *A Ford, not a Lincoln* (Hutchinson, London, 1976), in *New Society*, 11 March 1976.
31 A. Hamilton, 'Federalist Paper no. 70', in A. Hamilton, J. Madison, and J. Jay, *The Federalist Papers*, intro. C. Rossiter (Mentor, New York, 1961), p. 424.
32 J. M. Burns, *Presidential Government: Crucible of Leadership* (Houghton Mifflin, Boston, Mass., 1973), pp. 3–31, 112–17, 132–3.
33 W. D. Burnham, 'American politics in the 1970's: beyond party?' in J. Fishel (ed.), *Parties and Elections in an Anti-party Age: American Politics and the Crisis of Confidence* (Indiana University Press, Bloomington, 1978), p. 336.
34 L. Fisher, *Constitutional Conflicts between Congress and the President* (Princeton University Press, Princeton, 1985), p. 332.
35 R. E. Neustadt, *Presidential Power: the Politics of Leadership* (Wiley, New York, 1960), p. 185.
36 C. Rossiter, *The American Presidency*, rev. edn (New American Library, 1960), p. 250.
37 Burns, *Presidential Government*, p. 326.
38 G. C. Edwards and S. J. Wayne, *Presidential Leadership: Politics and Policy Making* (St Martin's Press, New York, 1985), p. v.
39 M. Lerner, *America as a Civilization: Life and Thought in the United States Today* (Jonathan Cape, London, 1958), p. 397.
40 R. S. Hirschfield, 'The power of the contemporary presidency', in R. S. Hirschfield (ed.), *The Power of the Presidency: Concepts and Controversy* (Atherton, New York, 1968), p. 245; see also H. M. Roelofs, 'The American polity: a systematic ambiguity', *Review of Politics* 48, 3 (1986), p. 341.
41 J. A. Califano, Jr, *A Presidential Nation* (W. W. Norton, New York, 1975), p. 297.
42 Califano, *A Presidential Nation*, p. 5.
43 G. E. Reedy, *The Twilight of the Presidency* (Mentor, New York, 1970), p. 28.
44 Reedy, *The Twilight of the Presidency*, p. 28.
45 Reedy, 'The Presidency in 1976: focal point of political unity', in W. C. Havard and J. L. Bernd (eds), *200 years of the Republic in Retrospect* (University Press of Virginia, Charlottes-

ville, 1976), p. 229.
46 Burnham, 'American politics in the 1970s: beyond party?', in Fishel (ed.), *Parties and Elections in an Anti-party Age*, p. 338.
47 L. Heren, 'Power to the populists?' *Times*, 10 June 1972.
48 T. Lowi, 'Presidential power: restoring the balance', *Political Science Quarterly* 100, 2 (1985), p. 185.
49 E. E. Cornwell, Jr, *Presidential Leadership of Public Opinion* (University of Indiana Press, Bloomington, 1965), p. 4. See also R. A. Brody and B. I. Page, 'The impact of events on Presidential popularity: the Johnson and Nixon administrations', in A. Wildavsky (ed.), *Perspectives on the Presidency* (Little Brown, Boston, Mass., 1975), pp. 136–48; S. Kernell, P. W. Sperlich, and A. Wildavsky, 'Public support for Presidents', in Wildavsky (ed.), *Perspectives on the Presidency*, pp. 148–81; J. E. Mueller, 'Presidential popularity from Truman to Johnson', *American Political Science Review* 64, 1 (1970), pp. 18–34; S. Kernell, 'Explaining Presidential popularity', *American Political Science Review* 72, 2 (1978), pp. 506–22; J. A. Stimson, 'Public support for Presidents: a cyclical model', *Public Opinion Quarterly* 40 (1976), pp. 1–21; G. C. Edwards III, *Presidential Influence in Congress* (W. H. Freeman, San Francisco, 1980), pp. 86–115; Edwards and Wayne, *Presidential Leadership*, pp. 90–136; L. Sigelman, 'Gauging the public response to presidential leadership', *Presidential Studies Quarterly* 10 (1980), pp. 427–33; G. Hodgson, *All Things to all Men: the False Promise of the Modern American Presidency* (Penguin, Harmondsworth, 1984), pp. 196–261; T. Lowi, *The Personal President: Power Invested, Promise Unfulfilled* (Cornell University Press, Ithaca, 1985); S. Kernell, 'The Presidency and the people', in M. Nelson (ed.), *The Presidency and the Political System* (Congressional Quarterly Press, Washington, D.C., 1984), pp. 233–63; Kernell, *Going Public: New Strategies of Presidential Leadership* (Congressional Quarterly Press, Washington, D.C., 1986).
50 E. J. Hughes, *The Living Presidency: the Resources and Dilemmas of the American Presidential Office* (Penguin, Baltimore, 1974), p. 69.
51 Burns, *Presidential Government*, pp. 239–75; Burns, *Roosevelt: the Lion and the Fox* (Harcourt Brace, New York, 1956), pp. 183–208; L. W. Koenig, *The Chief Executive*, 3rd edn (Harcourt Brace Jovanovich, New York, 1975), pp. 293–325; H. K. Smith, 'A strong thread of moral purpose', in Burns (ed.), *To Heal and to Build: the Programs of Lyndon B. Johnson* (McGraw-Hill, New York, 1968), pp. 1–18; R. Nisbet, *Twilight of Authority* (Heinemann, London, 1976), pp. 3–74.
52 Burns, *Presidential Government*, pp. 259, 323.
53 Rossiter, *The American Presidency*, rev. edn, p. 81.
54 J. Locke, *Two Treatises of Government*, intro. P. Laslett (Cambridge University Press, Cambridge, 1960), p. 384.
55 *United States* v. *Curtiss-Wright Export Corporation* 299 U.S. 304 (1936).
56 A. Wildavsky, 'The two Presidencies', in A. Wildavsky and N. W. Polsby (eds), *American Governmental Institutions: a Reader in the Political Process* (Rand McNally, Chicago, 1968), p. 94.
57 See E. S. Corwin, *The President: Office and Powers, 1787–1948: History and Analysis of Practice and Opinion*, 3rd edn, rev. (New York University Press, New York, 1948), pp. 207–317; L. Fisher, *President and Congress: Power and Policy* (Free Press, New York, 1972), pp. 175–235; A. M. Schlesinger, Jr, *The Imperial Presidency* (André Deutsch, London, 1974), pp. 35–67, 100–26; D. N. Abshire, 'Foreign policy makers: President vs. Congress', in D. N. Abshire and R. D. Nurnberger (eds), *The Growing Power of Congress* (Sage, Beverly Hills, 1981), pp. 43–71; C. H. Pritchett, 'The President's constitutional position', in T. E. Cronin (ed.), *Rethinking the Presidency* (Little Brown, Boston, Mass., 1982), pp. 117–38; G. J. Schmitt, 'Executive privilege: presidential power to withhold information from Congress', in J. M. Bessette and J. Tulis (eds), *The Presidency in the Constitutional Order* (Louisiana State University Press, Baton Rouge, 1981), pp. 154–94; J. K. Javits with D. Kellermann, *Who Makes War: the President versus Congress* (William Morrow, New York, 1973); Hirschfield (ed.), *The Power of the Presidency*, pp. 170–98; J. A. Nathan and J. K. Oliver, *Foreign Policy Making and the American Political System*, 2nd edn (Little Brown, Boston, Mass., 1987), pp. 21–62; Edwards and Wayne, *Presidential Leadership*, pp. 289–310.
58 For example, see J. McDiarmid, 'Presidential inaugural addresses – a study in verbal symbols', *Public Opinion Quarterly* 1 (1937), pp. 79–82; J. W. Prothro, 'Verbal shifts in the

American Presidency: a content analysis', *American Political Science Review* 50, 3 (1956), pp. 726–39.
59 See S. E. Ambrose, *Rise to Globalism: American Foreign Policy, 1938–1980*, 2nd rev. edn (Penguin, Harmondsworth, 1980), pp. 92–224; L. S. Wittner, *Cold War America from Hiroshima to Watergate* (Praeger, New York, 1974), pp. 30–58, 86–110, 141–69; J. W. Spanier. *American Foreign Policy since World War II*, 8th edn (Holt Rinehart & Winston, New York, 1980), pp. 15–70; B. J. Bernstein, 'American foreign policy and the origins of the Cold War', in B. J. Bernstein (ed.), *Politics and Policies of the Truman Adminstration* (Franklin Watts, New York, 1974), pp. 15–77; T. Hoopes, *The Devil and John Foster Dulles* (Little Brown, Boston, Mass., 1973), pp. 62–74, 89–123, 303–17, 394–414, 480–91; R. D. Schulzinger, *American Diplomacy in the Twentieth Century* (Oxford University Press, New York, 1984), pp. 201–88.
60 See D. Easton and J. Dennis, 'The child's image of government', in S. V. Monsma and J. Van Der Slik (eds), *American Politics: Research and Readings* (Holt Rinehart & Winston, New York, 1970), pp. 22–40; F. I. Greenstein, 'What the President means to Americans: Presidential "choice" between elections', in J. D. Barber (ed.), *Choosing the President* (Prentice-Hall, Englewood Cliffs, 1974), pp. 121–47. R. S. Sigel, 'Images of the American Presidency: Part II of an exploration into popular views of Presidential power', *Midwest Journal of Political Science* 10, 1 (1966), pp. 123–37; F. C. Arterton, 'The impact of Watergate on children's attitudes toward political authority', in D. Caraley (ed.), *American Political Institutions in the 1970s: a Political Science Quarterly Reader* (Columbia University Press, New York, 1976), pp. 29–48; Greenstein, 'The benevolent leader revisited: children's images of political leaders in three democracies', *American Political Science Review* 69, 4 (1975), pp. 1371–98.
61 Easton and Dennis, 'The child's image of government', in Monsma and Van Der Slik (eds), *American Politics*, p. 38.
62 Easton and Dennis, 'The child's image of government', p. 38.
63 R. M. Pious, *The American Presidency* (Basic Books, New York, 1979), p. 6.
64 See J. E. Mueller, *War, Presidents and Public Opinion* (Wiley, New York, 1973), pp. 208–13.
65 R. F. Kennedy, *Thirteen Days: the Cuban Missile Crisis* (Pan Books/Macmillan, London, 1969).
66 L. B. Johnson, *The Vantage Point: Perspectives of the Presidency, 1963–1969* (Weidenfeld & Nicolson, London, 1971), pp. 513–29; 'The bomb halt decision', photographic essay by Yoichi Okamoto, *Life*, 11 November 1968.
67 R. M. Nixon, *The Memoirs of Richard Nixon* (Grosset & Dunlap, New York, 1978), pp. 724–44; H. Kissinger, *The White House Years* (Weidenfeld & Nicolson, London, 1979), pp. 1446–57.
68 H. S. Truman, *Year of Decision, 1945* (Hodder & Stoughton, London, 1955), pp. 347–57; R. F. Haynes, *The Awesome Power: Harry S. Truman as Commander-in-Chief* (Louisiana State University Press, Baton Rouge, 1973), pp. 46–62; A. Cooke, 'Truman', *Listener*, 11 January 1973.
69 E. C. Hargrove, *Presidential Leadership: Personality and Political Style* (Macmillan, New York, 1966), p. 5.
70 See J. D. Barber, *The Presidential Character: Predicting Performance in the White House* (Prentice-Hall, Englewood Cliffs, 1972); Hargrove, *Presidential Leadership: Personality and Political Style*; Hargrove, *The Power of the Modern Presidency* (Knopf, New York, 1974), pp. 33–78; A. L. and J. L. George, *Woodrow Wilson and Colonel House: a Personality Study* (John Day, New York, 1956); A. L. George, 'On analysing Presidents', *World Politics* 26, 2 (1974), pp. 234–82; D. Kearns, 'L. Johnson's political personality', *Political Science Quarterly* 91, 3 (1976), pp. 385–409; R. C. Tucker, 'The Georges' Wilson re-examined: an essay on psychobiography', *American Political Science Review* 71, 2 (1977), pp. 606–18; D. Winter, 'What makes Jimmy run? An examination of the personalities of American presidential candidates and their predecessors', *Psychology Today* 2, 7 (1976), pp. 35–8; F. I. Greenstein, 'A President is forced to resign: Watergate, White House organization, and Nixon's personality', in A. P. Sindler (ed.), *America in the Seventies: Problems, Policies, and Politics* (Little Brown, Boston, Mass., 1977), pp. 50–101; M. Nelson, 'The psychological Presidency', in Nelson (ed.), *The Presidency and the Political System*, pp. 156–78.
71 Barber, *The Presidential Character*, p. 445.
72 See J. H. Qualls, 'Barber's typological analysis of political leaders', *American Political*

73 Pious, *The American Presidency*, p. 417.
74 G. McConnell, *The Modern Presidency* (St Martin's Press, New York, 1967), pp. 1, 2, 14, 15.
75 Hughes, *The Living Presidency*, pp. 56, 73–4. See also Rossiter, *The American Presidency*, rev. edn, pp. 38, 102–3; Schlesinger, *The Imperial Presidency*, pp. ix, 277, 410; W. F. Mullen, *Presidential Power and Politics* (St Martin's Press, New York, 1976), pp. 251–63; T. H. White, *Breach of Faith: the Fall of Richard Nixon* (Jonathan Cape, London, 1975), pp. 322–43. See also H. Finer, *The Presidency* (University of Chicago Press, Chicago, 1960), p. 111; and B. Hinckley, *Problems of the Presidency: a Text with Readings* (Scott Foresman, Glenview, 1985), pp. 37–41.
76 For example, see Abraham Holtzman, *Legislative Liaison: Executive Leadership in Congress* (Rand McNally, Chicago, 1970); J. H. Kessel, *The Domestic Presidency: Decision-making in the White House* (Duxbury, North Scituate, 1975); E. R. Tufte, *The Political Control of the Economy* (Princeton University Press, Princeton, 1978); Edwards, *Presidential Influence in Congress*.
77 Rossiter, *The American Presidency*, rev. edn, p. 38.
78 R. Dawkins, 'The necessity of Darwinism', *New Scientist*, 15 April 1982.
79 E. E. Cornwell, Jr, *The American Presidency: Vital Center* (Scott Foresman, Chicago, 1966).
80 T. Roosevelt, 'The "stewardship theory"', in Hirschfield (ed.), *The Power of the Presidency*, p. 82.
81 Roosevelt, 'The "stewardship theory"', in Hirschfield (ed.), *The Power of the Presidency*, p. 82.
82 *In re Neagle* 135 U.S. 1 (1890).
83 See Schlesinger, *The Imperial Presidency*, pp. 278–330; C. V. Crabb, Jr, and P. M. Holt, *Invitation to Struggle: Congress, the President and Foreign Policy* (Congressional Quarterly Press, Washington, D.C., 1980), pp. 5–32; J. Lehman, *The Executive, Congress and Foreign Policy: Studies of the Nixon Administration* (Praeger, New York, 1976), pp. 1–18; Hargrove, *The Power of the Modern Presidency*, pp. 123–74; N. A. Graebner, 'Presidential power and foreign affairs', in C. W. Dunn (ed.), *The Future of the American Presidency* (General Learning Press, Morristown, 1975), pp. 179–201; J. Spanier and E. M. Uslaner, *Foreign Policy and Democratic Dilemmas*, 3rd edn (Holt Rinehart & Winston, New York, 1982), pp. 25–66; C. H. Pyle and R. M. Pious, *The President, Congress, and the Constitution: Power and Legitimacy in American Politics* (Free Press, New York, 1984), pp. 233–390; F. D. Wormuth and D. B. Firmage with F. P. Butler, *To Chain the Dogs of War: the War Power of Congress in History and Law* (Southern Methodist University Press, Dallas, 1986); W. La Feber, 'The constitution and United States foreign policy: an interpretation', *Journal of American History* 74, 3 (1987), pp. 695–717.
84 Hargrove, *The Power of the Modern Presidency*, pp. 154–5, 164.
85 Burns, *Presidential Government*, p. 81.
86 See Burns, *Presidential Government*, pp. 78–97; 'History reappraises past Presidents', *Congressional Quarterly Guide to Current American Government*, fall 1976 (Congressional Quarterly Press, Washington, D.C., 1976), pp. 39–45; M. B. Parsons, 'The Presidential rating game', in Dunn (ed.), *The Future of the American Presidency*, pp. 66–91; G. M. Maranell, 'The evaluation of Presidents: an extension of the Schlesinger polls', *Journal of American History* 57, 1 (1970), pp. 104–13; Hargrove, *The Power of the Modern President*, pp. 4–12; S. J. Wayne, 'Great expectations: what people want from Presidents', in T. E. Cronin (ed.), *Rethinking the Presidency* (Little Brown, Boston, Mass., 1982), pp. 185–99; R. G. Hoxie, 'Presidential greatness', in P. C. Dolce and G. H. Skau (eds), *Power and the Presidency* (Scribner, New York, 1976), pp. 216–8.
87 Corwin, 'The aggrandizement of Presidential power', in Hirschfield (ed.), *The Power of the Presidency*, p. 224.
88 Corwin, 'The aggrandizement of Presidential power', p. 215.
89 C. Rossiter, *Conservatism in America: the Thankless Persuasion*, 2nd edn, rev. (Vintage, New York, 1962), pp. 191–2.
90 Rossiter, *The American Presidency*, rev. edn, pp. 79, 228.

91 D. W. Brogan, *Politics and Law in the United States* (Cambridge University Press, Cambridge, 1941), p. 50.
92 Hirschfield, 'The power of the contemporary Presidency', in Hirschfield (ed.), *The Power of the Presidency*, p. 247.
93 Corwin, *The President: Office and Powers*, 4th edn, rev. (New York University Press, New York, 1957), p. 307.
94 Brogan, *Politics and Law in the United States*, p. 74.
95 White, *Breach of Faith*, p. 337. See also C. L. Clapp, *The Congressman: his Work as he Sees it* (Brookings Institution, Washington, D.C., 1963), pp. 50–103; J. S. Saloma III, *Congress and the New Politics* (Little Brown, Boston, Mass., 1969), pp. 169–95; M. E. Jewell and S. C. Patterson, *The Legislative Process in the United States* (Random House, New York, 1966), pp. 339–57; J. S. Clark, 'Representing the people', in G. Goodwin, Jr (ed.), *Congress: Anvil of American Democracy* (Scott Foresman, Glenview, 1972), pp. 37–49; R. F. Fenno, 'US House members in their constituencies: an exploration', *American Political Science Review* 71, 3 (1977), pp. 883–917; 'Running for re-election is a full-time job', *Congressional Quarterly Guide to Current American Government*, spring 1980 (Congressional Quarterly Press, Washington, D.C., 1980), pp. 53–60; D. G. Tacheron and M. K. Udall, *The Job of the Congressman: an Introduction to Service in the House of Representatives*, 2nd edn (Bobbs-Merrill, Indianapolis, 1970), pp. 63–94; W. J. Keefe, *Congress and the American People*, 2nd edn (Prentice-Hall, Englewood Cliffs, 1984), pp. 16–20, 185–92; R. F. Fenno, *Home Style: House Members in their Districts* (Little Brown, Boston, Mass., 1978); A. J. Mikva and P. B. Saris, *The American Congress: the First Branch* (Franklin Watts, New York, 1983), pp. 326–41.
96 D. R. Mayhew, *Congress: the Electoral Connection* (Yale University Press, New Haven, 1974), p. 54.
97 W. E. Binkley, *President and Congress*, 3rd edn, rev. (Vintage, New York, 1962), p. 381.
98 C. Miller, *Member of the House: Letters of a Congressman*, ed. J. Baker (Scribner, New York, 1962), p. 110.
99 W. Wilson, *Congressional Government: a Study in American Government*, intro. W. Lippmann (Meridan, New York, 1956), p. 62.
100 H. Heclo, 'Introduction: the Presidential illusion', in H. Heclo and L. M. Salamon (eds), *The Illusion of Presidential Government* (Westview, Boulder, 1981), p. 5.
101 S. P. Huntingdon, 'Congressional responses to the twentieth century', in D. B. Truman (ed.), *The Congress and America's Future* (Prentice-Hall, Englewood Cliffs, 1965), pp. 18–19.
102 Huntingdon, 'Congressional responses to the twentieth century', in Truman (ed.), *The Congress and America's Future*, p. 21. See also N. J. Ornstein, 'Causes and consequences of Congressional change: subcommittee reforms in the House of Representatives, 1970–1973', in N. J. Ornstein (ed.), *Congress in Change: Evolution and Reform* (Praeger, New York, 1975), pp. 88–114; R. H. Davidson, 'Subcommittee government: new channels for policy making', in T. E. Mann and N. J. Ornstein (eds), *The New Congress* (American Enterprise Institute, Washington, D.C., 1981), pp. 99–133; Ornstein, 'The open Congress meets the President', in A. King (ed.), *Both Ends of the Avenue: the Presidency, the Executive Branch, and the Congress in the 1980's* (American Enterprise Institute for Public Policy Research, Washington, D.C., 1983), pp. 185–211; L. C. Dodd and B. I. Oppenheimer, 'The House in transition: partisanship and opposition', in L. C. Dodd and B. I. Oppenheimer (eds), *Congress Reconsidered*, 3rd edn (Congressional Quarterly Press, Washington, D.C., 1985), pp. 34–64; C. J. Deering and S. S. Smith, 'Subcommittees in Congress', in Dodd and Oppenheimer (eds), *Congress Reconsidered*, 3rd edn, pp. 189–210; G. Easterbrook, 'What's wrong with Congress?', *Atlantic*, December 1984; P. Woll, *Congress* (Little Brown, Boston, Mass., 1985), pp. 91–148; Mikva and Saris, *The American Congress*, pp. 123–40.
103 J. E. Schwarz and L. E. Shaw, *The United States Congress in Comparative Perspective* (Dryden, Hinsdale, 1976), p. 152. See also Schwarz and Shaw, *The United States Congress in Comparative Perspective*, pp. 118–91; D. B. Truman, *The Congressional Party: a Case Study* (Wiley, New York, 1959), pp. vii, 247–9; R. H. Davidson and W. J. Oleszek, *Congress and its Members* (Congressional Quarterly Press, Washington, D.C., 1981), pp. 383–6; J. F. Bibby, T. E. Mann, and N. J. Ornstein, Vital Statistics on Congress, 1980 (American Enterprise Institute, Washington, D.C., 1980), pp. 103–4; Keefe, Congress and the American People, 2nd edn, pp. 122–9.
104 Mayhew, *Congress: the Electoral Connection*, p. 100.

105 H. D. Price, 'The Congressional career – then and now', in N. W. Polsby (ed.), *Congressional Behavior* (Random House, New York, 1971), pp. 14–27; Polsby, 'Institutionalization in the US House of Representatives', *American Political Science Review* 62, 1 (1968), pp. 144–68; Price, 'Congress and the evolution of legislative professionalism', in Ornstein (ed.), *Congress in Change*, pp. 2–23; D. Rothman, *Politics and Power: the United States Senate, 1869–1901* (Harvard University Press, Cambridge, Mass., 1966), pp. 111–58; S. Kernell, 'Toward understanding 19th century Congressional careers: ambition, competition, and rotation', *American Journal of Political Science* 21, 4 (1977), pp. 669–93; C. S. Bullock III, 'House careerists: changing patterns of longevity and attrition', *American Political Science Review* 66, 4 (1972), pp. 1295–1300; R. Struble, Jr, 'House turnover and the principle of rotation', *Political Science Quarterly* 94, 4 (1979–80), pp. 649–67; M. P. Fiorina, D. W. Rohde, and P. Wissel, 'Historical change in House turnover', in Ornstein (ed.), *Congress in Change*, pp. 24–49; C. S. Bullock and B. A. Loomis, 'The changing Congressional career', in Dodd and Oppenheimer (eds), *Congress Reconsidered*, 3rd edn, pp. 65–84.
106 R. B. Ripley, *Congress: Process and Policy* (W. W. Norton, New York, 1975), p. 23.
107 G. C. Jacobson, *The Politics of Congressional Elections*, 2nd edn (Little Brown, Boston, Mass., 1987), pp. 28–9.
108 E. R. Tufte, 'The relationship between seats and votes in two party systems', *American Political Science Review* 67, 2 (1973), pp. 540–54.
109 M. P. Fiorina, 'The case of the vanishing marginals: the bureaucracy did it', *American Political Science Review* 71, 1 (1977), pp. 177–81; Fiorina, *Congress: Keystone to the Washington Establishment* (Yale University Press, New Haven, 1977); G. R. Parker, 'The advantage of incumbency in House elections', *American Political Quarterly* 8, 4 (1980), pp. 449–64; D. Arnold, *Congress and the Bureaucracy* (Yale University Press, New Haven, 1979).
110 A. I. Abramowitz, 'A comparison of voting for US Senator and Representative in 1978', *American Political Science Review* 74, 3 (1980), pp. 633–40; G. C. Jacobson, 'The effects of campaign spending in Congressional elections', *American Political Science Review* 72, 2 (1978), pp. 469–91; T. E. Mann and R. E. Wolfinger, 'Candidates and parties in Congressional elections', *American Political Science Review* 74, 3 (1980), pp. 617–32; Jacobson, *The Politics of Congressional Elections*, 2nd edn, pp. 25–96; E. N. Goldenberg and M. W. Traugott, *Campaigning for Congress* (Congressional Quarterly Press, Washington, D.C., 1984).
111 J. A. Ferejohn, 'On the decline of competition in Congressional elections', *American Political Science Review* 71, 1 (1977), pp. 166–76; A. Cover, 'One good turn deserves another', *American Journal of Political Science* 21, 3 (1977), pp. 523–43; A. Cover and D. Mayhew, 'Congressional dynamics and the decline of competitive Congressional elections', in L. C. Dodd and B. I. Oppenheimer (eds), *Congress Reconsidered*, 2nd edn (Praeger, New York, 1977), pp. 62–82; W. D. Burnham, 'Insulation and responsiveness in Congressional elections', *Political Science Quarterly* 90, 3 (1975), pp. 411–35; N. J. Candice, 'The effect of incumbency on voting in Congressional elections, 1964–74', *Political Science Quarterly* 74, 4 (1978–9), pp. 665–78; R. H. Salisbury and K. A. Shepsle, 'US Congressman as enterprise', *Legislative Studies Quarterly* 6 (1981), pp. 559–76.
112 N. W. Polsby, M. Gallaher, and B. S. Rundquist, 'The growth of the seniority system in the US House of Representatives', in Polsby (ed.), *Congressional Behavior*, pp. 172–202; R. E. Wolfinger and J. Hollinger, 'Safe seats, seniority, and power in Congress', in R. L. Peabody and N. W. Polsby (eds), *New Perspectives on the House of Representatives*, 2nd edn (Rand McNally, Chicago, 1969), pp. 55–77; G. Goodwin, Jr, 'The seniority system in Congress', *American Political Science Review* 53, 2 (1959), pp. 412–36; B. Hinckley, *The Seniority System in Congress* (Indiana University Press, Bloomington, 1971), pp. 3–18; Ripley, *Power in the Senate* (St Martin's Press, New York, 1969), pp. 41–50.
113 Polsby, Gallaher, and Rundquist, 'The growth of the seniority system in the US House of Representatives', in Polsby (ed.), *Congressional Behavior*, p. 13.
114 Hinckley, *The Seniority System in Congress*, p. 112.
115 Goodwin, *The Little Legislatures* (University of Massachusetts Press, Amherst, 1970), p. 126.
116 Hinckley, *The Seniority System in Congress*, pp. 36–46; W. J. Keefe and M. S. Ogul, *The American Legislative Process*, 3rd edn (Prentice-Hall, Englewood Cliffs, 1973), p. 476; M. J. Green, J. M. Fallows, and D. R. Zwick, *Who Runs Congress?* (Bantam/Grossman, New York, 1972), pp. 58–62.
117 Quoted in W. Millinship, 'Congressional "Rogues' Gallery" by Nader', *Observer*, 22 October 1972.

118 Brogan, *Politics and Law in the United States*, pp. x, xii.
119 G. Orfield, *Congressional Power: Congress and Social Change* (Harcourt Brace Jovanovich, New York, 1975), pp. 3, 9.
120 Hinckley, *The Seniority System in Congress*.
121 J. L. Sundquist, *Politics and Policy: the Eisenhower, Kennedy, and Johnson Years* (Brookings Institution, Washington, D.C., 1968); R. C. Moe and S. C. Teel, 'Congress as policy-maker: a necessary reappraisal', *Political Science Quarterly* 85, 3 (1970), pp. 443–70; R. B. Ripley and G. A. Franklin, *Congress, the Bureaucracy and Public Policy*, rev. edn (Dorsey, Homewood, 1980); Woll, *Congress*, pp. 405–54; L. Fisher, *The Politics of Shared Power: Congress and the Executive* (Congressional Quarterly Press, Washington, D.C., 1987); C. O. Jones, 'Policy contributions of Congress', in D. C. Kozak and J. D. Macartney (eds), *Congress and Public Policy: a Source Book of Documents and Readings* (Dorsey, Homewood, 1982), pp. 422–30; M. Derthick and P. J. Quirk, *The Politics of Deregulation* (Brookings Institution, Washington, D.C., 1985), pp. 96–146; J. Spanier and J. Nogee (eds), *Congress, the Presidency and American Foreign Policy* (Pergamon, New York, 1981); E. S. Muskie, K. Rush, and K. W. Thompson, *The President, the Congress and Foreign Policy* (University Press of America, Lanham, 1986).
122 M. S. Ogul, 'Congressional oversight: structures and incentives', in Dodd and Oppenheimer, *Congress Reconsidered*, 2nd edn (Congressional Quarterly Press, Washington, D.C., 1981), pp. 317–31; J. D. Aberback, 'Congressional oversight', in Kozak and Macartney (eds), *Congress and Public Policy*, pp. 389–402; M. D. McCubbins and T. Schwartz, 'Congressional oversight overlooked: police patrols versus fire alarms', in M. D. McCubbins and T. Sullivan (eds), *Congress: Structure and Policy* (Cambridge University Press, Cambridge, 1987), pp. 426–40; F. M. Kaiser, 'Congressional oversight of the Presidency', in R. H. Davidson (ed.), *Congress and the Presidency: Invitation to Struggle* (Sage, Newbury Park, 1988), pp. 75–89.
123 A. R. Clausen and C. E. Van Horn, 'The Congressional response to a decade of change: 1963–1972', *Journal of Politics* 39, 3 (1977), pp. 624–66; L. N. Rieselbach, *Congressional Reform* (Congressional Quarterly Press, Washington, D.C., 1986), pp. 79–148.
124 Orfield, *Congressional Power*, introduction and pp. 3–12, 23–46; W. J. Oleszek, *Congressional Procedures and the Policy Process* (Congressional Quarterly Press, Washington, D.C., 1978), pp. 168–73; 'Rules under Chairman Pepper looks out for the Democrats', *Congressional Quarterly Guide to Current American Government*, spring 1986, pp. 57–61.
125 L. A. Froman, Jr, *The Congressional Process: Strategies, Rules, and Procedures* (Little Brown, Boston, Mass., 1967), pp. 183–218; Oleszek, *Congressional Procedures and the Policy Process*, pp. 10–11, 137–45, 216.
126 Orfield, *Congressional Power*, p. 18.
127 M. Foley, *The New Senate: Liberal Influence on a Conservative Institution, 1959–1972* (Yale University Press, New Haven, 1980), p. 231.
128 See, for example, Green, Fallows, and Zwick, *Who Runs Congress?*, pp. 1–5.
129 J. S. Clark, *Congress: the Sapless Branch* (Harper & Row, New York, 1964), p. 246.
130 A. Bierce, quoted in Hughes, *The Living Presidency*, p. 20.
131 T. C. Sorensen, *Watchmen in the Night: Presidential Accountability after Watergate* (MIT Press, Cambridge, Mass., 1975), p. xi.
132 Hughes, *The Living Presidency*, pp. 20–1.
133 Hargrove, *The Power of the Modern Presidency*, p. 8.
134 A. King, 'Executives', in F. I. Greenstein and N. W. Polsby (eds), *Handbook of Political Science*, vol. 5, *Governmental Institutions and Processes* (Addison-Wesley, Reading, Mass., 1975), p. 174.
135 W. Wilson, *Congressional Government*, intro. W. Lippmann, p. 57.
136 S. C. Patterson, 'The semi-sovereign Congress', in A. King (ed.), *The New American Political System* (American Enterprise Institute, Washington, D.C., 1978), pp. 125–6.
137 Pious, 'Is Presidential power poison?', *Political Science Quarterly* 89, 3 (1974), pp. 637–9.
138 Pious, *The American Presidency*, p. 14.
139 R. K. Huitt, quoted by R. L. Peabody, 'Research on Congress: a coming of age', in R. K. Huitt and R. L. Peabody (eds), *Congress: Two Decades of Analysis* (Harper & Row, New York, 1969), p. 68.
140 See, for example, J. E. Jackson, *Constituencies and Leaders in Congress: their Effects on Senate Voting Behavior* (Harvard University Press, Cambridge, Mass., 1974); D. R. Mayhew, *Party*

Loyalty among Congressmen: The Difference between Democrats and Republicans, 1947–1962 (Harvard University Press, Cambridge, Mass., 1966); A. R. Clausen, *How Congressmen Decide: a Policy Focus* (St Martin's Press, New York, 1973); R. F. Fenno, Jr, *Congressmen in Committees* (Little Brown, Boston, Mass., 1973); J. W. Kingdon, *Congressmen's Voting Decisions*, 2nd edn (Harper & Row, New York, 1981); Ripley and Franklin, *Congress, the Bureaucracy, and Public Policy*; J. E. Schneider, *Ideological Coalitions in Congress* (Greenwood, Westport, 1979).

141 T. E. Cronin, *The State of the Presidency*, 2nd edn (Little Brown, Boston, Mass., 1980), p. 84.
142 A. Rosenthal, 'The effectiveness of Congress: the Congressional institution', in G. M. Pomper (ed.), *The Performance of American Government: Checks and Minuses* (Free Press, New York, 1972), p. 162.
143 Huntington, 'Congressional responses to the twentieth century', in Truman (ed.), *The Congress and America's Future*, p. 7.
144 J. C. Donovan, *The Policy Makers* (Pegasus, New York, 1970), p. xv. See also W. E. Binkley, 'The President as chief legislator', in S. Bach and G. T. Sulzner (eds), *Perspectives on the Presidency: a Collection* (D. C. Heath, Lexington, 1974) pp. 302–19; L. H. Chamberlain, *The President, Congress, and Legislation* (Columbia University Press, New York, 1946); Pious, *The American Presidency*, pp. 147–70; Hargrove, *The Power of the Modern Presidency*, pp. 201–36; S. Wayne, *The Legislative Presidency* (Harper & Row, New York, 1978); R. M. Christenson, 'Presidential leadership of Congress', in Cronin (ed.), *Rethinking the Presidency*, pp. 255–70; J. L. Sundquist, *The Decline and Resurgence of Congress* (Brookings Institution, Washington, D.C., 1981), pp. 127–54.
145 Quoted in J. J. Johannes, 'The President proposes and Congress disposes ... but not always: legislative influence on Capitol Hill', *Review of Politics* 36, 3 (1974), p. 356.
146 Senator H. H. Baker, Jr, 'What Presidential powers should be cut?', in C. Roberts (ed.), *Has the President too much Power?* (Harper's Press, New York, 1974), p. 42.
147 Senator M. O. Hatfield, Newsletter supplement, 'Presidential power', January 1973.
148 Clausen, *How Congressmen Decide*, pp. 2–3.
149 Huntington, 'Congressional responses to the twentieth century', in Truman (ed.), *The Congress and America's Future*, p. 6.
150 Huntington, 'Congressional responses to the twentieth century', pp. 16–31.
151 Woll, *Congress*, p. 39.
152 E. L. Levine and E. E. Cornwell, Jr, *An Introduction to American Government*, 3rd edn (Macmillan, New York, 1975), p. 172.
153 S. K. Bailey, *Congress in the Seventies* (St Martin's Press, New York, 1970), p. 107.
154 N. C. Thomas and K. A. Lamb, *Congress: Politics and Practice* (Random House, New York, 1964), p. 134.
155 Huitt, 'Congress: retrospect and prospect', in Havard and Bernd (eds), *200 Years of the Republic in Retrospect*, p. 229.
156 See J. C. Wahlke, H. Eulau, W. Buchanan, and L. C. Ferguson, *The Legislative System* (Wiley, New York, 1962); Jewell and Patterson, *The Legislative Process in the United States*, pp. 1–27; Schwarz and Shaw, *The United States Congress in Comparative Perspective*, pp. 11–20; L. A. Froman, 'Organization theory and the explanation of important characteristics of Congress', *American Political Science Review* 62, 2 (1968), pp. 518–27; R. F. Fenno, Jr, 'The Appropriations Committee as a political system', in R. L. Peabody and N. W. Polsby (eds), *New Perspectives on the House of Representatives* (Rand McNally, Chicago, 1963), pp. 79–108; J. Cooper, 'Congress in organizational perspective', in Dodd and Oppenheimer (eds), *Congress Reconsidered*, pp. 140–59; R. H. Davidson and W. J. Oleszek, 'Structural innovation in the US House of Representatives', *Legislative Studies Quarterly* 1, 1 (1976), pp. 37–65; C. O. Jones, 'How reform changes Congress', in S. Welch and J. G. Peters (eds), *Legislative Reform and Public Policy* (Praeger, New York, 1977), pp. 11–29.
157 R. H. Davidson and W. J. Oleszek, *Congress against Itself* (Indiana University Press, Bloomington, 1977), p. ix.
158 Rossiter, *Conservatism in America*, 2nd edn, rev., p. 79.
159 Clark, *Congress: the Sapless Branch*, p. 234.
160 Clark, *Congress: the Sapless Branch*, p. 107.
161 White, *Breach of Faith*, p. 337.
162 Bailey, *Congress in the Seventies*, p. 107.

163 D. Stockman, quoted in H. Smith, *The Power Game: How Washington Works* (Collins, London, 1988), p. 688.
164 Ripley, *Congress: Process and Policy*, p. 291.
165 Davidson and Oleszek, *Congress against Itself*, p. 55.
166 Fenno, 'If, as Ralph Nader says, Congress is "the broken branch", how come we love our Congressmen so much?', in Ornstein (ed.), *Congress in Change*, p. 281.
167 L. C. Dodd, 'Congress and the quest for power', in L. C. Dodd and B. I. Oppenheimer (eds), *Congress Reconsidered* (Praeger, New York, 1977), p. 278.
168 Huitt, 'Congress: retrospect and prospect' in Havard and Bernd (eds), *200 Years of the Republic in Retrospect*, p. 225.
169 Sundquist, *The Decline and Resurgence of Congress*, p. 161.
170 Sundquist, 'Congress and the President: enemies or partners?', in Dodd and Oppenheimer (eds), *Congress Reconsidered*, p. 242.
171 Rieselbach, *Congressional Reform*, p. viii.
172 R. Bolling, *House Out of Order* (E. P. Dutton, New York, 1965).
173 B. Eckhardt and C. L. Black, Jr, *The Tides of Power: Conversations on the American Constitution* (Yale University Press, New Haven, 1976), pp. 12–38.
174 W. Lippmann, quoted in R. Sherrill, *Why they Call it Politics: a Guide to America's Government*, 2nd edn (Harcourt Brace Jovanovich, New York, 1974), p. 112.
175 Jacobson, *The Politics of Congressional Elections*, p. 210.
176 D. Lockhard, *The Perverted Priorities of American Politics* (Macmillan, New York, 1971), pp. 123–67.
177 Green, Fallows, and Zwick, *Who Runs Congress?*, p. 4.
178 Christenson, 'Presidential leadership of Congress', in Cronin (ed.), *Rethinking the Presidency*, p. 255.
179 Davidson and Oleszek, *Congress against Itself*, p. ix.
180 J. M. Burns, 'The power to lead', in D. L. Robinson (ed.), *Reforming American Government: the Bicentennial Papers of the Committee on the Constitutional System* (Westview, Boulder, 1985), p. 160.
181 D. K. Price, *America's Unwritten Constitution: Science, Religion, and Political Responsibility* (Harvard University Press, Cambridge, Mass., 1985), p. 132.
182 Sundquist, *The Decline and Resurgence of Congress*, p. 159.
183 J. F. Manley, 'Policy-making in the House', in J. F. Manley (ed.), *American Government and Public Policy* (Macmillan, New York, 1976), p. 149.
184 A. R. Clausen and R. B. Cheney, 'A comparative analysis of Senate–House voting on economic and welfare policy: 1953–1964', *American Political Science Review* 64, 1 (1970), pp. 138–52.
185 See H. C. Mansfield, Sr, 'The dispersion of authority in Congress', in H. C. Mansfield (ed.), *Congress against the President* (Academy of Political Science, New York, 1975), pp. 1–19; Dodd and Oppenheimer, 'The House in transition', in Dodd and Oppenheimer (eds), *Congress Reconsidered*, pp. 32–40; S. Haeberle, 'The institutionalization of the subcommittee in the United States House of Representatives', *Journal of Politics* 40, 4 (1978), pp. 1054–65; T. E. Cavanagh, 'The dispersion of authority in the House of Representatives', *Political Science Quarterly* 97, 4 (1982–3), pp. 623–37; E. L. Davis, 'Legislative reform and the decline of Presidential influence on Capitol Hill', *British Journal of Political Science* 9, 4 (1979), pp. 465–70.
186 L. N. Rieselbach, *Congressional Reform in the Seventies* (General Learning Press, Morristown, 1977), p. 14.
187 Ripley, *Congress: Process and Policy*, p. 243.
188 D. Cater, *Power in Washington: a Critical Look at Today's Struggle to Govern in the Nation's Capital* (Random House, New York, 1964), p. 143.
189 Fenno, 'If, as Ralph Nader says, Congress is "the broken branch", how come we love our Congressmen so much?', in Ornstein (ed.), *Congress in Change*, p. 280.
190 Califano, *A Presidential Nation*, p. 21.
191 E. S. Griffith, *Congress: its Contemporary Role*, 4th edn (University of London Press, London, 1967), p. 41.
192 R. Neely, *How Courts Govern America* (Yale University Press, New Haven, 1981), p. 73.
193 W. Weaver, *Both your Houses: the Truth about Congress* (Praeger, New York, 1972), pp. 282,

286.
194 C. M. Hardin, *Presidential Power and Accountability: Toward a new Constitution* (University of Chicago Press, Chicago, 1974), p. 4.
195 For example, see Sundquist, 'Congress and the President: enemies or partners?', in Dodd and Oppenheimer (eds), *Congress Reconsidered*, pp. 222–43; Donovan, *The Policy Makers*, pp. 57–75; White, *Breach of Faith*, pp. 322–43; Hirschfield, 'The power of the contemporary Presidency', in *The Power of the Presidency*, pp. 238–55; Saloma, *Congress and the new Politics*, pp. 59–92; Huntington, 'Congressional responses to the twentieth century', in Truman (ed.), *The Congress and America's Future*, pp. 5–31; J. Spanier, 'Introduction – Congress and the Presidency: the weakest link in the policy process', in Spanier and Nogee (eds), *Congress, the Presidency and American Foreign Policy*, pp. ix–xxxii; J. L. Nogee, 'Congress and the Presidency: the dilemmas of policy-making in a democracy', in Spanier and Nogee (eds), *Congress, the Presidency and American Foreign Policy*, pp. 189–200; D. J. Vogler and S. R. Waldman, *Congress and Democracy* (Congressional Quarterly Press, Washington, D.C., 1985), pp. 39–59; C. O. Jones, 'Presidential negotiation with Congress', in King (ed.), *Both Ends of the Avenue*, pp. 96–130.
196 Rieselbach, *Congressional Reform in the Seventies*, p. 14.
197 Griffith, *Congress: its Contemporary Role*, p. 8.
198 B. Hinckley, *Stability and Change in Congress*, 2nd edn (Harper & Row, New York, 1978), pp. 195–208.
199 Orfield, *Congressional Power*, p. 9.
200 Orfield, *Congressional Power*, p. 1.
201 Orfield, *Congressional Power*, p. 306.
202 Mann and Ornstein, 'Introduction', in Mann and Ornstein (eds), *The new Congress*, p. 1.
203 P. Woll, *American Bureaucracy* (W. W. Norton, New York, 1963), p. 142.
204 See Woll, *American Bureaucracy*, pp. 142–73; Cronin, *The State of the Presidency*, 2nd edn, pp. 223–52; J. D. Aberbach and B. A. Rockman, 'Clashing beliefs within the executive branch: the Nixon Administration bureaucracy', *American Political Science Review* 70, 2 (1976), pp. 456–68; G. T. Allison, 'The power of bureaucratic routines', in F. E. Rourke (ed.), *Bureaucratic Power in National Politics*, 3rd edn (Little Brown, Boston, Mass., 1978), pp. 116–34; Cronin, 'Presidents as chief executives', in R. G. Tugwell and T. E. Cronin (eds), *The Presidency Reappraised* (Praeger, New York, 1974), pp. 234–65: Rourke, *Bureaucracy and Foreign Policy* (Johns Hopkins University Press, Baltimore, 1972), chs. 1, 3; M. H. Halperin, *Bureaucratic Politics and Foreign Policy* (Brookings Institution, Washington, D.C., 1974), pp. 63–83, 235–93; H. Heclo, 'Issue networks and the executive establishment', in King (ed.), *The new American Political System*, pp. 87–124.
205 Fisher, *The Politics of Shared Power*, p. 219.
206 Edwards and Wayne, *Presidential Leadership*, p. 345.
207 D. M. Berman, *In Congress Assembled* (Macmillan, New York, 1964), p. 400.
208 Fenno, 'Strengthening a Congressional strength', in Dodd and Oppenheimer (eds), *Congress Reconsidered*, p. 263.
209 Burns, *Presidential Government*, p. 241.
210 D. B. James, *The Contemporary Presidency* (Pegasus, New York, 1969), pp. xi–xii.
211 S. Hyman, quoted in Rossiter, *The American Presidency*, rev. edn, p. 250.
212 Roosevelt, 'The "stewardship theory"', in Hirschfield (ed.), *The Power of the Presidency*, p. 82.
213 Huntington, 'The democratic distemper', in N. Glazer and I. Kristol (eds), *The American Commonwealth – 1976* (Basic Books, New York, 1976), p. 24.
214 Huntington, 'The democratic distemper', p. 24.
215 Mullen, *Presidential Power and Politics*, p. 1.
216 Wildavsky, 'The past and future Presidency', in Glazer and Kristol (eds), *The American Commonwealth – 1976*, p. 58.
217 Thomas and Lamb, *Congress: Politics and Practice*, p. 126.
218 See D. R. Mathews, 'United States senators – a collective portrait', in S.C. Patterson (ed.), *American Legislative Behavior: a Reader* (Van Nostrand, Princeton, 1968), pp. 131–2; L. N. Rieselbach, 'Congressmen as "small town boys": a research note', *Midwest Journal of Political Science* 14, 2 (1970), pp. 321–30; Rieselbach, *Congressional Politics* (McGraw-Hill, New York, 1973), pp. 29–30.

219 Thomas and Lamb, *Congress: Politics and Practice*, p. 126.
220 Weaver, *Both your Houses*, p. 292.
221 L. Lipsitz, *American Democracy* (St Martin's Press, New York, 1986), p. 338.
222 D. S. Broder, 'The case for responsible party government', in Fishel (ed.), *Parties and Elections in an Anti-party Age*, p. 24.
223 Wilson, *Congressional Government*, intro. Lippmann, p. 31.
224 Wilson, *Congressional Government*, intro. Lippmann, p. 29.
225 Mullen, *Presidential Power and Politics*, p. 3.
226 Cronin, *The State of the Presidency*, 2nd edn, p. 188.
227 Califano, *A Presidential Nation*, p. 11.
228 Burns, *Presidential Government*, pp. 78–97; Hargrove, *The Power of the Modern President*, pp. 4–12; S. J. Wayne, 'Great expectations: what people want from Presidents', in Cronin (ed.), *Rethinking the Presidency*, pp. 185–99.
229 Locke, *Two Treatises of Government*, intro. Laslett, p. 392.
230 Quoted in Abshire, 'Foreign policy makers: President vs. Congress', in Abshire and Nurnberger (eds), *The Growing Power of Congress*, pp. 50–1.
231 Hirschfield, 'The power of the contemporary Presidency', in Hirschfield (ed.), *The Power of the Presidency*, p. 238.
232 Burns, *Presidential Government*, p. 81.
233 Quoted in N. de B. Katzenbach, 'Comparative roles of the President and the Congress in foreign affairs', in Bach and Sulzner (eds), *Perspectives on the Presidency*, p. 354.
234 Quoted in Corwin, *The President: Office and Powers*, 3rd edn, pp. 330–1.
235 See S. M. Hartman, *Truman and the 80th Congress* (University of Missouri Press, Columbia, 1971), pp. 186–210.
236 Nixon (ed.), *The White House Transcripts: Submission of Recorded Presidential Conversations to the Committee on the Judiciary of the House of Representatives by President Richard Nixon*, intro. R. W. Apple (New York Times Co./Bantam Books, New York, 1974), p. 80.
237 *Newsweek*, 25 January 1971.
238 Quoted in Schlesinger, *The Imperial Presidency*, p. 123.
239 Corwin, 'Dissolving the structure of our constitutional law', in R. Loss (ed.), *Presidential Power and the Constitution: Essays* (Cornell University Press, Ithaca, 1976), pp. 149–50.
240 Sorensen, *Watchmen in the Night*, p. 5.
241 Schlesinger, *The Imperial Presidency*, p. 275.
242 H. Heclo, 'Congressional problems', *New Society*, 7 February 1974.
243 Quoted in A. T. Mason, 'America's political heritage: revolution and free government – a bicentennial tribute', *Political Science Quarterly* 91, 2 (1976), pp. 203–4. For one of the most emphatic expositions on the Founding Fathers' distrust of human nature, see R. Hofstadter, *The American Political Tradition* (Jonathan Cape, London, 1967), pp. 3–17.
244 J. Madison, 'Federalist Paper no. 10', in Hamilton, Madison, and Jay, *The Federalist Papers*, intro. Rossiter, p. 80.
245 Madison, 'Federalist Paper no. 47', in Hamilton, Madison, and Jay, *The Federalist Papers*, intro. Rossiter, p. 301.
246 See Schlesinger, *The Crisis of Confidence: Ideas, Power and Violence in America* (André Deutsch, London, 1969); J. T. Patterson, *America in the Twentieth Century: a History since 1939*, Part II (Harcourt Brace Jovanovich, New York, 1976), pp. 449–519; T. R. Dye, *The Politics of Equality* (Bobbs-Merrill, Indianapolis, 1971), pp. 111–41, 175–214; M. Cohen and D. Hale (eds), *The New Student Left*, (Beacon, Boston, Mass., 1967); R. M. Scammon and B. J. Wattenberg, *The Real Majority* (Berkley Medallion, New York, 1972), pp. 35–83, 235–58; L. Chester, F. Hodgson, and B. Page, *An American Melodrama: the Presidential Campaign of 1968* (André Deutsch, London, 1969); A. H. Miller, 'Political issues and trust in government, 1964–1970', *American Political Science Review* 68, 3 (1974), pp. 951–72; B. Crick, 'The strange death of the American theory of consensus', *Political Quarterly* 43, 1 (1972), pp. 46–59; R. E. Pynn (ed.), *Watergate and the American Political Process* (Praeger, New York, 1975); J. Schell, *A Time of Illusion* (Knopf, New York, 1975); J. A. Lukas, *Nightmare: the Underside of the Nixon Years* (Viking, New York, 1976).
247 R. Egger, *The President of the United States*, 2nd edn (McGraw-Hill, New York, 1972), p. 4.
248 Reedy, 'The Presidency in 1976: focal point of political unity?', in Havard and Bernd (eds), *200 Years of the Republic in Retrospect*, p. 228.

249 See R. N. Goodwin, 'Advise, consent, and restrain: dismantling the Presidency', in Manley (ed.), *American Government and Public Policy*, pp. 352–63; Cronin, 'Making the Presidency safe for democracy', in Manley (ed.), *American Government and Public Policy*, pp. 363–72; Schlesinger, *The Crisis of Confidence*, pp. 286–300; Schlesinger, *The Imperial Presidency*, pp. 208–419; F. G. Hutchins, 'Presidential autocracy in America', in Tugwell and Cronin (eds), *The Presidency Reappraised*, pp. 35–55; R. E. Neustadt, 'The constraining of the President: the Presidency after Watergate', *British Journal of Political Science* 4, 3 (1974), pp. 383–97; H. S. Commager, *The Defeat of America: Presidential Power and the National Character* (Simon & Schuster, New York, 1974); J. W. Fulbright, 'The decline – and possible fall – of constitutional democracy in America', in Bach and Sulzner (eds), *Perspectives on the Presidency*, pp. 355–64; Fulbright, *The Arrogance of Power* (Penguin, Harmondsworth, 1970), pp. 52–70; Roberts (ed.), *Has the President too much Power?*, pp. 39–60, 96–109, 185–221.

250 T. Lowi, 'Representation and decision', in T. J. Lowi (ed.), *Legislative Politics USA*, 2nd edn (Little Brown, Boston, Mass., 1965), p. xiv.

251 R. A. Dahl, *Pluralist Democracy in the United States: Conflict and Consent* (Rand McNally, Chicago, 1967), p. 142. The question of whether the relationship of the Congress to the Presidency is of a strict zero-sum nature is a dispute which shows no sign of ever abating. It is significant that commentators go to the lengths that they do to point out that 'the President's loss is not automatically Congress's gain. No automatic laws of nature like the swing of a pendulum are involved' (Hodgson, *All Things to all Men*, p. 119). 'In absolute terms the power of both branches has risen historically' (S. C. Patterson, R. H. Davidson, and R. R. Ripley, *A More Perfect Union: Introduction to American Government*, Dorsey, Homewood, 1979, p. 428). Therefore, 'if one branch is up, the other is not necessarily down' (R. H. Davidson, 'The Presidency and Congress', in Nelson, ed., *The Presidency and the Political System*, p. 381). These efforts to correct the public's perception, however, are confronted by both the appeal and the apparent logic of that initial outlook of balance to which the revisionists apply themselves. The tide seems to run against them. The imagery of the seesaw continually insinuates itself back into the picture – sometimes even into the terms of description of those who are seeking to dislodge it. The debate continues and does so within a context still firmly set amongst the perspectives of balance. 'The old notion of separation of powers implies, for many people, a seesaw power struggle' (H. Smith, *The Power Game*, p. 15). 'In legislative as well as non legislative matters, Congress can be a formidable opponent. The balance tilts back and forth' (B. I. Page and M. P. Petracca, *The American Presidency*, McGraw-Hill, New York, 1983, p. 270). For example, 'predominance in the making of foreign policy has shifted back and forth between the two institutions' (H. Purvis, 'Introduction: legislative–executive interaction', in H. Purvis and S. J. Baker, eds, *Legislating Foreign Policy*, Westview, Boulder, 1984, p. 1). 'The relationship between President and Congress, then, yields temporary winners and losers' (Davidson, 'The Presidency and Congress', in Nelson, ed., *The Presidency in the Political System*, p. 389). To Allen Schick the existence of a balance is simply a matter of self-evident logic. 'Congress and the President are "two on a seesaw", with the ascendance of one usually matched by the descendance of the other. It would be naive to regard political power as sufficiently elastic to accommodate the competing ambitions of the two branches. If Congress controls, the executive is constrained; if the executive is dominant, Congress is docile' (A. Schick, 'Politics through law: Congressional limitations on executive discretion', in King, ed., *Both Ends of the Avenue*, p. 181).

252 A. Wildavsky, in Bickel *et al.*, *Watergate, Politics and the Legal Process* (American Enterprise Institute, Washington, D.C., 1974), p. 35.

253 See Hughes, *The Living Presidency*, *passim*.

254 See W. W. Lammers, *Presidential Politics: Patterns and Prospects* (Harper & Row, New York, 1976), pp. 27–54; F. Kessler, *The Dilemmas of Presidential Leadership: of Caretakers and Kings* (Prentice-Hall, Englewood Cliffs 1982), pp. 30–49; Page and Petracca, *The American Presidency*, pp. 39–61.

255 Schlesinger, *The Imperial Presidency*, p. viii.

256 P. E. Arnold and L. J. Roos, 'Toward a theory of Congressional–executive relations', *Review of Politics* 36, 3 (1974), p. 411.

257 A. M. Schlesinger, in D. Caraley, C. V. Hamilton, A. T. Mason, R. A. McCaughey, N. W. Polsby, J. L. Pressman, A. M. Schlesinger, Jr, G. L. Sherry, and T. Wicker, 'American political institutions after Watergate – a discussion', *Political Science Quarterly* 89, 4 (1974–5), p. 731.

258 Koenig, *The Chief Executive*, 3rd edn, p. 153.
259 *Time*, 12 February 1973.
260 Fulbright, 'The decline – and possible fall – of constitutional democracy in America', in Bach and Sulzner (eds), *Perspectives on the Presidency*, p. 359.
261 Fulbright, 'The decline – and possible fall – of constitutional democracy in America', p. 355.
262 Sundquist, discussion of 'The imperial President and the resurgent Congress: myth or reality?', in W. S. Livingston, L. C. Dodd, and R. L. Schott (eds), *The Presidency and the Congress: a Shifting Balance of Power?* (University of Texas Press, Austin, 1979), p. 70; Sundquist, *The Decline and Resurgence of Congress*, p. 35.
263 Sundquist, *The Decline and Resurgence of Congress*, p. 36.
264 Sundquist, *The Decline and Resurgence of Congress*, p. 35.
265 Eckhardt and Black, *The Tides of Power*, p. 36.
266 Kessler, *The Dilemmas of Presidential Leadership*, p. 46.
267 Schlesinger, in Caraley *et al.*, 'American political institutions after Watergate – a discussion', *Political Science Quarterly* 89, 4 (1974–5), p. 731.
268 R. H. Davidson, D. M. Kovenock, and M. O'Leary, *Congress in Crisis: Politics and Congressional Reform* (Wadsworth, Belmont, 1966), p. 27.
269 Quoted in *Time*, 15 January 1973.
270 Senator M. O. Hatfield, Newsletter supplement, 'Presidential power', January 1973.
271 Koenig, *The Chief Executive*, 3rd edn, p. 237.
272 A. J. Bickel in A. J. Bickel, C. S. Hyneman, R. M. Scammon, H.H. Wellington, A. Wildavsky, J. Q. Wilson, and R. K. Winter, Jr, *Watergate, Politics and the Legal Process* (American Enterprise Institute, Washington, D.C., 1974), p. 32.
273 Hutchins, 'Presidential autocracy in America', in Tugwell and Cronin (eds), *The Presidency Reappraised*, p. 53.
274 B. W. Tuchman, foreword to Javits with Kellerman, *Who Makes War*, p. vii.
275 Cronin, 'Making the Presidency safe for democracy', in Manley (ed.), *American Government and Public Policy*, p. 369.
276 Lehman, *The Executive, Congress and Foreign Policy*, pp. 14–15.
277 R. Evans, Jr, and R. D. Novak, *Nixon in the White House: the Frustration of Power* (Vintage, New York, 1972), p. 11.
278 E. A. Kolodziej, 'Congress and foreign policy: through the looking glass', in W. R. Nelson (ed.), *American Government and Political Change: a Contemporary Reader* (Oxford University Press, New York, 1970), p. 102.
279 *The Prize Cases* 67 U.S. 635 (1863).
280 The passages below are drawn from the edited extracts of the Senate debate on the Cooper–Church amendment published in E. P. Dvorin (ed.), *The Senate's War Powers: the Debate on Cambodia from the Congressional Record* (Markham, Chicago, 1971).
281 Dvorin (ed.), *The Senate's War Powers*, pp. 8, 9, 10.
282 Dvorin (ed.), *The Senate's War Powers*, pp. 35, 165.
283 Dvorin (ed.), *The Senate's War Powers*, p. 39.
284 Dvorin (ed.), *The Senate's War Powers*, p. 98.
285 Dvorin (ed.), *The Senate's War Powers*, p. 112.
286 Dvorin (ed.), *The Senate's War Powers*, p. 116.
287 Dvorin (ed.), *The Senate's War Powers*, pp. 113, 116.
288 Dvorin (ed.), *The Senate's War Powers*, pp. 174, 208.
289 Dvorin (ed.), *The Senate's War Powers*, p. 66.
290 Dvorin (ed.), *The Senate's War Powers* p. 156.
291 J. Rothchild, 'Cooing down the war: the Senate's lame doves', *Washington Monthly*, August 1971, pp. 13–15.
292 Lehman, *The Executive Congress and Foreign Policy*, pp. 68–71.
293 Lehman, *The Executive, Congress and Foreign Policy*, p. 73. See also N. G. Levin, Jr, 'Nixon, the Senate and the war', *Commentary*, November 1970, pp. 71–3.
294 See Schlesinger, *The Imperial Presidency*, pp. 187–8; Lehman, *The Executive, Congress and Foreign Policy*, p. 68; Dvorin (ed.), *The Senate's War Powers*, pp. 204–5.
295 See T. F. Eagleton, *War and Presidential Power: a Chronicle of Congressional Surrender* (Liveright, New York, 1974), pp. 141–67; T. M. Franck and E. Weisband, *Foreign Policy by Congress* (Oxford University Press, New York, 1979), pp. 13–23; Schlesinger, *The Imperial*

Presidency, pp. 195–8.
296 L. Fisher, *Presidential Spending Power* (Princeton University Press, Princeton, 1975), pp. 111–14; T. Ingram, 'The billions in the White House basement', in Bach and Sulzner (eds), *Perspectives on the President*, pp. 334–6.
297 See the Mansfield amendment to the Military Draft Extension Bill, *Congress and the Nation*, vol. III, *1969–1972: a Review of Government and Politics* (Congressional Quarterly Press, Washington, D.C., 1973), pp. 916–17.
298 Schlesinger, *The Imperial Presidency*, p. 196.
299 Congressional Quarterly, *Congress and the Nation*, vol. IV, *1973–1976: A Review of Government and Politics* (Congressional Quarterly Press, Washington, D.C., 1977), pp. 890–2.
300 Schlesinger, *The Imperial Presidency*, pp. 197–8; Kissinger, *The White House Years*, p. 1383.
301 E. Richardson, quoted in Eagleton, *War and Presidential Power*, p. 157.
302 Quoted in Franck and Weisband, *Foreign Policy by Congress*, p. 18.
303 'Did the CIA fail America?' R. Helms interviewed by K. Harris, *Observer*, 9 December 1979.
304 G. Wills, 'The CIA from beginning to end', *New York Review of Books*, 22 January 1976.
305 T. Wicker, 'Destroy the monster', *New York Times*, 12 September 1975.
306 V. Marchetti and J. D. Marks, *The CIA and the Cult of Intelligence* (Coronet Books, London, 1974); P. Agee, *Inside the Company: CIA Diary* (Penguin, Harmondsworth, 1975); D. Wise, *The American Police State: the Government against the People* (Random House, New York, 1976), pp. 183–257; J. Marks, *Search for the Manchurian Candidate: the CIA and Mind Control* (Allen Lane, Harmondsworth, 1979); S. Schlesinger and S. Kinzer, *Bitter Fruit: the Untold Story of the American Coup in Guatemala* (Doubleday, New York, 1982); J. Stockwell, *In Search of Enemies: a CIA Story* (W. W. Norton, New York, 1978); 'Intelligence agencies under fire for Watergate role', *Congressional Quarterly Guide to Current American Government*, fall 1973, pp. 58–65; H. S. Commager, '"Intelligence": the constitution betrayed', *New York Review of Books*, 30 September 1976; A. Lewis, 'The honorable, murderous gentlemen of a secret world', *New York Times*, 23 November 1975; G. Crile III, 'The Mafia, the CIA and Castro', *Washington Post*, 16 May 1976; R. S. Cline, *The CIA under Reagan, Bush and Casey: the Evolution of the Agency from Roosevelt to Reagan* (Acropolis, Washington, D.C., 1981), pp. 247–60.
307 Wills, 'The CIA from beginning to end', *New York Review of Books*, 22 January 1976.
308 T. Powers, *The Man who Kept the Secrets: R. Helms and the CIA* (Weidenfeld & Nicolson, London, 1980), p. 258.
309 R. Helms, quoted in 'Round the table with four men from CIA', *Times*, 6 November 1978.
310 Wicker, 'Destroy the monster', *New York Times*, 12 September 1975.
311 See Cline, *The CIA under Reagan, Bush and Casey*, pp. 117–19; Marchetti and Marks, *The CIA and the Cult of Intelligence*, pp. 36–7.
312 See L. Fisher, *The Constitution between Friends: Congress, the President and the Law* (St Martin's Press, New York, 1978), p. 188; Fisher, *Presidential Spending Power*, pp. 214–23.
313 Franck and Weisband, *Foreign Policy by Congress*, p. 116.
314 Franck and Weisband, *Foreign Policy by Congress*, p. 116.
315 They were (i) the House Appropriations Subcommittee on Defense; (ii) the House Armed Services Subcommittee on Intelligence; (iii) the Senate Appropriations Subcommittee on Defense; and (iv) the Senate Armed Services Subcommittee on Central Intelligence.
316 W. Colby and P. Forbath, *Honorable Men: my Life in the CIA* (Hutchinson, London, 1978), p. 18.
317 Marchetti and Marks, *The CIA and the Cult of Intelligence*, p. 317.
318 Marchetti and Marks, *The CIA and the Cult of Intelligence*, p. 374.
319 *Report to the President by the Commission on CIA Activities within the United States* (Manor, New York, 1975), p. 14.
320 Commager, '"Intelligence": the constitution betrayed', *New York Review of Books*, 30 September 1976.
321 For example, see Wills, 'The CIA from beginning to end', *New York Review of Books*, 22 January 1976.
322 A. Lewis, 'Only Congress itself', *New York Times*, 18 September 1975.
323 T. Wicker, 'The dark at the top', *New York Times*, 23 September 1975.
324 T. I. Emerson, 'Control of government intelligence agencies – the American experience', *Political Quarterly* 53, 3 (1982), p. 283.

Notes

325 Senator F. Church, 'The CIA needs stronger Congressional supervision', in *Point Counterpoint: Readings in American Government* (Scott Foresman, Glenview, 1979), p. 273.
326 Wise, *The American Police State*, pp. 408–9.
327 Cline, *The CIA under Reagan, Bush and Casey*, pp. 288–9.
328 Marchetti and Marks, *The CIA and the Cult of Intelligence*, pp. 404–5.
329 H. H. Ransom, 'Congress and the intelligence agencies', in Mansfield (ed.), *Congress against the President*, p. 166.
330 J. M. Oseth, *Regulating US Intelligence Operations: a Study in Definition of the National Interest* (University Press of Kentucky, Lexington, 1985), pp. 164–73.
331 For example, see Javits with Kellerman, *Who Makes War*, pp. 262–73.
332 'Veto of the war powers resolution', 24 October 1973, in *Public Papers of Presidents of the United States: Richard Nixon, 1973* (United States Government Printing Office, Washington, D.C., 1975), p. 893.
333 See Eagleton, *War and Presidential Power*, pp. 184–225; Schlesinger, *The Imperial Presidency*, pp. 301–7; J. Spanier and E. M. Uslaner, *Foreign Policy and the Democratic Dilemmas*, 3rd edn (Holt Rinehart & Winston, New York, 1978), pp. 67–70. For commentary on how the resolution has affected the Presidency's position in foreign policy-making since its passage, see R. Scigliano, 'The war powers resolution and the war powers', in Bessette and Tulis (eds), *The Presidency in the Constitutional Order*, pp. 120–4, 143–9; Pyle and Pious, *The President, Congress and the Constitution*, pp. 361–72; Fisher, *Constitutional Conflicts between Congress and the President*, pp. 284–325; Nathan and Oliver, *Foreign Policy Making and the American Political System*, 2nd edn, pp. 168–88.
334 Dodd, 'Congress and the quest for power', in Dodd and Oppenheimer (eds), *Congress Reconsidered*, p. 294.
335 Wills, 'The CIA from beginning to end', *New York Review of Books*, 22 January 1976.
336 They were the Senate Select Committee to Study Governmental Operations with Respect to Intelligence Activities under the chairmanship of Senator Frank Church (D.—Idaho) and the House Select Committee on Intelligence under the chairmanship of Congressman Otis Pike (D.—N.Y.).
337 Colby and Forbath, *Honorable Men*, p. 21.
338 Colby and Forbath, *Honorable Men*, p. 458.
339 Crabb and Holt, *Invitation to Struggle*, p. 157 (my italics).
340 L. K. Johnson, *A Season of Inquiry* (University Press of Kentucky, Lexington, 1987).
341 Franck and Weisband, *Foreign Policy by Congress*, p. 115. For similarly dogmatic reassurances, see H. G. Zeidenstein: 'As a civilian agency, the CIA is outside the jurisdiction of the War Powers Resolution. Consequently, the Resolution does not require the President to inform Congress of covert CIA operations.... This gap was plugged by other measures compelling CIA accountability to selected Congressional committees' ('The reassertion of Congressional power: new curbs on the President', *Political Science Quarterly* 93, 3, 1978, p. 398); and J. M. Orman: '*By law* [i.e. the Hughes–Ryan amendment, 1974] *the President must inform Congress of all covert operations in a "timely fashion"*. The importance of this fundamental change in the Presidential secrecy system cannot be overemphasized. For the first time Congress recognized that Presidents do have the power to engage in covert operations in the name of national security *only* if Congress is informed in an appropriate fashion by the President' (*Presidential Secrecy and Deception: beyond the Power to Persuade*, Greenwood, Westport, 1980, p. 50).
342 See A. Lewis, 'CIA: baby and bathwater', *International Herald Tribune*, 29 January 1980; T. Wicker, 'Killing freedom to save it', *International Herald Tribune*, 11 August 1980; 'New guidelines for oversight of CIA enacted', *Congressional Quarterly Almanac, 96th Congress, 2nd Session, 1980*, vol. XXXV (Congressional Quarterly Press, Washington, D.C., 1981), pp. 66–71; *Congressional Quarterly Weekly Report*, 11 July 1981, pp. 1243–6; P. E. Tyler and D. B. Ottaway, 'CIA rebuilds covert role under Director Casey', *Washington Post*, published in *Guardian Weekly*, 13 April 1986; J. Ranelagh, *The Agency: the Rise and Decline of the CIA* (Weidenfeld & Nicolson, London, 1986), pp. 648–83; D. L. Clark and E. L. Neveleff, 'Secrecy, foreign intelligence, and civil liberties: has the pendulum swung too far?', *Political Science Quarterly* 99, 3 (1984), pp. 493–513.
343 A difference in perspective reflected in Phillippa Strum's remark that Congress's 'functions are derived more from the idea of checks and balances than from separation of powers'

(*Presidential Power and American Democracy*, Goodyear, Santa Monica, 1979, p. 28).
344 Letter responding to House Judiciary Committee subpoenas requiring production of Presidential tape recordings and documents, 10 June 1974, in *Public Papers of Presidents of the United States: Richard Nixon, January 1st to August 9th, 1974* (United States Government Printing Office, Washington, D.C., 1975), p. 481.
345 Lehman, *The Executive, Congress and Foreign Policy*, p. 3.
346 V. Davis, 'Presidential politics and the policy process: the President's key players', in S. C. Sarkesian (ed.), *Presidential Leadership and National Security: Style, Institutions, and Politics* (Westview, Boulder, 1984), p. 103.
347 Sundquist, *The Decline and Resurgence of Congress*, p. 275.
348 Franck and Weisband, *Foreign Policy by Congress*, p. 155.
349 Cronin, 'The Imperial Presidency re-examined', in Livingston, Dodd, and Schott (eds), *The Presidency and the Congress*, p. 37.
350 Sundquist, 'Congress and the President: enemies or partners?', in Dodd and Oppenheimer (eds), *Congress Reconsidered*, p. 227.
351 Sundquist, 'Congress and the President: enemies or partners?', p. 229.
352 Davidson, Kovenock, and O'Leary, *Congress in Crisis*, p. 10.
353 Thomas and Lamb, *Congress: Politics and Practice*, p. 26.
354 Hughes, 'The Presidency after Watergate', in Roberts (ed.), *Has the President too much Power?*, p. 16.
355 Dodd, 'Congress and the cycles of power', in Livingston, Dodd, and Schott (eds), *The Presidency and the Congress*, p. 58.
356 Corwin, *The President: Office and Powers*, 3rd edn, p. 330. See also P. Herring, *Presidential Leadership* (Farrar & Rinehart, New York, 1940), p. 136.
357 'Carter vs. Congress: institutional conflict', *Congressional Quarterly Guide to Current American Government*, fall 1978, p. 75.
358 Levine and Cornwell, *An Introduction to American Government*, 3rd edn, p. 115.
359 Johannes, 'From White House to Capitol Hill: how far will the pendulum swing?', in D. C. Saffell (ed.), *American Government: Reform in the post-Watergate Era* (Winthrop, Cambridge, Mass., 1974), p. 102.
360 Johannes, 'From White House to Capitol Hill: how far will the pendulum swing?', p. 102.
361 Cronin, 'The Imperial Presidency re-examined', in Livingston, Dodd, and Schott (eds), *The Presidency and the Congress*, p. 38. For a generation American opinion had been conditioned into an acceptance and an appreciation of a strong and growing Presidency as a matter of need. 'The shift of initiative toward the executive ... had come about because it had to' (D. B. Truman, *The Congressional Party*, p. 7); 'survival in an essentially anarchical international system ... requires a single source of authority so that a state can, if necessary, act speedily, secretly, with continuity of purpose or, when demanded with flexibility.... In short, the primacy of the executive in foreign policy was essentially a response to the nature of the state system.... The need for a powerful Presidency seemed obvious' (Spanier and Uslaner, *Foreign Policy and the Democratic Dilemmas*, 3rd edn, pp. 2, 217); 'the only party that seems to have the organic capacity to go out and make these commitments is the President ... organizationally and structurally he's the one who *can* do it' (Eckhardt and Black, *The Tides of Power*, pp. 42, 56). And yet, after apparently becoming accustomed to the notion of 'a shift in the balance between President and Congress ... to summarize 175 years of history' (Burns, 'Dictatorship – could it happen here?', in Roberts, ed., *Has the President too much Power?*, p. 242), it is conspicuous that, during the Imperial Presidency crisis, perceptions of the legislative–executive relationship changed dramatically. It was not merely a recognition that 'there is nothing preordained or irreversible about the shift of power to the President' (Fisher, *President and Congress*, p. 238), or the rediscovery that 'the predominance of one or other branches ... ebbed and flowed' (Lehman, *The Executive, Congress and Foreign Policy*, p. 21). It was marked by an acknowledgement of the existence of a strictly mechanical agency: an agency whose processes could only be observed and experienced, as the following illustrative passages make clear. 'The recent assertion of power by Congress raises the question: is the balance of power ... shifting toward Congress? Or does the Congress's renaissance signal only a modest shift, a redress of an imbalance that will result in two more equal partners?' (J. B. Anderson, 'Tension of the Presidency', in J. C. Hoy and M. H. Bernstein, eds, *The Effective President*, Palisades, Pacific Palisades, 1976, p. 46). 'The pendulum may have come to rest'

(Frank and Weisband, *Foreign Policy by Congress*, p. 62). 'More recent complaints about "drift" in domestic policy, foreign affairs, and economic management in the Carter White House might indicate that, in the aftermath of Watergate, the pendulum of power had swung too far from the President in the direction of Congress' (Kessler, *The Dilemmas of Presidential Leadership*, p. 47). 'Some people used to complain about what they called an "imperial presidency", but now the pendulum has swung too far in the opposite direction. We have not an imperial Presidency but an imperiled Presidency' (President G. R. Ford, quoted in 'Imperiled, not imperial', *Time*, 10 November 1980).

362 'Carter vs. Congress: institutional conflict', *Congressional Quarterly Guide to Current American Government*, fall 1978, p. 75.
363 Lehman, *The Executive, Congress and Foreign Policy*, p. 23.
364 'Address to the nation announcing decision to resign the office of President of the United States', 8 August 1974, in *Public Papers of Presidents of the United States: Richard Nixon, January 1st to August 9th, 1974* (United States Government Printing Office, Washington, D.C., 1975), p. 627.
365 White, *Breach of Faith*, p. 222.
366 C. V. Hamilton, in Caraley *et al.*, 'American political institutions after Watergate – a discussion', *Political Science Quarterly* 89, 4 (1974–5), p. 724.
367 Schlesinger, *The Imperial Presidency*, p. 269.
368 Hughes, 'The plausible dream of zealots', *Time*, 19 August 1974.
369 Koenig, *The Chief Executive*, 3rd edn, p. 407.
370 Commager, 'The constitution vindicated', in Commager, *The Defeat of America*, p. 153.
371 Commager, 'The constitution vindicated', pp. 155, 153.
372 *New York Times*, 9 August 1974.
373 'Remarks on taking the oath of office', 9 August 1974, in *Public Papers of Presidents of the United States: G. Ford, August 9th to December 31st, 1974* (United States Government Printing Office, Washington, D.C., 1975), p. 2.
374 Franck and Weisband, *Foreign Policy by Congress*, p. 6.
375 'Carter vs. Congress: institutional conflict', *Congressional Quarterly Guide to Current American Government*, fall 1978, p. 75.
376 Sundquist, 'Congress and the President: enemies or partners?', in Dodd and Oppenheimer (eds), *Congress Reconsidered*, p. 229.
377 C. W. Dunn, 'Epilogue: apocalypse of the night watchmen', in Dunn (ed.), *The Future of the American Presidency*, p. 322.
378 E. Richardson, *The Creative Balance: Government, Politics, and the Individual in America's Third Century* (Hamish Hamilton, London, 1976), pp. 84–5.
379 Franck and Weisband, *Foreign Policy by Congress*, p. 159. This mood was reflected in the appearance of a large number of exhaustive studies into the separation of powers and, in particular, into the jurisdictional disputes concerning the delineation of the three branches. For example, see R. Berger, *Executive Privilege: A Constitutional Myth* (Harvard University Press, Cambridge, Mass., 1974); Berger, *Impeachment: the Constitutional Problems* (Harvard University Press, Cambridge, Mass., 1973); Fisher, *President and Congress*; Fisher, *The Constitution between Friends*; L. Henkin, *Foreign Affairs and the Constitution* (Foundation, Mineola, 1972); A. D. Sofaer, *War, Foreign Affairs and Constitutional Power: the Origins* (Ballinger, Cambridge, Mass., 1976); W. T. Reveley III, 'The power to make war', in F. O. Wilcox and R. A. Frank (eds), *The Constitution and the Conduct of Foreign Policy: an Inquiry by a Panel of the American Society of International Law* (Praeger, New York, 1976), pp. 83–125; Wilcox, *Congress, the Executive, and Foreign Policy* (Harper & Row, New York, 1971).
380 Wilson, *Constitutional Government in the United States*, p. 56.
381 Schlesinger, *The Imperial Presidency*, p. 1.

Chapter 5. A government of laws, men and machines

1 P. B. Kurland, *Watergate and the Constitution* (University of Chicago Press, Chicago, 1978), p. 179.
2 *Buckley v. Valeo* 424 U.S. 1, 121 (1976).
3 Kurland, *Watergate and the Constitution*, p. 164.

4 M. K. Udall, 'A Democrat looks at the Presidency', in C. W. Dunn (ed.), *The Future of the American Presidency* (General Learning Press, Morristown, 1975), p. 238.
5 J. Lehman, *The Executive, Congress and Foreign Policy: Studies of the Nixon Administration* (Praeger, New York, 1976), p. 31.
6 W. Kendall, 'Democracy: the two majorities', in W. F. Buckley, Jr (ed.), *American Conservative Thought in the Twentieth Century* (Bobbs-Merrill, Indianapolis, 1970), p. 258; F. I. Greenstein, *The American Party System and the American People*, 2nd edn (Prentice-Hall, Englewood Cliffs, 1970), pp. 86–112. For a more recent interpretation on this theme, see D. J. Vogler and S. R. Waldman, *Congress and Democracy* (Congressional Quarterly Press, Washington, D.C., 1985), pp. 1–22.
7 G. S. Wood, *The Creation of the American Republic, 1776–1787* (University of North Carolina Press, Chapel Hill, 1969).
8 Wood, *The Creation of the American Republic*, p. 603.
9 Wood, *The Creation of the American Republic*, p. 606.
10 Wood, *The Creation of the American Republic*, p. 604.
11 Wood, *The Creation of the American Republic*, p. 606.
12 Wood, *The Creation of the American Republic*, p. 604.
13 L. Banning, 'Republican ideology and the triumph of the constitution, 1789–1793', *William and Mary Quarterly* 31, 2 (1974), p. 173.
14 L. Banning, 'Republican ideology and the triumph of the constitution, 1789–1793', p. 173.
15 Wood, *The Creation of the American Republic*, pp. 608, 604.
16 W. B. Gwyn, *The Meaning of the Separation of Powers: an Analysis of the Doctrine from its Origin to the Adoption of the United States Constitution* (Tulane University Press, New Orleans, 1965), p. v.
17 Gwyn, *The Meaning of the Separation of Powers*, p. vi.
18 Kurland, *Watergate and the Constitution*, p. 169.
19 C. E. Merriam, *Systematic Politics* (University of Chicago Press, Chicago, 1945), p. 175.
20 J. S. Clark, *Congress: the Sapless Branch* (Harper & Row, New York, 1964), p. 22.
21 M. Capek, *The Philosophical Impact of Contemporary Physics* (Van Nostrand, New York, 1961), pp. xii–xiii.
22 Capek, *The Philosophical Impact of Contemporary Physics*, p. xiii.
23 A. Koyre, *Newtonian Studies* (Chapman & Hall, London, 1965), p. 23.
24 D. J. Manning, *Liberalism* (J. M. Dent, London, 1976), p. 16.
25 Manning, *Liberalism*, p. 143.
26 G. C. Lodge, *The New American Ideology* (Alfred A. Knopf, New York, 1976), p. 114. See also the view of John C. Donovan, who believes that in the American inheritance there is 'a vaguely Newtonian–mechanistic view of social processes' (p. 20) which contains 'a kind of automatic checking and balancing of one powerful group interest against the other' (p. 28), *The Policy Makers* (Pegasus, New York, 1970).
27 Koyre, *Newtonian Studies*, p. 22.
28 S. Black, *The Nature of Living Things: an Essay in Theoretical Biology* (Secker & Warburg/Heinemann, London, 1972), pp. 7–12.
29 J. H. Ferguson and D. E. McHenry, *The American System of Government*, 10th edn (McGraw-Hill, New York, 1969), p. 376.
30 A. de Tocqueville, *Democracy in America*, trans. H. Reeve, intro. H. S. Commager (ed.) (Oxford University Press, London, 1946), p. 207.
31 'Thomas Jefferson on judicial review', in B. Schwartz (ed.), *A Basic History of the United States Supreme Court* (Van Nostrand, Princeton, 1968), pp. 110–12.
32 See R. A. Dahl, 'Decision-making in a democracy: the Supreme Court as a national policy-maker', *Journal of Public Law* 6 (1957), pp. 279–95; R. Funston, 'Supreme Court and critical elections', *American Political Science Review* 69, 3 (1975), 795–811; H. J. Abraham, *The Judiciary: the Supreme Court in the Governmental Process* (Allyn & Bacon, Boston, Mass., 1965), pp. 116–17. R. McCloskey, *The American Supreme Court* (University of Chicago Press, Chicago, 1960), pp. 19–20.
33 M. S. Evans, *Clear and Present Dangers; a Conservative View of America's Government* (Harcourt Brace Jovanovich, New York, 1975), p. 104.
34 M. Shapiro, 'The Supreme Court: from Warren to Burger', in A. King (ed.), *The New American Political System* (American Enterprise Institute for Public Policy Research, Washington,

D.C., 1978), p. 179. See also M. Shapiro, 'Judicial activism', in S. M. Lipset (ed.), *The Third Century: America as a Post-industrial Society* (University of Chicago Press, Chicago, 1979), pp. 109–31; A. Bickel, *The Supreme Court and the Idea of Progress* (Harper & Row, New York, 1970); P. B. Kurland, *Politics, the Constitution and the Warren Court* (University of Chicago Press, Chicago, 1970).

35 N. Glazer, 'Towards an imperial judiciary', in R. B. Ripley and G. A. Franklin (eds), *National Government and Policy in the United States* (Peacock, Itasca, 1977), p. 232. See also J. D. Casper, 'The Supreme Court and national policy making', *American Political Science Review* 70, 1 (1976), pp. 50–63; D. L. Horowitz, *The Courts and Social Policy* (Brookings Institution, Washington, D.C., 1977); Horowitz, 'Are the courts going too far?', *Commentary*, January 1977, pp. 27–44; Kurland, *Politics, the Constitution and the Warren Court, passim*; Kurland, 'Towards a political Supreme Court', *University of Chicago Law Review* 37, 1 (1969), pp. 19–46; Kurland, 'Government by judiciary', *Modern Age* 20 (1976), pp. 358–71; D. Fellman, 'The separation of powers and the judiciary', *Review of Politics* 37, 3 (1975), pp. 374–5; L. J. Theberge (ed.), *The Judiciary in a Democratic Society* (D. C. Heath, Lexington, 1979); R. C. Cortner, *The Supreme Court and the Second Bill of Rights: the Fourteenth Amendment and the Nationalization of Civil Liberties* (University of Wisconsin Press, Madison, 1981); C. Wolfe, *The Rise of Modern Judicial Review: from Constitutional Interpretation to Judge-made Law* (Basic Books, New York, 1986); W. Berns, 'Government by lawyers and judges', *Commentary*, June 1987, pp. 17–24.

36 R. Sherrill, *Why they Call it Politics: a Guide to America's Government*, 2nd edn (Harcourt Brace Jovanovich, New York, 1974), p. 167.

37 R. J. Harris, 'Judicial review: vagaries and varieties', in W. C. Havard and J. L. Bernd (eds), *200 Years of the Republic in Retrospect* (University Press of Virginia, Charlottesville, 1976), p. 207.

38 *Congressional Quarterly Guide to Current American Government*, spring 1982, p. 122. For his comments on the same theme, see E. S. Corwin's review of B. F. Wright, *The Growth of American Constitutional Law*, in *Harvard Law Review* 56, 3 (1942), p. 487.

39 R. H. Jackson, *The Supreme Court in the American System of Government* (Harper & Row, New York, 1955), p. 61.

40 R. Neely, *How Courts Govern America* (Yale University Press, New Haven, 1981), p. 216. Neely enlarges upon the role of the courts on p. 113. 'In their interactions with the legislative branch, the courts are generally *positive*, to compensate for the inherent negativism of a legislature; in their interactions with the executive branch they are basically negative, to compensate for that branch's inherently *positive* orientation. The essential mission of the courts ... involves supplying balance'.

41 Neely, *How Courts Govern America*, p. 217.

42 S. C. Patterson, R. H. Davidson, and R. B. Ripley, *A More Perfect Union: Introduction to American Government* (Dorsey, Homewood, 1979), p. 561. See also H. Ball, *Courts and Politics: the Federal Judicial System* (Prentice-Hall, Englewood Cliffs, 1980), pp. 78–9; C. S. Hyneman, *The Supreme Court on Trial* (Atherton Press, New York, 1963), pp. 120–1; S. Krislov, *The Supreme Court in the Political Process* (Macmillan, New York, 1965), p. 105; R. Funston, *A Vital National Seminar: the Supreme Court in American Political Life* (Mayfield, Palo Alto 1978), p. 65; I. H. Carmen, *Power and Balance: an Introduction to American Constitutional Government* (Harcourt Brace Jovanovich, New York, 1978), p. 41; Ferguson and McHenry, *The American System of Government*, p. 358.

43 C. L. Black, Jr, *The People and the Court: Judicial Review in a Democracy* (Prentice-Hall, Englewood Cliffs, 1960), p. 170.

44 Rufus Davies, 'The "federal principle" reconsidered', in A. Wildavsky (ed.), *American Federalism in Perspective* (Little Brown, Boston, Mass., 1967), pp. 3–4.

45 J. Madison, 'Federalist Paper no. 37', in A. Hamilton, J. Madison, and J. Jay, *The Federalist Papers* (Mentor, New York, 1961), p. 228.

46 Madison, 'Federalist Paper no. 37', in Hamilton, Madison, and Jay, *The Federalist Papers*, p. 228.

47 Madison, 'Federalist Paper no. 39', in Hamilton, Madison, and Jay, *The Federalist Papers*, p. 246.

48 Madison, 'Federalist Paper no. 47', in Hamilton, Madison, and Jay, *The Federalist Papers*, p. 302.

49 Madison, 'Federalist Paper no. 51', in Hamilton, Madison, and Jay, *The Federalist Papers*, p. 323.
50 See E. S. Corwin, *The Twilight of the Supreme Court* (Yale University Press, New Haven, 1934), ch. 1.
51 See M. Grodzins, *The American System* (Rand McNally, Chicago, 1966); D. J. Elazar, *American Federalism: a View from the States* (Crowell, New York, 1966); Elazar, *The American Partnership* (University of Chicago Press, Chicago, 1962).
52 J. M. Burns and J. W. Peltason, *Government by the People: the Dynamics of American National, State and Local Government*, 3rd edn (Prentice-Hall, Englewood Cliffs, 1957), p. 118.
53 M. Ways, '"Creative federalism" and the great society', in D. J. Elazar, R. B. Carroll, E. L. Levine, and D. St Angelo (eds), *Co-operation and Conflict: Readings in American Federalism* (Peacock, Itasca, 1969), p. 620.
54 M. D. Reagan, *The New Federalism* (Oxford University Press, New York, 1972), p. 157.
55 W. Anderson, 'The federal equilibrium and the states', in D. J. Elazar *et al.* (eds), *Co-operation and Conflict*, p. 59.
56 Burns and Peltason, *Government by the People*, 3rd edn, p. 120.
57 L. D. Epstein, 'The old states in a new system', in King (ed.), *The new American Political System*, p. 338.
58 See M. Grodzins, *The American System*, pp. 8–9; Grodzins, 'Centralization and decentralization in the American federal system', in R. A. Goldwin (ed.), *A Nation of States: Essays on the American Federal System* (Rand McNally, Chicago, 1961), pp. 1–23.
59 Reagan, *The New Federalism, passim.*
60 K. C. Wheare, *Federal Government*, 4th edn (Oxford University Press, London, 1963), p. 10.
61 M. J. C. Vile, 'Federal theory and the "new federalism"', *Politics: Journal of the Australasian Political Science Association* 12, 2 (1977), p. 1.
62 Grodzins, *The American System*, p. 289.
63 Vile, 'Federal theory and the "new federalism"', *Politics* 12, 2 (1977), p. 3.
64 P. King, *Federalism and Federation* (Johns Hopkins University Press, Baltimore, 1983), p. 67.
65 Grodzins, 'The federal system', in A. Wildavsky (ed.), *American Federalism in Perspective*, p. 259.
66 J. L. Sundquist with D. Davis, *Making Federalism Work: a Study of Program Co-ordination at the Community Level* (Brookings Institution, Washington, D.C., 1969); Reagan, *The New Federalism*, pp. 3–28, 145–68.
67 K. Prewitt and S. Verba, *An Introduction to American Government*, 3rd edn (Harper & Row, New York, 1979), pp. 530–1.
68 D. L. Levine and E. E. Cornwell, Jr, *An Introduction to American Government*, 3rd edn (Macmillan, New York, 1975), p. 31.
69 R. A. Dahl, *Pluralist Democracy in the United States: Conflict and Consent* (Rand McNally, Chicago, 1967), p. 173.
70 Commission on Intergovernmental Relations, *A Report to the President* (Government Printing Office, Washington, D.C., 1955), p. 56, quoted in Grodzins, 'Centralization and decentralization in the American federal system', in Goldwin (ed.), *A Nation of States*, p. 17.
71 Burns and Peltason, *Government by the People*, p. 120.
72 Grodzins, 'The future of the American system', in Elazar *et al.* (eds), *Co-operation and Conflict*, pp. 63, 71.
73 R. T. Seager, *American Government and Politics: a Neoconservative Approach* (Scott Foresman, Glenview, 1982), p. 71.
74 Ferguson and McHenry, *The American System of Government*, 10th edn, pp. 84, 86.
75 N. Rockefeller, 'Freedom and federalism', in J. A. Burkhardt, S. Krislov, and R. L. Lee (eds), *The Clash of Issues: Readings and Problems in American Government*, 7th edn (Prentice-Hall, Englewood Cliffs, 1981), p. 60.
76 S. H. Beer, 'The future of the states in the federal system', in P. Woll (ed.), *American Government: Readings and Cases*, 7th edn (Little Brown, Boston, Mass., 1981), pp. 92, 99.
77 F. S. Griffith, *The American System of Government*, 6th edn (Methuen, New York, 1983), p. 182. An interesting variation on this theme is provided by Laurence O'Toole, who translates the federal balance into one between 'generalists (whose responsibility is to a geographic area or general government) and specialists (who focus on specific functions that are parts of modern governments, perhaps at multiple levels). Frequently, efforts to modify the inter-

governmental system are aimed at shifting the balance between these two groups or emphases' ('American intergovernmental relations: concluding thought', in L. O'Toole, ed., *American Intergovernmental Relations*, Congressional Quarterly Press, Washington, D.C., 1985, p. 306).

78 'Annual message to the Congress on the state of the union', 22 January 1971, *Public Papers of the Presidents of the United States: Richard Nixon, 1971* (United States Government Printing Office, Washington, D.C., 1972), pp. 54, 53.

79 M. N. Danielson, A. M. Hershey, and J. M. Bayne, *One Nation, so many Governments* (D. C. Heath, Lexington, 1977), p. 7.

80 Danielson, Hershey, and Bayne, *One Nation*, p. 7. See also R. Nathan, C. Adams, Jr, and associates, *Revenue Sharing: the Second Round* (Brookings Institution, Washington, D.C., 1977); D. J. Elazar, 'The rebirth of federalism: the future role of the states as polities in the federal system', *Commonsense* 4, 1 (1981); Elazar, 'Can the states be trusted?', in Burkhardt, Krislov, and Lee (eds), *The Clash of Issues*, pp. 82–6; I. Sharkansky, *The Maligned States*, 2nd edn (McGraw-Hill, New York, 1977); D. H. McKay, 'Fiscal federalism, professionalism and the transformation of American state government', *Public Administration* 80, 1 (1982), pp. 10–22.

81 For the same theme in President Reagan's 'new federalism' see C. E. Barfield, *Rethinking Federalism: Block Grants and Federal, State and Local Responsibilities* (American Enterprise Institute, Washington, D.C., 1981); R. S. Williamson, 'A review of Reagan federalism', in R. B. Hawkins (ed.), *American Federalism: a new Partnership for the Republic* (Institute for Contemporary Studies, San Francisco, 1982), pp. 89–120. See also J. Sununu, 'The spirit of federalism: restoring the balance', in *Intergovernmental Perspective* (Advisory Commission on Intergovernmental Relations, Washington, D.C., 1988).

82 F. E. Rourke, 'Grappling with the bureaucracy', in A. J. Meltsner (ed.), *Politics and the Oval Office* (Institute for Contemporary Studies, San Francisco, 1981), p. 127. See also E. J. Hughes, *The Living Presidency: the Resources and Dilemmas of the American Presidential Office* (Penguin Books, Baltimore, 1974), pp. 181–95; P. Woll, *American Bureaucracy* (W. W. Norton, New York, 1963); T. E. Cronin, *The State of the Presidency*, 2nd edn (Little Brown, Boston, Mass., 1980), pp. 223–96; Cronin, 'Presidents as chief executives', in R. G. Tugwell and T. E. Cronin (eds), *The Presidency Reappraised* (Praeger, New York, 1974), pp. 234–65; R. F. Fenno, Jr, *The President's Cabinet* (Harvard University Press, Cambridge, Mass., 1959); H. Heclo, *A Government of Strangers* (Brookings Institution, Washington, D.C., 1977); J. D. Aberbach and B. A. Rockman, 'Clashing beliefs within the executive branch: the Nixon administration bureaucracy', *American Political Science Review* 70, 2 (1976), pp. 456–68; F. E. Rourke, *Bureaucracy, Politics and Public Policy* (Little Brown, Boston, Mass., 1969); J. Helmer, 'The Presidential office; velvet fist in an iron glove', in H. Heclo and L. M. Salamon (eds), *The Illusion of Presidential Government* (Westview, Boulder, 1981), pp. 51–65; D. K. Price, *America's Unwritten Constitution: Science, Religion, and Political Responsibility* (Harvard University Press, Cambridge, Mass., 1985), pp. 99–128; R. Rose, 'The President: a chief but not an executive', *Presidential Studies Quarterly* 7 (1977), pp. 5–19.

83 Woll, *American Bureaucracy*, p. 165.

84 Cronin, 'Presidents as chief executives', in Tugwell and Cronin (eds), *The Presidency Reappraised*, pp. 240–1. See also H. Seideman, *Politics, Position and Power: the Dynamics of Federal Organization* (Oxford University Press, New York, 1975); S. Hess, *Organizing the Presidency* (Brookings Institution, Washington, D.C., 1976); R. L. Cole and D. A. Caputo, 'Presidential control of the senior civil service: assessing the strategies of the Nixon years', *American Political Science Review* 73, 2 (1979), pp. 399–413; R. P. Nathan, *The Plot that Failed: Nixon and the Administration Presidency* (Wiley, New York, 1975); M. H. Halperin, *Bureaucratic Politics and Foreign Policy* (Brookings Institution, Washington, D.C., 1974); Halperin, 'Why bureaucrats play games', *Foreign Policy* 1, 2 (1970), pp. 70–90; L. Berman, *The Office of Management and Budget and the Presidency, 1921–1979* (Princeton University Press, Princeton, 1979); D. C. Mowery, M. S. Kamlet, and J. P. Crecine, 'Presidential management of budgetary and fiscal policymaking', *Political Science Quarterly* 95, 3 (1980), pp. 395–425; R. C. Wood, 'When government works', in A. Wildavsky (ed.), *Perspectives on the Presidency* (Little Brown, 1975), pp. 393–404; R. Rose, *Managing Presidential Objectives* (Macmillan, London, 1977); R. E. Neustadt, 'Presidency and legislation: the growth of central clearance', *American Political Science Review* 48, 3 (1954), pp. 641–71; R. S. Gilmour,

'Central legislative clearance: a revised perspective', *Public Administration Review* 31, 2 (1971), pp. 150–8; R. Randall, 'Presidential power versus bureaucratic intransigence: the influence of the Nixon administration on welfare policy', *American Political Science Review* 73, 3 (1979), pp. 795–810. K. J. Meier, *Politics and the Bureaucracy: Policymaking in the Fourth Branch of the Government* (Duxbury, North Scituate, 1979), pp. 145–52. T. Moe, 'The politicized Presidency', in J. Chubb and P. Peterson (eds), *The New Direction in American Politics* (Brookings Institution, Washington, D.C., 1985), pp. 235–71; F. Rourke, 'The Presidency and the bureaucracy: strategic alternatives', in M. Nelson (ed.), *The Presidency and the Political System* (Congressional Quarterly Press, Washington, D.C., 1984), pp. 339–62; L. Lynn, 'The Reagan administration and the reticent bureaucracy', in L. Salamon and M. Lund (eds), *The Reagan Presidency and the Governing of America* (Urban Institute Press, Washington, D.C., 1984), pp. 339–80.

85 P. Woll, 'Constitutional democracy and bureaucratic power', in Woll (ed.), *American Government*, p. 426.

86 Cronin, *The State of the Presidency*, 2nd edn, p. 224.

87 Cronin, 'The swelling of the Presidency', in R. E. Pynn (ed.), *Watergate and the American Political Process* (Praeger, New York, 1975), p. 207. See also Cronin, ' "Everybody believes in democracy until he gets to the White House ...": an examination of White House–departmental relations', in N. C. Thomas (ed.), *The Presidency in Contemporary Context*, pp. 193–236; G. E. Reedy, *The Twilight of the Presidency* (Mentor, New York, 1970); Hess, *Organizing the Presidency*, pp. 158–78; R. J. Sickels, *The Presidency: an Introduction* (Prentice-Hall, Englewood Cliffs, 1980), pp. 172–92; D. Rather and G. P. Gates, *The Palace Guard* (Harper & Row, New York, 1974); J. Dean, *Blind Ambition* (Simon & Schuster, New York, 1976); 'How Nixon's White House works', *Time*, 8 June 1970; T. H. White, *Breach of Faith: the Fall of Richard Nixon* (Jonathan Cape, London, 1975), pp. 108–68, 322–43; J. Hart, *The Presidential Branch* (Pergamon, New York, 1987), pp. 176–97; G. Church, 'The President's men: how his inner council functions – and occasionally malfunctions', *Time*, 14 October 1981; J. H. Kessel, 'The structures of the Reagan White House', *American Journal of Political Science* 28, 2 (1984), pp. 231–58; G. Hodgson, 'Not for the first time: antecedents of the "Irangate" scandal', *Political Quarterly* 58, 2 (1987), pp. 125–38; T. Draper, 'The rise of the American junta', *New York Review of Books*, 8 October 1987; J. Tower, E. Muskie, and B. Scowcroft, *The Tower Commission Report: the Full Text of the President's Special Review Board* (Bantam, New York, 1987).

88 S. P. Huntington, 'Congressional responses to the twentieth century', in D. B. Truman (ed.), *The Congress and America's Future* (Prentice-Hall, Englewood Cliffs, 1965), p. 17. See also Woll, *American Bureaucracy*, pp. 124–5, 138–41, 172–3; R. H. Davidson, 'Congress and the executive: the race for representation', in A. de Grazia (ed.), *Congress: the First Branch of Government* (Doubleday Anchor, New York, 1967), p. 383; N. Long, 'Bureaucracy and constitutionalism', *American Political Science Review* 46, 3 (1952), pp. 808–18; P. Van Riper, *History of the United States Civil Service* (Row Peterson, Evanston, 1958); V. Subramaniam, 'Representative bureaucracy: a reassessment', *American Political Science Review* 61, 4 (1967), pp. 1010–19; Rourke, *Bureaucracy, Politics and Public Policy*, pp. 1–38, 63–86, 135–53; S. Krislov, *Representative Bureaucracy* (Prentice-Hall, Englewood Cliffs, 1974); K. J. Meier and L. G. Nigro, 'Representative bureaucracy and policy preferences', *Public Administration Review* 36, 4 (1976), pp. 458–70; Meier, *Politics and the Bureaucracy*, pp. 169–75.

89 P. Woll and R. Jones, 'Bureaucratic defense in depth', in Pynn (ed.), *Watergate and the Political Process*, pp. 216, 217, 224.

90 Long, 'Bureaucracy and constitutionalism', *American Political Science Review* 46, 3 (1952), p. 818.

91 S. E. Ambrose, 'The military and American society: an overview', in S. E. Ambrose and J. A. Barber, Jr (eds), *The Military and American Society* (Free Press, New York, 1972), p. 18. See also S. E. Ambrose, 'The military impact on foreign policy', in Ambrose and Barber (eds), *The Military and American Society*, pp. 121–36; M. H. Halperin, 'The President and the military', in Wildavsky (ed.), *Perspectives on the Presidency*, pp. 487–99; L. H. Gelb, 'Vietnam: the system worked', *Foreign Policy* 1, 3 (1971), pp. 140–67; K. C. Clark and L. J. Legere (eds), *The President and the Management of National Security* (Praeger, New York, 1969); A. C. Enthoven and K. W. Smith, *How Much is Enough? Shaping the Defense Program, 1961–1969* (Harper & Row, New York, 1971); A. Kanter, *Defense Politics: a Budgetary Perspective*

(University of Chicago Press, Chicago, 1979); R. Holbrooke, 'Presidents, bureaucrats and something in-between', in A. Lake (ed.), *The Vietnam Legacy: the War, American Society and the Future of American Foreign Policy* (New York University Press, New York, 1976), pp. 142–65; S. C. Sarkesian, 'A final word', in *Defense Policy and the Presidency: Carter's First Years* (Westview Press, Boulder, 1979), pp. 330–2.

92 A. Yarmolinsky, *The Military Establishment: its Impacts on American Society* (Harper & Row, New York, 1971); S. Lens, *The Military-Industrial Complex* (Kahn & Averill, London, 1970); D. M. Shoup, 'The new American militarism', *Atlantic Monthly*, April 1969; Congressional Quarterly, *The Power of the Pentagon: the Creation, Control and Acceptance of Defense Policy by the US Congress* (Congressional Quarterly Press, Washington, D.C., 1972); J. K. Galbraith, *How to Control the Military* (Doubleday, New York, 1969); C. W. Mills, *The Power Elite* (Oxford University Press, London, 1956), pp. 171–224; T. R. Dye, *Who's Running America? Institutional Leadership in the United States*, 2nd edn (Prentice-Hall, Englewood Cliffs, 1976), pp. 65–9; Donovan, *The Policy Makers*, pp. 136–67; 'Military-industrial complex', *Congressional Quarterly Weekly Report*, 24 May 1968; W. Proxmire, *Report from Wasteland* (Pall Mall, New York, 1970); Proxmire, *Uncle Sam: the Last of the Big Time Spenders* (Simon & Schuster, New York, 1972), pp. 65–89; I. Katznelson and M. Kesselman, *The Politics of Power: a Critical Introduction to American Government* (Harcourt Brace Jovanovich, New York, 1975), pp. 151–97; W. McGaffin and E. Knoll, *Scandal in the Pentagon* (Fawcett, New York, 1970); B. M. Russett, *What Price Vigilance? The Burdens of National Defense* (Yale University Press, New Haven, 1970); M. Janowitz, *The Professional Soldier: a Social and Political Portrait* (Free Press, Glencoe, 1960), pp. 347–414. G. Adams, *The Politics of Defense Contracting: the Iron Triangle* (Transaction, New Brunswick, 1982); L. J. Dumas, 'The military burden on the economy', *Bulletin of Atomic Scientists*, October 1986, pp. 22–6; B. D. Berkowitz, *American Security: Dilemmas for a Modern Democracy* (Yale University Press, New Haven, 1987), pp. 14–21.

93 E. F. Sherman, 'Accountability and responsiveness of the military establishment', in L. N. Rieselbach (ed.), *People vs. Government: the Responsiveness of American Institutions* (Indiana University Press, Bloomington, 1975), p. 241.

94 Sherman, 'Accountability and responsiveness of the military establishment', in Rieselbach (ed.), *People vs. Government*, p. 272.

95 Yarmolinsky, *The Military Establishment*, p. 36.

96 Yarmolinsky, *The Military Establishment*, p. 25.

97 J. W. Fulbright, *The Pentagon Propaganda Machine* (Vintage Books, New York, 1971), p. 149.

98 See A. Wildavsky, 'The two Presidencies', in A. Wildavsky and N. W. Polsby (eds), *American Governmental Institutions: a Reader in the Political Process* (Rand McNally, Chicago, 1968), pp. 93–102; S. P. Huntington, *The Common Defense* (Columbia University Press, New York, 1961); Rourke, *Bureaucracy, Politics and Public Policy*, pp. 143–7; R. H. Dawson, 'Innovation and intervention in defense policy', in R. L. Peabody and N. W. Polsby (eds), *New Perspectives on the House of Representatives* (Rand McNally, Chicago, 1963), pp. 273–303; I. M. Destler, 'National security advice to US Presidents: some lessons from thirty years', *World Politics* 29, 2 (1977); C. Wolf, Jr, 'Military-industrial simplicities, complexities and realities', in S. C. Sarkesian (ed.), *The Military-Industrial Complex: a Reassessment* (Sage, Beverly Hills, 1972), pp. 25–52; Sarkesian, *Beyond the Battlefield: the new Military Professionalism* (Pergamon, New York, 1981), pp. 237–65; J. Buck, 'The establishment: an overview', in Sarkesian (ed.), *Presidential Leadership and National Security: Style, Institutions, and Politics* (Westview, Boulder, 1984), p. 65.

99 Huntington, *The Soldier and the State: the Theory and Politics of Civil–Military Relations* (Harvard University Press, Cambridge, Mass., 1957), p. 456.

100 J. K. Galbraith, 'How to control the military', in D. V. J. Bell, K. W. Deutsche, and S. M. Lipset (eds), *Issues in Politics and Government* (Houghton Mifflin, Boston, Mass., 1970), p. 224.

101 Galbraith, 'How to control the military', p. 225.

102 Galbraith, 'How to control the military', p. 227.

103 R. E. Neustadt, *Presidential Power: the Politics of Leadership* (Wiley, New York, 1960), pp. 86–107; E. E. Cornwell, *Presidential Leadership of Public Opinion* (Indiana University Press, Bloomington, 1965); D. Grabner, *Public Opinion, the President and Foreign Policy* (Holt

Rinehart & Winston, New York, 1968); H. Purvis (ed.), *The Presidency and the Press* (Lyndon B. Johnson School of Public Affairs, Austin, 1976); M. B. Grossman and F. E. Rourke, 'The media and the Presidency: an exchange analysis', *Political Science Quarterly* 91, 3 (1976), pp. 455–70; M. B. Grossman and M. J. Kumar, *Portraying the President: the White House and the News Media* (Johns Hopkins University Press, Baltimore, 1981); T. Lowi, *The Personal President: Power Invested, Promise Unfulfilled* (Cornell University Press, Ithaca, 1985); S. Kernell, *Going Public: new Strategies of Presidential Leadership* (Congressional Quarterly Press, Washington, D.C., 1986).

104 Grossman and Kumar, *Portraying the President*, p. 5.
105 D. S. Broder, 'The Presidency and the press', in Dunn (ed.), *The Future of the American Presidency*, p. 264.
106 P. H. Weaver, 'The new journalism and the old – thoughts after Watergate', in Ripley and Franklin (eds), *National Government and Policy in the United States*, p. 54.
107 D. Fritchey, 'The Presidency as I have seen it' (special supplement), in Hughes (ed.), *The Living Presidency*, p. 341.
108 A. M. Schlesinger, Jr, *The Imperial Presidency* (André Deutsch, London, 1974), p. 273.
109 Grossman and Kumar, *Portraying the President*, p. 324.
110 D. P. Moynihan, 'The President and the press', in Tugwell and Cronin (eds), *The Presidency Reappraised*, p. 151. For a similar concern, similarly expressed, see R. L. Bartley: the 'press is very likely freer than it ever has been.... The problem is that we're at the end of one pendulum swing, and we worry about how far it will go when it swings back the other way' (quoted in 'New concerns about the press', *Fortune*, April 1975).
111 Grossman and Kumar, *Portraying the President*, p. 323.
112 Quoted in 'Has the press done a job on Nixon?', *Columbia Journalism Review*, January/February 1974, p. 52.
113 R. M. Entman, 'The imperial media', in Meltsner (ed.), *Politics and the Oval Office*, p. 80. See also T. Bethell and C. Peters, 'The imperial press', *Washington Monthly*, November 1976, and J. Kraft, 'The imperial media', *Commentary*, May 1981.
114 Grossman and Kumar, *Portraying the President*, p. 16.
115 W. D. Burnham, *Democracy in the Making: American Government and Politics* (Prentice-Hall, Englewood Cliffs, 1983), p. 50.
116 T. J. Lowi (ed.), *Legislative Politics USA*, 2nd edn (Little Brown, Boston, Mass., 1965), p. vii.
117 Burns and Peltason, *Government by the People*, p. 305.
118 Burns and Peltason, *Government by the People*, p. 306.
119 Mills, *The Power Elite*, p. 246.
120 J. S. Wright, 'The role of the courts: conscience of a sovereign people', in K. M. Schmidt (ed.), *Government in Action* (Dickenson, Belmont, 1966), pp. 231–2.
121 Sherrill, *Why they Call it Politics*, p. 167.
122 A. Lewis, 'The changing role of the Supreme Court of the USA', in L. Lipsitz (ed.), *American Government: a Book of Selected Readings* (Allyn & Bacon, Boston, Mass., 1967), p. 414.
123 Lehman, *The Executive, Congress and Foreign Policy*, p. 214.
124 Lehman, *The Executive, Congress and Foreign Policy*, p. 217.
125 Cronin, 'The Imperial Presidency re-examined', in W. S. Livingston, L. C. Dodd, and R. L. Schott (eds), *The Presidency and the Congress: a Shifting Balance of Power?* (University of Texas Press, Austin, 1979), p. 16.
126 Quoted in H. Sidey, 'Checking and balancing', *Time*, 2 May 1983. The vision of balanced policies emanating from balanced institutions can produce differing responses. Congress's renewed interest in international affairs 'offered hope that *balance and reason* [my italics] would be restored to foreign policy' (I. M. Destler, L. H. Gelb, and A. Lake, *Our own worst Enemy: the Unmaking of American Foreign Policy*, Simon & Schuster, New York, 1984, p. 142). Seen in another context, however, the prospect of balanced policies represented more of a vice than a virtue. 'Arguably, U.S. policy should either provide real, effective help to the contras or make peace with the Sandinista regime. Splitting the difference makes no particular sense. Yet this has been the result of an incredible and delicate balance between those who favour effective aid and those who do not. In short, there is *no* rationale to the middle course; it is simply the result of the balance of forces in the Congress' (J. T. Bergner, 'Organizing the Congress for national security', *Comparative Strategy* 6, 3, 1987, p. 298). Whatever the benefits or otherwise of such policies, what is noticeable about both these types of state-

ment is the clear underlying belief in the conjunction of moderate policies with the automatically moderating effect of interacting institutional units.
127 Huntington, *The Soldier and the State*, p. 400.
128 Huntington, *The Soldier and the State*, p. 419.
129 Huntington, *The Soldier and the State*, p. 400.
130 M. Lerner, *America as a Civilization: Life and Thought in the United States today* (Jonathan Cape, London, 1958), p. 403.
131 See Woll (ed.), *American Government*, p. xiii.
132 Lehman, *The Executive, Congress and Foreign Policy*, p. 217. Similar ambivalence can be detected in many accounts of American government. In respect to the Presidency and Congress, for example, R. H. Davidson and W. J. Oleszek allude to the mysterious nature of the relationship. They go on to pose the following question. 'Where does the balance of power lie? There is no easy answer' (*Congress and its Members*, Congressional Quarterly Press, Washington, D.C., 1981, p. 307). The point being made however, is that an answer exists. It is just that the answer is a difficult one to acquire. Hugh Sidey's observation provides a slightly different variation in that he links the existence of balance to historical experience, only to withdraw it by a qualification that virtually removes the possibility of balance ever having existed. 'A moment when a satisfactory balance existed between the presidency and the forces outside that seek to diminish it has rarely if ever occurred' ('Fragmentation of powers', *Time*, 6 July 1987).
133 See pp. 167–72.
134 T. I. Emerson, 'The danger of state secrecy', in Pynn (ed.), *Watergate and the American Political Process*, pp. 59, 60, 59.
135 For example, see T. Wicker, 'Destroy the monster', *New York Times*, 12 September 1975; and Garry Wills, 'The CIA from beginning to end', *New York Review of Books*, 22 January 1976.
136 S. Turner, 'Agency is a "whipping boy"', *Guardian Weekly*, 18 December 1977. This faith in such a conjunction is reminiscent of President Kennedy's statement on the subject: 'clearly, the two principles of an informed public and of confidentiality within the government are irreconcilable in their purest forms, and a balance must be struck between them' (quoted in T. M. Franck and E. Weisband, 'Introduction: executive secrecy in three democracies: the parameters of reform', in Franck and Weisband, eds, *Secrecy and Foreign Policy*, Oxford University Press, New York, 1974, p. 5).
137 J. Cropsey, 'Conservatism and liberalism', in R. A. Goldwin (ed.), *Left, Right and Center: Essays on Liberalism and Conservatism in the United States* (Rand McNally, Chicago, 1967), pp. 43–4.
138 J. M. Burns, *The Deadlock of Democracy: Four-party Politics in America* (Calder, London, 1963), p. 264.
139 P. H. Weaver, 'Liberals and the Presidency', *Commentary*, October 1975.
140 E. C. Hargrove, 'Presidential personality and revisionist views of the Presidency', *American Journal of Political Science* 17, 4 (1973), p. 820.
141 Lowi, *Legislative Politics USA*, p. xix.
142 N. J. Ornstein, 'The constitution and the sharing of foreign policy responsibility', in E. S. Muskie, K. Rush, and K. W. Thompson, *The President, the Congress and Foreign Policy* (University Press of America, Lanham, 1986), p. 35.
143 D. L. Clarke and E. L. Neveleff, 'Secrecy, foreign intelligence, and civil liberties: has the pendulum swung too far?', *Political Science Quarterly* 99, 3 (1984), p. 493.
144 J. A. Nathan and H. A. Oliver, *Foreign Policy-making and the American Political System*, 2nd edn (Little Brown, Boston, Mass., 1987), p. 237.
145 R. E. Osgood, *Ideals and Self-interest in America's Foreign Relations: the Great Transformation of the Twentieth Century* (University of Chicago Press, Chicago, 1964), pp. 1–23.
146 Griffith, *The American System of Government*, pp. 181, 183, 184.
147 White, *Breach of Faith*, p. 325.
148 Cronin, 'The Imperial Presidency re-examined', in Livingston, Dodd, and Schott (eds), *The Presidency and the Congress*, p. 39.
149 L. W. Koenig, *The Chief Executive*, 3rd edn (Harcourt Brace Jovanovich, New York, 1975), pp. 407–8.
150 Lowi, *Legislative Politics USA*, p. ix.
151 C. Rossiter, *Conservatism in America: the Thankless Persuasion*, 2nd edn, rev. (Vintage

Books, New York, 1962), p. 75.
152 I. H. Carmen, *Power and Balance: an Introduction to American Constitutional Government* (Harcourt Brace Jovanovich, New York, 1978), p. 51.
153 W. LaFeber, 'The constitution and United States foreign policy: an interpretation', *Journal of American History* 74, 3 (1987), p. 696.
154 N. Rockefeller, 'Freedom and federalism ', in Burkhardt, Krislov, and Lee (eds), *The Clash of Issues*, 7th edn, p. 61.
155 Jackson, *The Supreme Court in the American System of Government*, pp. 61–2.
156 Price, *America's Unwritten Constitution*, p. 145.
157 Udall, 'A Democrat looks at the Presidency', in Dunn (ed.), *The Future of the American Presidency*, p. 239.
158 Quoted in Wood, *The Creation of the American Republic*, p. 604.
159 Quoted in A. J. Bickel, C. S. Hyneman, R. M. Scammon, H. H. Wellington, A. Wildavsky, J. Q. Wilson, and R. K. Winter, Jr, *Watergate, Politics and the Legal Process* (American Enterprise Institute, Washington, D.C., 1974), p. 33.
160 A. Wildavsky, 'System is to politics as morality is to man: a sermon on the Presidency', in Wildavsky (ed.), *Perspectives on the Presidency*, p. 526.
161 Mills, *The Power Elite*, p. 242.
162 Lerner, *America as a Civilization*, p. 399.
163 W. H. Riker, *Democracy in the United States*, 2nd edn (Macmillan, New York, 1965), p. 342.
164 M. R. Cohen, *American Thought: a Critical Sketch* (Collier, New York, 1962), p. 164.
165 L. Fisher, *President and Congress: Power and Policy* (Free Press, New York, 1972), p. 1.
166 Huntington, *The Soldier and the State*, p. 191.
167 D. P. Moynihan, 'Imperial government', *Commentary*, June 1978.
168 Saeger, *American Government and Politics*, p. 71.
169 Griffith, *The American System of Government*, p. 185.
170 L. Fisher, *Constitutional Conflicts between Congress and the President* (Princeton University Press, Princeton, 1985), p. 329.
171 L. Fisher, *The Politics of Shared Power: Congress and the Executive* (Congressional Quarterly Press, Washington, D.C., 1987), p. ix.
172 Evans, *Clear and Present Dangers*, p. 102.
173 H. Sidey, 'The quiet counterforce', *Time*, 17 March 1975.
174 J. Reston, *New York Times*, 27 November 1966.
175 Quoted in *Television and the Presidency*, presented by T. H. White, broadcast by the British Broadcasting Corporation, 19 January 1985.
176 H. Smith, *The Power Game: how Washington Works* (Collins, London, 1986), p. 656.
177 Woll, *American Bureaucracy*, p. 176.
178 See White, *Breach of Faith*, and R. N. Goodwin 'Advise, consent, and restrain: dismantling the Presidency', in J. F. Manley (ed.), *American Government and Public Policy* (Macmillan, New York, 1976), pp. 352–63.
179 Schlesinger, *The Imperial Presidency*, p. 417.
180 T. C. Sorensen, *Watchmen in the Night: Presidential Accountability after Watergate* (MIT Press, Cambridge, Mass., 1975), p. 74.
181 Schlesinger, *The Imperial Presidency*, p. 405.
182 Cronin, 'The Imperial Presidency re-examined' in Livingston, Dodd, and Schott (eds), *The Presidency and the Congress*, p. 38.
183 G. E. Reedy, *The Twilight of the Presidency* (Mentor, New York, 1971), pp. 160–82; K. P. Phillips, 'An American parliament', *Harper's*, November 1980; T.R.B., 'Turbulence ahead', *New Republic*, 20 July 1974; J. L. Sundquist, 'Parliamentary government and ours', *New Republic*, 26 October 1974; C. M. Hardin, *Presidential Power and Accountability: Towards a new Constitution* (University of Chicago Press, Chicago, 1974), pp. 9–20, 163–98; H. S. Commager, *The Defeat of America: Presidential Power and National Character* (Simon & Schuster, New York, 1974); Sorensen, *Watchmen in the Night*, pp. 85–116; W. F. Mondale, *The Accountability of Power* (McKay, New York, 1975); D. S. Broder, *The Party's Over* (Harper & Row, New York, 1972); J. K. Javits with D. Kellerman, *Who Makes War: the President versus Congress* (William Morrow, New York, 1973); E. C. Hargrove, *The Power of the Modern Presidency* (Knopf, New York, 1974), pp. 275–337. 'The mechanisms for controlling friction between President and Congress' (K. W. Thompson, 'The President, the Congress, and

foreign policy: the policy paper', in Muskie, Rush, and Thompson, eds, *The President, the Congress and Foreign Policy*, p. 8) are still being looked for. See J. L. Sundquist, *Constitutional Reform and Effective Government* (Brookings Institution, Washington, D.C., 1986); D. L. Robinson (ed.), *Reforming American Government: the Bicentennial Papers of the Committee on the Constitutional System* (Westview, Boulder, 1985).

Chapter 6. Epilogue

1 J. L. Sundquist, *Politics and Policy: the Eisenhower, Kennedy and Johnson Years* (Brookings Institution, Washington, D.C., 1968), p. 510.
2 E. S. Griffith, *The American System of Government*, 6th edn (Methuen, New York, 1983) p. 181.
3 C. H. McIlwain, *Constitutionalism: Ancient and Modern*, rev. edn (Cornell University Press, New York, 1947).
4 See McIlwain, *Constitutionalism*, pp. 124–46; McIlwain, 'The fundamental law behind the constitution of the United States', in C. Read (ed.), *The Constitution Reconsidered* (Columbia University Press, New York, 1938), pp. 3–14; G. Sartori, 'Constitutionalism: a preliminary discussion', *American Political Science Review* 56, 4 (1962), pp. 853–64: G. Maddox, 'A note on the meaning of "constitution"', *American Political Science Review* 76, 4 (1982), pp. 805–9.
5 M. Cranston, 'The destiny of democracy', *Times Literary Supplement*, 4 June 1976.
6 D. S. Broder, 'The case for responsible party government', in J. Fishel (ed.), *Parties and Elections in an Anti-party Age: American Politics and the Crisis of Confidence* (Indiana University Press, Bloomington, 1978), p. 22.

Index

Adams, J. 16–17, 25, 225
Afghanistan 175
Age of Reason 5
Alembert, J.L. d' 12
Ambrose, S. 212
American Political Science Association's Study of Congress Project 119
Arendt, H. 32
Aristotle 27–8, 31–2

Bailey, S. 125
Bailyn, B. 13–14, 25, 55
balanced government, origins of: British 24–7, 244; Classical 27–8, 31, 45, 245; Renaissance 28; seventeenth- and eighteenth-centuries 29–31; American 15–19, 23–4, 72–9
Barber, J. 99–100
Beard C. 78
Beer, S. 38
Bellamy, E. 247
Berlin, I. 11
Bickel, A. 157
Binkley, W. 111
biological paradigm of American government: 38–41, 80–1, 88–90, 135–6, 139, 149–53, 191, 230; rise of 41–3, 78, 120–1, 133–7, 139, 141–3, 148–50, 158–9, 183, 191, 268; decline of 145, 147–8, 151–4, 156–7, 159–60, 166–9, 172–3, 175–7, 179–85, 192–9, 268
biology 81–8, 123–5
Black, C.L. 204
Black, S. 85
Blackstone, W. 25
Bolingbroke, H. St J. 25
Boorstin, D. 22–3

Borelli, G. 7
Bronowski, J. 11, 87
Burnham, W.D. 216
Burns, J.M. 92, 216

Califano, J. 92
Cambodia 161–6
Central Intelligence Agency 167–75, 222
Central Intelligence Agency Act (1949) 169
Church, F. 160, 171
Cicero (M.) 28, 45
Civil War 76, 112–13
Clark, J. 125
Clausen, A. 128
Cline, R. 172
Cohen, B. 15
Colby, W. 169, 174
Cold War 97, 167, 170, 178, 221
Commager, H.S. 14, 179
'Commonwealthman' tradition 29–31
Congress: and organic unity 110–12, 126–7; individual variation 112–16; vitalism 116–19, 125; adaptation/evolution 120–2, 124, 130, 132, 149
Connif, J. 24
Coolidge, C. 106–7
Cooper–Church Amendment (1970) 160–2, 166
Copernicus, N. 6
Cornwell, E. 94
Cranston, A. 161
Croly, H. 78, 247
Cromwell, O. 103
Cronin, T. 178, 220
Cuban Missile Crisis 98

281

Index

Dahl, R. 40
Darwin, C. 80–1, 85–8, 90, 102, 123, 185
Darwinian evolution 80, 85–90, 102, 123–4, 135–6
Davidson, R. 126
Davies, R. 204
Dellums, R. 115
Dennis, J. 87
Descartes, R. 8, 82
Dijksterhuis, E.J. 11
DNA 83, 85
Dodd, L. 126
Dunn, C.W. 181

Eagleton Amendment (1973) 165
Easton, D. 97
Eisenhower, D. 106
Emerson, T. 171
Enlightenment 3, 5, 12–14, 21, 23–24, 27, 32, 46
Entman, R. 216

Federalist Paper 37 61
Fenno, R. 126
filibuster (US Senate) 115
Ford, G. 180
Founding Fathers 2–6, 13–23, 27, 40, 44, 46–9, 51, 54–7, 59–61, 78–9, 144–5, 148, 151, 161–2, 168, 179–80, 187–8, 190, 194–5, 197, 233
Franck, T. 181
Franklin, B. 16
Fritz, K. 28
Fulbright, J.W. 155, 160, 213

Galbraith, J.K. 213
Galileo, G. 6
Gay, P. 14
George, H. 247
Gilbert, F. 16
Gilbert, W. 7
Glorious Revolution 24, 29–30
Gordon, T. 29, 31
Gore, A. 160
Grazia, A. de 70–1
Griffith, E. 130
Gulf of Tonkin Resolution (1964) 159, 163–4, 166
Gwyn, W.D. 55

Hamilton, A. 91, 96
Hardin, C. 130

Hargrove, E. 99, 117, 224
Harrington, J. 30–1
Hartz, L. 22–3
Hatfield, M. 156
Heren, L. 93
Hinkley, B. 131
Hirschfield, R. 92, 109
Hofstadter, R. 16
Hollis, T. 29
Holmes, Justice O.W. 43
House of Representative Rules Committee 115
Huitt, R. 119, 126
Hughes, J.E. 101, 117, 179
Hume, D. 12–13, 19
Huntington, S. 42, 111, 122, 134, 221
Hutchins, F.G. 157
Huygens, C. 8
Huxley, J. 82–3

'imperial Presidency' 106, 142, 146, 148, 153, 156, 172, 175, 177–8, 182–4, 191–2, 229–30, 232
In re Neagle (1890) 104
Iranian Revolution 175

Jackson, R.H. 203, 225
Javits, J. 161
Jefferson, T. 61, 96, 144, 168, 200, 226
Johannes, J. 178
Johnson, L.B. 99, 140, 143, 147, 155–6, 159
Jones, R. 211

Kammen, M. 19
Kennedy, J. 98–9
Kenyon, C. 24
Kepler, J. 6–7
King, A. 117–18
Koenig, L. 179
Kurland, P. 190

Landau, M. 16, 46–7
Lehman, J. 220–1
Lerner, M. 221, 226
Lewis, A. 171
Lincoln, A. 104, 139
Lippmann, W. 18
Locke, J. 5–6, 22, 37, 55, 96
Lolme, J. de 25
Long, N. 212
Lowi, T. 94, 150, 216

Index

Machiavelli, N. 28
McConnell, G. 101
Madison, J. 16–17, 24, 41, 61, 65, 71, 74, 144–5, 168, 205–6
Mansfield, M. 160
Marcell, A. 30
Marchetti, V. 172
Marks, J.D. 172
Mayhew, D. 110
mechanistic paradigm in American government: 38, 72–7, 125–36, 147–57, 159–60, 166–9, 172–3, 175–7, 179–85, 192–7, 224–31, 232–7, 264, 276; Supreme Court 200–4, 219; mass media 213–16; military 212–13; Federalism 204–10, 223; Federal bureaucracy 210–12; CIA 167–72, 174–5, 222–3; war powers 173, 220; Watergate 179–82
Miller, Justice S.F. 104
Miller, C. 111
Mills, C.W. 226
Milton, J. 30
mixed government 27–9, 59
Molesworth, R. 29
Montesquieu, C.L. de S. 18–19, 24–5, 40, 55
Mosier, R. 17

National Security Act (1947) 169
New Deal 37–8, 41, 208
New Federalism 209–10
Newton, I. 2–13, 16–18, 20–1, 45–9, 80–1, 123, 180–2, 185–6, 188–9, 197
Newtonian mechanics 3–11, 14–27, 32, 44–50, 52, 73, 79, 81, 123–4, 181–2, 186–9, 193, 196, 198–9, 231, 239
Neustadt, R. 51, 92
Neville, H. 30
Nixon, R.M. 99, 140, 143, 147, 158–9, 162–3, 166, 168, 175–6, 178–81, 183, 210–12, 215

Office of Management and Budget 169, 216
Oleszek, W. 126
Orfield, G. 131
organicism 110
Ornstein, N. 221

Packwood, R. 156
Paley, W. 25

Pargellis, S. 17
Paris Peace Accord (1972) 163, 165
Parrington, V. 78
Patterson, S.C. 119
Peltason, J.W. 216
Pentagon 216
Pious, R. 101, 119
Plato, 27–8
Pocock, J.G. 31
Pole, J.R. 18
Polybius 27–8, 31, 45
Pope, A. 12
Presidency and Congress as a biological–mechanical duality 26–35, 41–2, 108–10, 116–17, 119–20, 122, 125–35, 140–2, 146–55, 159–62, 168–9, 171–2, 174–85, 193, 268
Prewitt, K. 68
Puritan Revolution 29, 242

Ransom, H.H. 172
Reagan, R. 221
Reedy, G. 92
Richardson, E. 165, 182
Rieselbach, L. 126, 130
Ripley, R. 126
Roberval, G. 7
Robinson, J.A. 46–8
Roche, J.P. 23
Rockefeller Commission 170
Roosevelt, F.D. 37, 137, 156
Roosevelt, T. 103, 104
Rossiter, C. 16, 106–7, 225
Rousseau, J-J. 110
Royce, J. 247

Schlesinger, A. 19, 143, 230
separation of powers 39–44, 50–2, 53–73; checks and balances 181–4, 189–91, 193–8, 228–9, 234, 236; textbook traits: brevity 54; historical oversimplification 54–6; conceptual oversimplification 56–8; ambiguity of separation of powers/checks and balances relationship 58–67; diagrammatic representation 67–72
Sidney, A. 30
Smith, J.A. 78
Solberg, W. 17
Sorauf, F. 33–4
Sorenson, T. 230
South East Asia Treaty Organization 164

Index

Springer v *Government of the Philippine Islands* (1928) 43
Stockman, D. 126
Sunquist, J. 126, 156, 181
Supreme Court 200–4, 206, 210, 212, 219, 229
Symington, S. 161

Tacitus (C.) 28, 45
Thomas, N.C. 32
Trenchard, J. 29, 31
Tribe, L. 18
Truman, H. 99, 140, 156
Tydings, J. 161

US Constitution 13–14, 16, 46, 67, 74–6

Verba, S. 68
Vietnam 99, 146, 159–61, 163, 184, 214

Vile, M.J. 35, 55, 60

War Powers Resolution (1973) 173, 220
Warren era 43, 219
Watergate 143, 156, 158, 166–7, 178–9, 181, 184, 214, 215
Weisband, E. 181
Wheeler, H. 32
White, T. 125
Whitehead, A.N. 84
Wicker, T. 171, 216
Wildavsky, A. 96, 226
Wills, G. 174
Wilson, W. 18, 41, 80–1, 88–90, 98, 100, 102, 104, 107, 111, 118, 136, 185
Wise, D. 171
Woll, P. 211, 221, 229
Wood, G. 55, 194

Yarmolinsky, A. 213